MW00878346

The End Never Comes

Part Two
of
An
American
Odyssey

by
Liam Burnell

Cover art by Liam Burnell
Interior by M.C. Burnell

1. WACHUSSET

I awoke to a gentle breeze and the daily euphoria of birds celebrating the sun's return. I sat up and began to work the soreness out of my spine and hips. Sleeping on plywood was rough for a guy as skinny as me. I probably woke up forty times every night just long enough to shift positions, so morning always came as a welcome reprieve from the uncomfortable bed. Of course, my daytime activities were still mostly limited to whatever could take place on my two-and-a-half by eight-foot platform.

I looked over the side, but the forest floor was still hidden in darkness. There I was some eighty feet up in a giant white oak tree on the side of a mountain in central Massachusetts. Two buckets hung just below my platform. One was full of food, and the one at the other end was filling up with poop. I reached down and hauled up the poop bucket to start my morning routine.

It was a delicate dance trying to squat over a bucket on a tiny plywood platform eighty feet above the ground. The platform was hanging from a notch in the tree by six lengths of rope- one in each corner and one at the midpoint of each of the long sides. They all converged to a single point over the center of the platform sort of enclosing me in a loose cone of rope. Another series of knotted ropes pulled the bottom of the platform snugly against the tree's trunk for stability, but I could still make it tip some if I put too much weight out on one of the long ends. Not to mention the whole tree would sway back and forth in the wind.

I lived in the tree-top for a total of six days, and in all that time I never did find an expedient way to poop. I was supposed to wear my climbing harness at all times for safety, but it's really tricky to pull your pants down while wearing a climbing harness. That meant un-hooking myself during the only real dangerous move I tended to make on an average day. I found a relatively safe way to do it, but it took a long time.

By moving my bedding to one end, and sitting the bucket right in the center of the platform, I could hang on to several of the ropes at the same time and dangle-squat myself right over it. That meant that both my hands were clinging to ropes, leaving none free to operate a roll of toilet paper. The next step was to move the bucket back to the end of the platform and get into a kneeling position in the middle so I could wipe. I would have preferred to squat, but with all the motion of the tree and the gaping gaps between the six ropes; oh, and the fact that I am usually still half asleep when I shit, it just didn't seem worth it.

The first time I tried all this, I still tripped up dangerously on my own pants. After that I developed a strategy of pulling one leg all the way out of my pants so my ankles wouldn't be bound together. The whole potty break routine turned into a painstaking process that could carry on for nearly a half an hour. I am not afraid of heights, but I was acutely aware that I did not want to fall from that height, so everything I did up there was slow and steady.

***

Well, every good book should start with somebody pooping, preferably right on the first page, so now that we're off on the right foot, I should explain how I came to be living in a tree platform. Central Massachusetts is a hilly place with a few larger mountains and one great mountain called Wachusset. In New England, great mountains that stand all by themselves are called "monadnocks," and Wachusset is one of the best examples of a monadnock you will find anywhere. Besides being the biggest mountain around for many miles, Wachusset is also a state park, a ski resort, and one of the oldest forests in the state. The forest there had not been harvested since before the war for independence.

The political situation regarding land use on Mount Wachusset is very contentious and I feel like I need to explain a bit of that background to set the stage for this story. First of all, only 5.5% of the land in Massachusetts is open to the public as park-land where people can go and be out of doors without asking permission from the land-owners. There are only fourteen other states with less public land than Massachusetts, and most of them are places like Iowa and Texas where most of the outdoorsmen know their neighbors and don't have any trouble gaining access to privately-owned land.

As anyone in the northeast surely knows, Massachusetts is not like that. Now I'm not a hater. There are lots of sweet people in Massachusetts, but there are also a lot of people who come across like they are frustrated, fed-up, and selfish. Up in Maine, people call them "Mass holes." I don't think it would occur to them to talk to a rural land-owner because they don't talk to strangers at all. They don't even make eye contact. Even if they tried, there are a lot of rural land-owners in Massachusetts who wouldn't answer the door if someone knocked anyway. I guess you would have to mail them a request and hope they respond. Some Mass-holes might feel comfortable trespassing, but the lack of developed parking lots on private land usually forces them into the handful of tiny state parks and the Cape Cod National Seashore.

All they really need to feel better is a little bit of fresh air and some exercise. Quite a few of my friends up in Maine were actually rehabilitated Mass-hole refugees. It usually only takes one summer of farm-work to get it all out of their system. There are many happy stories of Mass-holes who have been cured, but the Boston area is still a bottomless fountain of passive-aggressive frustration. For the untold millions who still suffer, a brisk hike through the ancient forest of Wachusset is one of a precious few opportunities for real happiness and peace of mind.

I'm trying to make you laugh with jokes about Mass-holes, but seriously, they are like God's reminder to us of what happens when people are deprived of a healthy outdoor experience.

Of course, skiing is another way to get outside and raise a person's heart rate, and Wachusset is by far the closest ski resort of any satisfying size to the Boston metro area. Two ski trails were carved into the mountain's north slope by the Civilian Conservation Corps in the 1930's. They were operated as a public resource until the 1980's when a family of millionaires was given a lease to use the mountain's north slope for the purposes of private enterprise. Immediately following the lease, a giant complex of lodges and parking lots were constructed at the mountain's base, and twenty more ski trails were hacked into the forest, horribly fragmenting about a third of the forested land inside the park. I am not familiar with any stories about what controversy this may have created, but I assume there was a bitter struggle between the skiers and the more nature-minded environmentalists, all to the benefit of the millionaires who built the ski resort.

By the year 2002, demand for skiing opportunities had exceeded the supply that the Wachusset resort could provide, and the state approved the company's proposal to carve several more trails into the shrinking forest. The environmentalists complained vehemently, but all their e-mails fell on deaf ears. When sending e-mails turned out not to be enough, they were effectively defeated and left with yet another thing to be dissatisfied about.

By random coincidence, the nearby city of Fitchburg was home to several friends I had met on the protest circuit. They had grown up hiking on Mount Wachusset and they were very proud to see the return of an almost-ancient forest right there in their backyard. When the Sierra Club efforts to save the forest failed, they decided to take matters into their own hands and block the forest from being cut with a series of tree-sits. They were only three people though, and they had none of the materials or experience necessary to build a tree-sit, so they called up to Maine for support, and that is how I became involved.

In case you are unfamiliar with the terminology, a tree-sit is a tactic that activists use to try to prevent the forests they love from being cut down. People live on tiny platforms up in the trees, and when the loggers come to cut the trees down, they have to choose between sacrificing the lives of the tree-sitters, or giving up on those particular trees. If the tree-sits are located in just the right places, they will block the loggers' access to many other trees further up the slope.

Tree-sitting has turned out to be a fairly successful tactic. It was developed in the late eighties in the ancient Douglas Fir forests of the Oregon Cascades, and there were so many successful tree-sits there throughout the nineties that the Oregon State Police trained an entire branch of its agency in tree-climbing and methods of extracting protesters from the tree-tops. To date, only one tree-sitter has ever been killed by a logger, and several more have died from their own clumsiness. Many have been arrested and some are serving long sentences.

While law enforcement in the temperate rainforest of the Pacific Northwest were well versed in busting tree-sits, no such thing had ever been attempted in the state of Massachusetts before, so it seemed like we had a good chance.

The call for help came in the last week of July, sometime in the late morning. By that evening we had rustled up four volunteers- enough to fill a car. Most notably, we had an expert tree-climber among us who had been stockpiling ropes and other gear just in case of an emergency like this. We left that same evening and arrived in central Mass at about one-o'clock in the morning.

Mount Wachusset is located in the tiny township of Princeton, just west of Fitchburg, and an old man there in Princeton had provided his home to us as a base camp for our operations. We slept the first night and spent the following day gathering more supplies, cutting plywood, and reinforcing the bottoms with two-by-fours. Our friends had a detailed map of the cutting plan, so our strategy was to build two sits blocking what would be the access road leading to the rest of the cut. Due to various state regulations, the month of August was the only time that the ski company would be allowed to cut, so we figured we only had to clog up the bottleneck for one month, and that would buy the legal campaigners another whole year to defeat the project in court if they could. It was still three days until the first of August, and we were ready to deploy.

We waited until after dark and then drove to a place on the mountain's lower slope where a small dirt maintenance road branched off the larger county road and disappeared into the darkness up the slope. There were no structures nearby where people could see us unloading, but there was no telling when the next car would pass by on the road. Needless to say, we didn't want any witnesses to our strange nocturnal activities, so as soon as our vehicle stopped, we burst out in a frenzy of unloading. Five people were crowded into a car that could only legitimately hold four, along with a couple hundred pounds of supplies and two large wooden platforms strapped to the roof. Everything was shuttled into the safety of the shadows as quickly as possible and then the driver sped away. By random luck, no one else had passed by on the road to witness our deployment.

Four of us were left behind to carry the gear up the maintenance road and set up the sits. We stacked the platforms on top of each other and piled all the gear on top of that. Then, with one person on each corner, we would lift the whole mess and scurry up the road as quickly as we could. We could usually go about 200 feet at a time before we had to sit the load down and spend several minutes catching our breath and stretching. The dirt road traversed the mountain's north slope while angling slightly uphill, steadily gaining elevation. After about five of those cycles, we came to the first of several wide ski trails we would have to cross.

The trail was lit up like a baseball stadium by a series of massive floodlights mounted on and around the ski lodges down below. The lodges were only about a quarter mile down the hill. It seemed pretty unlikely that there would be anyone in the lodges at that time of night in the summer season, and even less likely that they would be looking up at the grassy, flood-lit ski slopes. Even so, I still felt incredibly vulnerable shuffling across the brightly-lit corridor of grass at such a slow pace.

Liam Burnell

The ski slope was wider than the usual intervals we had been taking in between our breaks, but none of us wanted to stop in the middle so we just kept straining all the way to the beckoning darkness of the forest. We had all dressed in the darkest clothing we could find, but the line of sight between us and the lodges was so direct and the lights were so bright, I don't even think it would have made much difference. At last, we made it back to the safety of the shadows and collapsed in a huffing, puffing heap. We listened for sirens, but none came. Apparently no one was watching, just as we had hoped.

Eventually we regained our strength and continued on. We crossed one or maybe two smaller ski trails, also brightly lit and with ample views of the lodge complex. Then we came to the mother of all ski slopes. We were still much closer to the bottom of the mountain than we were to the top. All the smaller trails up the hill fed into one big trail that widened into a great sloped field in their final approach to the lodges, and we were going to have to cross it. The locals informed us that the spot where we would be setting up on was just on the other side of that field. We took a few moments to rest and psyche ourselves up. Then on the count of three we grunted a collective grunt and shuffled out into the light.

The waddling, shuffling pace of four people straining together to move a heavy load left us exposed for what felt like an eternity. The lights were bright enough to make the grass grow. Half way across I looked down and realized that there were whole sections of the lodge complex that I hadn't been able to see before. An amused janitor or security guard could have been watching us from any one of a hundred windows.

Three quarters of the way across I started to worry that my forearms might give out causing me to drop my corner of the load. With more than a hundred feet to go, I started voicing my concerns to the others. Through the clenched teeth of their own exertion, they all offered me encouragement and shot down my hint that maybe we should take a quick break out in the light. The pain in my fingers and forearms was overwhelming, but I resolved to keep going. My friends kept whispering a steady mantra of, "Hang in there buddy," and "We're gonna make it," all the way until we finally crash-landed into the safety of darkness. My forearms would be sore for most of the next week.

Our hosts disappeared up the hill on a scouting mission for a while, and then came back to lead us to a colossal tree that they had previously identified

6

as a good candidate for a tree-sit. After bushwhacking another hundred yards or so straight up a steep slope through the darkened forest, we were finally done carrying our ridiculous burden.

There before us in the glow of the flashlights was the trunk of a truly enormous white oak. The four of us together could not have wrapped our arms around it. I have occasionally seen oak trees get that big in city parks or in people's yards, but no one ever lets them get that big out in the forest. It was almost like the trees in the paintings at the Shinnecock Museum. Our hosts told us that in all their years of exploring on Mount Wachusset, this was the biggest tree they had ever seen. Not only that, but it was right near the bottom end of the proposed new ski trail.

A hollowed-out rotten streak several feet wide ran up the down-hill side of the trunk as far up as we could see. That caused some concern that it might not be a safe tree to inhabit, but after a moment of consideration, we decided that it was sturdy enough.

Approaching from the downhill side, we soon discovered another interesting feature of the old grandma tree. A whole colony of white-faced hornets had made their home in a hole right at the tree's base. I had never heard of white-faced hornets in particular, but everyone else agreed that they packed the most painful sting of any northeastern insect species. This would add another layer of challenge to our project, but we all agreed that the hornets would make wonderful allies when the police came to try to extract our sitter.

To begin with, our climber simply went around the uphill side, a good ten feet away from the hornets at least, and started up. He fashioned a piece of rope that was just slightly longer than the circumference of the tree, wrapped it around the trunk, and clipped both ends of it to his climbing harness. Then he wrapped his legs as far around the mighty trunk as he could, pulled tightly on the rope, and began to inch his way up. Each time he would get his body up to the level of the rope, he would squeeze tight with his legs to hold himself in place and then let the rope go slack so he could attempt to fling it a little higher up the trunk with a whipping motion. Then he would pull the rope tight again and repeat the process. The method was called "girthing" and it looked like an amazing test of athletic endurance. He only seemed to gain about a foot with each cycle and he had to go up about a hundred feet. I'm not sure what he did once he started to encounter branches because I couldn't see up that high. The old oak had grown up in the close company of other tall trees, so its trunk towered up into the obscurity of darkness with no branches in sight. I think it took our climber about an hour to get to the place where he decided to build the sit.

After that he lowered a much longer rope that he had carried up on his back and started calling us on the walkie-talkie to request that we tie various other items to the end of it. One by one we sent extra ropes, metal fasteners, a snack, and eventually one of the big wooden platforms up into the darkness.

At some point he accidentally dropped a long piece of rope and it landed right on the hornet nest. We all ran away down the hill expecting the hornets to attack. Then came the voice over the radio, "Oh shit! Can you guys send that rope back up to me," followed a few seconds later by the beckoning end of the elevator rope dangling into view. We told him to hang on a minute while we figured out how to get the rope back from the hornets.

We shined a flashlight on the rope and crept up on it like terrified children. Once we got close enough to see the hornets, it looked like they were in a fairly slow and torpid state due to the chill of the late night. Still, there were hundreds of them and they had all crawled out on to the offending rope, probably trying to sting the shit out of it. After the three of us on the ground had hesitated and vacillated a moment beyond what would have been dignified, one of the local guys endeavored to grab hold of the rope with a long stick. The hope was that if we pulled on it very slowly, the hornets would all hop off and wander back to be near their nest. I don't remember the exact sequence of events, but at some point, something went wrong and a bunch of the hornets took flight.

The next thing I remember, there was something buzzing inside the hood of my jacket followed immediately by the sudden pain of a hornet sting on the left side of my face. I took off running through the dark forest repeatedly slapping the side of my own head. I whacked myself over and over, but the damn bug kept buzzing right in my left ear, inside my hood. Somehow, I just couldn't seem to deal it a fatal blow. As long as the buzzing kept up, I kept panicking, and as long as I kept panicking, I kept running. For a brief moment, I actually popped out onto the brightly-lit ski trail and started running across it. After a few paces, I realized what I was doing and dove back into the shadows. I finally just bore down with my left hand and ground the sturdy hornet to death, crushing it against the back of my jaw. Wow. That was a lot more effective than flailing in panic. At that point I had quite a few stings on the left side of my neck and one from a different hornet on my right wrist, plus my ear was swollen and ringing from all my pummeling. In my spastic flailing, I had added my own strength to the hornet's attack on the side of my head. Psychologically defeated by an insect!

When I got back to my friends, they were both covered with hornet stings too and we all had a good laugh about it. Part of the rope was still laying in the damn hornet's nest, but we had gotten most of it, and the free end had a good long lead on it. We had to move slowly, but we got the rest of the rope without any more problems. Then we had to wait another long while for the bugs to calm down and go back inside their hole before we could get close enough to the tree to send the rope back up. Hopefully our friend up in the tree wasn't falling asleep!

After that there wasn't much for the ground crew to do, so we sat in the leaves occasionally drifting off to sleep. As the dawn approached, the air got cold and damp and I remember being too cold to sleep. Our intrepid climber finally lowered himself on a rope right at dawn and declared that the sit was ready. He was halfway done. He was tired, but he wanted to keep working until the second one was done too.

Our hosts explained that in order for us to most effectively block the proposed logging road, we would have to put the second sit down the hill, in between the first one and the maintenance road that we had come in on. We had already scouted out and chosen a tree earlier in the night so we wouldn't waste any time. It was smaller than the mighty matriarch that we had put the first sit in, but it was still a giant tree in its own right. It was another white oak, like most of the biggest trees on that slope, and it took three of us stretching to wrap our arms around the base of its trunk.

The forest filled with the light of an overcast day as our climber girthed his way inch by inch up the mighty tree trunk. It was a nerve-wracking thing to observe because we were close enough to the little road for our climber to be seen or heard determinedly humping his way up into the canopy. At last, he found the place he wanted to put the second platform, and we spent the next fifteen minutes conspicuously shuttling supplies up the rope. Someone went down to the road just to make sure the coast was clear before we sent the big wooden rectangle spinning and wobbling up through the forest canopy. At last, our climber and all his supplies were safely hidden high up in the tree top and it was still too early for most Americans to be awake.

After that, my two friends on the ground were tired and they wanted to go home and get some sleep. There was no reason for all four of us to be there anymore, so I volunteered to stay behind on ground-support and they bushwhacked up the hill.

Just after they left, the inevitable cold drizzle began to fall. I radioed the climber and he said the rain would slow him down a little, but he was still determined to get the job done. I hunkered down under a bush and tried to stay warm. It was my job to stay vigilant for any sign of a security risk and to send an occasional snack up the rope for the guy who was actually doing things. I was bleary with sleep-deprivation and shivering in the damp cold. The rain never increased beyond a drizzle, but it was steady enough that everything was saturated after a few hours, including my clothes.

A handful of hikers came by on the road, but we were well hidden and no one noticed us. The drizzle finally let up in the early afternoon, but the sky remained cloudy, damp and cold. After what felt like an army shift, the climber radioed and asked if anyone would notice him rappelling down the rope. The second sit was done. I checked the road and gave him the green light. When he arrived on the ground, I had never seen a more thoroughly exhausted person. He had been working for about eighteen consecutive hours, preceded by a full day of being awake. Suddenly my own fatigue semed like child's play.

It was about four o'clock in the afternoon, still more than five hours until it would start to get dark, so we couldn't just waltz back across the ski trails the way we had come in. Now we were going to have to climb to the top of the mountain!

A paved road winds up the southern slope so that tourists can enjoy the view from the top of Mount Wachusset. The parking lot at the top was truly the next closest place we could get to where a driver could pick us up, so we called for a ride, shouldered our packs, and started up. I was a little dizzy just from being awake for two consecutive days, but otherwise I found the physical activity a welcome break from sitting and shivering. It was the first time I had been warm enough in about fourteen hours.

For my tree-climbing friend it was the grand finale to a tweaked-out bender of workaholic exercise. We had to go about a mile straight up the steep north face of the mountain, bushwhacking the whole way to remain hidden. A couple times, we had to use all four limbs to scramble up over piles of loose, moss-covered boulders. When we reached the first of the boulder fields, my exhausted friend burst out into a fit of hysterical giggling that carried on for a moment beyond the limits of sanity. From then on, we cracked stupid jokes and giggled ourselves the rest of the way to the top like a couple of giddy children at a sleep-over party. The sun came out just as we arrived at the parking lot. Our ride was waiting for us with praises and hugs, and my buddy passed out as soon as his butt hit the car seat.

***

The night we showed up from Maine, I had made it clear that I didn't want to be one of the tree-sitters. In my mind, sitting in a tree platform was a prima donna position for people who wanted to get all the glory without having to do much of anything. I was much more interested in delivering food and supplies to the sitters because that seemed more exciting.

The morning after the sits were built, I awoke to a situation that required a bit of compromise. My hosts cooked me a huge delicious breakfast and then explained why they needed me in the tree. All three of the other people who had come down from Maine with me had to return home that day and resume their normal lives. One of the locals was already installed in the big tree with the hornets. One of the others was the designated "media coordinator" for the entire campaign and they needed to stay on the ground to be near the telephone and to meet with members of the press if necessary. The only other person left besides me was desperately afraid of heights, so I agreed to put my prejudice aside and do what was best for the team.

I was retrained on how to hook up my climbing harness and how to climb a free-hanging rope. By mid-morning I was deployed from the parking lot atop the mountain with a huge, sketchy-looking backpack full of gear. If any of the tourists at the parking lot thought about it, they may have wondered why I was carrying so much stuff into a park where no overnight camping was allowed, but I didn't encounter any rangers, and it only took me a few minutes to get off the trail and into the woods where I was all by myself. I descended the same stripe of forest that we had come up through the day before. As I passed the giant hornet tree, I radioed a greeting to the woman who was already in position up there. A short ways below it, I came to a rope dangling neatly to within a foot of the ground, just as we had left it. I hooked up my harness and the little piece of rope below it for my foot-sling, and began my slow ascent into the canopy.

First you stand up in the foot sling and slide the rope that attaches your climbing harness to the main rope as far up as you can reach. Then you lean back and sit into the climbing harness which attaches around your waist. Once all the weight is off your feet, you reach down and slide that lower knot up as far as it will go. Then you repeat that process as many times as it takes to get up. Both the foot-sling and the climbing harness are attached to the main rope by knots that won't slip when pulled from the side. It took me several minutes to get up to the platform in that fashion, and once I was up, I pulled the loose rope up behind me.

There I was in my new home. My hosts had assured me that reinforcements would arrive soon and then I would be back on the ground doing what I wanted. It seemed likely that they were right, but for the meantime, I would live in a treetop indefinitely.

I had a sleeping bag, lots of tarps and a "bivvy-sack" that was basically a tube of nylon with breathable mesh at the head end that I could crawl into and zip closed around me like a tiny tent. I had one pad to cushion my back from the plywood platform, but it was not very adequate. I was always glad when the first light of dawn gave me an excuse to sit up again. I started off with a couple days-worth of food in my backpack, and my bucket of food arrived the next day along with many words of encouragement.

I was nestled in a crotch of the tree where the main trunk divided into three main leaders. The platform felt very secure, and it offered me a spectacular view of that level of the forest. The three main leaders divided into a multitude of smaller branches just above me and the tree continued on for about thirty feet above my position. I was almost entirely enclosed in the canopy. From where I sat, I could only see a few patches of sky, and when I looked down, I could only see a couple small patches of the ground. Birds and squirrels were my constant companions throughout the daylight hours. It gave me a beautiful new perspective on the forest that I will always appreciate, but it also didn't take long for me to get really bored.

There was literally nothing to do. Slapping mosquitos became my primary pastime. I always assumed that mosquitos would stay close to the ground, but there actually seemed to be more of them up in the tree-tops.

All we really had to eat were military MRE's- "Meals Ready to Eat." Either some soldier or veteran had hooked us up, or there was a good deal on them at the Army surplus store. I don't know. I did get a variety of snack foods to fill in between meals, but every breakfast, lunch and dinner was cold cheese ravioli from a metal bag. The bags were like aluminum foil only heavy, as if they were made out of lead. I had to reassure myself every time that the Army would not be careless enough to pack its soldiers' rations in lead containers, but I could never be certain. Careless exposure to toxic materials being one of the hallmarks of American military service after all.

During the first couple days I received a lot of radio transmissions from the other tree-sitter up the hill. She seemed to be pretty overwhelmed by the experience and she called me to express her concern over all sorts of trivial little things. Eventually I became short with her and I insisted that she try to relax a little bit. After that I got fewer calls. I had a pen and a notebook with me, and I started writing letters to everyone I could think of. I passed the first two days in utter boredom writing letters, slapping mosquitos, eating cold Army food and learning how to squat over the shit-bucket.

Day three was the first of August, the day when logging was scheduled to begin. Suddenly, before dawn a team of Boston activists showed up and started digging a trench across the dirt road just down the hill from me. They had heard about our tree-sits and felt inspired to try to blockade the road in solidarity. It sounded like there were somewhere in the range of five to ten people clanking away in earnest with shovels and pick-axes. I could only see little bits of the scene through gaps in the canopy, but I could tell they dragged logs out of the woods onto the road and hung up a banner.

It was very exciting to hear such energy and enthusiasm in support of our cause, but their efforts came well beyond the last minute, and they didn't really stand a chance. To set up and maintain the kind of road blockade they were attempting, you need several days of preparation before the authorities show up. In their case, they got a little less than three hours. Shortly after sunrise, the police arrived and by that time the blockade was only in the beginning stages of being built. Several people refused to move and they were quickly arrested. The rest dispersed quickly and went back to Boston. Apparently, the police hadn't heard about our tree-sits because they never even came looking for us. By eight o'clock in the morning all the activists and all the police were gone and the forest returned to silence.

Our media team had sent out a press release at six in the morning and then called us to tell us to expect another flurry of activity. Sure enough, a small team of security guards came up from the ski lodge a few hours later. They stumbled around craning their necks, and eventually they spotted both of us. As I recall, once they had located us, they just turned around and left without saying a word.

Just before noon, a reporter from the Leominster/Fitchburg paper came out and attempted to interview us. I told her I was not educated enough to do interviews and I gave her the number for our media coordinator. She said she had already talked to our media person and she implored me to answer some questions. I kept declining and eventually conceded to let her photograph me as a compromise. The reporter then proceeded up the hill where my companion cheerfully accommodated her and answered her questions. I could hear most of what they were saying considering that they had to shout just to hear one another. I called her on the radio afterwards to scold her for the breach of protocol, but I doubt she actually did any harm. The reporter didn't ask her any questions about our strategy or about the history of the ancient forest or anything like that anyway.

That afternoon a television crew came out from Boston and that was highly amusing. The anchor-woman was dressed for the studio, so it was hilarious to watch her stumbling through the forest in her high-heeled shoes and her glittering gold dress. Her blond hair was so coiffed that from my perspective eighty feet above, she looked like Dolly Parton. They set up in one of the little spaces of ground that I could see and filmed the awkward anchor-woman while she gave a sensational account of tree-sitters on Mount Wachusset. The camera swung my way briefly, and I gave them a big grin while waving a defiant fist in the air. That was all they needed, so then they packed up and proceeded up the hill to the other sit. I couldn't see them after that, but several minutes later I heard one to the male camera technicians give out an anguished shriek of pain as if he had been stung by a white-faced hornet.

The next morning several police officers came out from the town of Princeton and hollered legal threats up to us. I don't remember exactly what they threatened, but I remember them trying to sound as intimidating as they could. I was amused because it was obvious that they could only make good on their threats if they could persuade me to come down my rope to a place where they could actually reach me. I laughed and gave them a big, sarcastic, "Okay! You do that then!"

My friend up the hill was genuinely frightened by their threats, so I spent a good bit of time with her on the walkie-talkie afterwards trying to reassure her that she couldn't be charged with grand-treasonous-terrorism (or whatever) if the cops couldn't reach her.

The cops didn't stay for long. We hosted several more reporters that day, and they were all frustrated that I wouldn't give them a proper interview. Having been trained in political campaigns for years, I knew that we had a media coordinator so that we wouldn't put out conflicting or irrelevant stories that might confuse the public. I also knew to refer all the reporters to our media person and I knew to get their contact information so our media person could call them too.

Late in the afternoon an older man came out to ask me some questions on behalf of a local newspaper and we went through the same routine. He stood in the little space where he could see me and at one point, he started backing up to get a better view, tripped over a log, and fell on his ass. I laughed a little to myself, but then quickly recovered my manners and asked if he was alright. He was fine. He asked me some strangely personal questions and then left feeling very frustrated. I had recently reminded my buddy up the hill about our reporter protocol, so she dealt with him very well also.

He left complaining that we had both been really "dodgy" and how did we expect him to write a real article if we wouldn't even talk to him, etc. Our media representative called him the next day and it turned out that he was the chief of the Princeton police department. Apparently, I had caught him off guard when I asked for his phone number, and he didn't even think to make up a fake one. My campaign training had paid off, and I got to tell everyone triumphantly that I had seen the chief of police fall on his ass!

That night the forest floor came alive with strange sounds. There were no lights, but we kept hearing twigs snap as if people were walking around and several times, we heard the distinct sounds of people cutting through wood with handsaws. The other tree-sitter called on the radio, and for once I could relate to her feelings of concern. What the hell was going on down there? I yelled down, "We can hear you!" a couple times, but there was no response. Sometimes intervals of ten or fifteen minutes would go by without a sound and then the activity would resume. It kept up for much of the night and it was really unsettling. Since there were no lights, I had to imagine they were using night-vision technology to find their way around. None of the bright light from the ski trails penetrated in to our location.

Right in the middle of all that, we got a call on the radio telling us that we were about to get a food delivery. A fourteen-year-old kid from the failed road blockade had stayed behind to help us and was right below me on the road with a big bag of food for each of us. I told him we were pretty sure that an unknown number of creepy people were lurking in the woods right in the vicinity at that moment and he should just get the hell out of there and bring us our food some other time. We already had several days-worth of food anyway. But he insisted. He seemed to think that would be the last chance to deliver our food rations for a long time. He sounded very emotional over the walkie-talkie, so I conceded and dropped my rope down.

For whatever reason, the people who were creeping around in the woods that night decided not to pounce on him, but I was terribly worried about him. I don't think I have ever seen someone do such a courageous thing, let alone a fourteen-year-old kid. We both got our food deliveries and then he took off running back down the road. He forgot to let go of the call button on his radio for a long way, so we could hear the clomping of his footsteps and his terrified breathing for the next couple of minutes as he ran back to the main road. Finally, he remembered to let go of the button and the radio went silent. Then a minute later he called back to tell us he had made it safely back to his ride and they were headed out. I breathed a huge sigh of relief. It takes a big heart to do something that brave. I will never forget that kid, and I have always imagined that he grew up to be quite a warrior.

Overwhelmed by curiosity, I descended my rope the next morning to see what had happened. I stopped about fifteen feet above the ground for quite a while, surveying the area to see if anyone was going to jump out and get me. Finally assured that it was safe, I touched down on the ground and looked around. A fair amount of underbrush had been removed and I found several places where saplings had been cut off at their base. My theory was that a team of night-vision commandos had come and set up some kind of surveillance system, but I couldn't find any little cameras or transmitters or any of that. It was seriously weird. Obviously, the military would not respond to a situation like that, but there are such things as high-tech private security contractors. Would a ski resort really want to pay for all that though? I was stumped. There wasn't really anything else I could do, so I climbed back up my rope and moved on with my life.

I thought about my situation and realized that in the event of an extended siege, I would run out of water long before I ran out of food. I had several extra tarps and a lot of bailing twine, so I decided to build a rainwater collection system. I was all rigged into my safety harness, but it was still terrifying to clamber up the thinner branches and dangle out over the huge open space below me. It took several hours, but I eventually managed to rig the tarp up into a half-funnel shape with the open side facing up. Right where the water would flow out at the bottom, I attached a two-liter soda bottle with the top cut off to catch the water. The bottle hung in a spot where I could reach it without even leaving the safety of the platform. Perfect!

The following morning, we were greeted with the clatter of a huge array of earth-moving equipment that came to repair the little ditch that the Boston activists had dug across the road. It was a ridiculous case of overkill. Any four-wheel-drive vehicle with high clearance could have driven right through the ditch, and two men with shovels could have repaired it in less than a day. Instead, they brought half a dozen pieces of equipment including dump-trucks, graders, and steam-rollers.

Whenever citizens stand up and fight the expansion of some industry, it's always a victory if we can cause them to spend a bunch of extra money on something, because it bleeds their bank account. Still, the road construction that day was so excessive, I can't help but think they must have found a way to charge it to the Massachusetts taxpayers. Wachusset is a state park after all.

By four o'clock in the afternoon, they still hadn't finished repairing the foot-deep ditch, but a great thunderstorm blew in and forced them to abandon their work. All at once, the horrid rumble of their equipment stopped and was quickly replaced by the beautiful rumble of nearby thunder.

The next hour and a half ended up being one of the more spiritual experiences of my life. Lightning crashed all around and the wind came in mighty gales, swinging my tree-top back and forth in a great arc. My platform never budged from the safety of its moorings, but the tree-top swung every which way in the swirling storm. I never felt like I was in any danger of falling, but I did get to go for a wilder ride than anything you would pay for at the county fair. I hung on like a bull-rider at the rodeo and whooped like a Portland street bum with every thunderclap.

I'm not the kind of guy who gets off on adrenaline rushes like bungee-jumpers or rock-climbers. What thrills me are tangible manifestations of nature's power. Thunderstorms are always a special treat for me, but to be held aloft into a thunderstorm in the embrace of a mighty oak tree was

17

beyond anything I ever imagined I would experience.

I also got wet. The rain poured down for almost an hour, and for a brief moment we even got a little hail. I ended up with a full bottle at the bottom of my rainwater-collector. The water was a strange green color and full of little bits of bark and leaves, but I was eager to try it anyway. To my surprise, it was horribly bitter with the flavor of oak tannins. I'm not sure why so much tannin seeped out of the tree into my water supply, but I was proud of my self-sufficiency, so I ended up drinking most of it anyway despite the disgusting flavor.

The road construction crew finished up the next morning and left us in peace and quiet for the rest of the day. A hiker from some nearby town found us and told us that she thought we were heroes and we should keep up the good work. She had brought her eleven-year-old son with her to look at us. Apparently, our media campaign was working.

That night I got a call from our people on the ground to report that they had received a flood of phone calls from local citizens who were thanking us, commending our courage and initiative, and in some cases offering support. People had offered to send money and supplies, and best of all they had found a replacement for me to sit in the tree-top. He would be up in the morning.

I spent one last night on the hard wooden platform, and right on time a big guy with a big beard, wearing a red and black-plaid skirt showed up to replace me. I'm not sure a skirt was the best choice of clothing for climbing trees, but I kept that to myself. I just made sure not to look up at him as he shimmied away up the rope. (I suppose he probably had an easier time dealing with the poop-bucket than I had.) Our transfer went smoothly, and I hiked back to the top of the mountain where my ride was waiting. Time in the tree-top passed so slowly, I felt like I had been up there for weeks, but altogether it had only been six days and six nights.

***

Back on the ground I finally got a chance to deliver supplies like I had originally wanted. My first mission turned out to be even more exciting than I had imagined. It was late-morning and we had just finished delivering food to the big uphill tree when we heard the rumble of several four-wheelers roaring out from the ski-lodge complex down the hill. We hustled down to the lower tree, and by the time we had tied the bag to the end of the new sitter's rope, it was obvious that the off-road-vehicles were coming towards us. Maybe the night-vision commandos had set up some kind of motion sensor and we had tripped it. From the sounds of it, the four-wheelers were approaching up the dirt maintenance road from the east.

I had a buddy with me who was one of the central Mass locals. He figured it would be too risky to hike back up to the parking lot on the mountain top. He knew the mountain like the back of his hand and he suggested that if we ran west, we would only have to cross two more ski trails and then we would make it to a wide-open forest stretching on for miles.

I followed his lead and we crashed through the bushes and down onto the little road. We turned left, away from the sound of the approaching vehicles, and burst into a dead sprint. Luckily, we had just unloaded our packs, so we were not burdened by any extra weight. We were running up the gentle slope of the road, but I was so full of adrenaline that it felt like level ground. We came to the first ski trail in just a few short paces and I was relieved to see that it was just a narrow one. The off-road-vehicles were revved up to full throttle and it sounded like they were almost on top of us. I looked over my shoulder, but they were still out of sight. We sprinted through another stripe of forest and then burst out into another ski trail.

"This is the last one!" my buddy hollered.

That was good news, but I was still pretty worried. The last ski trail was another impossibly wide stretch of grass easily four times as wide as the one we had just crossed. We were both running just as fast as we could and by some happy coincidence that put us shoulder to shoulder with no one lagging behind. We were still about twenty running paces from the forest when I looked back to see two cops and a security guard emerge from the forest behind us and start across the open trail on their four-wheelers. There could no longer be any doubt that we had been spotted.

At last, we made it to the edge of the clearing and my friend made an abrupt right turn, leaping down the embankment on the downhill side of the road. I followed one pace behind him and by some miracle we both managed to stay on our feet. Now we were crashing down a steep slope, dodging small trees, leaping over thigh-high boulders and crashing straight through thickets of brush. It was one of the most athletic performances of my life. I can't believe neither of us tripped or twisted an ankle.

In the next instant, we heard the motors pull up and stop on the road above us. Just in the nick of time, we came to a much larger boulder and dove behind it. The cops shut off their engines. I lay there panting for a moment and then wriggled on my belly to peek around the side of the rock. I kept my face pressed against the ground and peered through the many twigs of some plant, keeping myself hidden. The cops had dismounted and were standing on the road looking and pointing right at the rock where we were hiding.

Just then, my buddy decided he needed a peek too, and he stuck his whole head right up over the top of the rock. Shit! I slapped at his leg and hissed at him to get down, but I didn't really need to tell him. The first thing he saw when he poked his head up was both cops and the security guard looking right at him. He ducked back down and then, following my lead, he found a much safer vantage point through the twigs of a bush around the other side of the outcrop.

We watched and waited, catching our breath and bracing for the attack. The cops just stood there murmuring to each other and pacing back and forth on the road. If they had run down the hill towards us, it would have taken them less than ten seconds to close the gap, but they just didn't seem to be that motivated. In fact, their body language seemed to suggest that they were actually afraid to enter the forest. I'm certain that they knew exactly where we were, but something was keeping them glued to the road. Eventually, they got back on their machines and rolled away down the hill.

We were ecstatic. We had escaped! My buddy turned to me with a crazed look of excitement and disbelief.

"Did you see that? They were scared of us!"

To this day I am not certain what happened, but I have to admit that the three armed men up on the road above us really had appeared to be frightened. Or at least nervous.

My friend continued through a wicked grin, "The forest is a dangerous place for a cop you know!"

We hiked west for about three hours down the steep slope, over swamps, and through thickets without following the slightest semblance of a trail. At last, we emerged onto a large state highway and called for a ride. Within twenty minutes, we were whisked away to safety.

I have told that story to a lot of people over the years and it turns out that quite a few people have similar stories of police calling off the chase as soon as the person they're chasing makes it to the forest. (Oregon's tree-climbing cops are the notable exception.) The prevailing wisdom seems to be that police will only keep chasing you as far as they can drive in a vehicle. As soon as you get off the road, you're home free.

Of course, that would be different if you committed a real crime where you actually hurt someone. The people I hang out with don't commit those kinds of crimes. We mostly commit minor property crimes in our efforts to defend nature and oppressed people from relentless exploitation by the world's most powerful companies. Our actions are often illegal, but they are not immoral and I think many police must understand that on some level. It is their job to bust us and they will give whatever effort they must in order to get paid, but deep down I think a lot of them couldn't care less if some billionaire is prevented from making an extra buck or two. There are a few cops out there who are zealously driven to defend their masters' property, but I think they are a minority.

2. DISCLAIMERS

Alright. This is the sequel to *Bug Food* and it won't make a whole lot of sense if you haven't read that book first. This is essentially just the second half of that story, but I feel like it needs its own introduction and disclaimers. The two books together tell the tale of a young man full of ideology setting out on a grand impossible quest to save the world. It is a coming-of-age story and I am still very proud to have such a collection of wild experiences that make up the true story of how I came of age. Of course, for a young person to grow and learn, they also have to make some mistakes.

By some coincidence, the first half of my story is mostly cute and charismatic, and all of my most embarrassing mistakes are clustered in the second half. I guess I failed to quit while I was ahead so to speak. I intend to be honest about what I did and what I learned from it because I think honesty is really important, but I am not quite as excited to share all of these stories as I was in the first book.

I'll give you an example. During my first year of adventuring, I met lots of other radical people who gave me whole stacks of zines and even a few books to read all advocating for different methods of rebellion. In those days, shoplifting from big-box stores and other corporate chain stores was one of the most common rebellious tactics I read about. There were entire zines and chapters of books devoted to the study of out-smarting the security systems at various stores. Of course, none of those methods should ever be applied to small, locally-owned stores because they are not the problem. For stealing to be virtuous, one must only steal from the rich, like Robin Hood.

Well, I had never shoplifted anything before, but suddenly it seemed like an important skill to learn. In 2003, there was a particular big-box store that had reached the verge of world-domination. It was the largest corporation on the planet, and there were only 21 countries with more money and power than that company. It was on an aggressive campaign to wipe out our nation's diversity of local businesses and replace it with sterile homogeneity. And it was winning. It looked like we had to do something fast, or pretty soon that store would be the only place left where we could buy anything. Always low prices? Sure, until all the competition has been destroyed, and then they can charge whatever they want.

I saw it as my patriotic duty to fight the advance of that behemoth corporation, and the radical literature had given me something concrete I could actually do toward that end. There was just one small problem with shoplifting. I was travelling and living out of a backpack. I already had everything I needed and I couldn't really carry any more stuff. What was I to do? Steal stuff and then leave it in the dumpster?

I decided that I had to try to hit that company's profit margin in some way even if shoplifting wasn't practical. That line of thought led me to what seemed like an even better tactic. The megastores already had sophisticated security systems devoted to the prevention of shoplifting anyway. Why challenge all that surveillance when I didn't even need the stuff. I decided that I could take a much bigger bite out of the profit margin by simply destroying products inside the store and leaving them there. Then I could hit big, expensive items that I could never smuggle out the door while exposing myself to significantly less risk.

It seemed brilliant at the time, and so I left a mild trail of destruction down the East Coast from Massachusetts to Virginia. Almost every time I happened across one of those stores, I forced myself to gulp down the fear, go inside and break stuff. Of course, nothing in those stores is very expensive, so it took a long time for the numbers to add up. The electronics department was always too heavily guarded, so I couldn't get in there to sabotage anything. The best move I found was to grab a pair of wire-cutters out of the hardware department, wander over to the sporting goods section and casually cut the brake-lines on the bicycles. The bicycles only costed $60 a-piece, but twenty of those did add up. The most expensive thing I ever hit was a $400 vacuum cleaner, easily rendered cordless by that same pair of wire cutters. That only happened once though because it was the only time I ever found one that had been taken out of its box. Over the course of that summer and fall, I tallied up several thousand dollars-worth of damage and felt satisfied that I was doing my part to fight the corporate monster.

At the time of my sabotage campaign, that company was paying its peon employees six dollars an hour. Years later, I made friends with one of those employees, and he explained to me that he and all his coworkers would receive bonuses at the end of every month. It wasn't much, but it was a big deal for people who were only making six an hour. Those bonuses come out of a fund, and the money from that same fund was used to cover any losses from shoplifting or vandalism. If there had been no shoplifting or vandalism in a given month, then the bonus could be substantial, but I put dent in the employees' monthly bonuses at the stores where I broke all those bicycles. It was like I threw a rock up at the advancing battle-ship, but my rock fell short and landed on the heads of the innocent people standing in front of me. The CEOs and shareholders used their peon employees as a human shield to protect their profit margin from me.

If anyone who worked at those stores ever reads this, I want to apologize. I probably didn't cost any individual employee more than about ten bucks, but I probably *did* impact several hundred people in that way. That sucks and I'm sorry. I won't ever make that mistake again.

Diversity is what makes cultures, ecosystems, and economies strong. Homogeneity leads to instability and collapse. Ceding control of entire markets to a single corporation is not something we can afford to do if we want our culture to stand the test of time. If there is some way to stop capitalist businesses from metastasizing into global forces of homogeneity, and some way to preserve a diversity of small businesses, then capitalism could be a beneficial system. I would work for that.

As long as it remains an enshrined institution of might-makes-right, where the biggest bully takes all, then I will seek ways to rebel. I think it's wrong for investors and CEOs to profit from other people's work. In my struggle to right these wrongs, I need allies, and I would be likely to find some allies among the peon employees at a big box store. Every human being has potential power. America's millions of service employees may not be using their power at the moment, but it is there, and there is a wide array of potential catalysts that might inspire them to use it. Treating innocent people like enemies can only produce more enemies. So, I really screwed that up.

I guess that was the worst mistake I had to confess, and we already got it over with, so it should all be downhill from here.

I hope I can make this as entertaining as possible, but my goal is not just to entertain. I'm still trying to change your life. I want to say something so compelling that it inspires you to make positive lifestyle changes. Maybe you could stop hoarding excess wealth and use some of it to help your community. Maybe you could make friends with a poor family and let them live in your giant, empty house. If you're not rich, maybe you could stop paying for silly bling to make yourself look rich and save up money to buy land instead.

You could grow gardens in the city. You could stop using electricity and fossil fuels. You could take your used Tesla batteries and dump them in Elon Musk's driveway.

Maybe what you really need to do is stick up for yourself and stop letting some dominant douche bag take advantage of you. Maybe you need to stop being a dominant douche bag and trust people to make their own decisions. The possibilities are endless. It might be delusional for me to think I could inspire people to change their lives, but I wouldn't be motivated enough to write a whole book if I didn't think there was at least a chance.

I'm going to explain a lot more of my philosophical motivations than I did in *Bug Food*. This might be the last book I ever write, so I have to get it all out of my system. This is going to be challenging for people who believe the history they learned in school, and for people who don't believe that the media would hide important information from them. It's going to be challenging for people who don't believe that our government would hurt people in other countries and keep it a secret from us, or that American businesses would take advantage of the bad situations our government creates in other countries. It will also be challenging for people who believe the corporate-funded advertisers who call themselves scientists. I know I see things really differently than most Americans, and I don't want to sound too cocky, but I'm also pretty sure I'm right. Sorry if I end up offending you.

In my wildest dreams, I would convince Americans to stop taking politicians and the mainstream media so seriously. Some people prefer their media liberal, while others like it conservative, but either way, they are being led astray by treacherous, dishonest people who are trying to take advantage of them.

I really like a lot of the liberals and a lot of the conservatives I've met. I think most of us are good people, and we can accomplish wonderful things when we work together. I want to see us team up to boycott foreign imports and work together to re-localize our economies. That project would show us that we have a lot of common ground, and it would solve many of the other major problems that we currently face.

The mainstream media is just going to keep us focused on whatever issues bring out the most emotional disagreement between liberals and conservatives. That and whatever they can think of to frighten us enough that we will hide in our houses and order everything we need from Amazon. They've already whipped us into enough of a frenzy to sell us all manner of bullshit from border walls to fake, "green" power plants. What's next? Another civil war? The sky is not falling, but it might if we keep letting the fear-mongers lead us around by our noses and herd us into rival factions.

With so much false information and so little honesty being provided, it can be a very daunting prospect to figure out what you actually believe. I just want to reassure you that it can be done and urge you not to give up.

No one can ever take away the value of your own experiences and observations. Unless you are tripping on some bad drugs, you can always trust the information you get from your senses. For this to work though, you have to detach your senses from the glowing screens of the phone, computer, and television. Go travelling if you can afford it. Get outside. If you live in the country, go to town. If you live in a city, visit the country. Work at different jobs. Having first-hand experience of a given subject makes it much harder for someone to trick you in relation to that subject.

You have to get to know lots of different kinds of people too. I know it feels easier to find a safe clique of like-minded people and hide out from everyone else, but don't do it! That's a shortcut to ignorance and bad decisions. Next thing you know, you're judging people you've never met, and voting for the government to control them. That can actually screw up their lives, so you end up being an asshole with bad karma, and you have to live in fear. I just wanted to warn you about that pitfall because I fell in it, and had to work my way back out.

***

I have a couple more quick disclaimers and then I can get back to the story. While *Bug Food* was mostly filled up by my character, this second half of the story involves a lot more situations where I am operating among a crew of awesome characters. Unfortunately, many of those people have asked me not to mention them at all in my books even under a fake name.

The same type of people who ordered the massacre of tens of thousands of anti-capitalist South Americans in the 1970's are still in power in our country today, so many of my allies believe that their lives would be in danger if the boss gangsters knew about them. In writing this book, I am making a conscious choice to stick my neck out, but it would be wrong of me to drag anyone else into this risk without their consent.

Unfortunately, that means there will be many places in this story where someone awesome did something awesome and I will not even do so much as hint to you about it. There are also a bunch of stories where I am the main character, but they would still be impossible to recount without the supporting characters, so I will just have to leave them out. It's going to be really difficult to figure out what I can and can't say. I've never had this kind of limitation put on my storytelling before and I'm not sure how it's going to work. I will try to smooth over the gaps so they aren't too awkward, but I will also need to deviate from the truth just a little. Deviating from the truth is something I never want to do when I set out to tell a story, but I don't know how else to get around the security issue. I apologize and I hope you understand the nature on my limitations here.

Just know that in any given chapter, there is quite likely something really interesting happening involving some really inspiring character who I am keeping secret. Please don't hesitate to use your imagination.

***

Lastly, this story took place almost two decades ago. I describe a lot of urban scenery that has changed in the time since then. For example, Newark New Jersey has gotten a total makeover since I walked through it back in 2003. I don't know which places have changed and which ones haven't, and my writing style sounds awkward if I convert all the setting descriptions into the past tense. All this is to say that if you read something that is no longer accurate, that doesn't mean I'm lying. It just means my verb tense is off.

Oh yeah. And there's almost no mention of masturbation in this episode, but there's a lot more pee and poop. Have fun!

3. BLACKOUT HOTTIES

Leominster and Fitchburg are a pair of cities sitting right next to each other in north-central Massachusetts. They make up the core of a metropolitan area that is home to about 150,000 people. As far as I could tell, their big claim to fame is having been the original home of Johnny Appleseed, who himself was famous not only for promoting agricultural self-sufficiency, but also for seducing teenage girls all over our young nation. It's a strange historical chapter, and a lot of people in Leominster/Fitchburg prefer to avoid it.

The cities enjoyed a brief period of prosperity during the middle decades of the 1900's when Massachusetts was the hub of America's booming plastics industry. Leominster/Fitchburg was home to more than a dozen "injection molding" factories producing everything from children's toys to car parts. Then most of the employees, and many of the other people in town got sick, and regulations were created to control pollution from the factories. Rather than spending the money to control their pollution, the owners closed their factories and build new ones in places like the Ohio Valley, the Gulf Coast, and the Third World where people still accept cancer as a necessary sacrifice to make in exchange for having a job. The people of Leominster/ Fitchburg were not willing to make such a sacrifice, and to this day many of them do not have jobs.

I was riding around somewhere in those cities with two of my friends from the Wachusset tree-sitting campaign when we decided to acquire some food for the sitters from a large corporate grocery store. We drove around back and parked in a fairly inconspicuous place behind one of the other stores in the strip mall. We were within sight of the loading dock where we could see many stacks of boxes and a couple of employees standing, chatting, and occasionally moving one of the boxes. My two accomplices told me to wait by the car and holler to them if there was any sign of danger, and then they proceeded to execute a maneuver that I will never forget.

One of them was an attractive young woman. It was a hot summer day and she was dressed appropriately, wearing a tight tank-top that didn't quite reach all the way down to the top of her pants. She left first and when she got to the loading dock, she engaged the employees there (both men) in some manner of conversation. She kept twisting her long reddish-brown hair around her index finger and shifting her weight so that one hip or the other was prominently displayed. They were too far away for me to hear what she was saying, but whatever it was it held both the loading dock employees in rapt attention for quite some time.

Meanwhile my other cohort, the same guy who I fled from the cops with in chapter one, walked up behind them and grabbed a heavy box off the top of one of the piles. It was a long walk back to the car, probably sixty paces at full stride, but he didn't look back over his shoulder once. He just kept looking at me while the grin on his face grew wider with each step. Once he had loaded the box into the car he looked back, saw that our other friend still had the store's employees totally hypnotized and went back for another box! After the second box, our hot friend withdrew to the car and we putted away with no one the wiser. It was amazing. I had never seen anything like it. Well to be fair, I probably had seen something like it before, but that was the first time I ever understood what was happening.

We examined the boxes and discovered that we had just acquired sixty pounds of fake chicken nuggets made out of soy. Perfect. They could be eaten raw up in the trees, and we could feed them to the many vegan volunteers we would probably end up having to accommodate.

Within a few days, volunteers were indeed showing up in a steady stream and I decided to say farewell to Mount Wachusset and the heroic people trying to save its old trees. It was already half way through August, and I felt secure that they had plenty of help. Anyway, I had to complete my solo-egotistical walking project.

I have wished ever since that I had stuck around. Apparently right after I left, the level of police harassment went through the roof. I heard that they hired a helicopter to hover over the sitters for long periods of time and put spotlights on them at night in an attempt to drive them out of the trees with discomfort. Interestingly, those are two of the exact same tactics that failed to intimidate tree-sitters out in Oregon before the state police there put together their tree-climbing division.

I heard that the sitters hung on tenaciously through the month of August and part way into September, until there was some credible threat that the state had found a climber to come and actually extract them from the trees. Hearing this, the sitters slipped out that night and avoided being arrested. They had succeeded in saving the trees for the month of August already, and supposedly state regulations would ban logging in the park for the next eleven months. Unfortunately, a local judge ruled that an exception should be made in that case, and the new ski trails were promptly cut that fall. The state regulations were intended to protect migratory birds, and that just isn't a very high priority when some millionaire is scheduled to make more money.

I assume the hornets put up a valiant fight of their own when it came time to cut down the grandmother tree. They probably incurred an additional cost of some pesticide application and maybe even some minor first-aid to the workers.

Even when we fail to save a special place from "development," I have learned to think of it as a partial success if we can cause the developers to spend more money than they planned on. Investors may not have any sense of the value of healthy ecosystems, but if they look at the numbers and see that an extra million dollars is getting spent on security every time they go to destroy some wild place, that creates the kind of incentive that they can understand. I don't know the exact numbers, but I heard that the state police presented the ski resort with a huge bill for all the extra man-hours, the helicopter, etcetera. There was also a boycott called on Polar Beverages which were owned by the same company and that may have hit them in the bank account some too.

Before I could return to a life of walking, I had to get a new pair of shoes. My feet were literally hanging out of gaping holes in the sides of both my shoes where the treads had separated from the tops. I had been talking to my friends there about my newfound interest in shoplifting, and they were full of encouraging advice. They helped psyche me up, gave me some helpful tips, and then drove me right to a K-mart where they waited in the parking lot with the car running.

I had tried shoplifting from several other places that summer, and it was always a nerve-wracking experience. I would find myself glancing all over the place, face flushed, hands sweating profusely, balking ten times before I actually followed through with the act. Stealing from K-mart was different though. I worked for K-mart for half a year back in 1997. Not only had they paid me $4.75 an hour, consistently scheduled me for thirty-eight hour weeks to avoid giving me benefits, and treated me like a perpetual sixth-grader, but they had also systematically shorted me on my last three paychecks. K-mart owed me and I could feel it. I also had an intimate understanding of their security system and I knew that their employees never receive bonuses under any circumstances. In K-mart, all that sweaty-handed nervousness was gone, replaced by a feeling of righteous payback.

I tried on several pairs of hiking sneakers and when I found the right ones, I simply put my old nasty shoes in the box that they came out of, put the box back on the shelf, and walked right through the door like Jane's Addiction. No one in K-mart noticed a thing so the getaway vehicle remained in place while one of my friends took a turn stealing stuff from another mega-store that shared the same parking-lot. Apparently it was that easy.

***

It only took me one day to walk from Princeton to Worcester and I found a beautiful route through the rugged, oak-covered hills of central Massachusetts. Approaching the city from the northwest I didn't pass through any of the sprawling suburbs that one usually finds surrounding American cities. It was just a bunch of open countryside full of farms, old houses, and quiet stretches of forest. For the last several miles I passed through the protected parkland that surrounds the city of Worcester's municipal water supply. The reservoir and the road were literally the only human developments there. Then very abruptly, I was in the city.

My friends hooked me up with other friends to stay with in Worcester and I had a great time. I spent three days working in gardens with inner-city children, and I'm pretty sure I got invited to big parties all three nights I was in town. Socializing with crowds of like-minded young people was a grounding and comforting thing to do, but it doesn't make much of a story, so I'll skip over my tales of Worcester here.

If you're visiting southern New England though, Worcester is not a place to be skipped. Half a million people live in Worcester and its surrounding suburbs. You can get there from Boston easily on the T commuter rail, and there is a gray area around the boroughs where it is hard to draw a line between the Boston 'burbs and the Worcester 'burbs. Still, Worcester is not just a small version of Boston. It is a unique city with its own distinct culture and a somewhat independent economy. There are a lot of interesting things to see and do there, but I'm not going to write a tourist brochure here either. I will point out that Worcester was the birthplace and childhood home of Abbie Hoffman who wrote better radical books than this one that you should check out.

***

I headed east towards Boston. That's where my list of zine subscribers left off. If I could make it back to Boston and start off again from there, then I would have an unbroken chain of people reading my writing that stretched from Maine to wherever I got to. My obsessive compulsive itch would at last be relieved and America would rise up from dungeon of economic oppression.

I got an early start the day I left Worcester and by mid-afternoon I was in a large town called Westborough. I went into a sandwich shop and discovered that the power was out all over town and had been out for hours. The shop owners gave me a free sandwich out of the cooler because they had to get rid of it before it spoiled. They had a battery-powered radio tuned to the news and it sounded like the apocalypse.

Apparently most of southern New England was in the dark as well as a large portion of upstate New York and possibly areas farther west. It was a huge sensation. The radio broadcasters had not sounded that emotional since 9/11. I guess it makes sense. For a culture that invests most of its religious faith in technology, a failure of the power grid can bring more than just a series of major logistical challenges. It can also cause terrifying feelings of insecurity.

It was a hot day, and it was even hotter inside the sandwich shop, so I moved right along. Just about a mile east of the center of town, a car passed by me and erupted in shrill feminine cheers as if the home team had just scored a touchdown. I looked up from my overheated daze to see a carload of pretty young women waving at me. I had recently replaced the "Freedom" sign on my back with a sign that said, "Love Earth." I had been worrying ever since that my message might be a little too cheesy, but the ladies in Westborough seemed to approve whole-heartedly. It was by far the best thing that had happened all day and it put a spring in my step just in time to climb a big long hill.

Then about twenty minutes later the same car came back the other way and pulled over right in front of me. Now there were only two young ladies. They were sisters, Claire and Maggie, and they had indeed thought that my sign had a good message. After some brief introductions, they told me about a perfect little swimming hole and invited me to go swimming.

Now it was a hot afternoon, and at that particular moment the day's heat had reached its pinnacle. It was that time around 3:30 when the heat from the morning hasn't left yet, but the afternoon heat crams right in on top of it anyway. A car load of wrinkly old men could probably have led me off to a swimming hole at that moment, let alone a car load of beautiful women. At their suggestion, I put my pack in the back seat and piled in beside it.

First we had to visit some of their other friends and then I had to sit in the hot car in a driveway for a while so they could talk to someone in private. On our way to these various places we got to know each other better. Both of them were still in high school which meant they were both too young for me to be thinking of them as hot adult women. I did my best to strain into a monk-like attitude of celibacy and preach about loving the Earth. On the way to the swimming-hole we passed by a cluster of ugly new office towers. The girls told me that had been their favorite forest when they were little and they told me how sad they had been when it got bulldozed and made into an office park.

After a while, we turned onto a narrow road with no traffic and followed it through several miles of secluded forest. Finally, we pulled over onto the narrow gravel shoulder and the girls got out. Through the trees, just down the hill to the right I could make out a shimmering surface of water. There was not so much as a trail to the swimming hole, but we pushed through tree limbs and climbed over fallen logs and when at last we reached the shore of the water, we came right out on a beautiful little beach. They told me it was the Hopkinton Reservoir- water supply for many of the surrounding towns, and the little beach was a secret shared by only a few of their closest friends.

No one hesitated to get in the water. I usually swim naked, but it seemed inappropriate in such company, so I left my boxers on. I figured I could just hang them up on top of my pack to dry in the morning. Claire had brought a tank top and a pair of loose nylon swimming trunks, but her little sister had come unprepared and she just ended up swimming in her underwear too. We swam all the way out to a little island where we rested up catching our breath and then sat and talked about many things.

Claire talked about how she was on track to become a veterinarian and even though she still had a year of high-school left, the administrators were letting her take pre-vet classes at the local community college. Maggie wanted to talk about how she could feel a revolution coming and her sense of how young people everywhere were on the verge of some huge spiritual awakening. It was really just what I wanted to hear coming from exactly who I wanted to listen to, and I got all wrapped up in a breathless conversation with Maggie about how the times they are a changin'. She seemed to be really inspired by the blackout, and by the fact that she had met her first ever wandering, prose-lytizing Earth-lover. I think we reached quite a few major spiritual epiphanies in the course of an hour or two.

Eventually we swam back to shore and resumed our conversation there. None of us had brought towels, so we had to sit there in our swimming out-fits until evaporation dried us off. By that time the beach and that whole side of the lake were in the shade of tall trees, so it took a while. I found a spot where I could lean against a tree, and crouched there as humbly as I could in my underwear. Claire took a seat several reasonable paces to my right, and then Maggie sat down on a rock right in front of me so close that it made my heart pound.

Now there is no way I can describe her appearance to you without being a creepy old pervert, but you have to know for the sake of the story that she was an amazing specimen. In her high-school yearbook she was probably voted most likely to inspire men to *kill* one another. There had to be MTV cameramen hidden somewhere filming us.

We continued our meaningful conversation, but I had trouble concen-trating on what I was saying, and my voice started to tremble a little. I did not want to become the next Johnny Appleseed, but that was the closest I had ever been to someone that pretty and we were both almost naked. She perched with her profile towards me in a perfect posture to display all of her most perfect parts, dripping with water in her mismatched bra and panties. I concentrated as much as I could trying not to glance at her figure, but it was impossible. For a while I tried maintaining eye contact, but we were so close together, that turned out to be even more arousing. I ended up mostly staring at the sand. If I got aroused everyone would notice, and nothing good could come of it. Maybe they would be offended, cuss me out and leave, or worse, they might call the cops. Maybe they would be pleased and I would end up doing something I would be ashamed of for the rest of my life.

Why oh why did no one like that take me to the secret swimming hole when I was in high school? Maggie had not mentioned her exact age, so my brain fought furiously to think of some way that she might be older, but to no avail. She certainly did look older, but realistically, she could only have been seventeen at most and it was much more likely that she was just sixteen. She might have only been fifteen. I had just turned twenty-six and that would just never be okay.

I'll never know whether or not Maggie was actually trying to seduce me. Deep down I'm pretty sure beautiful teen-age girls don't want to hook up with random guys they find walking down the side of the highway. My theory is Maggie had recently discovered how men were affected by her looks, and she was just experimenting to find out more about the scope of her abilities. I think Claire was there to make sure nothing dangerous happened. I wouldn't be surprised if she was gripping a pocket-knife in that interminable moment while her little sister sat dripping dry in front of me. I hope the experiment was as memorable for them as it was for me.

By some miracle I managed not to pop a boner, and finally after one of the more timeless moments of my life, we were all dry enough to put our clothes back on. We walked back to their car where the girls gave me my pack, hugged me a pleasant goodbye, and left me to camp in their lovely secret place. I would never have found such a beautiful camping spot left to my own devices, and that had to suffice as my only consolation for never getting laid back in high school.

4. PROVOKING THE IRE OF BOSTON

I was vaguely aware that the girls had taken me south, so I set off in a northerly direction first thing in the morning, wet underpants waving like a flag from the cross-bar on the top of my pack. Sure enough, within a few miles I got back to route 30 and turned east.

The blackout was still in progress and a lot of businesses had closed even though it was a weekday. At one point I passed by a transformer station where a bunch of utility workers were diligently hustling to restore power. I forged ahead into the thickening sprawl of Framingham, Cochituate, Natick and Weston. By the time I got to Cochituate, the power had either been restored or I had walked into an area where it hadn't gone out in the first place, and people were behaving normally.

Just as the sun went down, I found what appeared to be a perfect camping spot on the eastern edge of Weston. A cliff had been cut into the edge of a steep hillside to make room for a tangle of highways. I scrambled up around the edge of the cliff, and up above I discovered a broad stretch of forest. In spite of the fact that it was right in the thick of the Boston megalopolis, it didn't seem like anybody ever went there. It was a difficult place to get to and the native vegetation showed a corresponding lack of disturbance.

Unfortunately I couldn't find a single flat spot to set up camp on. I kept searching farther and farther up the hill, but if anything it was only getting steeper as I went up. At that time of day, I didn't have the energy for an intense uphill bushwhack into the darkening unknown, so I settled on the most level spot I could find and went to sleep. I didn't even set up my tent because there was hardly any space for it between all the bushes. There were only a handful of mosquitos in late August and I could tell it wasn't going to rain that night.

It was a well-secluded place to sleep that close to the core of a giant city, but I kept startling myself awake all night long anyway. Every time I rolled over or shifted positions, I would slide down the hill a few inches towards the highway. Every time that happened I would jolt awake in a panic thinking I was about to tumble over the top of the road-cut. In reality I was at least a hundred feet away from the top of the cliff. There were dozens of little trees and bushes blocking the way, and the slope wasn't really steep enough for me to slide all the way down it anyway. All of that was obvious whenever I was awake, but as soon as I fell asleep the anxiety would creep back in and wake me up. Between that and the constant rumble of the junction between I-90, I-495, route 30, and a major railroad line, I didn't get much sleep.

***

I had made arrangements to stay with some people in Boston, but I had been trying to call them for days to get directions to their house and I just couldn't seem to get them on the phone. I tried and failed again that morning and my spirits sank. Here I was marching right into America's least welcoming city again with no place to stay and no backup plan. Feeling sleep-deprived and grumpy as hell I found myself stumbling across the Boston College campus with a ferocious need to urinate. Just then it started to drizzle. It was the final straw. I just didn't care anymore, so I turned into a hedge and peed right in front of a couple dozen students who were hurrying this way and that. I turned my back to them, but I made no attempt to hide in the bushes or to be discreet in any way. I'm not sure what that really proved, but it took the edge off my grumpy attitude.

The drizzle only lasted for half an hour or so. Soon after that the sun came out and I crossed the line into Boston Proper in the familiar neighborhood of Brighton.

I was still stumbling headlong into the city wondering what the hell I was going to do when the powerful smell of rotting compostable garbage caught my attention. Looking up I realized that I had stumbled upon the infamous van belonging to Dan the Bagel Man. I didn't take the time to describe Dan the Bagel Man in my first book, but he was in fact the strangest of the many strange characters I met at the rotting Food Not Bombs house. Dan suffered from some intense mental disorder that I took for schizophrenia, and it made him really difficult to hang out with. It was as if there were way too many thoughts occurring in his head simultaneously and he would try to express all of them in a constant stream of highly agitated words. There was nothing anyone could say that would not add more stress to Dan's already heaping plate of stress. He didn't usually leave space for anyone to say anything anyway.

In spite of all that, he was a dedicated Food Not Bombs volunteer whose whole life revolved around the delivery of free food. Somehow in a city of nearly four million people, I had followed my nose right to Dan the Bagel

Man's van.

I sat down on the sidewalk and waited for him to return from whatever he was doing. Finding Dan the Bagel Man was not necessarily a solution to my problems. I knew that the old man, Eric had died and his house had been repossessed by the banks, so I wouldn't be able to stay there. I also couldn't stay with Dan because more than a couple hours with him would drive me crazy, but I reckoned he could take me to some place where other FNB volunteers were hanging out and I could improvise from there.

Sure enough after about half an hour of staking out his van, I came face to face with Dan the Bagel Man. He didn't remember me and it seemed to startle him that I knew who he was. But then, once we were reintroduced he didn't even blink when I asked if I could climb aboard the van and join him on his daily missions. Apparently anyone who could handle his reeking van and his schizophrenic chatter was good enough for him.

First we had to go pick up boxes of food from several different locations around the city. I have always been baffled by the layout of Boston's streets. Riding around shotgun with someone who really knows their way around Boston is better than a roller-coaster ride at the fair. There are no right angles anywhere, you can never go more than two blocks in any direction without having to turn, and most intersections involve more than two streets. Add that to the fact that everyone who drives there is eternally pissed off and it's quite a scene. A popular New England joke claims that Massachusetts is the only state whose driver's education manual actually shows students how to give opposing drivers the finger. If you put a neurosurgeon and a Boston cab driver next to each other and asked me who had the trickiest job, I'd point to the cabbie.

Navigating the back streets of this arcane maze, Dan proved to be a neurosurgeon in his own right, and we left a zigzagging trail of stench across every corner of the city. By mid-afternoon we had all the food and we arrived at a building full of fresh-faced young volunteers. All of the leather-clad Punks had disappeared and been replaced by college students. It was an odd transition, but the spirit of community remained intact and I made friends easily with the new crew.

One of the people I had been trying to get in touch with was the courageous kid who delivered food to our tree-sits that night while the night-vision commandos were lurking about. One of the FNB volunteers knew him well and they gave me directions to his house. When I asked if it was wise to just show up without any prior communication, they reassured me that whoever answered the door when I got there would become my friend and we would have a good time.

I showed up that evening to what turned out to be the kid's dad's house. I guess that made sense since most fourteen-year-olds don't have their own apartments. His dad was cool too and we ended up becoming friends just as the FNB volunteer had promised. I stayed with them for several days in the Jamaica Plain neighborhood surrounded by tons of artists, hipsters, and other cool White people. I helped with several more Food Not Bombs meals, worked in several community gardens, and drank a lot of beer with the hipsters. I also signed up over a dozen new subscribers to my zine.

One night I had stayed until ten or eleven o'clock cleaning up after a Food Not Bombs meal and then walked back to Jamaica Plain in the dark. My route took me through a poorly lit Puerto Rican neighborhood, and when I got back people were beside themselves with concern. They told me I was extremely lucky to have survived that neighborhood in the dark and I should never do that again.

I was astonished to find out that such a bunch of cool-looking people could turn out to be so full of racist fears. I recited all the best lines I could remember from *No More Prisons*, but to no avail. They insisted that for whatever I had heard, Boston was different. Boston's Black and Spanish-speaking ghettos were scary places where I really would get mugged and thugged and whatever other bad things a chicken-shit gringo could imagine. I guess if you look and act like a JP hipster, maybe you are in danger in other parts of the city.

To their credit, my actual hosts didn't participate in the onslaught of racist stereotyping, but the whole crew of people who were over visiting them ganged up against me and I ended up conceding the debate. The fact that they lived in Boston where I was just visiting did effectively trump all my theoretical points.

The next day I decided to walk around and find out for myself just how scary the non-White ghettos of Boston could be. I left my pack in Jamaica Plain, swiped a map from some pharmacy chain-store and wandered all over the deepest darkest ghettos of southern Boston. Some people gave me funny looks, and some others were directly rude to me, but that's just the way people in Boston act. By mid-afternoon I was satisfied that I had proven the silly JP hipsters wrong and I wandered downtown. I was hungry so I went to the Quincy Market and gorged on discarded gourmet leftovers until I was so full I had to sit on a park bench for about an hour rubbing my fat belly. By then it was getting late so I headed back towards JP.

My route took me right past the historic Fenway baseball stadium where a long line of Red Sox fans were waiting impatiently to buy tickets. The Sox's arch rivals, the New York Yankees were in town and it was a big deal to the fans. Hundreds of them were waiting up on a concrete platform about one story above street-level and the line stretched half-way down a long concrete ramp leading to the sidewalk I was walking on. It was less than an hour until game time. As I approached the bottom of the ramp, quite a few of the men in the line erupted in a belligerent cry of outrage. I looked up to see at least a dozen large angry men pointing at me, their faces contorted with rage, shouting angry curses.

Oh Shit! I was still wearing my Yankees hat! I had grown so accustomed to my New York disguise that I had worn it right into the capitol of Red Sox country. What a dumb move.

All in one motion I said, "Oh shit," swiped the offending hat off my head and started jogging away from the angry mob. Apparently that was a sufficient display of cowardice to appease them, and an approving cheer went up from the platform. I looked up to see that most of the bulls were smiling again and several of them had raised cans of beer in my direction as if in a toast.

Whew! Disaster averted. If someone had objected to a Pittsburgh Pirates hat like that I might have tried to stand my ground, but the New York Yankees could screw a pineapple for all I care. I had ceased thinking of my Yankees hat as a symbol of America's richest baseball team. I loved New York and I was proud to have lived by my wits there for an entire winter. To me the hat was more a symbol of my New York experience, but how were a bunch of drunken Red Sox fans supposed to know that? It was like I had worn a red sweatshirt to a bullfight.

I complain relentlessly about how nasty Boston people are, but I'm actually really lucky that they are such a forgiving lot. I had just spent the whole day wandering around the ghettos in a Yankees hat and only when I passed by the half-drunk crowd at Fenway did I finally get a real reaction.

5. A BIG HEART

Looking at my map that evening, I noticed the huge green swath of the Blue Hills Reserve separating Boston from its southern suburbs. When I asked about it, my hosts assured me that it would make a great camping place for me on my way out of town. I ended up drinking quite a bit with them that night, and I was too hung over to get moving first thing in the morning. I wasn't too worried though because the Blue Hills didn't look very far away on the map. It was afternoon before I finally got rolling and the first hour or so was pretty rough. Walking is a pretty good cure for a hangover though and eventually I walked off the alcohol's poisonous effects.

In the late afternoon, I walked through a hood called Dorchester that turned out to be more ghetto than any place I had found on my grand ghetto tour of the previous day. This time I had my Yankees hat respectfully stashed in my pack.

I made it to the boundary of the Blue Hills Reserve right around sunset. There was a big sign right at the trailhead that said "No Camping," and threatened legal consequences. That made me a little nervous, but I had come there to camp and the sun was setting. Another sign showed a topo map of the whole park. Looking at that map I could see that I was right at the base of a huge hill and it was a little less than a mile to the top. I decided I wanted to camp on top of the hill and without further hesitation I started up.

Quite a few people were coming down the same trail and it must have been obvious that a guy hauling a big backpack into the park after sunset was surely going to camp there. I just hoped no one would be up-tight enough to actually rat me out.

The hill was steep and long. Spurred on by the waning evening light, I hustled up it until I was soaked in sweat and practically gasping for breath. It was almost completely dark when the trail leveled off and I emerged into a rocky clearing where it suddenly seemed light again. There at the summit, the parks department had cleared several acres of forest to give hikers a view of the city. Or maybe the mountain was just naturally bald. I really couldn't tell one way or the other.

Either way, it was an amazing view. I don't remember ever being anywhere in Boston where I could look up and see a view of a nearby mountain, but here I was on top of a mountain looking right down on the nearby city. The lights were coming up as night fell, but they were softened by several miles of hazy smog.

Several other people were still up there enjoying what was left of the sunset, so I slithered down to the forests edge and hid until they left. The last pair of stragglers remained until well after dark and I got pretty irritated waiting for them. For some reason the hill-top was swarming with mosquitos and I just wanted to get in my tent. But I was determined to sleep right on the summit and I was determined not to be seen doing it, so I hung out and quietly squished bugs all over my face.

Finally they left and I set up camp by flashlight. In the dark I couldn't find an ideal spot. Where I ended up there was only a tiny bit of soil stretched over the bedrock, so my tent stakes had nothing to sink into. I ended up sleeping with my tent sagging and dangling all around me. Oh well. It was good enough for one night.

All of my stubborn lurking paid off when I awoke the next morning and unzipped my tent to greet a spectacular view of the city. In the night the air had cooled settling the smog and I could see every detail of the urban panorama to the north and the bay to the east. I packed up my tent first thing so I could plausibly deny that I had just slept there and the first hikers of the day arrived only moments later. Then the sun rose and its fiery glow reflected off the glass surfaces of some of the skyscrapers downtown. It was Boston sure enough, but somehow it was, well....... beautiful.

Coming down the mountain's south side the view was not so nice. Just south of the Blue Hills is a giant tangle of highway intersections that I had to pick my way through for a half an hour. Then it was hours of trudging through the soulless homogenous suburbs of Randolph and Avon. By afternoon I reached Brockton which is not a suburb, but a huge pocket of densely populated Spanish speaking ghetto. I guess it must have been an independent city before it was engulfed by Boston's suburbs.

I turned west in Brockton and then turned south again in Easton. Just around the time I was starting to really crave some supper I stumbled upon an odd little Chinese restaurant. The suburbs were starting to thin out into the countryside at that point and there were no other businesses around. I hadn't expected to find any food until I got to a town center of some sort, but there in the middle of nowhere was the world's tiniest restaurant. The kitchen, dining room, and restroom were all crammed into a space about the size of a two car garage. I sat at one of the two tables and enjoyed a generous meal. Then it was time to find a camping spot for the night.

The landscape was still fairly suburban, so I didn't get my hopes up for a nice secluded spot. Having thus lowered my standards, it wasn't long before I found something adequate. It was an abandoned garage with a big back yard totally grown over with bushes and weeds, and it was situated just right so that no one in any of the nearby houses would see me approach it. Without hesitation, I strolled up the long driveway and then slipped around the decaying old building into the backyard. From there I could see that there were no more houses behind it and the forest stretched on indefinitely. That was a pleasant surprise, so I decided to keep walking out into the woods and find a really nice camping spot. I had only gone a hundred paces or so before I changed my mind. Thick, thorny greenbriars were growing up everywhere and I was set upon by an uncanny swarm of mosquitos. It was by far the thickest cloud of mosquitos I had ever seen anywhere that late in the summer. In fact, there were more mosquitos there than you would find in the swamps of Maine in the spring time.

It felt unnatural and it gave me a weird feeling about the place. I stopped and set up camp in the first clear space I could find. So many mosquitos descended upon me in the five minutes that it took to set up my tent that I started to panic. These bugs were ferocious. Sometimes mosquitos are content to just hover around your face and buzz in your ears, but these ones were aggressively biting me all at the same time. The more I swatted at them, the longer it took to set up my tent and I found myself lurching around, dropping things clumsily and stumbling over the greenbriars. Once I finally got in the tent it took me half an hour to kill all the bugs that followed me in the door. I got a pretty good night's sleep after that though.

When I awoke in the morning, the skeeters were still waiting for me so I packed up as quickly as I could and postponed breakfast until I could get somewhere less buggy. Less than a mile down the road I came to a sign welcoming me into the Raynham Swamp nature preserve. It turns out that I had camped right outside of the largest network of swamp-land in the state of Massachusetts. The Raynham Swamp, also known as the Hocko-mock Swamp, spans the border of Bristol and Plymouth Counties and covers significant portions of five townships. It is much larger than the "Great

Swamp" where the Narragansetts hid out in nearby Rhode Island.

The road passed through several miles of wilderness wetlands. The forest canopy was pretty thick, but the trees all grew out of little hummocks of land with standing water in between most of them. It was gorgeous scenery to behold, especially in the early light of morning, but the bugs chased me out as quickly as I could move. I could swat them off my face and arms, but somehow they managed to land on my legs even as they swung back and forth in my hurried stride. Bending to swat them off my legs slowed me down too much and it was already too hot out for long pants. Anyway, I figured if I stopped long enough to dig a pair of long pants out of my pack and change into them, the mosquitos would devour me whole. At one point I had to stop and tie my shoe and even that was long enough for them to get a bunch of my blood. My only reprieve was the gust of wind that would swirl off the back of an occasionally passing car.

Sometime in the mid-morning I emerged from the nature preserve into yet another eerie location. All along the right side of the road was a vast field paved in asphalt. It must have been almost a square mile of nothing but old cracked pavement. There were no buildings and no one around. It was just a giant abandoned parking lot in the middle of nowhere. The only thing that I could think of was that maybe it had been built for racing cars, but then abandoned some ten or twenty years before I got there. It was a weird place but it had one advantage that I really appreciated at the time. The temperature differential between the sun cooked asphalt and the forest created enough of a breeze to blow away most of the mosquitos. It was a welcome relief, so I sat down in front of the bizarre scene and ate my breakfast.

After the world's largest abandoned parking lot, I passed a greyhound dog-racing stadium followed by mile after mile of post-industrial wasteland. Huge quarry pits, abandoned cement works and other industrial works that I couldn't identify lined both sides of the road. It was clear that much of Bristol county had been carried away to build the nearby cities of Boston and Providence. It was a stark reminder that for every high-tech collage of urban landscape, there is a corresponding place like Bristol County that has been destroyed in sacrifice.

I made it to the small city of Taunton by early afternoon and stopped for lunch in an Italian sandwich shop. By then the day was broiling in its own heat and it felt really unpleasant to be back in a city.

After lunch I struggled a couple more miles into the center of town where I found a big park and plunked down in the shade of an old tree. I decided it was too hot to carry on, so I should just stay there until the heat let up some. I ended up loitering there for hours, but I met a few people and signed them up for zines, so the time was not wasted.

After a while I met a reporter from the newspaper in Brockton. She was just out of college and she had been assigned to do a story about the people she found hanging out on the Taunton Green that afternoon. It sounded like a really mundane waste of time to me and I gave her a really short, almost grumpy interview.

It was still really hot, but I decided I better get a move on so as to be out of the city by nightfall. Taunton is a pretty compact city though and I made it out into the country in just a couple hours. I had run out of water, so I knocked on the door of a random house to ask for a refill. A girl of maybe thirteen came to the door, followed immediately by her father who was beside himself with amazement that I had walked there from Maine. He acted like it was the most incredible thing he had ever heard. He asked me a bunch of questions and after every answer I gave him he let out a huge, exuberant exclamation complete with dramatic facial expressions and hand gestures. His daughter had just returned from filling my water bottle when he blurted out, "Damn man! You must have some big balls!"

I had always been in the habit of watching my mouth around pubescent female children, so I immediately started to blush with embarrassment. Miraculously, I recovered with a witty response. Normally I think of witty responses about five minutes after their time has passed, but for once I responded on cue, "I think it has more to do with the size of my heart, sir."

I signed them up for a zine and they wished me good luck. Back on the road, I was headed west towards Providence. A mild breeze swept away all the raunchy heat of the afternoon quicker than I expected. It was a lovely evening for walking and the countryside was lovely too. Though I was only two towns away from Providence, there were no suburbs to be seen. Just farms and forest. As the sun went down, I set up camp under a stand of young white pines across the road from a big pasture full of horses. The soft bed of pine needles made the coziest resting place I had slept in for quite a while.

I made it back to Providence before noon on the following day.

6. SECRET HEADQUARTERS OF THE REBEL ALLIANCE

Before my third stop through Providence, I actually had the foresight to call ahead and make arrangements for a place to stay while I was in town. I had an invite to stay at a squatted building in a broken-down neighborhood called Olneyville.

Where there were houses, they were inhabited by poor Latino, Portuguese, and Black families, but much of the neighborhood was made up of abandoned factory buildings and some big bare stretches where old industrial works had been bulldozed out. Everything was made out of red brick and some of the industrial ruins were really old and weathered. Olneyville was the site of America's first industrial-scale glass production clear back in the 1600's. I'm not sure if any buildings remained from that long ago, but some of the abandoned structures looked more like something you'd expect to see in Europe than here in America.

The only real modern touch came from the beautiful graffiti that adorned many of the walls. There was a combination of ghetto-style throw-ups, and then the more intricate and multi-colored pieces by middle-class artists imitating and building upon the ghetto styles. Also, some artist had gotten ahold of dozens of old stop signs and got children from the neighborhood to design and paint cartoons on them. Then they put them up on poles or pasted them to abandoned brick walls all over the hood. It was a nice touch.

The Oak Street Squats, where I had arranged to stay, occupied a huge old red-brick factory. The building was only three stories, but each level had a double-high ceiling, so it was really pretty tall for a brick structure. Each level was divided into two long wings separated by a broad concrete stairwell that ran up the middle. Most of the sewing machines or whatever industrial equipment once produced things there had been removed, leaving the long cavernous spaces mostly empty.

I was told that the people occupying the building were like a federation of quite a few different crews of friends. Each one occupied its own section of the building and had its own way of doing things, and they didn't necessarily mingle much with the other groups. Some of the groups were going through some hard-drug phases, or so I heard, but they all stuck together on the principle that the city would have a harder time evicting such a large number of people.

The folks I stayed with lived on the west wing of the top floor. They were a gang of really talented artists. I think they said there were nine of them in all. I don't think I even got to meet all of them, but I really admired the home they had made. They were like fictional mad-scientists come to life and it all came out through the decoration of their own home. I knew I would not be able to remember all the details, so I actually grabbed a notebook and wrote down some of my bizarre findings in the Oak Street Squat. By some miracle, I have retained possession of that diary entry to this very day, and now I am very pleased to quote it to you verbatim.

Cavernous art space on the top floor of a once abandoned industrial building. Started as one giant room and the occupants built walls and smaller rooms inside it to suit their needs. From the look of it, the construction did not take place all at once, but rather as a series of projects over a period of years. In fact, there is a pile of lumber in the main room that is being made into something as I speak.

The ceiling is very high, and people have built quite a few lofts to make use of the vertical space. Some of the lofts are enclosed for privacy, and some are partially open. Some rooms on the ground floor are enclosed and some are not. Some of the lofts are accessible by stairs, others by ramps, and others just by ladders. One loft right in the center has a window with a view into the kitchen. Another series of lofts sits over top of a hallway. No two doorways are the same size. Some walls come halfway down from the ceiling. Other walls rise halfway up from the floor, and some walls stretch all the way from floor to ceiling. One wall of the kitchen is made entirely from salvaged window frames, shudders and venetian blinds. Due to their irregular shapes and sizes, there are quite a few gaps, and a potted plant hangs in one of the gaps. The rooms are full of a variety of different home-made work benches, tables and shelves, all different sizes and textures. The architecture is so complex that I feel like I am inside an Escher painting. I'm certain there are secret places in here that I don't know about!

The walls are decorated with a great variety of bright-colored paints, happy clouds, bizarre designs that remind me of Dr. Seuss, lots of stenciled, spray-painted birds and some hand-painted birds as well. A few places are decorated with different patches of wall-paper and different fabric scraps that seem to have been selected for their wild colors and patterns. While many of the walls are hanging with paintings, posters, and photographs, there are many other places where the art has been applied directly to the wall by a pattern of random whimsy.

Did I mention that these people are artists? Their art is all over the place. Paintings, photographs, zines, stickers, stencils, drawings, home-made clothing and costumes, home-made comics, stuffed mutant dolls, furniture, sculptures made out of all sorts of stuff, homemade bicycles, music, carpentry, and architecture seem to be their specialties. There's a bike repair shop in here. There's a wall devoted to old posters advertising concerts and parties that I'm certain were all epic experiences that I shouldn't have missed. The stereo is always playing obscene music that sets new standards for weirdness and the neighbors next door are usually jamming away in an effort to raise that bar again.

I can't possibly list all of the things that are hanging from the ceiling, but here are a few of my favorites: Cardboard cutouts of stormy clouds including a bolt of lightning; A large abstract sculpture made out of literally hundreds of empty soy-milk boxes; A series of papier-mache unicorns of identical design, but varying sizes; A collection of women's bras with strange objects (like bicycle horns) glued over the nipples; A toy pterodactyl with only one wing.

One loft is going up in cardboard cutout flames. The collection of costumes, hats and masks is breathtaking. There are about twenty-five bicycles in here and the parts to make quite a few more. Skateboards! Quite a few limbless, headless female mannequins. Tons of art supplies, tools and raw materials. I wonder if anyone is going to make anything out of all these duct-pipes?

Besides the human occupants, a dog, two cats, and a shitload of plants live here.

Perhaps the most impressive thing about this place is the telephone. The phone sits right by the front door on a little round table with a little plastic kindergarten chair to sit on while you talk. Surrounding this table is a fifteen-foot-tall cone made of chicken-wire, soft plastic, papier-mache, string and other materials. You enter through an arched doorway partially covered by strips of translucent, soft plastic. The interior of the plastic telephone grotto is lit by its own yellow-tinted light bulb. If you happen to look up while you're in there, you will be greeted by a terrifying herd of stuffed animals and monsters hanging from the ceiling and all looking right back at you.

I love it here! These people are obviously insane!

It could only have been better if they had held open hours for it to be a children's daycare/playhouse/museum. For all I know maybe they did. I was out in the city most of the time doing other fun things with Providence people. I stayed for four or five days, saw a bunch more shows, cooked more FNB meals, and helped repair bicycles. Providence bands were really into making music that you couldn't possibly dance to because the rhythm was all weird, but it was fun to go see them play anyway.

There was plenty of room for me to sleep in the mad-artist castle at night, but it was hot in there in the dog days of August, so I opted to sleep out on the fire escape in the fresh air. There were several fire escapes all on the southern wall. Most of the platforms were covered with potted garden plants and more weird art, but one had been left clear in case of an actual fire, and that's where I slept. It was almost as high above the ground as the tree platform I had slept in, but the fire-escape didn't sway back and forth and it was safely enclosed by many iron guard-rails.

I would awaken each morning to a stunning birds-eye view of several blocks worth of industrial ruins all grown over with moss and ailanthus trees. The left side of my view was framed by a great curving segment of some roaring interstate highway. The interstate was elevated on a big concrete ridge effectively blocking the view of whatever lay on the other side.

At night I would watch the planet Mars arc across the sky. People told me that Mars would be closer to the Earth that week that at any other time for the next several hundred years. They said it was a very significant time for people who believe in astrology. It was the summer of 2003, and it wasn't hard to get into the astrological groove with Bush, Blair, and Bin Laden all beating their chests and bringing war back like some horrible retro fad. Somehow I doubt the red planet actually has anything to do with the culture of military-imperial destruction, but those guys will jump on any excuse they can find.

***

In a sad postscript to all this, I heard the majestic madhouse of the Oak Street squats was evicted and bulldozed a few years after I visited there. Just like the Hostos-Crimmins garden it was too beautiful to survive in this profit-driven society.

For three and a half decades at the end of the twentieth century, a guy named Buddy Cianci reigned as mayor of Providence. He was a well-known mob-boss with connections to every organized crime racket in the city. He survived scandal after scandal and always came back to serve another term as mayor. In one notable incident, a dead body was found in the trunk of Buddy Cianci's car, wrapped in a rug from Buddy Cianci's house. Cianci claimed that the whole situation was a total mystery to him. He was acquitted by the judge and he resumed his mayoral duties. I shit you not.

Despite Buddy Cianci's superlative record of corruption, he couldn't have cared less about kids squatting abandoned factories in Olneyville. None of the squatters were old enough to remember a time before Cianci, but throughout his more recent terms, they had suffered only minor harassment from the PPD.

I think it was 2004 when someone by the name of Cicellini finally ousted old Buddy from the mayor's mansion. Cicellini was a fired-up reformer who was going to purge the city of Cianci-era corruption. He sounded good, but he turned out to be just another Democrat. The city would continue to be just as corrupt if not more so, but different people would benefit from the shake-down. For some reason the Oak Street squats had to be sacrificed in the transition. I think Cicellini was trying to prove that he was tough on something but I'm not really sure what the point was.

He evicted the squats in the middle of January, the coldest month of his first year as mayor. According to the folklore, there were usually about sixty people living there, and at times the population of that one building swelled to over a hundred. I heard estimates that about seventy people were there that winter when they got thrown out into the ice and snow. It is one of two instances I know of where New England landowners have evicted people from their homes in January, and both stand out in my mind as important examples of calculated cruelty.

7. HORROR SCENES WITH JILL

Enter a character who I will now call Jill. A couple of months earlier, during my vacation, I had been to a big social gathering where I met Jill. She was tall and skinny and pretty. I had only just barely made her acquaintance when she asked if she could come hiking with me. Of course, I was thrilled and I agreed heartily. The idea of anyone coming with me was exciting let alone a beautiful young woman, but there was something strange about the whimsical way that she asked that made me wonder a little. We were at the same gathering for the next four days, and in that time, we barely hung out together at all.

By the time I got to Providence, I hadn't heard from her in three months and I just assumed it wasn't going to happen. After Sweet Pea, I had learned to rein in my expectations a little bit. But then out of the blue, I got an e-mail that Jill was ready to join me and she wanted to know where I was. I responded, and she arrived a couple days later with her father who had driven her there all the way from the Hudson Valley region of New York. I felt bad and apologized to him for all the trouble he had gone through, but he didn't seem to mind. He was just extremely worried about his daughter and he begged and implored me to be careful and take good care of her. He was very polite, and he didn't do that threatening thing that some fathers do, but somehow, I still felt certain that I would bleed to death in his hands if anything bad happened to Jill.

I did my best to reassure him and then he drove all the way back to New York. Jill had arrived in the late afternoon, so we stayed one more night at the squat and departed in the morning. Before I knew Jill was coming along, my plan had been to follow the Blackstone River up to the small city of Woonsocket and then turn west towards Hartford, Connecticut. It wasn't the most direct route, but I was hoping to distribute some zines in Woonsocket. I asked Jill if she was up for some slight meandering or if she would rather head due west. She didn't care where we went, so we struck out for Woonsocket. Jill said she was in the habit of running several miles every day, so I felt reassured that she would be athletic enough to walk all over the place.

As we walked along, we got to know each-other better, but there was something awkward about our new partnership. Jill didn't share any of my opinions about politics or spirituality or the changes our society needs to make. It wasn't that she was against my ideas. She just didn't really think about those kinds of things, and so she had no opinion at all. I couldn't figure out why she would even want to come along with me on such an adventure, but I didn't want to discourage her, so I didn't mention it.

She was having a lot of trouble with her backpack, and we had to keep stopping and adjusting it. It was an old Army surplus pack that she had dragged out of her parents' basement and she had no idea how to use it. It looked like a pretty good pack to me, but I guess it probably wasn't the most comfortable design ever. Jill's hips started to chaff right away and she found the discomfort really overwhelming. She also felt overwhelmed by the exhaustion from walking and the pain in her feet and legs. We had only made it to Pawtucket when she reached a point of total despair.

She wondered aloud how she could be so weak when she did so much running at home. She was really hard on herself and I felt bad. I did my best to reassure her that her body would strengthen and I would be happy to go as slowly as she needed until then. It took her a long time to get her good spirits back and then for the rest of the day we hobbled along in short increments of walking, broken up by long rests full of sorrow and self-loathing. It felt like I had to coax her along every step of the way.

It was a slow pace, but we did make it out of the city by nightfall and we set up camp in a place called Lincoln State Park. Of course, the park had "No Overnight Camping" signs, but we just crawled into the dense forest and set up camp in my usual manner.

As the light of the day faded, Jill became visibly nervous. We crawled in the tent and talked for a while until the complete darkness set in and then Jill started to really freak out. She had never slept in the forest before and she didn't realize that little animals come out at night and scurry every which-way. Every time a mouse or a bug would rustle the leaves, she would exclaim in terror, "What was that!? Did you hear that!?"

I found myself explaining that the forest is a good place for all sorts of nocturnal creatures to live. Yes. I did hear that, and no, I didn't know what it was but I wasn't really worried about it.

Jill was still beside herself with fear, and she could not be consoled. I started to lose my patience and I began teasing her in an effort to diffuse my frustration. As if on cue, a nearby raccoon let out a long, gurgling growl straight out of a horror movie soundtrack. Jill screamed, grabbed onto me with both arms and clung to me by her fingernails. The raccoon startled me pretty good too, but I composed myself quickly in an effort to soothe my companion.

If you've never heard two raccoons cuss each other out, it really is quite an experience. They have an incredible range of scary rasping growling and barking sounds in their repertoire. They also do a sort of squirrel-like chatter, but with much more death-metal bass than a squirrel can do.

As it turned out, this raccoon was just getting warmed up. I hadn't even convinced Jill to pull her claws out of me before it launched into a prolonged streak of irate raccoon profanity. Then it started coming towards us.

Now I had heard two raccoons fight each other before, but I had never been directly cussed out by a raccoon myself. The closer it came, the harder it was to escape the conclusion that it really was upset with us. The situation was starting to feel pretty tense. I wondered if we had put the tent in some place that had caused it some terrible inconvenience or loss. The phrase, "Get the fuck out of here before I fuck you up," is way more intimidating in raccoon language than any other language I've ever heard. It sounded like some Germanic banshee-monster from the forest of the damned was coming to devour our babies.

I pushed Jill off of me so I could get out my knife and take up a defensive position. The raccoon kept getting closer, but it was moving very slowly and there seemed to be something wrong with its voice. Not that I really know what a raccoon's voice is supposed to sound like, but its roars and screeches sounded like they were gargling out through a whole bunch of mucous, and much of the time it seemed to be coughing. It sounded like an angry raccoon that was dying from some horrible upper respiratory infection.

The whole situation was getting overwhelmingly bizarre. I realized that without visual confirmation, I couldn't be sure that it really was a raccoon. All I knew from my ears was that some diseased animal in a state hysterical fury was coming to get us as soon as it could drag its tired, sick body across the last ten feet of space to our tent. I put my flimsy little sneakers on wishing I had a nice big pair of steel-toed boots. I didn't want to fight a sick raccoon or whatever evil banshee was out there, but I got ready 'cause it was a-comin'.

I was waiting for it to get just a little bit closer before I jumped out of the tent and attacked, but at the last second the mysterious demon halted its advance. It never did attack the tent, but instead it just sat there berating us with the most offensive sounds I have ever heard in my life. It shrieked and roared and chattered and cussed. It growled and snarled and hissed. Its sermon of hatred was regularly interrupted by fits of coughing. It would choke on some snot for a minute, then wheeze and gasp until it had recovered its strength and then resume tearing us a new asshole.

Jill looked like she had gone into a coma for a while, but the sick monster tirade went on for so long without escalating into real violence that she started to come out of paralysis. At length she found the courage to ask me what was going on. I had to admit that I had no idea. To this day I have not come up with a good explanation of what we experienced that night.

I wondered how much more of it we were going to endure. I didn't feel at all inclined to charge into the darkness and attack something that wasn't attacking me, but we sure weren't going to roll over and go to sleep either. The sound was really overwhelming.

Finally, the thing seemed to be tuckering itself out. It tried to maintain its intensity, but it kept coughing more and more, and at times it seemed to be literally gasping for breath. My heart and my adrenal glands stood down a notch from level one emergency. Steadily the monster became less frightening and more annoying. For Christ's sake buddy! Throw in the towel! You scared the shit out of us, but we didn't leave and now you've almost screamed yourself to death. Take a freakin' break!

Finally, the little bugger spluttered to a stop. It laid there wheezing and gurgling for quite a while and I thought it might just die right on the spot, but after a while it got up and dragged its weary ass back into the woods even slower than it had approached. What a weird night.

***

We woke in the morning to a steady rain and our spirits sank. I decided to skip Woonsocket and just head west toward Connecticut. Jill obviously wasn't up for any extra hiking and in the pouring rain, neither was I. That meant backtracking a couple miles to a place where we could get on a road with a good westerly course. Backtracking is always a bummer, but in this case it at least took us past a nice cafeteria-style restaurant where we could get out of the rain and eat some hot breakfast.

We were really wet and disheveled compared to the other customers and Jill wore a particular look of defeat on her face. At one point I got up to go to the bathroom, and when I came out, a man was bent over talking to her very quietly. As soon as she looked up at me, he flashed me a nervous glance and scurried away. Jill said that as soon as I went in the restroom he had hurried over and offered to rescue her. Apparently, he thought I had kidnapped her! I got a good laugh out of that, but Jill only smiled for a second.

The rain didn't continue for very long after breakfast. Going west we ended up back in the suburban ring of Providence. We passed the morning walking through garbage-strewn older suburbs, and by afternoon, we had reached the new layer of suburban sprawl on the city's northwestern corner. Our pace was slow with a lot of stopping. Like the previous day I spent hours trying to reassure Jill that her body would rise to the challenge if she kept pushing it, and I would walk beside her patiently in the meantime. We had sat down for a break in front of a huge new shopping-mall when she put my claims of bottomless patience to the test. It was only mid-afternoon, but Jill declared that she had reached the limit of her endurance, and she would not be able to move another step that day.

I looked around. We were sitting on a strip of grass in between a massive system of parking lots, and a four-lane suburban boulevard. More commercial buildings lined the other side of the road. We were not even in a good spot to sit for very long, let alone spend the night. As if to emphasize that point, a cop drove by right then and gave us a long suspicious look.

I told Jill that we could sit there for hours if she needed, but we were at least going to have to find a decent place to sleep. We argued about it some, and I don't really remember how the debate was resolved. I just remember sitting there feeling frustrated for a long time and then eventually convincing Jill to struggle on. She moaned and complained with almost every step, but somehow, we dragged ourselves a little further until we were no longer right in front of a mall. At last, we came to a tiny stretch of forest where nothing had been built yet and Jill collapsed. I had recovered my compassion by then and I did my best to make her comfortable. I showered her with praise for finding the strength to trudge that last mile or so to find a safe camping spot, and I set up the tent so she would have some place comfortable to lie down.

It was still hours until sunset, and it felt crazy to put up the tent so early. I could see right in the windows of two suburban houses from our tiny, inadequate hiding spot, and we were right at the intersection of two major roads. The sound of cars slowing down to turn made me a lot more nervous than the sound of cars just whizzing past.

At least my tent was not so conspicuous anymore. During my early-summer break I had spray-painted a nice brown and green camouflage pattern over the white nylon. I cleared out a spot between the browning branches of a large tree that had recently fallen and that was the best I could do to conceal us. If anyone saw us there, they decided just to let us be, and so we slept undisturbed.

A particular concern for Jill's health had been growing in the back of my mind. I had been with her for two whole days at that point and in all that time she had barely eaten anything. Over the course of two days, she had eaten about as much I usually eat in one meal. When she refused to eat any breakfast on the morning of the third day, I finally said something about it.

"You need some serious calories to go on a long-distance hiking expedition," I said. "Maybe if you ate more, you'd have more energy."

Jill explained that something was making her feel sick. The same sickness that was limiting her walking endurance was also suppressing her appetite. I kept pushing and suggested that it couldn't hurt to try eating a little bit. The worst that could possibly happen would be that she might vomit, and if she didn't, she might actually find that she had more energy for walking. Jill refused and then changed the subject. She insisted that she was going to walk much further that day and she wanted to get back on the road and prove it to me. She had never feigned so much enthusiasm before, so I obliged her and packed up quickly.

We were only back on the road for about an hour before the pain of exertion caught up to Jill again. She cursed herself mercilessly and apologized for slowing me down so much. We resumed our pattern of short walks in between long breaks. I suggested eating every time we sat down, but she wouldn't do it and she seemed to be getting really annoyed by my suggestions. Then sometime in the mid-morning, she literally collapsed into someone's driveway. She crawled over to the grass and started crying.

That's when I decided I was going to force her to eat something. Everything I had seen up until that point suggested to me that she lacked any kind of strength in her personality. I figured that anyone who pushed hard enough could force her to do anything they wanted. I got out my food, held it in her face and insisted in my best authoritarian dad voice that she eat it. A titanic verbal debate ensued. For the first time Jill showed me the real strength of her convictions. After a long battle of wills, I came to realize that Jill would starve herself if she damn well wanted and no one better try to tell her otherwise.

We had quite a fight right there on some stranger's front lawn, and eventually someone came out of the house to check on us. We apologized to them and then we apologized to each other. It had been a pretty cathartic scene and we ended up in a long, sincere hug. Then we picked up our packs and struggled along down the road as if nothing was any different.

We kept shuffling along between long breaks, and Jill kept up with the merciless self-criticism and apologies for slowing me down. It reminded me a lot of the way Sweet Pea had described herself as an anchor always slowing me down. The big difference was that Sweet Pea had marched twelve miles on her second day, and she was carrying at least three times as much weight in her pack. Unlike Sweet Pea, Jill really was slowing me down, but I felt really bad after yelling at her, so I was determined to show her all the patience and appreciation I could. It was just after noon when the whole south side of the road opened up into a beautiful wide-open forest. Although it was still early, I suggested we set up camp and let Jill get some rest. It was the first real undeveloped place we had come across and I figured I wouldn't mind killing some time there.

The place turned out to be a county park, so there was a nice trail system for us to follow and get away from the highway. We had been walking down the trail for probably a half mile before we came to a mowed clearing with a children's swing set in it. It seemed really strange to me because there was no road leading in there. Apparently, someone had carried all the parts in over the foot trail to set up a swing set out in the wilderness, and someone drove or pushed a lawnmower out there sometimes to mow the grass. We sat there for a while, swinging and contemplating the strangeness of the place. To my immense relief, Jill finally ate some food. Then we climbed up a steep bank on the uphill side of the clearing and set up camp in a dense thicket of evergreen saplings where we would be well hidden.

At some point that afternoon, I left Jill by herself to rest and wandered off to explore the park. There were two other trails leading to the mysterious clearing and I followed each one in turn. They both led through about a mile of lovely mature forest and they both ended at little parking areas. One of them was located just off the same highway we had been following only a couple miles further west, so I figured we could go out that way when we left.

Back at camp, the symptoms of Jill's mystery illness had gotten worse, and it was time for her to give up and go home. She told me she had been bitten by a tick just before she came out to meet up with me, and she was convinced that she had Rocky Mountain spotted fever. I was sad and frustrated to hear she was leaving me, but I was also relieved. After three days of walking, we were only about ten miles out of Providence. We weren't even half way to the Connecticut border. Truly I would be sad and lonely without Jill, but I really couldn't afford to walk so slowly if I wanted to get south before winter time.

***

It was about an hour after dark, and I had just begun to reassure Jill that every mouse rustling leaves was not a monster coming to get us when we heard a human voice shouting out in the woods. At first it was some distance away, but it was drawing closer, and as it did, we realized that they were shouting for help. This produced a very mixed bag of reactions inside our tent.

Jill gasped, "Oh my God!" and literally started quivering in terror. Meanwhile I turned on my flashlight and started putting on my shoes.

"Oh my God! No! What are you doing?" she hissed.

"Somebody needs help." I responded, thinking that was enough of an explanation.

"Help!" shouted the voice. It was even closer now. It sounded like a boy who had not quite gone into puberty yet or maybe an adult woman.

Just then Jill grabbed me with both arms and pulled me down into a prone position next to her.

"Don't go out there Leroy! You'll be killed and then I'll be all alone! Don't leave me alone here Leroy!" It was pure hysteria.

"Help!" The voice was even closer now.

"Listen," is hissed. "It's some poor lost kid and they need help. When someone calls for help you can't just sit there and hide from them!"

Jill started crying and then she took to whimpering the phrase, "please don't leave me," over and over again. I looked at her in the beam of my flashlight. She was trembling and weeping, and her eyes were unfocussed in a strange way that made her look really pathetic. I felt like I could actually see an aura of fear surrounding her head like the flickering black and white dots of static on an old-fashioned television.

"Help!" Now the voice was farther away. I felt my opportunity to help slipping away and immediately I was overcome by guilt. Jill clung to my arms and kept whimpering at me not to leave her. To my shame, I let my warrior's spirit succumb to her cowardice and I lay there with her doing nothing.

The voice shouting for help receded into the darkness for about ten minutes and then it turned back toward us again. At that point I realized that whoever it was didn't really need help anyway. Obviously, they weren't hurt if they were moving around so much. They were just lost in the dark and too stupid to keep going in the same direction for any length of time. Once again, they came right up to the little clearing with the swing set and Jill's level of panic rose to a crescendo as they approached. Then they turned back the way they had come from twice already and kept shouting, "help!"

Four times the lost fool wandered into the distance and four times they returned to the mysterious little swing-set clearing just below our camp. Each time they returned their cries sounded a little more desperate. I found myself getting mad at them whoever they were. They had walked far enough to get back to the highway twice already if only they would keep going in the same direction. Briefly I decided that whatever fool was dumb enough to get lost in such a small place deserved whatever scary ordeal they got as a result.

Then I realized that anyone who was that foolish would be very impressionable and it made me want to rescue him even more. I had a whole fantasy where I would walk up to the kid without using my flashlight, and greet him in a most cheerful way. I would soothe his fears with many gentle words and cheerful reassurances. Then, in the ten minutes it would take me to walk him out to the road, I would spin a tale about how I was part of a secret tribe of people who lived in the forest. I would tell him that he never need be afraid in the woods because nice, helpful people like me were always hiding just out of sight. Then I would tell him that we desperately needed the help of people like him to save our forest home from getting mowed down to clear the way for more suburban sprawl.

Spurred on by this mischievous impulse I got up to leave the tent a second time, and again Jill tackled me like a football player. She was still convinced that we were living out some scene in a horror movie. I got angry and called her a bunch of mean names. I told her she needed to stop watching so much T.V. and get out into the big wide world of reality. I lectured her at some length about how television created a sickness of fear, and how real-life experiences were the antidote to this sickness. Then, when all my lecturing energy was spent, I stayed in the tent with her, making me just another fool in the whole foolish situation. Finally, we heard the footsteps of some rescue worker walk through the little clearing and then off down the trail that the lost fool kept doubling back on. A few minutes later the shouting stopped. Then we heard two sets of feet walk back through the little clearing. They didn't say anything to each other.

The situation was resolved, but I still felt awful. Instead of learning to appreciate a mysterious secret tribe of forest people, the poor dumb kid learned to appreciate uniformed rescue workers. It might have even been a cop. Although I felt no fear in the situation myself, I had acted as a coward, and so I felt ashamed. I also felt real contempt for my walking partner and I was glad she would be leaving me in the morning. Lastly, I realized that fear puts tremendous limitations on the lives of many people. I realized that I was very lucky not to be one of those people and for that I should be grateful.

In the morning we walked out the western exit of the park and got back on the highway. After a short ways, we came to a little gift shop where Jill used the phone to call her father. The gift shop owners told us there was a little café just a couple miles further on, so we struggled on past a big reservoir and then a little farther until we reached the restaurant. I had a nice brunch, and Jill sat with me while I ate. A couple hours later, her father arrived and he seemed to be immensely relieved to be reunited with his daughter. I just felt bad that we had caused him to make another long crazy drive, but he didn't seem to mind at all.

We said farewell, and then I got back to walking for real. I was grumpy that I had wasted three days coddling such a weak-spirited person, but I was also heartbroken at the loss of her companionship. Just like when Sweet Pea left me, I found therapy in walking especially hard and fast, and I walked the rest of the way to Connecticut in one afternoon.

8. THE LION AND THE TINMAN

It was evening when I crossed the state line into Connecticut and I was out of water. Houses were pretty far apart, but I decided to skip over the first one I came to because there was an American flag on a free-standing pole and a Bush/Cheney campaign sign in the front yard. In my mind only dangerous lunatics would support Bush and Cheney, not people I would feel safe asking for water, but as I passed the house, a man in the driveway called out a friendly greeting to me. Then he asked me where I was going and I realized that I ought to put aside my prejudice and have a friendly conversation with the guy.

I was braced for another encounter like I had with old George back in Lisbon Falls, but it never came. This guy was a retired trucker and he absolutely loved to talk about travelling. He was fascinated to hear about my travels and he told me a couple crazy stories of his own. I tiptoed around all the philosophical motivations for my walk, and I didn't try to sign him up for a zine, but in hindsight I don't think it would have caused a problem. I'm sure he would have disagreed with my political perspectives, but I doubt he would have gotten upset. He was happy to refill my water bottle and before I left he loaded me up with two big tomatoes from his garden and a whole loaf of banana bread fresh out of the oven! I couldn't believe it. How could a guy with a Bush/Cheney sign in his yard be so nice?

In the last eighteen years since the end of my big walk, I have totally gotten over my fear of conservatives, because I have spent most of that time working on farms. Roughly two thirds of my coworkers at those jobs have been citizens of Mexico or Jamaica who migrate seasonally between here and their home countries, but the last third has been almost entirely made up of conservative White Americans who vote for Republicans.

As I've already mentioned, I grew up thinking I was a liberal, so it came as a real surprise to find out that conservative farm-workers are not a bunch of bigoted war-mongers. They are actually really nice people, and not just to me. They are just as nice to the non-White foreigners who work on the farms. I have even seen some of them keeping in touch with their foreign friends over the winter while those people are back home in other countries. They just seem to really appreciate anyone who is willing to come out and help on the farm. They think my political perspectives are totally crazy, but they appreciate me for the same reason I appreciate them. We are the ones who we can count on to get the essential work done.

Farm workers are my homies, and I will stick up for them if you try to take their guns away or raise their taxes. I will also stick up for my foreign farm friends if you try to block them from getting to their jobs here in the US.

When the empire collapses, the foreign workers will stop coming. At that point, the Rednecks will have to teach all of us how to do farm work, or we will literally run out of food.

All along, I was planning to use this encounter with the retired trucker to launch into a detailed explanation of why I am so opposed to Democrat and Republican politicians. I have volumes of specific information and analysis to demonstrate just how irredeemably corrupt both parties are, and it is one of my big priorities in life to get people to stop supporting them and stop taking them seriously. The trouble is, I don't want to publish a book full of negativity and cynicism. I have rewritten this chapter about six times now, and it just keeps coming out to be overwhelmingly depressing and disempowering. There just isn't anything nice to say about Democrats or Republicans, and if I write down even a fraction of the nasty things there are to report, no one will want to read my book. The rest of this book has been finished for weeks, and this chapter is what's holding it up, so I'm changing the plan. I'm going to keep all the ugly details to myself, and just give you a really basic overview in three little paragraphs.

The life goal of any politician is to think of ways to frighten the citizens so we will give up freedom and allow the government to take more and more control over our lives. Here in our country, big corporations are even more powerful than the government, so there is a secondary goal of getting us to spend as much money as possible on the products that the big corporations want to sell to us. The same corporations that sponsor our politicians own all our major media sources, so they are pretty effective at controlling what information we do and don't have access to. They use that control very strategically to manipulate us into making choices that will enrich their cronies, increase their level of control over us, and keep us at odds with our own neighbors.

People are less likely to voluntarily limit their own freedom, so the politicians have split into two rival factions. The Democrats can convince their voters to support new laws that limit the freedom to make the kinds of choices that conservative people tend to make. Republican voters can be persuaded to outlaw the types of choices that liberal people tend to make.

Without the influence of politicians and the media, we would generally get along with each other much better. We would all be a lot less frightened about things that aren't really a big deal, and we would function much better as a society. I hate it when people try to manipulate us by predicting disastrous future consequences if we don't change our ways. I don't want to be the kind of person who does that, but I do have to be honest. If we don't stop letting politicians and the media lead us around like a flock of sheep, we really are going to get ourselves into some terrible situations. Clearly we already have, but the more we follow the "leadership" of Democrats and Republicans, the worse it will get.

***

Just after the trucker's house, I found a rest stop on the side of route 44. It was a dirt parking lot with some picnic tables right next to a pleasant little river. It was past sunset and getting dark, so I walked through the rest stop and followed the river downstream. There was a solid trail made by fishermen and it stuck to the middle of a narrow strip of wild forest between the stream and a field full of corn that had grown to the height of my shoulders. It was not an ideal place for camping, but I figured it would be dark soon enough and no one would be out there at night. I sat down, ate some food and set up my tent.

Well, in the half hour it took for the day's last light to fade away, two different dudes stumbled across my camping spot. The first guy obviously didn't care. He was just travelling a long way in his car, and he needed to get out and walk around for a minute while he smoked a cigarette. But the second guy came from out of the cornfield and once he noticed me, he stopped and stared at me from a distance as if he thought I might be dangerous. I couldn't quite make out the look on his face in the dim light, but it seemed a little hostile.

I assumed he was the land-owner so I got up and started apologizing to him for trespassing. I walked up to him explaining myself and trying to be as friendly and non-threatening as I could, but then it turned out he was just another guy who had wandered out of the rest stop. As soon as he told me that, he turned and left abruptly. I didn't know how to interpret his behavior and it made me nervous. I wondered if the cops would show up next. I thought about leaving, but I was tired and it was dark. The anxiety kept me awake for a long time, but there were no more disturbances after dark.

When I'm traveling, I don't want strangers to know where I'm sleeping. It doesn't feel safe and so I can't get to sleep. I had slept in some sketchy spots before on my journey, but up until that night no one had ever actually spotted me. Suddenly I had been witnessed by no less than two people in one evening. Nothing happened, but I was stressed out about it for hours. I decided never to camp near a highway rest-stop again.

***

Northeastern Connecticut reminded me a lot of southern Maine. There were a lot of low, bumpy ridges with grassy swamps and clear, swiftly-flowing streams between them. The forest was full of big white pines, and the houses were spread out like countryside. There were even some old farm houses and trailer houses, and the people I met actually had an accent that reminded me of southern Maine. I know I kicked Connecticut out of New England in the last book, but I guess Windham County Connecticut should be allowed back in.

I walked through a large town called Putnam in the morning. There was a spectacular waterfall and an old mill building downtown. I looked at a map and saw that route 44 meandered to the south after that, but I could take a short-cut due west on route 144. Happy with that knowledge, I set out enthusiastically, but I didn't think to stop in Putnam and get any food. It turned out that route 44 wandered off to the south to make contact with several small towns while route 144 traversed the middle of nowhere. By midday I was starving and there was nothing around but forest and an occasional farm or an occasional mansion.

I recalled that I had let this happen the last time I had walked across eastern Connecticut too. I had gotten so used to seeing little corner stores every few miles in Massachusetts and Rhode Island, that I stopped carrying any food reserves. That works all the way from New Haven to Washington DC too, but there is a narrow strip across eastern Connecticut where you actually have to pack some food. Given a third chance, I will not forget.

Sometime in the mid-afternoon a couple of teen-age girls stopped in their car to see what I was doing. I signed them up for zines and begged for whatever food they had in the car. All they had was a half-eaten bag of chips, but that was better than nothing. The girls were growing up to be the Hippy-type and they thought my walk was wonderful. When they went to leave, one of them gave me a seashell and said it would give me something to remember her by. I held the shell and realized it had a little weight to it. Then I gave it back to her and said I couldn't carry any extra weight in my pack, but I would remember her anyway.

The girl gasped and her face fell in rejected disappointment. Oh no! I had broken her heart! I stammered some dumb thing that I don't remember, and they drove away. I should have just taken the damn shell and thrown it in the ditch after they left. Maybe I could have just carried it until the next time I met a high-school girl and then passed it to her. I got out my notebook and wrote down their names: Tiffany and Lilly. Somebody please tell Tiffany and Lilly that I still remember them even though I didn't take their shell.

I had nothing to eat all afternoon and it put me in a really foul mood. I told myself that it was good to fast sometimes to remind me what life is like for the millions of starving people around the world, but I still couldn't muster a genuine good attitude. Being hungry sucks.

I joined back up with route 44 in a town called Eastford. After that I started seeing stores and businesses again, but none of them sold food. I think I passed four antique shops and still not so much as a gas station with hot dogs and a microwave. I can't eat antiques!

It was evening when I passed by a bourgeois house where a middle-aged woman was getting into her car. I hollered a greeting to her and asked if there was anywhere to eat nearby. As soon as I said it I realized that I was hinting that maybe she could give me some food. She told me that there was a burger stand just over the crest of the next hill. Hallelujah! I was overjoyed.

I crested the hill a few minutes later and there was a real old-fashioned drive-up burger and ice cream stand. Guy Fieri was probably there, but that was before Triple D got famous, so I didn't recognize him. Instead I saw the woman who I had just accosted back at her house. She asked me about my travels and when I explained, she offered to buy me dinner. I was overwhelmed with emotion and I thanked her somewhat dramatically. After starving all day, the smell of burgers and ice cream was already pretty cathartic, but then to be offered some for free was just over the top.

We sat and ate together at a picnic table, and we had a good conversation about travels and politics. She was obviously a liberal, but I am always polite to liberals when they are feeding me some delicious grub.

She was all worked up about the recent blackout. Her house had been without power for two days and it had been a real trial. After describing a bit about what that was like, she glanced both ways nervously, leaned across the table and whispered to me that she thought the blackout was engineered intentionally by a conspiracy of oil companies as a means of pushing their agenda. Our conversation continued, but I'm not going to bore you with that because I want to make a point here.

Within a year after the blackout, investigative journalists uncovered a conspiracy of utility companies and showed how they had deliberately caused the blackout as a way to push their agenda. But even if that hadn't turned out to be true, why would that be something you have to whisper about? Why would someone be nervous that someone might overhear you saying that? Will the bourgeois neighbors think you're crazy and call you names? Will the thought police find out that you don't believe the party line and take away your bourgeois privileges?

That cowardice was what frustrated me the most about liberals. I didn't ask, but it's safe to assume the conservative guy who gave me the banana bread believed whatever dumb explanation Rush Limbaugh came up with for the blackout. The Muslims totally did it because they hate us. Du-uh!

Now here was a woman who figured out intuitively who was really behind the blackout, but she was too scared to even speak out loud about it let alone do anything. Both of those people were really nice to me and I liked them a lot. They were good Americans. (I'm not just saying that cause they gave me free food I swear!)

If only the liberals weren't such cowards and the conservatives weren't such suckers, our nation would be in really good shape. I felt like Dorothy leading the Lion and the Tin Man to find their lost organs. Don't you realize you already have courage in your hearts and brains in your heads? You just need to use them. Come on America! We need to team up and do something about the man behind the curtain.

9. PODUNK TOWN

The whole world looked rosy again with a belly full of burgers and ice-cream. The evening was mild and the New England countryside was lovely. About an hour later I found a thicket of wild grape vines along the side of the road. I don't actually know if grapes grow in the wild in North America, but those grapes looked wild. They were just out in the edge of the woods along the highway, and they were doing really well, even though it looked like no one tended to them. They were extremely tart and I could only eat a couple hand-fuls before my whole face puckered up and my tongue got sore. I love sour fruit though so I thought of the grapes as an exquisite treat that you only nibble in small quantity.

The sun went down and I ended up sleeping right behind the grapes. It looked like the kind of place that would be pretty damp in early summer, but it was dry enough by the end of August.

I walked many miles the next day without a single noteworthy experience to write about. The day was growing long when I came to a place called Bolton Notch State Park. A long, steep-sided ridge spanned the entire west-ern horizon, but right in the middle was a neat little notch where all the high-ways, roads and railroads crammed together to squeeze through on their way to Hartford. The summit of the ridge maintained the same level for many miles, like the Appalachians of Pennsylvania.

It was a beautiful place and I suddenly felt inspired to climb up the ridge and camp on top. There was no trail, but the oak forest had been left to grow for at least a century, so the trees were huge and spread out with very little undergrowth to tangle my steps.

Even so, it was a long and grueling ascent up the steep slope. Right near the top, the oaks thinned out and I had to push through some rhododendrons. I was huffing and puffing and covered with sweat, but the view from the top was well worth the effort. Most of central Connecticut stretched out in a panorama below me. The towers of downtown Hartford looked like chil-dren's toys below the blue-green ridges of the Berkshire Mountains beyond. I ate sardines and peanuts and then watched the sunset over the great valley. The ground was hard and rocky, but I slept with the satisfied heart of a man on top of the world.

In the morning I found a nice, easy trail down the west side of the ridge. An hour later I emerged at the trailhead parking lot and then plunged immediately into the thickening suburbs. Every major city in this country is surrounded by a cultural wasteland of suburbs, and they all give me an almost identical feeling of alienation, but somehow the eastern suburbs of Hartford felt even more desolate than most. I bet the teen-age suicide rate is really high there.

By the hottest part of the afternoon, I had cleared the bourgeois belt and arrived in a ghetto called East Hartford. It seemed to be a haven for African immigrants. Black people speaking exotic languages were everywhere and the shabby old apartment buildings were decorated with a variety of flags that I didn't recognize. There were also quite a few Brazilian flags.

I came to a bridge across the mighty Connecticut River and crossed into downtown Hartford, but after a few minutes I decided to cross back over to the African slum. I had been trying for days to find someone of a friendly political stripe to stay with in Hartford, but so far my search had turned up nothing. It was not late yet, but it was getting there and I was right in the core of another giant city. Huge office towers crowded right up to the levee on the west bank of the river, but across on the east side, some wise urban planners had left a broad swath of forest to absorb the great river's occasional floods. An extensive system of walls and fences separated the forested floodplain from the adjacent ghettos, but after an hour or so of probing around, I found a hole in the fence and slipped through.

Suddenly I was in a different world. It was like a little stripe of wilderness, just a bit wider than the length of a football field, stretching along the river bank all the way through the city. The whole space was shaded by a dense canopy of beautiful ancient trees. They were some kind of hardwood, but I never did manage to identify them. They all had deep, wavy furrows in their bark like the cottonwoods out West, but I don't think cottonwoods grow in the wet forests of the East. Despite the dense canopy, there was still a lot of bushy undergrowth perfect for hiding in. There were piles of garbage drifted up here and there, but they didn't really detract from the wild beauty of the forest.

I assumed that such a lovely, secluded place right in the middle of a huge city would be teeming with homeless people, but after wandering around for an hour, I hadn't found evidence of a single squatter's camp. There were just a couple of guys fishing down at the river and they looked like they would be leaving before dark. I found the total absence of other people very strange, and I worried that maybe the police came through on a regular basis to bust people for being homeless. Maybe a recent flood had cleared the area of its inhabitants?

I hid my camp in the densest cluster of bushes I could find. Soft, sandy river sediment made the ground very pleasant to lay on. The fishermen went home just before sunset, and I sat down in their place to admire the great swirling eddies of the Connecticut. What a cool place!

I sat there for hours watching the lights come on in the many angles and glass surfaces of the skyscrapers across the river. Hartford is America's insurance capital and at least a dozen insurance companies have built grand, towering headquarters there. Clearly, no expense was spared in the effort to give Hartford's skyline the most modern and affluent look of any city.

The rumble of the urban landscape drifted in from every direction, but in the foreground all was silent but for the gentle gurgling of the river. Nearly a million people call the Hartford area home, but right there in the exact center of the metropolis, I was perfectly alone. I sat enchanted by the scene for quite a while, and then at last I crawled back to my tent and slept, the security of the dark forest covering me like a warm blanket.

It would have been wise to start out early the next morning looking for new friends, but I felt like exploring the flood-plain, so I did that instead. I packed up my things, stashed them in the bushes and headed downstream. Before long I had to climb through another fence, and then I was in a public park. It was still forested though, so I kept following a paved trail downstream dodging joggers and people on bicycles.

After a while I came to a place where a small river called the Hockanum emptied into the Connecticut. There was a large wooden sign commemorating the Podunk Indians who once inhabited the valley. It said that the river confluence was once the site of a large Podunk village, and the first white settlers to the area built the town of Hartford to be near the Indians for the purposes of trade.

Now I have heard the phrase, "Podunk town" used many times to describe any small, boring town, but I had no idea that the word came from the name of an actual Indian tribe. I chuckled as I realized that Hartford, Connecticut must have been America's original "Podunk Town."

The riverside park ended there at the Hockanum, and beyond that the riverbank was crowded with ugly industrial sites, so I turned and went back the other way. When I got back to my camp, I walked right past and went exploring upstream. Before long I came to a railroad track and following that, I soon stumbled upon a pair of graffiti artists who were busy decorating a large concrete wall. I greeted them cheerfully and praised their work, but they only glanced up at me for a second. Neither of them said a word, and they both looked extremely paranoid. Their antisocial behavior was mildly insulting, but I told myself they must be on drugs so I shouldn't let it bother me. I walked on and left them to their work, but I came back a few hours later after they had left and took pictures of it. They really were beautiful, intricate, multi-colored pieces of artwork. Neither of them made any sense to me, but they sure did look cool.

I finally got back across the river around noon and resumed my quest to distribute zines and make friends. I ended up walking all over the city and I got the impression that Hartford is a very racially segregated place. In other cities nearby, like Boston, Providence, and New York, I had grown accustomed to seeing a lot of mixed-race people. In Hartford though, everyone was either Black as coal or White as snow with very few shades of brown in between. I'm not just talking about the fresh immigrants from Africa either. Even the American-born, English-speaking Black people did not appear to have ever mingled their genes with anyone of another race. It made me wonder what would keep all the different inhabitants of the same city isolated from each other for so many generations, but the explanation was all too obvious: racism. It gave me an uncomfortable feeling. In one Black neighborhood, quite a few people asked me if I was lost and offered to help me find my way back to the part of town where White people belong. Some of them seemed to be concerned for my safety, but others actually seemed to be upset at the sight of my White face.

It was in that neighborhood, somewhere in the northwestern part of the city that I found another large stretch of forest that had somehow been spared from development. I had signed up a few new zine-subscribers that afternoon, but I hadn't met anyone who I felt comfortable asking favors from, so I crawled into the bushes and waited for dark. There were a lot of children playing in the woods there, but no one calls the cops when Black children find a mysterious man out in the woods, so I didn't feel too nervous about it. By the time darkness came, none of them had noticed me anyway, so I set up my tent and slept right there.

It was noon the next day when I finally found some activist types serving Food Not Bombs in a park. They told me I had just missed a giant festival that had been sponsored by a dozen different activist groups from around the city. Apparently the day I had wandered into town there were hundreds of people out in Bushnell Park celebrating their freedom of speech, opposing all different kinds of oppression, handing out radical literature, and enjoying all kinds of free food. The organizers had called it the Hope Out Loud festival. It was an effort to bring together all different kinds of progressive people in an attempt to foster a sense of community and potentially inspire some cooperation. If I had walked a few more blocks into Hartford instead of turning around and hiding in the flood-plain, I would have found it.

I spent the rest of the day tagging along with the FNB volunteers. I let them drag me along to a meeting of the Peace and Justice League that evening where I got on the meeting agenda to make a shameless request for a couch to crash on. A painfully shy and awkward middle-aged man volunteered, and I rode in his car out to his house in West Hartford after the meeting. We tried to have one conversation, but talking to people obviously wasn't one of his strengths. It was late anyway, so we gave up trying to be social and I slept on the couch in his living room. I decided to leave Hartford in the morning and head south towards New Haven.

I stepped out into a cold wind that morning, and before long I noticed that the leaves on some of the trees were starting to show some yellow. That set off an alarm bell in my head. Here it was the first of September, the weather was getting cold, the leaves were turning yellow, and I was still putting around in the northern reaches of Yankee-land. Hadn't I made this same mistake last year? I pointed my face due south and made haste.

10. GOD'S FRENCH FRIES

With the aid of a stolen map I found a bicycle trail to walk on and that route revealed a much more human side of the suburbs. It was a weekend, so children were frolicking everywhere. The din of 30,000 lawn-mowers was not enough to drown out the sounds of their laughter and shouts, and my spirits lifted.

I was headed towards a smaller city called Middletown where folks in Hartford had recommended I meet the radical student activists at Wesleyan University. I figured I could get there in one day if I put my head down and marched. The bike trail ended in the outer ring of suburbs, so I found my way to route 99, the most direct route to Middletown. That worked well enough until it came time to cross several miles of swampy landscape called the Cromwell Meadows. There route 99 merged into a much larger highway called route 9. Suddenly I was looking at four lanes of high-speed traffic pinched tightly between concrete Jersey barricades without so much as a breakdown lane for me to walk on. Outside the barricades the loose gravel of the causeway sloped abruptly into the swamp.

I looked at my map for an alternate route and realized that it would take me many hours to skirt around the western side of the swamp. There was no way around the east side because the Connecticut River was right there. It was late in the afternoon and I was almost within sight of Middletown. The only alternative was a railroad track running parallel to route 9.

I backtracked a short ways to where I could access the tracks without wading through swamp, but it was still quite a struggle to push my way through the dense tangle of thorny vines that grew in the little trench between the road and the tracks. As I was inching my way through the brambly mess, a train roared past at top speed and I realized that the railroad tracks were not going to be much fun either.

It was quite a ways across the Cromwell Meadows, and the awkward spacing of the railroad ties slowed my pace. At one point I had to crawl down onto the steep gravel that elevated the tracks above the marsh to make way for another passing train. There was no way to avoid being spotted by the train conductor. Nor was there any way to avoid being spotted by the thousands of motorists who roared past me less than a stone's throw away on highway 9. Signs at regular intervals warned me that I was not only in danger of being splattered by a train, but I was also in danger of being arrested by police. The loud roar of traffic, the awkward spacing of railroad ties cramping my stride, and the obvious dangers both physical and societal, made this one of the more unpleasant hikes I can recall.

Right at the end, the gravel causeway gave way to a long trestle over open, flowing water. At that point if a train came along I would have had to climb on to the outside of the trestle frame and hang on, dangling backpack and all above the river until the train had passed. As it turned out, I made it across before any trains came along. It would have made a hell of a story if one had, but that's one crazy experience that I don't mind having missed out on.

The bridge ended right into the thick of a bombed-out ghetto neighborhood on the riverside edge of Middletown. I had not expected to find such a broken-down slum in a city that small, (Middletown is home to about 80,000 people.) Since then I have learned that incredible contrasts of poverty and wealth are one of the hallmarks of the Connecticut experience.

I quickly found my way to the university and checked my e-mail. I had tried to contact several students from a computer back in Hartford, but none of them had responded. I cursed them for being flakes, but I resolved to find them one way or another. I found a link to the university's telephone directory right on their homepage, and all the students' numbers were right there. Ha! You can run but you can't hide, you flakes!

Just then I realized I had spelled the word Wesleyan wrong, so no one had received my e-mails in the first place. Oops! Now who looked stupid?

The kids were great. They put me up in their apartment for the night and called all their friends to come over and meet me. I was staying with a couple young guys who helped organize a radical, anti-capitalist student group, and they boasted that they had been taking a crew of as many as forty people to recent protests in the area. There they would all dress in identical black clothes with their faces masked and practice maneuvers to defy the police.

I was thrilled to meet them and before long I found myself proudly sharing my own stories about the Seattle uprising back in 1999. When they heard that I was a veteran of the Battle of Seattle the kids were overwhelmed with excitement. They called a bunch more people and before long a spontaneous party had gathered in their apartment with me as the focus. I sat there all evening telling my stories to a large gang of wide-eyed, aspiring young dissidents in rapt attention. They were all in the range of five to eight years younger than me, and they treated me like a revered elder warrior. High points in my story provoked a chorus of enthusiastic wows and gasps. I had never been the focus of so much admiration in all my life. Twenty of them subscribed to my zine and I ended up with a wad of ones and fives big enough to choke a horse.

I felt right at home with the Wesleyan kids, but I knew I had a long way to go before winter, so I bid them farewell the very next morning. On my way out, one of them offered to buy me a bunch of food at the campus convenience store. There wasn't much there that I could take with me travelling but there was one product that looked like it would make good road food. It was called an Odwalla Bar and it was basically a little chewy lump of grain and sugar pressed into the shape of a candy bar and sealed in a colorful plastic wrapper. I loaded my food pouch to the brim with Odwalla Bars and headed west.

The urban zone of Middletown ended almost as abruptly as it had started, and I spent most of the morning walking through pleasant countryside. Around noon I came over the summit of a ridge with a spectacular view to the south and west. The climb up the ridge's east side had been gradual, but the west slope dropped off abruptly and the road had to switch back tightly on itself to maintain a gradient appropriate for wheeled vehicles. I could see from there that some parts of the ridge were even capped with high cliffs of black basaltic rock.

That's when I remembered my father's geology lessons from my youth and I recalled that the central valley of Connecticut is actually a graben. That's a geologic term meaning that at one point millions of years ago, the Earth's crust began to split open there like the Great Rift Valley of East Africa.

Sometimes continent-sized currents of hot, fluid rock far below the surface well up to the bottom of the solid crust. When it hits the solid underside of the crust, its current divides in two opposite directions and flows horizontally before it circulates back down into the depths. Since the crust is basically floating on top of this fluid, friction with the circulating fluid causes the crust to move as well. Over time, this motion will tear open a crack in the surface directly above the upwelling where the magma's current divides and pulls in two opposite directions.

Of course, this process is imperceptibly slow from the perspective of human life-spans, so there is never anything like a huge, open trench full of boiling lava at the surface. An active rift is currently dividing a long slice off the eastern edge of Africa, but there are permanent cities and villages in the bottom of the valley. The African Rift does experience frequent earthquakes and volcanic activity in some places, but it will be millions more years before the ocean floods in and the region of eastern Ethiopia, Somalia, Kenya, Tanzania, and Mozambique becomes a smaller continent drifting away from mother Africa. It is also possible that the currents pulling the rift open will change and the spreading will cease, leaving the continent intact for millions more years.

More often than not, when a rift splits the surface of a continental landmass, it runs out of energy before it actually cleaves the continent apart. While the valley is actively widening, it is called a rift, but once it has failed and stopped moving, it is called a graben. The Connecticut River Valley has been stable for many millions of years, but the basaltic cliffs remain as a testament to the volcanic activity that once occurred there. (The Hudson Valley of New York and the Rio Grande Valley of New Mexico are other examples of grabens, and there may be more in the U.S. that I am not aware of.)

Not far below the cliffs, I came to another small city called Meriden, this one home to about 50,000 people. I crossed a tangle of highway interchanges, and I was pushing through a desolate commercial strip when a man who was sitting in the outdoor seating area at a McDonalds called me over to eat with him. He was a slightly heavy, middle-aged Black man with a shiny bald head, and he said his name was God. He offered me some fries and engaged me in a truly odd conversation. I wish I had written down some quotes, because I cannot remember a single example anymore of what was so odd about it. He didn't ask a single one of the typical questions about how I got food or where I slept, and he definitely didn't compare me to Forrest Gump. He asked some really thought-provoking questions, but then he also talked about himself with a degree of self-absorption that suggested a mild mental illness.

At some point I asked him to spare the Earth from the wrath of the apocalypse. I intended it as a gentle tease about his name, but he didn't seem to take it that way. He just smiled wistfully and stared into the distance for quite a while, his face showing something akin to inspiration.

When he finally spoke again, he just changed the subject. He said he was about to release his debut album as a rap artist. It was to be a double CD and he was producing it on an independent label that he had started with his own resources. I was duly impressed. It takes a lot of work and a lot of heart to produce music on a home-grown independent label, but it is also by far the most legitimate way to make genuine art. I gave him lots of props and encouraged him to stay independent. Most rappers are self-obsessed to the point of mild mental illness, so I figured he had a good chance of making it.

After a while I wandered away pondering the cosmic strangeness of the experience. What if God *was* "just a slob like one of us," eating at McDonalds and making a double CD of rap songs all about himself? No one really knows. Good thing I had the presence of mind to ask him to cancel the apocalypse. He seemed to have liked the idea. Who knew saving the world could be that simple?

***

Meriden is another stop on the boogie-down ghettos of Connecticut tour, but one distinct feature sets it apart from the others. A spectacular cliff-topped mountain hangs over the city. Filling the entire northwestern horizon, it can be seen from almost every block in town. My map called it the "Hanging Hills," but that name didn't make sense to me. It did indeed hang, but the word "hills" implies more than one small lump in the Earth's surface. In contrast to that, I remember seeing one magnificent mountain with towering black cliffs along the southern face and a long talus slope of broken rock below them. In New England they would call this a Monadnock, but apparently here in the Mid-Atlantic the word for this feature was "hills." It was a true natural wonder and before I had walked halfway across town, I decided to climb up to the top.

It was four o'clock when I found the park entrance, and a big sign threatened legal consequences for anyone caught inside the gate after five. I would have to keep a cautious lookout for rangers. The park road wound several miles around the east side of the mountain, and I dodged into the bushes every time I heard an approaching car. The mountain's long shadow had spread across the road when I finally came to a trail leading up the northeastern slope. The slope was not as steep as the cliffs on the south face, but it was a long and rugged ascent nonetheless. It took me several hours to get to the top, and I passed at least a dozen hikers coming down long after the five-o'clock deadline.

Just before the top, there was a viewpoint where I could see all the way north to the towers of Hartford. Two days out of Hartford, I had forgotten it as a thing of the past, so I was quite surprised to find that I was still in sight of the place. I truly was on top of the highest mountain for many miles.

Only moments later I reached the top of the great southern cliffs, and from there I could see all the way south to the towers of New Haven. I'm pretty sure it was the only time in my life that I have ever seen two huge cities from the top of one mountain, not to mention the smaller city of Meriden in the foreground. I thought you would have to go to Japan to see something like that.

The view was slightly marred by a colossal American flag that hung from a towering metal pole right on the cliff top. I love my country with a passion, and I am proud to be an American, but to me, the red, white, and blue flag doesn't symbolize any of the things we have to be proud about. The flag has always been used as a tool to manipulate the most foolish Americans to perpetrate atrocities against the people of other nations, and against the indigenous tribes here at home. Honestly, there are a lot of people who see that flag and instantly feel unsafe, just like a Jewish person would feel seeing a Nazi swastika.

I examined the possibility of removing this offensive symbol from the otherwise beautiful mountaintop, but there was no rope I could cut, and I certainly couldn't do anything about the sturdy metal pole. Oh well.

I turned my back to the flag and admired the sunset panorama over the many ridges and cliffs of the Connecticut Graben. The whole sky seemed to turn salmon pink for several moments, and I felt the presence of my usual God sitting with me.

After the sunset colors had faded, I set up camp and lamented that I had forgotten to fill my water bottle before climbing up the mighty mountain. I had a little bit of water left, but not enough to quench my thirst after the long sweaty hike. I saved one swig for morning, and drifted off to sleep feeling parched.

I awoke with a throbbing head, just like you would expect after hours of being dehydrated. I lingered atop the mighty cliffs for a few more moments, noticing that the morning-side shadows brought a whole different beauty to the extensive landscape below me. Unfortunately, I had to go. I needed to find water badly.

I found a steep trail that plunged down a ravine right between two of the mighty cliffs. It was a much more direct route than the one I had taken on my way up, and I found myself back in the valley bottom in less than an hour. Suddenly the secluded forest trail emerged onto the side of a rushing, four lane highway, but right there was an elevated sidewalk-bridge spanning the rushing flow of traffic. It was an odd piece of infrastructure to find along a forest hiking path, but I certainly did appreciate its convenience.

Soon after that, I emerged onto a suburban street lined with houses, but it still seemed much too early in the morning to start knocking on doors. So I walked on. Sometime later I came to a Dunkin Donuts, but they refused to give me water unless I paid for something. By then I was enduring a truly agonizing headache, and I was incensed by their cruelty. I muttered some curses and stomped out.

Thankfully I came to a stream-crossing soon after that and at last I was able to quench my painful thirst. I always carried a hand-pumping water filter so I could drink out of streams without having to fear Giardia or any other water-borne illnesses. The rest of the day passed uneventfully as my headache slowly receded and I closed the distance to New Haven.

By late-afternoon, I had reached the base of another rocky-topped peak, so once again I climbed up and slept surrounded by spectacular cliff-top views. This mountain was called the Sleeping Giant, and it was familiar territory for me. I had spent a winter in New Haven three years prior, and I had climbed up that mountain several times before, but it was really cool to see it in the green shades of summer, and I had certainly never spent a night up there before. Now I was only one day out from New Haven, so I had a much better view of its skyline, and I could see the ocean beyond. Thick juniper bushes covered the top of the Sleeping Giant making for an interesting ecosystem that reminded me of the West.

***

I have already explained that my normal morning rituals usually include a dumping of the previous day's meals. The previous morning, when I awoke on top of the Hanging Hills, my body had offered nothing for this ritual so I skipped it. That happens every once-in-a-while, and I hadn't thought much of it, but now for the second day in a row, I awoke unable to poop. That never happens, so it seemed appropriate when I felt a corresponding pain in my abdomen. I realized that I had eaten nothing but Odwalla Bars and a handful of God's French fries during the last two days. They were very tasty, and they seemed to give me plenty of energy for hiking, but once inside my body, they didn't seem to want to come out.

I decided to give it a little more effort. I crawled back into the junipers, squatted, and strained. After a few minutes of heaving and sweating, I managed to multiply the pain in my abdomen to an overwhelming level, but still I could not poop. I pulled my pants up and lay there recovering from the painful exertion. I made a mental note to warn my zine-readers about the potential consequences of an all-Odwalla Bar diet, and I am making good on that intention now, many years later. I still had several more of the little snack-treats in my pack, but I resolved to eat something different before I consumed any more sugared oat-blobs.

Down in the New Haven suburb of Hamden, I stopped in a pizza joint for lunch and enjoyed some good old-fashioned cheesy-wheat. It's a little-known fact, but New Haven, Connecticut actually claims to be the city that invented Pizza. I doubt the validity of this claim, but it is at least true that most of the pizza joints in New Haven serve up a product that is far superior to the national standard. I mean to say that there is some damn good pizza in New Haven and the surrounding burbs. It wasn't until later that evening that my symptoms cleared up, but I am convinced that this greasy delicacy was the miracle cure that relieved my constipation.

11. NITEMARE ON JILL'S STREET PART TWO

My old friend was back in New Haven and it was great to catch up with her. She was starting on her final year as a Yale student and she lived in a big house off campus with quite a few other cool people. I only stayed there for two days, but by the time I left it felt like home.

I just happened to be in town for a giant protest organized by the Service Workers' International Union (SEIU.) They were striking against Yale University for higher wages and relief from various humiliating work conditions. I didn't write down all the specifics, and I don't remember them anymore. I just remember being impressed by how many people turned out for the protest. It was a grey and drizzly day, but there still must have been at least five thousand people marching in the streets. There were a lot of SEIU people and a lot of people from other unions, but there were also a lot of Yale students, and many more people who just appeared to be random folks from around the area. My new friends from Wesleyan were there too, all masked up and ready to rumble. I didn't realize so many people cared about the plight of service workers and I was really inspired. One of the people from the house I was staying in carried a sign that said, "Yale sucks!"

I decided I wanted to do something really courageous that day and early in the afternoon I saw my chance. At that point the crowd had stopped moving and everyone was standing still in the middle of a street in front of the university. Some police had driven into the mass of people and gotten stuck. With no way to move their car forward or back, they had gotten out of the vehicle and just left it there in the middle of the road. By the time I got there, I couldn't even tell where they had gone. Some cops were trying to form a barricade in front of a building and others were harassing protestors in various places, but none of them were anywhere near the stranded squad car.

I made my way towards the cruiser until I was standing right next to it. I looked all around gulping and feeling my adrenaline surge. After about five minutes of building up my courage, I bent down and pretended I was tying my shoe. The crowd of people was very thick around me, and as soon as I crouched down I was effectively out of sight to all but a few protestors right near me. I pulled out my pocket knife and plunged it into the cop car's tire up to the handle, but when I pulled it out, one short blast of air followed it and then the hole in the tire appeared to seal itself.

What!? I had pumped up a gallon of adrenaline for this? How could a tire seal itself? It was a real let down and I left the protest feeling defeated. Through later research, I discovered that many police departments use special high-tech tires that are virtually impossible to deflate. Word to the wise.

***

Sometime while I was in New Haven, I got an e-mail from Jill. She was feeling better and she wanted a second chance to be my walking partner. I figured there couldn't be any harm in that, so I gave her directions to the house where I was staying. Once again her poor father delivered her in person all the way from upstate New York.

Before we left town I made a point to stop by and see Stuart and Miss Kay again. I had taken a different route across eastern Connecticut to avoid getting bored, but I had merged back up with my previous route in New Haven specifically because I wanted to see those two. They had given me really generous donations, and I wanted to make sure they got their zines. As I recall, Stuart insisted on giving me another twenty bucks.

Jill and I walked along the beach in West Haven and she was really enchanted by the scenery. We stopped and got ice-cream, and it felt more like we were on a date than a trans-continental walk. Jill had demonstrated a healthy appetite several times already and I was relieved to let go of my impression of her as an anorexic. I guess she really had been sick the last time I saw her.

Farther down the beach, we were approached by a superlatively sleazy man who insisted that he could get us on television. He looked like a roadie from the Van Halen era who still hadn't figured out that the eighties were over. He had a curly pony tail of once-blond hair that had mostly gone grey. He wore tattered, cut-off jean shorts and a Hawaiian shirt, unbuttoned to reveal his sunburnt beer-belly and his thick mat of grey chest hair. His face was covered with three days-worth of stubble and he was sweaty all over.

He told us he had inside connections in the rock'n'roll industry, (of course.) He also said he knew people in television and he was sure he could make us rich and famous if we would just work with him. I wanted to ask him if he had ever given Jimmy Buffet a blowjob, but as usual I managed to stay polite even when it wasn't really necessary. He was really pushy, but he wasn't willing to keep pace with us for more than a few blocks on foot, so we eventually escaped without giving him any contact information. What a creep!

Soon after that we came upon a very strange zoological phenomenon. At first I thought my eyes were playing tricks on me, but after a while there was no denying it. Large, tropical-looking birds with long tails and bright blue and green feathers were sitting in trees, on telephone wires, and flapping all over the neighborhood. I have never been a bird-watcher, and I have never studied any details about different birds and their habitats, but I was pretty sure that these things were somehow out of place on the coast of Connecticut. After a while, we asked an old woman on her front porch and she confirmed my suspicion.

"Yup," she said, "Those are feral parakeets. Aren't they cool?"

Apparently so many parakeets had escaped or been discarded by their owners in New York and other nearby cities that they had actually found one another and formed a breeding, feral population. While they may not have been specifically adapted to that region of the world, they had done well enough to survive and even increase their numbers. It was definitely another weird American Odyssey moment.

Walking a few blocks away from the shore, Jill and I found a little stretch of forest right on the western edge of West Haven. It was only about the size of two city blocks, but the underbrush was thick enough to hide a tent, so we crawled in and made camp.

I had wondered before why someone like Jill, with no real political opinions would want to accompany me on such a journey, but that evening her motivations became clear. She liked me! We kissed and before long, we had followed through to the end of where our desires led us. As always, I was overwhelmed with gratitude for the most rare and pleasant experience. Jill may not have been very brave, or very strong, but she was very pretty. For a man my age that was probably the most redeeming quality a woman could possess, and if she was happy to share herself with me in that way, I couldn't imagine a better situation. I drifted off to sleep in utter satisfaction imagining that we would make a perfect team. I figured we would walk to the west coast and back, and the whole world would be saved by our heart-warming love story.

***

We walked across Milford the next morning and Jill was having an awful time with her shoes. She had only brought one pair of shoes with her and it was several sizes too small. She had no real explanation for why she had done this, and same as before, she was intensely critical of herself. She found the pain unbearable, and we had to stop frequently to soothe her feet. After a while, she tried walking barefoot, but that quickly became ridiculous. We were walking on hot asphalt strewn with gravel and all manner of garbage including broken glass.

Out the west side of Milford, we came upon a shopping plaza with a K-mart in it, and I suggested that we shoplift a new pair of shoes for her. Jill had never shoplifted anything before, and she was mortified by the suggestion. Somehow I was able to convince her though, so we stashed our packs in a big hedge at the edge of the parking lot and went inside. I coached Jill on how to change into a new pair and then walk out like it was no big deal, but when we went to leave she was obviously melting with fear and humiliation. Her attempt to act casual looked absurd. I had never seen her slouch so low. The loose way she let her arms swing, and the way she dragged her feet seemed to attract looks from customers and employees alike. Her face glowed red and displayed a look of absolute terror.

We had not quite gotten to the cash registers when a red-vested old woman circled quickly in front of us holding the box with Jill's old shoes in it.

"Ma'am! You forgot your shoes!" she barked angrily.

Just then three more red-vested K-mart peons surrounded us. Jill didn't say a word, but she obediently changed back into her old shoes without hesitation.

While she was doing that, I apologized profusely to the shriveled old employee and put in a quick plea that she refrain from calling the police. She didn't respond to anything I said, but instead told us that we were banned from their store forever. I agreed to her terms and hurried out the door dragging the quivering Jill behind me. We hurried back to our packs and hid in the hedge. No one had said whether or not they intended to call the cops, so I figured we better hide for a while just to be safe. I realized right away that the hedge would not really hide us at all if a cop was actually looking for us, but it took me a couple minutes to come to terms with that reality and decide what we should do about it. There was a larger patch of forest just across the street, but the street was four lanes of rushing traffic so thick you could scarcely have fired a bullet across it without hitting two or more cars.

Finally I gulped and dragged Jill out of the hedge. We pressed the "walk" button and waited for what felt like ten minutes. Finally the light turned red, the cars stopped, and the little white image of the walking person lit up. We dashed across the street and into the forest beyond. By then it was pretty obvious that the cops weren't coming, but we hid for a good while anyway. Jill and I fought over who was responsible for our ridiculous failure, each one of us trying to shoulder all the blame. I don't remember who won that debate. Obviously it didn't matter. I still felt like a total jerk. I should have just bought her a new pair of shoes. I had over two hundred dollars on me at the time.

After some thought, Jill borrowed my pocket knife and cut the tips of her shoes right off, so her toes could extend to their natural length. It was an innovative idea coupled with a decisive action. I was worried that the new structure of her shoes would lead to all new problems, but she didn't complain about her feet any more after that, so I guess it must have worked well enough.

Eventually we got back on the road and crossed the ever-lovely Housatonic River into Stratford. Jill kept on truckin' and the next thing I knew we were in Bridgeport. We were both pretty hungry and it was more or less dinner time, so we stopped in a little restaurant. I ordered my own food, but when the man asked Jill what she wanted, she just stared at him blankly. He kept prompting her politely, but she just kept stammering and looking around confused. I was also pretty confused, but then the look on her face told me that she couldn't understand what he was saying. It was an embarrassing moment, but I translated and eventually I just took over ordering food for her. We ate heartily and then went back out into the thickening slums of Bridgeport to look for a place to sleep.

After a short while, we came to a public library that also doubled as the intake office for a nearby homeless shelter. I knew we weren't likely to find any nice parks, or any people wealthy enough to have spare beds, so I suggested we stay in the shelter. Jill agreed and we went in.

I started answering questions and filling out paperwork, but when the woman questioned Jill, she just stood there awkwardly with that same confused look on her face. Once again she could not understand the person speaking to her. I tried to help, but the intake woman interrupted me. Seeing how dependent Jill was on me for her communication, the woman pointed out that the shelter was segregated into male and female sections. She explained that we would be separated until morning and asked if we really wanted to do that. Jill flashed me a look of absolute terror. Obviously we couldn't split up. I thanked the woman and we left.

Both the people whose speech Jill had failed to understand were Black, so I asked about the apparent pattern. Jill confessed that she literally couldn't understand Black people. I was shocked. I know urban Black Americans have a unique accent, but it had never occurred to me that any White American under the age of fifty would not be able to understand them. Didn't everyone listen to rap and watch Hollywood movies?

Once again Jill boiled over with self-loathing and she explained that she was "raised in a closet." I wondered why anyone would do that to their own children, but then I remembered that most Baby-Boomers had tried to raise their kids in isolation from other people. That still didn't make it a good idea, but it did mean it was a common phenomenon that I should try to be sensitive about. This was going to make things really awkward. We were right in the thick of Bridgeport on our way to other places like New York and Philadelphia. It was obvious that Jill was not only confused by Black people's dialect, but she was also scared of them.

I was troubled by the feeling that Jill was turning out to be more of a burden than a companion. How could a twenty-year-old woman have so little experience outside of her parents' house? Was that normal? Were my expectations totally unreasonable? In all of this negativity, I failed to notice the good news. We had come farther in this one day than we had in all four days combined back in Rhode Island. Jill's physical fitness had risen to the challenge, but her record-breaking walk had landed us right in the middle of Bridgeport at sunset. Of course, I was the one who led us into Bridgeport. Jill was just following along.

Without a plan or even much hope, we kept walking west. Night fell. It was only the second time I had ever been stuck out after dark still looking for a place to sleep and we were in the absolute least hospitable landscape anywhere. Jill had never been in a real ghetto before, much less wandering through a ghetto after dark with nowhere to go. I'm sure I don't need to carry on about how frightened she was. I kept apologizing and reassuring her that we would find somewhere safe to sleep if we just kept trying. I also tried to reassure her that this was not going to become a typical experience in our future travels.

At some point we stumbled upon the campus of Bridgeport University.

A conservative business school, BU was not the kind of place where we would be likely to find any activists, but it had to be worth a try. We found a dormitory and waited by the locked front door for someone to come by. After some time, a girl came out on her way somewhere. I stopped her and described our predicament. Then I asked if she knew of any place we might be able to stay for the night. She stared at me blankly, so I tried a more direct approach.

"Do you think anyone in this dorm would let us sleep on the floor in their room tonight?"

An emphatic "no" was her only response. At that point Jill spoke up and her pathetic, feminine tone of voice seemed to reach the college kid in a way that I hadn't. She thought for a moment and then pointed out into the darkness beyond a broad field of mowed grass.

"There's an abandoned house just over there. Some people say it's a crack house, but I don't really know." With that she turned back into the dormitory and pulled the door shut behind her. It seemed like she was on her way out when we first met her, but apparently she had changed her mind.

Jill and I walked across the field and into the darkness where we found a large abandoned house just as the kid had promised. The place was surrounded by unkempt trees and bushes, and it was so dark that I couldn't make out any details at first. A few short stairs led up onto the front porch and we stood below them for a couple minutes waiting for our eyes to adjust to the darkness. The place was oozing with bad vibes and I thought I caught a whiff of human feces. I am a brave man, but this seemed like a truly bad idea. There didn't seem to be anyone there, but there was no telling how many half-dead junkies might be laying in the corners. There was also no way of telling who might show up later.

"This is not good enough," I declared, and Jill sighed in relief.

We walked back into the light of the grassy field and sat down. Jill kept whimpering the same hysterical nonsense over and over. I don't remember the exact wording, but it was all variations on the theme, "What are we gonna do?" I advised her to get a grip and then tried to tune her out so I could think. Eventually I declared that we just had to keep looking. Jill wanted to continue her emotional breakdown and I really had to cajole her to get her moving.

We had gone east for one whole block when suddenly we were face to face with a pair of abandoned house lots that had grown over with trees. It was the kind of place I would have rejected in the daylight for being too small, but after several hours of wandering around in the darkness it looked like a beckoning oasis. The trees were not big and old with room between them for junkies and thugs to roam. They were all little saplings bunched so closely together that only crazy, desperate freaks like us would ever try to squeeze in between them. The lots were on a corner of two streets with one side open and one side closed off from the street by a tall, chain-link fence. Right near the inside of the fence, we found a clear spot just wide enough to set up the tent.

Jill was trembling and mumbling about how she couldn't take any more of this and she was going home in the morning. In the darkness I imagined her cross-eyed and drooling while she babbled. I had no patience for it, but I held my tongue. I had no kind words for her so I rolled over and went to sleep. I figured she would change her mind after a good-night's sleep.

It must have been about two in the morning when we were jolted awake by a more terrifying clatter of loud machinery than I could ever describe. It was like a Gatlin gun, five jackhammers, and forty chainsaws all powered by an eighty-six cylinder diesel engine with no muffler. It looked like Jill was screaming in terror, but I couldn't hear anything over the noise of the Armageddon machine. The ground beneath us was literally shaking.

I burst out the front of the tent to find a crew of men working in the road not fifteen paces away from us through the chain link fence. They were operating some enormous piece of equipment and they were all wearing hearing protection. It was utterly overwhelming. Their backs were turned towards us, and it seemed like the back of the machine was also turned towards us, so I never did manage to figure out what they were doing.

I crawled back into the tent were Jill was practically convulsing in horror. My eardrums rattled painfully against the side of my brain and I had to plug my ears. Obviously we were just going to have to endure this ordeal until it was over. We certainly couldn't go out and demand that they stop.

The cacophony continued. As I lay there vibrating, I found myself boiling with anger and frustration. No one would think of running loud equipment this late at night in the suburbs, but this was the ghetto. Life was supposed to suck for these people, so of course they would test the nuclear-powered sonic disruptor at two in the morning. Maybe there was some emergency with the sewer that had to be dealt with right then, but I was in no mood to contemplate such reasonable explanations at the time. The Earth-shattering clatter kept up for about an hour followed by a denouement of rumbling trucks. Then at last we were left in peace for the last couple hours of darkness.

In the morning Jill found a pay phone and called her father once again. He told her she could take the bus this time, so we asked around and learned that we were only a few blocks from the bus station. When we got there I finally let my anger boil over. I called Jill some nasty names and told her she needed to grow up. I don't remember the whole diatribe I gave her, but I remember it was horribly judgmental and mean. Jill said she felt like a failure, and I stomped away leaving her to wait for the bus with all the scary Black people.

I had only gone a couple blocks before I started to feel really bad. There was no reason for me to yell at her like that. What good could that do? It was my job to help Jill grow and expand the boundaries of her comfort zone. Instead I made her feel like a failure. That meant that I was a failure.

I walked along bumming out about what a jerk I had been, but I had something else weird to consider too. Why did all the most frightening things happen only when Jill was around? At this point the pattern was too solid to ignore, but there was no reasonable explanation for it. I had heard claims that personality and disposition will draw particular energies to particular people, but I always thought that was just some new-age hogwash. Now I had to admit that I had a bunch of real data pointing towards that conclusion.

Sweet Pea had been afraid of bugs and together we had been submerged in ticks. It was the most overwhelming bug experience I could ever remember. Jill's list of fears outnumbered the list of things she was comfortable with, and by some coincidence, almost every night we spent together something legitimately terrifying happened. Things like this hardly ever happened to me when I was alone. I thought of life as a fascinating adventure, and I consistently met with interesting new adventures every day. I also thought of myself as a desperately lonely man, and coincidentally all my female companions left me alone. Maybe there was something to this theory of Hippy-physics after all.

12. CARINA

Every time I got ditched by a hiking companion, I found solace in walking hard and fast. I really wasn't that different from Forrest Gump after all. The morning sun gave way to clouds and an unusually strong wind.

With the help of a stolen map, I found a route that took me right near the ocean. That meant that my afternoon turned into a tour of Coastal Connecticut's most opulent mansions, but I did get to catch occasional glimpses of the water and it was quite a sight. Even though it was only the Long Island Sound, the high winds had churned up big breaking waves like you'd expect to see on the open ocean. A misty drizzle came and went several times, but it never got serious enough for things to really get wet.

I had walked across most of the affluent suburb of Westport when I came to a particularly scenic view of the sound. The wind was fierce, but it was not at all cold and it had been hours since the last round of drizzle. I stopped for a moment admiring the view and letting the wind tear at my hair and clothing.

Just then a little brown Saab drove by and slowed conspicuously while the young woman who was driving gave me a long, curious inspection. I couldn't be sure, but I thought I had just seen the same car drive by moments earlier going the other direction. I wasn't usually that observant of cars, but the dilapidated old Saab stood out because it reminded me of Maine.

For some reason, that model of car is really popular among rich people on the coast of Maine. Whenever the little brown Saabs get old, the rich people discard them and they get scooped up by local high-school kids who patch them together with the proverbial duct-tape and bailing twine. When I left Maine, no fewer than three of my good friends drove old brown hoopty Saabs, and when I saw the same car circling me in Westport, I thought it might be one of them.

As it turned out, I was not yet friends with the driver of this car, but that was soon to change. I had walked another two blocks when the same car came back for a third pass, but this time it pulled into a driveway just in front of me and stopped. The driver got out and introduced herself. For this book, let's just call her Carina. She was an adult in her mid-twenties, but she was so short and skinny that she still might not have been allowed to ride the rides at the county fair. She said she could just tell when she saw me that I was doing something really interesting and after checking me out twice, she had finally summoned the resolve to stop and ask. When I explained my mission, her eyes lit up with inspiration. She wanted to know more, but she was extremely busy that day. She suggested that I stay at her apartment in Westport so that she could hear more about my adventures later.

I liked her suggestion at first, but when she told me where she lived my enthusiasm faded. I had already walked past that part of town and I didn't feel like I could afford to backtrack at all, being so far behind schedule as I was. When I explained my hesitation, Carina came up with a different plan. She was an extremely busy person in general, but in two days, she would have an entire day off work. She suggested that I call her the day after next, and she would come out to wherever I was and walk with me for the day. I couldn't imagine a more perfect plan, so I took her number and she hurried off to do some important thing.

My heart soared all afternoon. I had been mourning Jill's departure only moments before. Now, suddenly I was scheduled to have a new hiking partner. The highs and lows of life's emotional roller-coaster were making me dizzy.

As the day neared its finish I found myself in Norwalk, the full-sized city that I had only just discovered the year before. I remembered that I hadn't signed up a single subscriber to my zine the last time I passed through Norwalk, so I resolved to do better this time.

Just then a passerby on the street warned me that a hurricane was coming and I better get under cover. The wind, heat, and humidity had been steadily increasing all day, but somehow I had failed to recognize the obvious signs of an approaching tropical storm. Clearly I was going to have to make some friends and get under a roof before nightfall.

I spent some time wandering around in a foolish panic before it occurred to me to use my brain. Eventually I snapped out of it and found a telephone directory. Scanning for various non-profit groups, I found out that Norwalk was home to the offices of "E" magazine, a very glossy publication about environmentalist issues. I called and suggested that they interview me as some kind of eco-pilgrim who had randomly wandered through town on foot. The receptionist wasn't sure if anyone would want to interview me, but she suggested I come by the office and make a face to face proposal to some of the editors. She gave me directions and I felt very hopeful walking back across town to the E Magazine office.

My hope faded quickly when no one answered the buzzer. I stood outside the locked door for at least twenty minutes occasionally pushing the button while gusts of warm fog buffeted my backpack, pushing me around like an unwanted sail.

Eventually a young writer came back from her dinner break and let me in. She was very friendly, and she also seemed very familiar. It turned out that no one had heard the doorbell because it only rang in the receptionist's office and she had gone home at five. I was introduced to the handful of people who were working late and they all apologized for leaving me out in the weird weather. No one wanted to do a story about my walk for E Magazine, but they all signed up for zines. Then the writer who had let me in figured out that we had already met at a party in New York City the previous winter. Her husband was another writer in the same office and I had met both of them at the party. Before I could even ask, they insisted that I stay with them until the hurricane passed. I was saved!

The wife was determined to get some writing done, so the husband took me home and she showed up a couple hours later. They were both recent college graduates, slightly younger than me, but they lived in a full-sized bourgeois house in one of Norwalk's "nice" neighborhoods. I guess they were making good money working for the magazine. They fed me delicious dinner and we bonded over the fact that we had all been the biggest nerds in our respective high-schools. We had all shared the experience of being in the throes of utter teen-age depression when the band Nirvana became popular, suddenly making it cool to be a nerd. Our moment of glory had only lasted about three years, but it had been just long enough to get us through the really tough times. Having discovered this bond, my new friends put on some Nirvana right then and we stayed up late drinking beers and waiting for the hurricane.

I am also a real nerd for extreme weather, and I got all excited in anticipation of the storm, but it turned out to be a total let down. It rained some and the wind blew a little bit harder, but there was very little thunder and nothing extreme happened. I suppose if I had been out in a tent with some untested young woman then nature would have seen fit to lash the coast with unprecedented fury, but alas I was in a big, well-constructed house with no one to impress.

The weather had cleared up by morning, so I resumed my walk without delay. In the southwestern part of Norwalk I came across a huge abandoned building that had recently been a community college. I couldn't help but think what a cool squat that would make.

By afternoon I was wandering around Stamford trying to sign up zine subscribers, and by evening I was still in the dense urban core of Stamford with no place to stay. It was time to call Carina, so I called and she said not to worry. I could stay at her place. I described the location of the pay-phone I was calling from and she told me to wait right there. About half an hour later her little brown Saab pulled up to the corner. She parked and then treated me to dinner at a noisy sports bar across the street. Then we drove back to Westport to her apartment.

Carina lived in the top flat of a small, two-story building. The ground floor was a store that specialized in aquariums, fish, and other fish related pet-supplies. She explained that she paid for her apartment by cleaning the pet store downstairs. She also had several big tanks full of interesting fish in her apartment.

Getting to know Carina, I was truly impressed. Since our first meeting, I had sensed a wisdom and maturity beyond her years, and now that I got to hear her life story, I understood. She had grown up a hick in some little town out West, but some time in her mid-teens, she had followed a boyfriend into the city and gotten involved in a very serious drug scene. Before long she had hooked up with another man who was some kind of king-pin in an international drug-smuggling operation. She had been to most of the countries in South America and she had helped smuggle drugs into the United States so many times she couldn't even remember them all. Her tiny stature and her youthful good looks made a very non-threatening impression, and apparently that qualified her to carry bags just loaded with drugs through customs. While the men who accompanied her owned the drugs and made all the money off their sale, Carina was usually the one who actually carried the bag.

She described the spectacularly decadent lifestyle of her past, consuming all kinds of pills, cocaine, and other drugs, and being used sexually by all sorts of high-ranking gangsters. She told me that in one case she followed her boyfriend on a flight to South America just to go to a party, and then flew back the next day. When I asked her what country the party was in, she didn't even know. She said she was so cracked-out on different drugs that she partied all night without knowing or caring what country she was in.

Then one day a customs agent caught her at the border carrying an entire suitcase full of hash. She thought her life was over, but by some miracle she was able to bribe the agent. She got off with a sentence of only six months and a few thousand dollars in fines. Perhaps the agents had understood that she was only a pawn in the game, but in a system where the pawns usually receive the worst punishment, there really was no explanation for her good luck.

After that she decided to turn her life around. She knew she would never get another chance like that, so she left all her gangster friends behind and set about finding legal means of earning a living. Somehow, she had hooked up with an very rich family who needed a nanny, and she had moved to Connecticut to be near them. On the side she had started her own house-cleaning business and by the time I met her, she had built up a base of customers that kept her busy almost constantly. It had been years since she paid off her legal fines, and she was saving up money to go to college. She was also making payments on her mother's house because her mother had become disabled or something. I had never met a person so diligently determined to reform their own life.

She told me another story that left a long-lasting impression. One of her house-cleaning customers was a Westport police officer, and through his recommendation, she ended up cleaning house for several other officers on the same squad. Now one would think that anyone who hires a house-cleaner would have the sense to hide anything that they would want to keep a secret, but Carina said she had found conspicuous stashes of cocaine in every single one of the cops' homes. Being a dutiful maid, she left them all in place, cleaned around them and never said a word, but she couldn't resist telling me.

Cocaine gives people a ridiculous over-abundance of self-confidence. People on cocaine are certain that they are the coolest people to ever exist. They are right and everyone else is wrong. If a big man is high on cocaine, he won't hesitate to escalate into violence to prove his point. Even people who aren't cops will start to act like cops under the influence of enough cocaine, and it makes a lot of sense that cops would have a taste for such a drug. If you're about to kick in the door of someone else's house, beat the shit out of them, cuff them, and initiate legal procedures that will ruin the rest of their life, that's not the time for any thoughtful reflection or doubts. You would want to feel certain you're doing the right thing, get it done with a stimulating burst of energy, and then move on to the next bust. Any urges towards self-doubt or hesitation need to be suppressed and cocaine is the perfect drug to suppress them. I suspect that the percentage of police who are addicted to cocaine nationwide is probably pretty high. (No pun intended.) That would help explain why so many thousands of innocent people get incarcerated, beaten and shot every year.

Sometime in the late-late night, Carina finally declared that we ought to sleep. She gave me her bed to sleep in while she curled up on the couch across the room. As tired as I was, it took me a long time to get to sleep. My amazing new friend had given me so many things to think about. It was also strangely intimate to sleep in such an interesting woman's bed, so I tossed and turned all night to the gentle rumble of fish-tank aerators.

In the morning we walked to the commuter-rail station in Westport and rode ahead three stops to Stamford. The train station in Stamford was only a few blocks from where Carina had picked me up, so my walking route felt legitimately continuous in spite of the recent flurry of high-tech travel. We walked all day through western Stamford, Greenwich, Port Chester New York, and into Rye. The police were having a parade in Port Chester, but aside from that I don't remember a single detail of the scenes we walked through. I just remember the day as one long, uninterrupted, fascinating con-versation with Carina. We talked about life and death, nature and civilization, God and religion, men and women, relationships, love, revolution, and every-thing in between. I didn't try to sign up a single zine subscriber all day, but it didn't matter. I would not say that I fell in love, but I did feel a profound appreciation for Carina's company. I couldn't remember feeling such a sub-lime happiness in weeks or even months.

When the evening's shadows grew long, it was time for her to go. We found the train station in Rye, shared a moment of appreciative embrace, and said farewell. I never kept in touch with Carina, but that seems fine. I hope she is doing well.

It was only a few blocks after that when I found an adequate hiding place for the night. The Avon cosmetics corporation had a factory or perhaps a warehouse there and they had left a swath of forest around it to isolate the surrounding residents from their little industrial site. There was no fence around it so it made an ideal camping spot. I drifted off to sleep still basking in the glow of Carina's company even after she had left. What a life full of valuable experiences she had. It gave her a fascinating insight and a spiritual weight that I could feel just standing next to her.

I also appreciated that she had told me she would only be with me for one day. Knowing exactly what to expect, I had not gotten my hopes up for anything more, and so I had felt none of the anguish of loss when she left. The sadness of losing Jill only three days before seemed like a distant memory. It was a pleasantly warm night for that time of year, and I slept well with a big smile on my face.

13. KRS-ONE

I found a greenbelt park on my neat new map and followed it most of the way across Westchester County. No more plunging ahead into the unknown for me. I knew where I was going and I had a plan to stay at my friend Sha-King's apartment in the Bronx. I had been calling him from pay phones for days but I still hadn't gotten in touch. I had left plenty of messages though, and I knew it was the right number because he identified himself on the voice mail message. There was no way for him to call me back, so I just figured I should keep calling until I got ahold of him. I walked along into the thick of the Bronx assuming that he would eventually pick up the phone, and it would come as no surprise because I had left so many messages. I didn't know exactly where his apartment was, but I thought it was somewhere right in the center of the Bronx near Fordham and the zoo.

I came to the Bronx River Park which is right in that area and called again. Still there was no answer. The situation was starting to feel a little bit stressful. It was already too late to backtrack to the parks I had walked through that morning, and I hadn't told anyone else besides Sha-King that I was arriving back in the city. I waited for as long as I could stand, an interval of about an hour at best, and then called him back. I don't remember how many times I ended up calling, but eventually I got Sha-King on the phone.

He wasn't angry at *me* but he was in a bad mood nonetheless. He had just been evicted and he was sleeping on the floor at his grandmother's apartment. There was nothing he could do to help me.

I felt like a total idiot for assuming I could just crash at his place. It felt like a typical White-boy move to assume that my Black friends in the ghetto wouldn't be getting evicted or relocated at any random time. I apologized and expressed concern, but he didn't want to talk about it. He had to go.

So there I was back in the city at sunset with no place to stay. I considered my options. I could walk down to Paco and Luisa's place in Morissania and ring the buzzer. It would be dark by the time I got there, but it would not be terribly late. Still, who knew if they would be home or if they would even understand my voice through the cheesy little microphone at the door buzzer. Not only that, but I couldn't stand the thought of leeching off them anymore. I had grown to feel ashamed of the way I had lived in their home for two months the previous winter and contributed so little to the household.

I thought about other options but all of them made me feel like a leach. I could call up any number of other people and ride the subway to their parts of the city, but I just didn't want to. In every case it would only amount to asking someone to change whatever plans they had for the evening and redirect their energy into rescuing me from the dumb situation I had just brought upon myself. Anyway, skipping over miles of Bronx in a comfortable subway seat would effectively mean cheating on my walk.

I looked across the street at the Bronx River Park. There was a crew of about fifteen young men who I took for Dominicans rolling dice on the sidewalk, laughing and drinking beers. I didn't see any obvious gang colors or guns, but being all young men as they were, I still couldn't help but wonder if they were a gang.

The sun had gone down and it was starting to get dark. I had to make my move. I crossed the street and then looped around through the grass so as not to disturb the dice game on the sidewalk. Most of the vatos gaped at me like I had genitalia growing out of my forehead. I tried not to notice and stroll along like everything was normal.

I followed a broad gravel path that followed the river downstream. The Bronx River is really only a broad creek, splashing and gurgling down out of the ridges. The water is a strange, soapy-gray color, and the churning of the little rapids seems to release some odd-smelling gasses, but it provides a pleasant contrast to the grinding city nonetheless. Before long, I came to a place where wild vegetation had actually been left along either side of the path. There was very little space between the river and the path, and even in the waning light, there were still old men fishing at regular intervals. The other side of the trail was a thick jungle of aldery brush.

Eventually I gulped and plunged into the thicket. I found a spot where Japanese knotweed or some similar, bamboo-like plant had been flourishing. The hollow dead stems were brittle, and they crackled and crunched loudly under every step, but I found the noise reassuring. I was really nervous about someone sneaking up on me in the night, so I figured the crackling stems would serve as a security system to alert me if anyone tried anything sketchy.

By some coincidence, I stumbled upon a vaguely circular space about six paces across where all the knotweed had been cut down. Crackling dry stems covered the ground, but no plants were left standing. I imagined it must be a secret hiding place for some local kids. I selected a spot on the edge farthest from the trail, cleared out a bare space on the dirt, and set up my tent. I turned in for the night, but I was too wired to sleep at all.

I had slept out in gardens in the Bronx plenty of times, but they were all surrounded by fences higher than my head. I had grown accustomed to the Morissania and Saint Anne's Park regions of the Bronx, but now I was in a whole new neighborhood that I knew nothing about. What if this park was a hotbed for gang violence or crack or some other unknown dangerous vice of poor city people? I clutched my knife and worried.

Suddenly the dry stems crunched right nearby signaling an alarm! I burst out of the tent with my blade drawn ready for combat. AAAAAAAAAAAAAH!

A mangy alley cat was making its way back from the river. I stood there panting, my heart pounding and adrenaline oozing from every pore. I felt ridiculous but I still couldn't shake the fear that was consuming my mind. Something told me I just wasn't in a safe enough place to ever really relax.

About an hour later the reeds crackled again, and once again I sprang to attention like a defending warrior. This time it was a skunk. The skunk shambled away unconcerned, and I had crawled most of the way back into my tent when I saw something that made my heart stop. There in the reeds just an arms-reach beyond the far edge of the little clearing was the silhouette of a man. He was looking right at me and standing perfectly still.

The hair on my neck bristled. He must have been sneaking up on me very slowly, picking his way between the millions of crunchy sticks. I couldn't believe he had gotten so close without making some sound to alert me. I was very lucky that the skunk had roused me when it did. For an interminable moment neither of us moved a muscle. He must have been telling himself that I hadn't seen him, convinced that if he just held still, I would eventually go back to bed. I could see his silhouette clearly in the light of a dim lamp over the nearby foot path. He looked like a young-to-middle-aged Latino man. Maybe he was one of the men who had been playing dice earlier. Maybe he had seen my big backpack and thought there might be something in it worth stealing. That made sense. If he meant to hurt me, there would be no reason to sneak up on me. Why not just attack? Then again, maybe he did intend to hurt me and he just needed to build up his courage a little bit.

I have no sense of how much time I spent contemplating these things. It stands out in my memory as one of those truly timeless moments. It could have been ten seconds or five minutes for all I know. Eventually a gust of wind blew through making the stems sway back and forth. When the alders and bamboo around the stalking figure swayed, he actually loosened his stance and swayed gently with them. Did he really think he was that camouflaged, or was he messing with me?

Enough time elapsed that I realized he wasn't just going to leave. I had to do something to chase him away. I looked at myself. I was dressed in a t-shirt and boxer shorts. No pants. Bare feet. I held a small pocket knife in my right hand, but I had never tried to stab anyone before. I didn't know the first thing about fighting. He was well within range that I could have easily pegged him with a rock, but there were no rocks on the ground there, only dirt and flimsy little sticks. The odds were against me, but I had to do something.

Maybe if I made threatening wild animal noises, he would think I was insane and that would scare him away. I gave him my most ominous grizzly bear growl. Nothing. He didn't move. He didn't even say anything. Now it was obvious that he was messing with me. He was just going to stand there and stare me down until…. Until what?

Nothing good could possibly happen if I just sat there and waited. It also seemed like there was very little chance that anything good could happen if I lunged across the clearing and attacked him, but at least in that option there was a glimmer of hope. If the bastard could see that I was not a coward, that would surely count for something right? That was it. I had made up my mind.

Suddenly I stood up and charged across the small clearing in my most ruthless barefoot, Celtic berserker rage. It was probably the most macho thing I had ever done in my life. This guy had pushed me over the edge and he was going to pay.

I took the six-pace clearing in four paces, but before I had even reached the mid-point, the man vanished. He didn't run away. He just disappeared into thin air! Not to be distracted by metaphysical mysteries, I followed through with the attack. I finished my charge and plunged my knife into the alder branches and bamboo stems where he had just been.

Then I started laughing as I realized that he had never existed in the first place. It was all just a trick of the lights and shadows amplified through my paranoia until it became the dark urban boogey man out to get me. I went back to my tent, and there he was again, a collage of random leaves and sticks, backlit in just the right way to look like Jose Malvado (Spanish for Joe Evil) coming to avenge the sins of every gringo since Christopher Columbus.

I kept laughing. For years I had been mocking privileged White people for their fear of ghetto people. Who was I to talk? Who had just attacked an alder bush in his underpants?

I had made an enormous ass of myself, but no one else was there to witness it, so I just laughed and laughed. Who was the only motherfucker out in the Bronx River Park that night? It was me! I was alone. *I* was the boogey man hiding in the shadows! Growling like a bear! I felt like a dumbass and a badass all at the same time.

Suddenly a line from a KRS-One song popped into my head.

"While you were home with your mama, afraid of the dark-

I was out sleepin' in Prospect Park!"

After that I finally managed to sleep. Two more animals came crackling through the reeds before dawn finally broke, but I didn't feel compelled to attack them.

***

After that I decided I had to sleep out in Prospect Park too, just as some kind of hip-hop rite of passage. That morning I walked across the Tri-borough Bridge which takes almost an hour to walk from one end to the other and provides amazing views of the city the whole way. I spent a night or two with friends in Queens, and then it was time.

I had lived right near Prospect Park the previous winter when I stayed with the drag queen in Brooklyn. It's much bigger than the Bronx River Park and it's surrounded by gentrified neighborhoods that no one would write a rap song about. Still, if KRS had slept there, it must have been tough at some time in the past and I would not feel like a real hero until I had slept there too. I wandered around the park for hours unable to find any place that hadn't been mowed and manicured. Clearly it was not going to be easy to find a hiding spot.

Finally, I found a little ravine full of wild undergrowth. I got about half-way finished setting up my tent when I realized someone was watching me. He was a young Black man with his head shaved, but something about his presence seemed very non-threatening. I crossed the ravine, climbed to the little stone turret he was standing on and asked if I could help him.

"It depends," he said. "What are you looking for?"

I gave him a quizzical look to which he responded, "You know this is the cruisy area of the park, right?"

"No, what does that mean?"

"Oh." He thought for a moment, eyes wandering timidly. Then he tried to explain, "You know, men come here cruisin'. You know? Looking for each other."

"Oh shit," I said. "I'm just looking for a place to camp."

The man left politely, but I realized that if I was truly camped in the "cruisy" area of the park, he would likely not be the last person to see me there and misunderstand my intentions. Reluctantly I packed my things and moved along.

Prospect Park is really a vast park and I wandered for what seemed like hours without even coming close to the perimeter. Finally, I found a large stretch of real forest near the park's southeastern corner. I had to climb over a wrought-iron fence to get into it, but it felt reassuring to know that people wouldn't just randomly wander in there without some effort. It was starting to get dark so I picked a spot quickly and set up camp. I was far enough out in the woods that I could see nothing but wild trees and bushes in every direction. If it were not for the sounds of the city, I could have believed I was miles out in the wilderness. Compared to the Bronx River Park, this felt very secure. As I lay in my tent, I imagined that the park must have been much more dangerous back when KRS wrote that song. Then I realized that he never claimed it was dangerous. That was just something I had assumed. All he actually said was that he slept there.

Suddenly a man coughed right outside my tent. Whoa! I snapped to attention, grabbed my knife and scrambled out into a crouched position. The coughing came again and then it turned into a full-scale coughing fit. Someone was really sick and they were right nearby, but I still couldn't see them. The light outside was dusky but there was still some daylight left. I strained to focus my eyes in the direction of the coughing. Slowly I began to recognize an unnaturally straight line. I followed it to another line and then another. I gulped hard as I realized what I was looking at.

Somehow, I had pitched my tent less than ten paces up the gentle slope from another, much larger tent. It was masterfully camouflaged, not only in the way it was colored, but also in its positioning and the way the dead sticks had been arranged all around it. Instantly I imagined a deranged Vietnam veteran capable of killing me and skinning me all in one quick flick of the wrist. Maybe if I had not been in such a hurry to set up my own camp, I would have noticed his, but I hadn't and now it was almost dark- too late to move again. Why hadn't this guy said something when he heard me setting up right in his personal space? Maybe he had been asleep?

As the coughing continued, I felt somewhat reassured. He was obviously really sick. It wasn't hard to imagine him sleeping through the sounds of my arrival even if he had once been a badass survivor of jungle combat. After crouching at the ready for quite some time, I decided to just be as quiet as I could and leave at the crack of dawn. I slithered silently back into my tent and spent the next five minutes zipping the front flap shut inch by inch so as to avoid making that distinct zipper sound. The man had several more coughing fits throughout the night, but he never showed any sign that he had noticed me. Nor did he ever make any sounds that would indicate that he was coming out of his tent.

The thought of Vietnam veterans reminded me of my father. By now anyone reading this has probably noticed that I usually feel very comfortable in the darkness. I have my father to thank for that trait.

When I was only five years old, we lived in east Alabama where we had a big back yard. Like most five-year-olds, I was afraid of the dark and at some point, I had been making a big deal out of that fear, using it as an excuse to challenge bed-time and other such frustrating things. Finally, my dad got tired of it and decided that I was going to learn to appreciate the darkness.

He took me out into the back yard late one night and we waited together for our eyes to adjust. Most of the yard was clear, but one back corner was completely overgrown with honeysuckle and other vines. As our eyes adjusted to the darkness, most of the yard became dimly visible in the starlight and the ambient glow from our town, but that one corner remained hidden in an impossibly dark shadow. After some time, my father asked me to point to the scariest place in the whole yard, and without hesitating I pointed to the honeysuckle vines. He grabbed my hand and led me across the yard to that place. We circled around behind the mass of vines and then crawled in underneath them on our bellies. A space was hollowed out underneath where my sister and I would play during the day, and we crawled right in until we could see out the front, looking back across the yard towards the house.

I would never have dared go there by myself in the dark, but it didn't feel scary at all with my big, indestructible dad right there. I thought that was all he had to prove, but the lesson had only just begun. Next, he told me stories about some of his experiences in the Vietnam War. They are not my stories to repeat here, but I can assure you that my five-year-old mind was thoroughly blown.

After a substantial amount of that, he explained that he had survived the war and come home safely because he had learned to find the darkest, scariest-looking spots and hide in them. He pointed out all the details we could see out in the brighter part of the yard. Then he reminded me how we couldn't see any details of the honeysuckle thicket when we had been out there.

"Imagine if men with guns were looking for you trying to shoot you," he explained. "The darkest place you can find is the safest place you can find because they can't see you there. Not only that, but once you're in the darkest place, then your eyes adjust and you can see what they are doing out in the brighter places."

I'm paraphrasing because I don't remember his exact words forty years later, but I do remember the line, "The darkness is your friend."

I really took that lesson to heart. I can't claim that I lost all fear of the darkness right then and there, but that was the point when I started working on it in earnest. For the next ten years I was the kid who snuck up on the other kids in the dark and scared them into screaming hysteria. Judging by their reactions, very few of their parents had made it a real priority to help them overcome their fear of the darkness, so I feel lucky that my father did that for me. Before you were home with your mama afraid of the dark, and KRS-One was out sleeping in Prospect Park, my old man was hiding in a foreign jungle trying not to get shot by extremely motivated locals.

14. WHY YOU LITTLE!

Even after living in New York all winter, I still found myself getting hope-lessly lost in the outer boroughs, so I decided to get some maps. I was visiting a feminist bookstore that several of my friends had just opened up some-where in Brooklyn when I got the idea. There was a Walgreen's chain store just a few blocks down from their little storefront, so I stomped down there stressing out and pumping up my adrenaline.

The franchise was small and it was fortified with panoptic mirrors ring-ing the ceiling and security cameras everywhere. I ignored them and wan-dered around impatiently, looking for the maps. The aisles were cramped and crowded, and I kept getting stuck behind little clots of people. I wanted to get my business over with and my frustration kept mounting. Finally I found a few fold-out maps. I grabbed one of Queens and one of Brooklyn, and hastily stuffed them into my shorts, my belt pressing them against my belly, and my loose shirt hanging down over their tops. I had done this quite a few times already and it seemed like the way to go- at least in the summer when it was too warm to wear a jacket. I could see that a camera was looking at me, but I assumed no one would be watching me through it. The whole store was under surveillance anyway, so I turned my back to the camera as best I could and wasted no time.

At least, I intended to waste no time. As I rounded the corner of the aisle, there was a large, hunchbacked old man pushing a cart and blocking the entire passage. He was inching along at a pathetic pace, but even that seemed to be straining him. To go around him would have been rude verging on violent, as he was somehow so wide that he was almost touching both sides of the corridor. Well, this was a pharmacy. Certainly I should expect to see infirm people at a pharmacy.

I sighed reluctantly and traced my steps back around to the other end of the aisle. I had been near the exit before, but this route took me back through the middle of the store. I had to dodge several more slow-moving elders and I felt exasperation growing in my chest. Shoplifting made me really nervous. Why couldn't I just get the hell out of there?

By the time I made it to the front door, I was walking conspicuously fast, but it turned out to be a good thing anyway. About four paces from the door,

I heard a loud, male voice shout, "Excuse me, Sir!"

After two more steps, I saw a human shape running towards me out of the corner of my left eye. I got through the first door, but the Walgreens was built with a sort of airlock-style double front door. I had to stand still for a second before the motion-sensor activated the pneumatic pump and the automatic door slid open. The man rounded the corner into the airlock just as I bolted into motion through the first sliver of the opening door. I was starting to run, but he had already been running fast. He caught hold of my left elbow as I strode forward with my right leg. Our momentum pulled him out the door, but after a couple more steps he yanked me to a halt.

At this point we were both shouting angrily. He was accusing me of being a thief and I was shouting something to the tune of, "Let go of me you fuckin' creep!" I wrestled and struggled, but he was a very strong man. He obviously worked out a lot. If I had to guess, I'd say he was an immigrant from maybe Turkey, so all his shouting was coming across in broken English. He was threatening legal consequences and commanding me to go back into the store. I returned in kind threatening to sue him for assault. I had no idea if that would work, but I hoped it would sound intimidating.

Just then, the maps slid down into my shorts, out the bottom of one of my pant-legs, and onto the sidewalk. Dammit! I hadn't thought to tighten my belt in preparation for a wrestling match. What a slacker. As far as I was concerned the maps had been mine since the moment I put them in my pants, so I twisted defiantly towards the ground and got them back in my hand for a brief instant.

As I did, I felt the security guard closing on me from behind and trying to wrap me up in his arms. I dropped and spun evasively, but my right arm was still outstretched from grabbing the maps and somehow I didn't think to pull it in close. In the next turbulent moment, I accidentally slapped him right across the face with my maps, and the impact of his head knocked them out of my hand. The two maps flew high in the air. A pimply, teen-aged Walgreens peon had followed us out of the store, and when they landed, he scooped them up.

Meanwhile I grappled furiously with the guard and I almost escaped. I can't remember the whole sequence of maneuvers and counter maneuvers. All I remember was a quick cascade of opposing efforts. When it ended we were facing one another, breathing heavily, and the guard was only holding onto me by the now-empty right sleeve of my shirt.

The man returned to his legal threats and then he took to reciting the details of the procedure he was going to put me through. It involved going back into his office and filing paperwork. I wasn't about to do that. I repeated my legal threats, informing him that a security guard was never allowed to manhandle a customer under any circumstances. Shoplifting was no exception. I'm pretty sure that's true, but my point came out sounding a bit wordy and less convincing than it had the first time.

My upper torso was mostly bare at this point, and a small crowd of customers and employees was gathering around to witness our strange contest. I considered pulling the rest of the way out of my shirt and running for it, but I decided that I wanted to keep my shirt. It was a nice, light-weight, long-sleeved shirt. It looked good on me. I had worn it for many years and this over-zealous guard dog didn't deserve to keep it just because he caught me trying to shoplift. I put my right arm back through the sleeve, which meant voluntarily handing my right arm back to the guard. He grabbed my wrist with both his meaty paws, flexing his macho-man arms and squeezing until it hurt.

He kept repeating his procedures like a mantra and I felt obliged to keep shouting my defiance. I felt like I had lost a few points ranting about lawyers and courtrooms that I really knew nothing about, so I decided to change my approach.

"Come on man! You got your maps back. Now I get my arm back."

It seemed like a really sensible compromise to me. I hoped the other people standing around would agree and say something in my defense. They didn't. Instead the guard just kept tugging on my arm, determined to reel me in like a hooked fish. He kept shouting and I kept shouting. After several repetitions I gave up on my proposed compromise and just started berating him. I hurled all kinds of insults, some witty and some real dumb ones. I commanded him to let go of me like one would command a misbehaving dog. He was shouting his own commands at me in the same tone, and we carried on like that for several moments.

I had been staring into the man's eyes the whole time, trying to show him how determined I was to regain control of my own arm. Suddenly I looked up and refocused my eyes on the scene behind him. We were no longer on the sidewalk and the crowd of onlookers was farther away than I remembered. I realized that without even thinking about it, I had towed the big man a good ways out into the parking lot. Could it be? He had obviously done years of weight-training on his buff chest and arms. Had he really forgotten to work out his lower half?

I hadn't. I had just used my lower half to walk more than a thousand miles. I stopped shouting and smiled. We were going to play tug-of war with my right arm as the rope. Maybe once we got to the end of the Walgreens property he would be able to understand that he had no right to physically detain me.

I put my legs in low reverse gear and commenced to tug in earnest. In an instant the man's face turned from anger to wide-eyed astonishment. It was obvious to both of us that I was going to overpower him in the battle of leg-strength. He turned back to the crowd and shouted, "Call the cops!" The pimply kid jumped to attention and ran inside. The guard skidded along on his heels steadily dragging in the direction I wanted to go. He spluttered random curses at me, but he couldn't catch his breath long enough to really say anything coherent.

Now I'm not sure if I can really explain just what a triumphant moment that was for me. I had been the skinny, wimpy kid my whole life. Here was a big, puffy-chested bully trying to dominate me and I was beating him in a battle of physical strength. That was the first time I had ever experienced anything like that, and it may never happen again. I will always look back on it as a highlight.

It took a minute or so, but eventually we got to the sidewalk marking the boundary between Walgreens property and the city of New York property. I still hadn't figured out how to get the bastard's hands off my wrist, but I wasn't about to give up now. As a tactic though, I decided to pretend to give up. I was pretty winded after all that wrestling and tugging, so I played it up. I feigned an expression of weary defeat as I slowly relaxed. Finally I stopped pulling altogether, went slack, and said, "Okay. (puff, puff, puff.) You got me."

I hadn't imagined this cheap deception would work, but it did. The guard didn't let go of me, but he loosened his grip significantly and turned as if to lead me back to the store, to his office, to begin the procedure he had been telling me about for so long. He seemed so relieved for the struggle to be over that he just wanted to believe me even though he should have known better.

In a flash, I twisted my sore wrist out of his grip and took off running up the street. Immediately I realized that I had made another stupid mistake. I wore a low-top pair of skateboarder sneakers in those days, and I kept the laces loose enough that I could just slide them on and off like slippers. Now I was facing a situation where running at top sprint on the balls of my feet would literally cause me to run out of my shoes. Instead I had to take big goofy, loping strides and try to land each step flat-footed. Oh what a cursed, inept, bumbling slacker!

The meaty ogre gave chase and he was right on my heels. I looked back to see his teeth bared in an expression of exasperated fury. Together we charged up the sidewalk with the back side of the Walgreens to our left. To the right, across the street, we ran past the length of an NYPD precinct with about half a dozen unoccupied squad cars out front. I smiled thinking that the situation couldn't get much more ridiculous. Luckily, there were no actual police officers outside at that moment, and no one came popping out the door just then. Hopefully I would remember to give thanks to the spirits of luck the next time I found a spare moment.

Somehow in spite of my impaired pace, I had managed to put a few strides between me and the lagging security oaf. I guess he was just getting tired. I was tired too, but my freedom was at stake. I think that added a level of motivation to my struggle that he just couldn't match. When we came to the end of the block, I ran on across the street and he finally gave up. As I looked back, he waved his angry finger at me one last time and shouted, "Why you little…..!" and then trailed off unable to come up with a noun nasty-enough to express his frustration. It made me wonder if he had been learning to speak English by watching Bugs-Bunny and Yosemite Sam cartoons and I howled with laughter.

I had beaten him! You can't take away my freedom asshole! I'll fight back. I ran two or three more blocks all the way back to my friends' bookstore, laughing the whole way. I had never prevailed in such a triumphant way before. I felt indestructible.

I never heard any police sirens before or even after I ducked into the bookstore. Nonetheless, my friends did not hesitate to let me hide in the back store-room for a while. There were two people back there going through boxes of books anyway, so it gave me someone to hang out with and regale with my heroic story.

***

I was a real action-hero for sure, but alas, I still didn't have any maps of New York City. I had heard tell that if a person gets caught shoplifting, they have to get back on the horse right away afterwards. If they don't, they run the risk that a crippling anxiety will set in and prevent them from ever trying it again. I had always been impaired by my anxiety anyway, so I made up my mind to get my new maps right away.

The next day I was visiting someone in lower Manhattan. I staked out a chain bookstore and set up a fairly elaborate escape plan. There was a dark alleyway running parallel to the avenue that the store fronted on, and in preparation for my mission, I hid a hat and a jacket in the alley. Then I tied my shoes tightly and cinched my belt tight on my hips.

Inside the store, I found the maps right in front of the checkout counter. It was a fairly small space for a chain store, but everything has to squeeze a bit to fit into lower Manhattan. There were only two cashiers working the exit, but the rack of maps was in plain view of both of them. They were both young men who looked like college students. One of them greeted me cordially and asked if he could help me find anything.

"No thanks," I tried to maintain a casual coolness while my pulse accelerated even more.

This was frustrating. These guys had nothing to do but stand there and chat with me. How the hell was I going to steal anything? I browsed the maps and sweated profusely. My hands felt clammy. I sweated and browsed and smiled awkwardly at the employees. I had gathered up a stack of five maps, one for each borough of the city. (New York is so big that you can't really show all of it in one map without losing some important details.) It would have been silly to put them in my pants with everyone right there. I realized that my move was going to look hopelessly sketchy no matter what I did, but I couldn't give up now or my will to shoplift would be broken forever. At least that was the theory.

Finally a customer came up to ring out and both the cashiers engaged her in conversation, apparently relieved to have something at all to do. I was only a few paces from the door, so I just left. I held the stack of maps in my hand for all the world to see and walked right through the door. As I crossed the threshold, I heard one of them squeak, "Hey…. Wait!" but it was nothing like a forceful command.

Outside, the sidewalks were bustling with pedestrians and I thought it would look bad to burst out the front of a store running, so I walked quickly but casually to the corner. Once I made it around the corner, I broke into a run and then quickly ducked into the alley. No one was around to see me change into the hat and jacket, or to see me tuck the maps into my belt. I don't think anyone had even tried to pursue me out of the store, but it didn't hurt to be careful. I walked the length of the alley and emerged on the next street as a different guy without any maps. Another block and I was completely lost in the crowd.

Now the victory was truly complete. Not only had I battled a beast of a security guard and won my freedom, but I had also kept my shoplifting streak alive and acquired maps of the entire city of New York. I still have those maps too. I collected several dozen maps of various East-Coast cities on my journey. Whenever my stash got too heavy, I would put the old ones in a package and mail them to my parents for safe-keeping. I always made sure to trace my walking route with a highlighter before I sent them away, so I will always have a fairly accurate record of where I went.

15. LIBERTY

Somehow in spite of the deepening chill of autumn, I managed to dawdle around New York City for three more weeks before I finally resumed my journey. Just one year earlier, the pace of my travelling had slowed significantly because I was nervous about going into the city. Now I couldn't bring myself to leave.

I rode the free ferry from Battery Point to Staten Island and walked along the eastern edge of the island. I was still technically in New York, but it was a part of the city I had never seen before. I walked along for hours following the gentle curve of the island's fringe until the east shore faded into the south shore. The day had been overcast, but by the time I reached the island's southern shore, the clouds had begun to lift revealing the long shadows of evening. I found my way to a large park belonging to the federal government called the Gateway National Seashore. The situation was perfect for camping. There were no guards or gates to pass through and there was almost a mile of untrammeled forest to hide in.

There were still a couple hours of daylight left, so I stashed my backpack in the woods and walked down to the beach. The southern shore of Staten Island faces out into the open Atlantic and catches the full strength of the ocean's waves. Being right there within the city limits, I assumed the beach would be crowded with other people, but when I got there I was all alone. Just to the east there was a long string of what looked like abandoned summer cottages. It would make sense for summer camps to be vacant in the fall, but these places all had boards over the windows as if they had been left behind permanently. Their paint was peeling and weeds had grown up through cracks in the porches. It was a mysterious place, and I wandered the streets of the abandoned tourist village for quite some time trying to figure out what to make of it. I was tempted to break into one of the cottages and sleep there just for the sense of adventure, but eventually I decided not to. With such a secure alternative awaiting me in the wild forest just down the road, it didn't make sense to risk being arrested for breaking and entering.

I went back to the beach and sat there for a long time soaking in the beauty and watching the steady stream of ships on their way to and from New York's busy harbor. Thinking about the route I intended to walk across the

111

continent, I realized that this would be my last view of the wide-open Atlantic. I would probably see some of the Chesapeake Bay, but this would be my last view of big waves crashing on sand until I reached the coast of California several years in the future. Thinking these thoughts, I did my best to soak up the ocean's spirit and hold it in my heart.

***

It rained some over the night but it had finished by morning. I set off north across the middle of the island. I found a large corporate bookstore and acquired maps of most of the counties in northern New Jersey.

That afternoon I spent several hours walking around the outside of the Fresh Kills Landfill in the western marshes of Staten Island. I had heard that it was one of the largest landfills on the planet and I had also heard that it could be seen by astronauts orbiting Earth in the Space Shuttle. I wanted to take a picture of this monument to modern American culture to put in my zine, but alas I never found a good view of it. It may look spectacular from outer space, but from the ground it just looks like a big grassy embankment. There were no vantage points where I could see more than a small segment of it at any one time. I ended up not taking any pictures and feeling like I had wasted several hours of valuable time.

Late in the afternoon I found the Bayonne Bridge and crossed into New Jersey. A cold wind was blowing that afternoon and high up on the bridge it chilled me to the bone. Rather than heading straight for Philadelphia, I wanted to walk a zigzag across northern Jersey in the hopes of signing up more zine subscribers. That meant I would head north to Bergen County first, then skirt around the north end of the Meadowlands, and then make a southwesterly line through Newark and beyond to the rest of the country. Shivering in the wind high above the harbor I began to question the wisdom of delaying any longer before heading south. It was the last day of September.

I touched down in the city of Bayonne, New Jersey and within a few short blocks I came upon a confusing scene of pure Americana. Standing on a dirty street-corner in a ghetto part of town were three huge White men with shaved heads wearing intimidating outfits of leather and denim. They were covered with tattoos and I immediately noticed a large swastika tattooed on the back of one of their calves. They all looked like Nazis anyway, but the swastika seemed to confirm my fears.

The confusing part was that two of them were listening with obvious enthusiasm while the third one recited a rap. I didn't recognize the song, and I got the impression that the guy had written it himself. As I passed by them, I couldn't quite catch what the man was rapping about, but his flow was tight and he didn't miss a beat. Not only was he rapping, but he was good at it. Given the obvious association between rap and Black-American culture I never expected to see Nazis rapping, but the longer I've lived in this country, the more I have learned to expect nothing less than infinite variety.

Right around sunset, I came to the park on the shore of the harbor closest to the Statue of Liberty. The park was little more than a vast mowed lawn and an even bigger parking lot where tourists board the ferries taking them out to Ellis Island. Though New York City unquestioningly claims the Statue of Liberty as one of its tourist attractions, it actually sits on a tiny island much closer to the shore of Jersey City. Very few tourists were around at that time of the evening and I was glad because it gave me an opportunity to slip into a hedge and set up camp for the night. It would have been too conspicuous to set up my tent, so I just rolled out my sleeping bag on the ground and then wrapped it up in my tarp like a burrito. It was uncomfortably cold that night to the point that I had trouble sleeping. I awoke on October first to frost and a spectacular view of Lower Manhattan with the Statue of Liberty in the foreground.

Lady Liberty was on high alert so soon after the terrorist bombings. Guards were posted all over the ferry docks to screen all the visiting tourists for bombs and warnings were posted everywhere. It all served to heighten the sense that our nation was under siege by hateful lunatics bent on destroying everything we hold dear as Americans. To me it was an obvious public relations move intended to hide the fact that the terrorists of September 11th had actually struck highly strategic targets.

The Pentagon is the headquarters of the U.S. military which has terrorized almost every nation on the planet. The World Trade Center was one of the headquarters of the economic system that extracts valuable resources from the Third World without adequate compensation, and imports them to the First World to maintain our relative luxury. The Statue of Liberty is a monument intended to celebrate our nation's legacy of sheltering and nurturing foreign refugees. One of these things is not like the others. That's why it was not a target on September 11th and that's why it probably won't ever be a target.

I started walking right at sunrise, and I crossed the rest of Jersey City during that time of the morning when everyone is too busy to stop and talk to a wandering pilgrim. In Union City I met a Venezuelan man and had a whole conversation in Spanish. By the end of it, I had convinced him to buy a subscription to my zine even though it was written in English. It was interesting to think of my zine being used as part of someone's efforts to learn English.

As I kept going to the north, the land rose higher and higher. By mid-afternoon I was walking along the top of an impressive cliff that towered over the Hudson. In the city of Fort Lee almost everyone was Korean. I don't speak a word of Hangul so I couldn't sell anyone a zine. In Englewood I turned west and plunged into the thick of New Jersey suburbia. This was Bergen County, the richest part of New Jersey, but the route I was on took me through a series of fairly standard middle-class neighborhoods.

In the late afternoon I passed through a large park where someone had built a miniature replica of the World Trade Center as a memorial. It was like a white plastic model of the twin towers about as tall as a grown man. Right in the same park there were a couple of guys flying remote controlled model airplanes, and I couldn't help but wonder if they felt at all tempted to do a miniature reenactment of the WTC bombings.

I made it to Hackensack that evening where I was surprised to find a densely-packed city center with a few tall office buildings and public housing projects surrounded by ghetto neighborhoods. For some reason I had expected all of northern Jersey to be a homogenous landscape of middle-class suburbs, but in reality it is dotted with older urban centers.

Folks back in New York had hooked me up with an ally to stay with in the town of Lodi and it took me until after dark to find his house. It had been an exceptionally long day of walking, but I did my best to stay up for a while longer and get to know my host once I had finally found him. He was a member of a semi-underground organization called Anti-Racist Action (ARA). The ARA was made up almost exclusively of young, White men and their mission was to keep track of Nazis and other racist hate groups and sometimes to confront them with violence. It seemed like a noble cause to me and I pledged my support. When I told the guy about the Nazis I had seen rapping in Bayonne he wasn't amused at all. He just wanted me to describe every detail I could remember about them and the location where I had seen them.

We got out the map of Hudson County and I tried to figure out the exact intersection where I had spotted the hip-hop Nazis while my host took notes.

The man was gravely serious. He claimed that northern New Jersey was a hotbed of racist organizing and his little gang was fighting an uphill battle. Most of the police in that region were known to have White-supremacist tendencies, so the ARA had to be very secretive about their activities. He also said that northern New Jersey had seen a huge wave of immigration from Poland in the last decade and an alarming percentage of the new Polish neighbors were affiliated with Nazis and other White racist groups. After receiving this briefing on the local racist situation, I felt like I was spending the night in a secret rebel safe-house surrounded by enemies.

In the morning I set off across Garfield and into Passaic. Passaic, New Jersey is another historic city that has long since been engulfed by the sprawling suburbs of New York. Its densely-packed core sports a handful of skyscrapers and a multitude of old tenements full of Puerto-Rican and Dominican people. After seeing several hundred-thousand brown-skinned people speaking Spanish I felt a little less worried about the Nazi menace. That afternoon though, I passed through a really affluent town called Nutley where everyone was White and it seemed like almost all of them were blond. Then it was on to Newark where everyone was Black. It was a stark reminder that the North was never forced into racial integration the way the South was.

I had a phone number for someone to stay with in Newark, but I hadn't been able to get ahold of them up to that point. I found a working pay-phone amid the office towers downtown and called again, but once again I got no answer. Not knowing what else to do, I wandered on into the southern reaches of the city. By that time in my life, I had grown pretty accustomed to Black ghettos, but I had never seen anything like south Newark. A fair majority of the structures were gone, either burned down or simply collapsed. In some places, the city had bulldozed the rubble away, but in other places, huge piles of debris remained, giving the impression of a war zone. Chest-high weeds grew in clumps between the piles of broken bricks, and there were no fences around the vacant lots like there were across the river in New York. Even the buildings that remained looked to be on the verge of collapsing.

Perhaps the most alarming thing about the neighborhood was the incredible density of population. With so many of the buildings gone, one would expect many of the residents to move away to some other place where there was more shelter available, but the streets and sidewalks of Newark were as thick with pedestrians as any block in lower Manhattan. In many places, I had to walk at a slow pace to avoid bumping in to people. The implication seemed to be that all those people lived together in the few crumbling brick tenements that remained.

At one point I stopped and talked to a group of old men who were sitting out on a stoop and I asked them why so many buildings were gone. They said that some of them had burned down in unrelated incidents, but the majority of them had burned down during two apocalyptic riots back in the summer of 1967. They believed the conflicts had been incited by government provocateurs as part of an experiment to see how well the police could contain a riot. Both the incidents stretched on for multiple days and nights while armies of White cops attacked tens of thousands of angry Black protestors. The old men didn't think that people had intentionally destroyed their own homes, but since Molotov Cocktails were one of their primary weapons, a lot of buildings caught fire. With firefighters unable or unwilling to enter the area, fire spread quickly from one building to the next and whole blocks burned to the ground. All three of the men who I approached had been in the riots and even thirty-five years later, it was still very emotional for them to tell the story. I feel like I learned as much from the expressions of fear and anger on their faces as I did from their words. The streets of Newark had given me the impression of a war zone, and as it turned out, that impression was valid. The way those old men described it, a war really had taken place there.

Literally everyone I saw in Newark was Black. In addition to that obvious similarity, most of them also had really similar hairstyles. I would estimate that four out of five people there all had their hair done up into hundreds of thin little dreadlocks that hung down from their heads like black spaghetti. Since then, I have seen the style in other cities, and I have been told that it's called "poo sticks," but the first time I ever saw it was in Newark in 2003. I found it really attractive and it was hard for me not to ogle at all the hot people passing by me on the sidewalk. Given the city's history of racist violence, you might expect a tall White guy like me to encounter some hostility there, but I never did. Most people just ignored me, and the people I did interact with were all totally friendly.

There was only one person who really gave me a hard time and that was a horrifying crack zombie who spent an hour or so trying to convince me she was a prostitute. I was wandering from pay-phone to pay-phone trying to find one with a live dial-tone when she accosted me begging for money. Her face and arms were covered with scabs and her skin was stretched so tightly over her skeleton that she almost looked like a corpse. I tried to be polite despite her appearance. It was obvious that she was a drug addict of some sort, so I didn't really want to give her any money, but she was so persistent that I gave her a dollar just hoping she would go away. Unfortunately that dollar only inspired her more, like a shark catching a real whiff of blood. After that she insisted that I should pay her for sex or at least a blow job. She got right in my face and she kept touching me. I couldn't help but wonder if she had any contagious diseases. I kept trying to ignore her and walk away, but she followed me around the city for blocks.

I was still focused on my quest for a pay-phone and after some time I found one that worked. I put my last coins into it and called the number for the person I was supposed to stay with that night, but before anyone could answer, the crack zombie wrapped her arms around my waist and shoved her face into my crotch! I recoiled in horror, dropping the phone and stumbling backwards. I almost fell down and laughter erupted from the nearby crowds on the sidewalks.

After that the woman insisted that I give her five dollars for a blow-job and she wouldn't back down. Now I have never hired a prostitute for any purpose, but I'm pretty sure a blow-job costs more than five dollars. Anyway, no John in his right mind would let a pestilential vector like that touch his private parts for a million bucks. She was out of her mind. It seemed like she intended to blow me right there on the sidewalk in front of everybody. She kept commanding me to open up my pants, and whenever I slowed down enough for her to catch up, she would reach for my belt in an attempt to do it herself. Finally, I got out a five dollar bill and held it out in front of her. I told her she could have it, but only if she promised to leave me alone. It took some negotiation, but at long last she agreed to my terms. She promised to leave and I gave her the five. Then she went right back to badgering me about blow-jobs. That was when I realized I was simply going to have to flee.

I took off running and for a minute she actually gave chase. I could hear dozens of people laughing at the sight of the weird White boy running scared from the emaciated, scabby-faced crack whore. My face turned red with shame, but I did eventually escape. Even carrying my heavy backpack it was pretty easy to out-run a person who was that close to the verge of death. Anyway, she already had six dollars, and I think that's probably enough to get a hit of crack.

When I was at last certain that I had managed to ditch the nasty ho, I sat down on the curb to collect my thoughts. The sun was getting low and there I was, stuck in the most desperate ghetto I had ever seen without anywhere safe to sleep. I sat there for about an hour watching a man across the street make dozens of calls on his cell phone. Periodically, someone else would show up, the two of them would walk away, and then the man would return by himself a few minutes later and resume making phone calls. I got the distinct impression that he was dealing drugs, but I didn't really care. I was out of change for the pay phones and he had a phone I might be able to borrow.

I waited for a lull in his business activities and then I approached him to ask if I could make a quick call. He didn't mind lending me the phone for a minute, but alas I still couldn't get an answer. I thanked the drug dealer and wandered off. I gave up on my Newark contact and started searching in earnest for a place to spend the night. This was obviously going to be the most fucked-up ghetto camping I had ever attempted, but I still felt oddly at peace about it. Ever since I had attacked that malevolent shadow in the Bronx River Park, I had felt fundamentally safer around poor people and the neighborhoods where they lived. It was as if my worst fears had manifested in that shadow and I had stabbed them and killed them. Now they were just gone.

I wandered along through the waning light of evening. The sidewalks were still crowded with people and it seemed impossible that I might sneak into anywhere without being noticed. I came upon a huge field of weeds where two whole blocks worth of buildings were missing. The weeds grew in thick clumps as high as my shoulders, and I got the idea that if I waded out into them and crouched down, I would be hidden to all the world.

I picked my way cautiously out into the thicket, worrying a little that I might stumble across a dead body or someone else who was already hiding there, but there was no one. When I finally got to the middle of the field, it seemed like a good enough spot, but there was still one major problem. At least half the people back on the sidewalk had watched me pick my way in there, and many of them were still gawking at me with confused and concerned expressions. Well that wouldn't work now would it? I could crouch down out of sight, but I couldn't really consider myself to be "hiding" if the whole neighborhood knew right where I was. Feeling defeated and a bit embarrassed, I bushwhacked back out to the sidewalk and continued on.

Night fell and I was still the lone White guy wandering the bombed-out streets of Newark carrying a backpack. At least the darkness had inspired most of the people to go indoors. With fewer witnesses I might be able to sneak into a hiding spot unnoticed. Of course there would also be fewer witnesses if someone decided to jump me, but I did my best not to worry about that.

Finally I rounded a corner to the sight of a pitch-dark horizon several blocks away. When I got there, a sign welcomed me to Weequahic Park. There had still been a few random pedestrians treading the sidewalks of southern Newark, but as soon as I set foot in the park, I was all alone. As my eyes adjusted I realized that it wasn't completely dark after all. A network of paved pathways crisscrossed the park and they were lit by old lamps that stood on poles only slightly higher than my head. The dim light of old incandescent bulbs trickled out through frosted glass panes held inside ornately sculpted rectangular cages of wrought-iron. The eerie yellow light revealed a landscape of manicured hedges, sculpted trees, and ornate benches of carved stone. I couldn't see much beyond a large earthen mound. The side facing me was an intricately-carved stone wall with a door in it that made it look distinctly like a crypt. It was surrounded by a whole assortment of strange ornamental plants.

None of the pathways followed a straight line in any direction. I wandered around for a few minutes looking for some scrap of wild forest and found none. Perhaps if I had delved deeper into the heart of the park I may have found the welcoming darkness of some real woods, but it seemed just as likely that I might stumble upon Count Dracula's castle. There were plenty of long, spooky shadows for me to hide in right there in the near corner of the park.

I crawled into the darkest spot I could find and rolled out my sleeping bag. It would have been a bit too conspicuous to set up my tent, but no one would spot my sleeping bag unless they were searching the ground with a flashlight. No one would inadvertently trip over me either because I crawled under the low-hanging branches of some ornamental evergreen tree. After lying still for a few minutes, I felt secure that no creeping criminals were going to get me, but there still wasn't any hope for true relaxation. It turned out that I was camped on a hillside overlooking the runway at Newark International Airport, so every few minutes the ground would shake to the sound of an airplane coming or going. During take-offs, I could feel the sound waves vibrating through my entire body, not to mention my eardrums. The din of the jets kept me awake until late at night, and it started up again at the crack of dawn, but I did get a few hours of good sleep while the airport was closed.

In the morning I wandered back to the north to snap a few pictures of the ruined city. I had wanted to take pictures the previous afternoon, but I didn't feel safe flashing my camera around in front of the multitudes of impoverished people. Somehow I felt less likely to be mugged by the kind of folks who you find up and about early in the morning. After I got a few good shots of half-collapsed buildings, I turned back south, walked through the Weequahic Park and out the other side.

As I emerged from the park, I just happened to come out onto the edge of a basketball court where two guys were playing a little early-morning one-on-one. When the guy with the ball saw me, he stopped dribbling and shouted angrily at me.

"Man, what the hell are you doin' kid? Get the hell out of there! That's Weequahic Park kid! People get killed in there every week! It's dangerous in there!"

I wasn't sure what to say. I think I said something stupid like, "Well I didn't get killed." I thought about boasting to him that I had just spent the whole night in there and I had spent much of it in a totally vulnerable state of unconsciousness, but then I thought better of it. He cussed me out some more for being so stupid. I thanked him for the warning and then proceeded on my way.

For some reason the encounter got me thinking about freedom as a grand philosophical concept. Nothing had stopped me from walking across Newark or sleeping in Weequahic Park. The fact that I had done those things proved that I had freedom and I felt a palpable sense of liberty that thrilled me right to my core. I thought of George W. Bush and what would happen if he tried to walk across Newark. He literally couldn't do it. They would have to bomb the city for days in advance, and he would still need to be accompanied by battalions of soldiers. I was free to walk wherever I wanted because I was not an enemy of the people. I was one of the people. There were only a handful of places in the world where George Bush could go without a huge entourage of security guards. That same handful of places would literally be the only places where I would not be free to wander around by myself as long as I pleased. The power that the people like George Bush sought made them the enemies of almost all the other people on the planet, and that trapped them inside their defensive fortifications. I realized that anyone that rich or powerful would never know the feeling of real freedom.

In hindsight, it was a pretty over-simplified way to think about my own freedom. A significant portion of the freedom I experienced in Newark came from a phenomenon called White privilege. When criminals in the ghetto were hunting for victims, they were most likely to leave me alone out of fear that the police would work much harder to protect White people than to protect other colors of people. Even if that isn't true, it's a common enough perception to keep White people safer from crime. There really isn't anywhere in this country where I wouldn't be safer than the average Black person.

That said, I still think it's important to recognize that our hierarchical social structure limits the freedoms of the rich and powerful as well as those of the poor. Sure, they can bomb Yemen or hop on a private jet to Tahiti whenever they feel like it, but they can never just wander off into the woods by themselves and take a piss. They will never know what it's like to have sex with someone who isn't trying to dig gold out of them. Instead of friends, they are surrounded by con-artists and brown-nosers all trying to piggyback on their power. They can't just walk down the street without a crew of body-guards and they sure as hell can't sleep in Weequahic Park.

Hierarchy literally hurts all of us, including the "winners" who sit at the top of the pyramid. The only way to have true freedom is to grow out of hierarchy, to evolve into an egalitarian society where no one holds any financial or legal power over anyone else. It is a level of liberty that our culture has never known, but we can envision it and we can reach for it as our highest goal.

16. THE END NEVER COMES

I had an epiphany one afternoon on my way across New Jersey. It was one of those rare moments when the divine truth of reality crashes into your mind like a tidal wave, washes out all the cluttered misconceptions, and leaves you with only the most solid bedrock of truth, clean and serene. Your mind loses control and your emotions swirl. A catharsis happens, and then you emerge with new abilities like a butterfly from the cocoon. Young people are particularly prone to these sudden expansions of consciousness, and a young person on an adventurous walkabout is almost certain to stumble upon some experience that flips their proverbial wig. But it still came right out of the blue for me, when I was least expecting it.

First of all, I wasn't Siddhartha on some soul-searching, selfish quest for enlightenment. I was trying to be Paul Revere and round up the rebels to fight tyranny. The whole world was gonna learn something from me damnit!

I felt like our whole culture was sinking like the Titanic, but the captain and the crew insisted that everyone pretend it wasn't happening. Some people didn't even realize they were in danger. I felt like Soundgarden screaming, "The wreck is goin' down! Get out, before you drown!" I literally felt bound by duty to warn as many people as I could and then help organize emergency procedures. My whole life was a mission, and it was literally a mission to save the world.

That's why I set out walking. I had to change the way our culture thinks about the natural world. I had to show them that life is sacred and we are part of a big sacred life-cycle. I had to spread the concept that we are not separate from the animals, plants, bugs, and fungi. Together with them, we make up one sacred life, and when we fight against them, we hurt ourselves too. I had to free our culture from the techno-utopian fantasy that we could improve our lives by separating ourselves from nature and retreating into an artificial environment. Technology can't save us from nature, because nature is what actually keeps us alive. Those who would sacrifice nature for the dream of being saved by technology have made some spectacular short-term gains, but in the long run, they are putting us all in peril.

It is easy for me to remember and articulate those feelings because I still feel much the same way now. The big difference is that in my youth I lived in a perpetual state of anxiety over the fear that the world was literally going to end. This worry plagued me until it defined my personality. I rarely got a full night's sleep because of all the worries on my mind.

It was obvious that an elite cadre of madmen were doing their damnedest to rule the world. They may not have completely succeeded yet, but it was evident that they were working on it with a dogged determination. They needed an ever-expanding supply of resources to feed their war machine and the natural world was expected to provide and sacrifice. They waged wars all over the world just to gather more resources to be able to wage more war. All their humanitarian P.R. lines were obviously just cheap bullshit. What kind of insanity would lead a person to try to conquer the world? Who would send armies to kill and die for such a goal?

I came of age in a time when the most homicidally insane and least trust-worthy humans on the planet held power over every significant institution of our society. They set up a global economy in their own insane image and then fought ruthlessly to impose their order on every obscure corner of the world. The hot guts of Iraqi and Afghani people splattered through the air on a daily basis. Here in the homeland, everywhere I turned there were clear cuts and quarry holes, dams, airports and power lines. The Earth itself was being bled dry to feed the lunatic's quest for power. It had been almost two centuries since their creed wiped out the bison as a means of conquering the native people of the plains, but that same attitude towards nature and humanity still prevailed. It was obvious that they didn't understand the value in maintaining the delicate balance of nature. The catastrophic danger of disrupting the Earth's ecosystems didn't faze them. Maybe they didn't realize it could happen, like they had a collective blind-spot as one of the symptoms of their mental disorder. Maybe they knew a disaster was coming, but they believed they were going to escape in space-ships like some kind of science fiction story. Maybe they believed they would be saved by angels and deliv-ered to some comfortable heaven. I didn't know, but I knew they were on the verge of getting us into deeper shit than we had ever seen before.

Some of my associates tossed around the idea that the global warlords were actually aliens from outer space come to enslave the Earth. Other peo-ple, including some of my close friends contended that the elite humans were motivated by a powerful form of evil and that they were actually trying to destroy or enslave everything that was good. I never took much interest in the alien theories, but the evil human theory was both highly plausible and deeply distressing. Left to my own devices, I preferred to believe that humanity suffered from a mental illness. I still prefer that explanation now because mental illness seems more curable than pure evil, but I have to admit that I don't really know, and the defenders of the Pure Evil theory do have volumes of evidence to support their belief.

Either way, the possibility that a combination of human mistakes might wipe out all life on Earth was fundamentally unsettling. It didn't matter whether they did it on purpose to fulfill the evil quest of some bizarre cult or whether they stumbled into it in a state of blind insanity. Either way it was a terrible thing of the gravest spiritual significance.

At that age I had figured out that life in all its forms was the one truly divine thing. To boil it down, life was God and the human race was in danger of destroying God. They had to be stopped by any means before it was too late, but the challenge of stopping them was almost insurmountable. It was essential to figure out what motivated the bad people because that would affect what kind of strategy we would use to stop them. My brain twisted in knots trying to figure out these philosophical and strategic details. It chewed on the problem day and night while my nerves strained under the relentless fear that the world itself was ending. My own death was insignificant, but the death of all living things was too much to bear. God needed me to do something right away, but what? I worried about it a lot.

I don't remember, but it's quite likely that I was thinking similar thoughts one pleasant afternoon as I walked across the soulless suburbia of north Jersey. Suddenly a confusing sight interrupted my thoughts, whatever they had been. Off to the right, through a chain-link fence that had essentially become a trellis for wild vines, I could make out an extensive green field. In the distance, I saw the familiar shape of big rectangular buildings, but there was something odd about their colors and textures. I approached the fence to peek through a hole in the vines and my view of the scene became clear.

Stretched out before me was the panorama of a full-sized suburban mall, completely abandoned. All the signs had been taken down, so I couldn't tell what stores used to be there, but it was easy to imagine Sears and Macy's and other big department stores bustling with 1960's era shoppers. The buildings still remained, but they had changed dramatically in the time since they were abandoned. The vast, flat surfaces of concrete were intended to be featureless, but over the years nature had added a rich texture to the tall walls of the mall. They had darkened with asymmetrical mildew stains ranging in color from black to a dull orange. Here and there, the drab mildew was broken up by smatterings of lively green moss. The roof had grown over with grass and weeds, and the acres of parking lot surrounding the buildings were in the process of becoming lush fields. In the foreground I could still see big chunks of ground that were sealed under asphalt, but in the distance all that was hidden by a rolling green grassland, highlighted by the fiery-yellow flowers of the autumn goldenrod bloom bobbing gently in the breeze. In more than a few places the vertical concrete walls of the abandoned buildings had cracked open and grass and weeds had sprouted from the cracks.

Here was a full-sized retail center in the process of being destroyed by plants, the most passive of all living things. Life wasn't on the verge of being destroyed by human technology. God wasn't even breaking a sweat! All those worries and fears that had kept me restless for so many years were all based on an illusion and the illusion shattered in the moment I laid eyes on the Chia-Mall. As my stress evaporated, waves of glee and relief washed in to fill the hole it left behind, followed by a sense of security like I had never known. It was as if the original divine spirit sheltered me in its mighty embrace and whispered in my ear that "everything is gonna be alright." I still lived on a planet where crazy humans fought to destroy nature and replace it with a homogenous artificial environment, but suddenly I understood that they didn't even have the slightest chance of success.

The architecture of the massive retail center was based on psychological science. Big clean rectangles branded with stylish company names were supposed to attract customers to the stores. For people who believed in the industrialist world-view of progress and prosperity through consumerism, the mall's clean, flat surfaces and hard right angles would inspire comfort, confidence and even pride. If someone outside of that cultural bubble had a different reaction, it didn't matter to the people who built the malls. After all, anyone who didn't like it didn't have to shop there.

Unfortunately, for those of us who can feel the divinity of nature, the big square shapes trigger emotions of fear, anger, and depression. It's not just malls of course. Everywhere we turn, we see our beautiful divine home being devoured by highways and smokestacks, suburbs and power-lines. Every day, more of the Earth's glorious diversity gets bulldozed and replaced by the homogenous landscape of efficient profit. For the first twenty-six years of my life, I watched this process of economic growth devour so much of my homeland that I almost lost my mind. It was obvious that the monster's appetite would never be satisfied.

In all that time, it never occurred to me that life would grow right back over the big ugly concrete shapes. I had seen plenty of pictures of Roman ruins. I had seen roads split open by grass and I had seen abandoned old cabins in the desert with sagebrush growing inside them, but somehow the implications of all that data had escaped me. I still thought that once a beautiful, natural place became developed, it would be ruined forever. I think it was because the mall was such an icon of the artificial industrial landscape that when I saw one decaying, it finally snapped me out of my apocalyptic nightmare.

The mall could not have been older than my parents and was most likely abandoned sometime within my lifetime. It had only taken a few years for the parking lot and even the buildings to sprout a thickening cover of grasses and goldenrods. If this site were left to age as long as a Roman ruin, there would be no trace of it. Suddenly my mind filled with visions of abandoned super-highways turned to grasslands and crumbled power-plants being devoured by ivy.

Now I know that it is highly unlikely that the Chia-Mall of Woodbridge New Jersey will be left to decay for thousands of years. I would be surprised if it hasn't already been bulldozed and built over with some abominable new strip-mall. We happen to be living in a time when the infrastructure of industrial capitalism is expanding at an unprecedented rate. It's not hard to understand why I thought the world was ending. Nor is it wrong to be alarmed at the size and speed of this industrial expansion. It is still a terrible idea to destroy God's diversity and replace it with concrete. It's just silly to worry that developments of that kind represent a permanent change in the landscape. Industry may indeed be able to ruin a place for longer than I will live, but life will continue to thrive on the grand scale. We cannot create anything so toxic that plants won't eventually grow back over it.

We do cause species to go extinct all the time and once a species is gone it is gone forever. That is a truly shameful and tragic mistake that we should have stopped making years ago. Even so, new species will evolve to fill whatever niches are left vacant in the ecosystem. From the perspective of the geologic time scale, all of this ecological catastrophe that we are witnessing is happening in the blink of eye. It was made possible by the discovery of fossil fuels and it can only continue until those fuels run out. If capitalist culture is allowed to proceed towards its desired trajectory, it will burn through all of that fuel in a few short generations and then the Earth will be left to heal at the same steady rate that it always does.

Don't be fooled by the daily barrage of news stories heralding the arrival of some new savior technology that is going to bring about a state of eternal high-tech civilization. Those are all just part of the industrialist mythology intended to keep us praying to the church of techno-utopia. They are nothing more than advertisements trying to sell us the next new gimmick. The internal-combustion engine, running on fossil fuel is still the basis of our entire industrial infrastructure.

Let's imagine that humans do manage to develop a new energy source that actually extends our ability to power high technology beyond the era of fossil resources. Let's imagine that our population just keeps growing and the wild, natural places keep shrinking until the whole world looks like Western Europe. As humans and our food crops make up an ever-greater portion of the Earth's biomass, new species will simply evolve to eat us. Every time the human population grows, we look that much more delicious to the other organisms. That's how life works. Anything that lives becomes food for something else that lives. At this point it would be impossible for any new large predators to come along, but we are sitting ducks for things like viruses, bacteria and fungi. The more we isolate ourselves from nature, the weaker our immune systems become, and the more we crowd into cities, the more we shorten the vectors for contagion. The only reason we haven't already fallen to some pandemic infection is because our rise to dominance has been so short-lived. Evolution doesn't work quite that fast.

Also don't forget that every time we expand our industrial infrastructure, we create more habitat for seagulls, rats, roaches, and whatever other new species are evolving to live off our waste. I feel confident that life will adapt to whatever changes we bring about.

Of course, I don't want to see large numbers of my fellow humans wiped out by a disease, or starve and die fighting over a rapidly dwindling food supply. I will still devote my life to the effort of trying to persuade you all to stop making the mistakes that will inevitably lead to those ends. I will just be able to take a calm and collected approach to it now that I've realized that life will go on one way or another. Never again will I flail about in a panic worrying about the end of the world. The end never comes! There is no disease that would wipe out every last one of us. The strong would survive and we would grow back from there.

17. BORN TO RUN

The next city south of Newark is called Elizabeth and it is another urban center that I would describe as more of a satellite city than a suburb. It was much less impoverished than Newark or even Passaic and Hackensack, and it was the first city I came to in New Jersey where different races of people seemed to be somewhat integrated. The city was very clean and well-maintained, but by the same token it felt rather sterile and boring. The small river that flowed through town was confined inside an angular concrete trench. I had a great conversation with a nice young White guy whose clothing and tattoos identified him as part of the heavy-metal subculture. He was one of several people who bought subscriptions to my zine before I continued on past Elizabeth.

Next came a huge industrial zone known as Linden. The road I followed carved a perfectly straight line across the town dividing the industry from the residential zone. All along the right side were miles of virtually identical little brick duplexes with little lawns. Across the street were miles of smokestacks, warehouses, and incomprehensibly complicated networks of metal tubes. It took half an hour to walk past a Merck Pharmaceutical factory and it was there that I encountered the most unique odor I have ever smelled. I am at an absolute loss for words to describe the sensation tickling my nostrils that afternoon, and I suspect that there really aren't any in the English language. It was clearly a chemical smell, but beyond that you will have to use your imagination. (Or travel to Linden, NJ if you are really curious.) I found the smell more interesting than unpleasant, but I certainly wouldn't want to live across the street from its source.

I was walking past a limousine rental business when a bitter dispute between two men in the parking lot erupted into a fist-fight. Both men were Arabs and they were screaming at each other in Arabic. Once the fists started flying, half a dozen other Arab men who were present intervened, but it still took them a while to pull the combatants off one another.

That afternoon I met a food-truck driver who gave me three free egg-and-cheese sandwiches. New Yorkers refer to his particular kind of food truck as a "roach-coach." I'm not sure where the name comes from, but the food they serve is particularly bad. It's all prefabricated sandwiches like the kind you would find sealed in plastic in a gas station and heat up in a microwave.

Roach-coach drivers make a living providing food at construction sites or other locations where large numbers of workers have no better options for their lunch break. The man I met in Linden had just come home after the lunch rush, and the sandwiches he gave me were the left-overs that hadn't sold. They were cold and soggy, but it was still a nice gesture and I gobbled them down immediately. It was not long after that when I found the legendary Chia-Mall and had my epiphany.

The man's attempt to help me failed miserably a couple hours later when I was beset by wrenching abdominal pain and periodic outbursts of diarrhea. By then I had passed into a vast landscape of homogenous suburbia called Woodbridge. I spent most of the afternoon sitting in the grass in front of a Taco Bell with my whole body clenched around the pain in my abdomen. Every fifteen minutes or so, I would run inside to use the bathroom. After a couple hours, the pain began to subside and the intervals between my visits to the toilet got longer.

It was then that I met Angie. She was stomping along the road in the grass where a sidewalk should have been and when she saw me sitting there holding my guts she could just tell that I would be sympathetic to her plight. Angie was the embodiment of all suburban teen-age frustration. All of the world's most unreasonable bullshit had somehow heaped itself on top of her, and there was nothing she could do about it but complain. She worked as a waitress and a busser at a diner just down the street where only moments earlier she had gotten into a titanic fight with the cook, the manager, the other waitresses, and some of the customers to boot. She was the only one in the place with any competence or dignity and what was worse, none of the others even understood that. One of these days they were going to piss her off so badly that she was going to leave for good, and without her they would be totally screwed. In fact, maybe today would be that day. She had stormed out in the middle of her shift but she doubted she would be fired because she had done this several times before and not been fired. Clearly they understood that the restaurant would not survive without her, but for some reason they couldn't bring themselves to show her any respect while she was there. Well they weren't going to get away with it this time. She wasn't about to crawl back in there and finish her shift. She was going to walk all the way over to her boyfriend's house and let him know just how mad she was that he hadn't come out to pick her up in his car. In a town full of assholes, he was probably the biggest asshole of them all but this time she was going to straighten him out for real.

She had already put up with so much bullshit, and not just from her job and her boyfriend. Her parents were assholes too. As a matter of fact, the whole town could just kiss her ass. No one in Woodbridge appreciated her and what they really deserved was for her to just disappear. She knew there was a better world out there somewhere. One of these days she was just going give Woodbridge the finger and leave.

The paragraphs above are my weak attempt to recreate Angie's frustrated soliloquy, but the real thing was far longer and more passionate. It was like ten minutes of volcanic eruption, beautiful and awe-inspiring in its god-like power. It would have also been terrifying had any of her angst been directed at me, but it wasn't. I was just a random person who was in the right place at the right time to provide a sympathetic ear, like a therapist only much more effective. Clearly I wasn't from around there, and that made me exactly the ally she was looking for. For some time all I had to do was nod and grimace in understanding, but after a while the tempest of frustration began to subside and there were small opportunities for me to speak.

I confirmed that there was a big awesome world out there. I told her that I had also grown up in culturally bleak suburbs and I could totally relate to the feeling of needing to escape. It was exactly what she needed to hear at that moment, and I can't describe how cool it felt be there for some random teen-ager right when they needed it the most. We ended up talking for about an hour, sitting in the grass in front of the strip mall. Angie did most of the talking, but I was able to provide occasional bits of inspirational wisdom. Everything Angie said was utterly typical for a teen-age American, but that didn't make it any less meaningful or justified.

Adolescence is the time in our lives when we find out that our whole culture is full of shit. The adults were lying all along. All our discipline and hard work isn't going to pay off. We really have been betrayed and the happy ending isn't coming. The only hope for redemption is to rebel. A teen-ager going through this stage is suffering more emotional trauma than they ever thought possible. To them it is an unprecedented level of pain, but it's still a beautiful phase to behold, because you know that they will rebel and persevere, and in some indirect way their rebellion will help to redeem all of us.

At least I could tell that Angie was going to persevere.

After about an hour, she thanked me with a big hug and continued on her way. She didn't go back to finish her shift at the diner, or to her boyfriend's house. She was off to plan her eventual escape from Woodbridge. She walked away with her head held high in determination and once again I heard Bruce Springsteen in my head singing, "Tramps like us, baby we were born to run!"

The musical scoring was particularly appropriate because Springsteen was born and raised in the suburbs of north Jersey in a town called Perth Amboy. I'm not sure where I picked up that tidbit of information because I have never owned a Springsteen album or been a particular fan. Still as a scholar of American pop-culture, I have to acknowledge that he made a very significant contribution. After contemplating just how significant "The Boss" may have been to the very culture I was hoping to influence, I decided to take a slight detour and walk through Perth Amboy. It was a few miles south of what would have been the most efficient route, but suddenly it seemed important. If I could soak up a real taste of Bruce Springsteen's home town, maybe I would be one step closer to becoming an American folk hero myself.

I made it into Perth Amboy at sunset, and luckily I stumbled right into a little park full of wild New Jersey woods. I set up my tent on a bed of freshly-fallen autumn leaves. All the trees above me were painted with the beautiful colors of fall, but I wasn't really in the right state of mind to appreciate the majesty of it. Mostly it just felt like a stressful reminder that winter would not wait while I meandered around. I did go through quite a bit more of Perth Amboy in the morning, and it just looked like an older version of the Suburbs.

After my little detour I got back on a south-westerly course towards New Brunswick, Trenton and Philadelphia. Before long the suburban thoroughfare I was following emerged onto a bridge over the widest and most complex system of highways I have ever seen. Crossing above them I counted fifteen lanes of asphalt, all bustling with traffic. Now the first thing you may imagine would probably be seven lanes going one way and then eight going the other way, but it was nowhere near that simple. There was an eight-lane divided highway with four north-bound and four south-bound lanes in the middle, but it was sandwiched between seven more lanes that were all divided individually or in pairs by high, chain-link fences and cement barricades. In some cases the barriers divided lanes that were going in opposite directions as one might expect, but in other cases parallel lanes of traffic going in the same direction were divided from one another. I can't fathom what would make such complexity necessary and I really doubt that it was necessary at all. I think most people who have driven on New Jersey's network of highways can testify that it is far more complex than it needs to be. I tried to photograph the bizarre tangle of highways from the overpass above, but it was too wide to fit in the frame of the camera lens.

***

I had an actual destination to aim for that day. Folks in New York had given me a phone number for a guy named David in New Brunswick and he actually answered his telephone. I spent the day walking through Edison, Metuchen, and Highland Park. The bland pattern of suburban neighborhoods was periodically interrupted by huge swaths of industrial landscape. At one point I caught a view of the filthy-looking estuary of the Raritan River, full of old rusty barges and the decaying remains of docks.

By late afternoon I had made it to New Brunswick where I found David without any difficulty. He was just getting off work and we walked together back to his apartment. We dropped off my backpack and rested for a few minutes. Then David put me on his spare bicycle and gave me a tour of the whole city.

New Brunswick New Jersey is the headquarters of the Johnson and Johnson Corporation and literally all of the office towers downtown are part of the J&J campus. David explained that most of the city's imposing skyline had just been built within the last ten years. The first several stops on our tour were locations where cool places had recently been destroyed to make way for the J&J expansion. When David was a child, the coolest place for all the kids to hang out was an arcade which has since been torn down to make room for a huge glass-fronted office tower. Then we were off to look at a parking lot where the city's best Punk-rock venue had recently stood.

After David had thoroughly impressed upon me that Johnson and Johnson was devouring New Brunswick like a monster, we rode off to see some parts of town where the local color was still shining through. We saw three volunteer-run community gardens built on lots where buildings burned down, and then we went to the site of a newly-established farmer's market. It was a relief to see that the community was growing in that way despite the corporate cancer eating away at its core. We harvested vegetables at one of the gardens and then rode home to cook them and eat them for dinner.

David had spent several years travelling within the same protest circuit as me. He had been on campaigns to protect beautiful wilderness areas out West and he had been to all the cool cities where like-minded radicals accumulate, but in his late twenties he decided that the best thing he could do was to go home to New Jersey and put his ideals into practice there. He told me that places like Portland Oregon, Asheville, and Madison didn't need any more people like him, but New Brunswick needed him desperately so home he went.

I was really impressed and I told him so. I really respect anyone who hangs tough in their home town even when the vast majority of people there hold opposing political or social views. It's fun to vacation in places like Portland Oregon, but then it always occurs to me that all the weirdoes who migrated there to find safety in numbers are only contributing to a sad lack of weirdoes in the Sacramentos and Charlottes of the world. Sometimes I get really judgmental about all the weak-hearted people running for the safety of the herd. Then I have to remind myself that I spent almost two decades hiding out in the organic-farming mecca of the East, 3,000 miles away from my childhood home in the distinctly uncool desert region of Washington. Back when I met David I still thought of that old home as the eventual destination at the end of my long walk. In my mind I was about to start on the same hard-core endeavor as him, and I looked up to him as a real source of inspiration.

David also helped me get access to a computer where I discovered an e-mail from Aresh back in New York. He was compiling a book full of stories about all the gardens that his organization had attempted to save, and he wanted me to write the chapter about the Hostos-Crimmins garden. I was glad to accept the responsibility and I figured the sooner I did it, the better I would remember the details. David was able to sneak me into a lab at the local campus of Rutgers University and I spent the whole next day writing a thirty-page account of the beautiful garden and its sad demise. I e-mailed it to Aresh the next night. I have never heard another word about the book, but I assume it was published with my account in it somewhere.

It took me until the wee hours of the morning to finish writing and editing my piece, so I ended up sleeping through the entire first half of the next day. I didn't get on the road until afternoon, but I only planned to walk a few miles that day anyway. I had friends to visit in East Brunswick as well, and that was the very next town down the road.

The End Never Comes

East Brunswick is a high-class suburb with larger houses that are much more architecturally unique than the cookie-cutter developments in places like Linden. Despite the upper-class feel of the place, I found it very pleasant because the houses were located on large lots, and many of the residents preferred to leave their land growing with wild forest instead of mowed lawns.

My friends there were people I had met on the protest circuit. I had been to their house before on some road trip, and I actually found my way back to it just from my memory of the place. I hadn't called for directions, or to announce my arrival. I thought it would be really fun to show up at their door unannounced, having just walked there from a distant state. I couldn't wait to see the looks on their faces. What a surprise! I would be the most unexpected guest ever.

Then I arrived to find that my friends were out of town for the whole week. It was a real let-down, but their house-mates were nice and they said I was welcome to spend the night there anyway. Gracious as they were, my hosts were all graduate students and they had to spend the night studying like fiends. Having no one to hang out with, I spent my evening in the company of their three or four large dogs who all insisted on snuggling with me where I slept on the floor.

Halfway through the following day's walk, I actually started to find some farms and some real stretches of forest. After orbiting the city of New York for another whole month, I was finally moving on.

18. LABOR HISTORY

I got an early start walking and took a westerly direction. Later in the morning I passed by several large farms which made for a welcome change from the previous days of unbroken suburbs. I didn't expect the gap between the New York sprawl and the Philadelphia sprawl to be much if anything, so I stopped and ate in a place where I could admire the view of one of the farms.

Not long after that I stumbled upon a very pleasant surprise. I was headed west looking for an old country road that I had found on my map of Middlesex County. When I got there, I would turn left and follow the road on its very straight southwesterly course for many miles. The road continued to the edge of Mercer County where the map ended, but I hoped it would continue on its straight path all the way to Trenton.

When I finally encountered the road, I could see there was a tree-lined body of water just beyond, so I crossed over to get a look at it. There, running parallel to the road was an old abandoned canal with a dirt bicycle path running alongside. This was a wonderful discovery because it meant I would get at least part way to Trenton without having to dodge cars or stumble along on the uneven slope of the gravel shoulder. Also, it was an unpleasantly hot day for early October and the canal was nicely shaded by old hardwoods.

Before long I came to a little building with signs and information about the canal. It was called the Delaware and Raritan Canal and it was now owned by the state of New Jersey as part of the state parks system. Interpretive signs explained how the canal connected the Delaware River to the Raritan River and how this route had been used to ship thousands of tons of coal from the mines of northeastern Pennsylvania to New York City in the 1800's. It was built in the 1830's and used to ship all kinds of cargo until it eventually closed in the 1930's.

Other signs told the tale of the men who dug the canal, and those were the stories that really captured my imagination. Most of the workers had been recruited from Ireland, nut no one actually knew how many men had worked there. The estimates ranged from 3,000 to 5,000. They were packed into squalid bunk-houses where they were fed two meals a day consisting of nothing but corn-meal. All day long they were set to the toil of cutting trees, digging up stumps, and then digging the great trench itself. They worked six days a week earning only pennies each day. They worked through cold winters and hot summers, and the summer heat often brought with it the danger of contagious disease.

Hundreds of workers died one summer during an outbreak of Asiatic cholera, and dozens more died from periodic outbreaks of malaria, dengue, and typhus. Still more died from work-related injuries or simply from exhaustion and malnourishment. The company that built the canal made no efforts to provide medical attention to any workers who fell sick or suffered injuries. Those who were left standing could bury the dead in their free time if they wanted to. The state park signs estimated that about 700 men died building the D&R Canal, but again no one really knows because no one cared enough to keep track. Somewhere in the range of one-out-of-four to one-out-of-seven men who worked on the canal died on the job. Even by the best estimate, that is a horrible statistic.

The story of those mistreated Irish workers really got to me. It inspired me to learn more about our nation's labor history, and I have read a lot about that topic in the years since my big walk. Sadly, in its time the D&R Canal was not some kind of anomaly. All over our young nation, immigrant workers were sacrificed by the tens of thousands to build railroads, canals, and bridges, and to mine ore. Women were used in textile mills and other manufacturing jobs where they were locked inside for long shifts and regularly exposed to toxic materials. They were lured on to ships with the promise of prosperity and freedom, and once they discovered the harsh reality of their virtual enslavement here in America, they found themselves trapped with no means of return home.

Of course, our nation was built by actual slaves from the beginning. Hundreds of thousands of African people were captured, and those who survived the trip across the ocean were used for hard core farm labor and other types of labor. Their owners were expected to keep them alive, but the slaves would never be paid, or ever allowed to own themselves, and their children would be born into the same situation. They were treated like farm animals, or in many cases even worse, being publicly whipped, or even executed for all sorts of mistakes ranging from the real to the imagined. It may well have been the most hideous style of slavery ever perpetrated by the human race, but I'm pretty sure most people already know about this.

A lot of other types of people were also used in terrible ways to build this country. I'm not sure their stories are quite as well known, so I want to tell some of them here. If we understand that all of our ancestors suffered, and we see the patterns that caused that suffering, the we can team up and avoid being harmed the same way in the future.

A great many Europeans were also put to work without any pay, and many of them were also captured against their will. English prisons were overflowing with peasants who were arrested for the crimes you would expect starving and destitute people to commit. After the colonies were established, English authorities shipped many of the convicts off to this continent to be used as slaves. It was also common for the English to raid the Celtic nations of Scotland, Ireland, and Wales to capture slaves for use in the New World. England had already been colonizing and enslaving the people of those nations for nearly a millennium at that point, and their racist perceptions of the Celts were comparable to their racist perceptions of the Africans.

Unlike the Africans, the European slaves would be free to go if they could complete a specific period of years known as a term of indenture. The terms were generally set for periods of either three years, five years, or seven years. Poor Europeans who wished to migrate to the American colonies were offered a ride across the ocean in exchange for a term of indenture. Thousands more Celtic and English people were lured into unpaid labor this way, as well as thousands of Germans. Life was so difficult in Europe back then that many people actually thought this sounded like a good deal. It is estimated that before the war for independence, at least half of all the White immigrants to the British-American colonies came as servants.

The trouble was, before they could become free, the servants had to survive their terms of indenture. Some slave-owners were gentle and generous, but the majority were ruthless, calculating economists who knew how to squeeze every last drop of work out of the people they owned. More slaves, both Black and White, were imported to Virginia and Maryland than the rest of the colonies combined. It was there that they were used to grow tobacco, a cash crop that nobody actually needed, but that made the early American ruling class fabulously wealthy.

Tobacco plants are heavy feeders that impoverish the soil quickly. You can only grow tobacco in the same place for seven years before you have to move on and cultivate new soil. In early Virginia and Maryland, that meant cutting thick forests of 1,000-year-old hardwoods and then tearing out stumps bigger than we will ever see in our modern lives. Black slaves were generally used for planting and harvesting the tobacco, because the owners would pace them to work for thirty or forty productive years. A slave who was used for clearing land would likely be broken and useless after just a few years, so this work generally fell to the slaves who were not owned for life. None of the slaves were adequately fed, clothed or sheltered, and they were often set to work with inadequate tools. Many thousands of indentured servants never lived to see their term of slavery end.

Some of the servants signed up voluntarily, some were captured, and some were convicted of crimes, but once they were here, the courts treated them all as if they were criminals to be rehabilitated. It was very common for the courts to add extra years to the servants' terms of indenture as punishment for disobedient behavior. This was especially common among the Celts because so many of them were captured, and because the English masters knew just how to piss them off and inspire rebellious behavior. A great many Celts ended up being worked as slaves for longer than seven years. Many lived to a ripe old age and still died in slavery.

Of course, many Scottish and Irishmen managed to escape and survive in the western frontier wilderness of the Appalachian Mountains. When their captive counterparts were eventually freed, they usually ended up in the mountains too because all the good land near the coast was already taken. Freed servants weren't given land, money, or even a new pair of shoes when they were finally released. They were just turned out with nothing but their tattered clothing and expected to find a legal means of survival. Many freed people were caught stealing food within their first weeks of freedom and sentenced to do more time.

This indignity was born on the shoulders of so many people, that eventually many thousands chose to rebel in violence and throw off the English oppressors. After the American Revolution, indentured servitude was abolished for White immigrants. Sadly, our new nation kept its southern Black slaves in chains and blew its chance to start off on the right foot. The newly-freed Irish became the new police force of New York City where they reigned racist terror on the Black population for generations.

Most of the freed servants and their descendants were pushed further into the mountains where they shivered in shacks and learned how to eke out a living growing corn, hunting and fishing. Crippled by their own racism, they usually failed to make friends with their benevolent Indian neighbors. One thing led to another and they ended up in perpetual danger from the ongoing war that they started.

Over time, the Scots-Irish settlers killed off most of the Indians in Appalachia, the South, and the Ohio Valley. Normally, an expanding empire would pay professional soldiers to do this most dangerous kind of work, but the settlers of the American frontier took it upon themselves.

Meanwhile, America's ambitious entrepreneurs needed more workers to set up the ever-expanding industrial infrastructure back East. For whatever reason, they preferred to use the African slaves for farm labor and domestic service, and not so much for building industry. Virtually none of the White people who were already here could be lured into the festering work camps of the early industrial projects. They could see first hand that the pay was too low, and the work was too dangerous, so the captains of industry turned back to Europe for fresh blood.

Word of the conditions here in America rarely made it back across the wide ocean, so the recruiting agents for the companies had an easy time seducing new immigrants with tales of limitless freedom and gum drop hills. In many cases they only had to make America sound like a peaceful place to make it a welcome refuge from the war-torn feudal kingdoms of Germany.

In the 1830's, the English rulers caused a devastating famine in Ireland, and that led to a whole new wave of desperate workers who could be exploited. The workers were paid, but only enough that their lives would remain in a constant state of emergency. They died sick and malnourished, crushed in mines, or their lungs full of dust from the materials in the factories. The 700-or-so Irishmen who died building the Delaware and Raritan Canal stand testament to that era.

As the supply of desperate and gullible people began to dwindle in Germany and Ireland, the business tycoons found thousands more in Italy.

By the time their industrial project spread to the Midwest, most people in western Europe had been warned about the scam. That was no problem. The tycoons simply started a mass-migration of Slavs from almost every nation in Eastern Europe.

The same company that employed the immigrants sold them rotten food that had been disguised with chemicals and diluted with fibrous fillers like sawdust. No other food was available in the remote mining towns. Even in cities, immigrants rarely had time to walk to other parts of town where products of a higher quality were sold. Very few knew anything about the big, English-speaking cities that existed outside their little industrial ghettos. The companies sold the immigrants pathetically flimsy houses with no insulation or sewerage systems and signed them up for payment plans that they could never actually pay off. By the time the newcomers learned to read English and discovered they had been swindled, it was too late. They had already signed.

The industrial titans had only just begun to tap the impoverished hordes of Eastern Europe when the southern Blacks were "freed" to become the next victims of the wage-slave migration scam.

In the late 1800's the unions made a strong stand for workplace safety and better pay, but alas no one in the unions spoke Chinese, so another new race of exotic people who no one trusted was brought in to industrialize the West. Thus, America became a global melting pot of oppressed people all boiling and toiling to provide for the luxury of the aristocracy and the increasing comfort of a new middle-class.

This middle class was also a product of social engineering designed to show that America was a free society with the opportunity for class advancement. A small percentage of the poor who were the most intelligent, disciplined, and selfish were given more pay and easier work. I specify that they were selfish, because most of the intelligent and disciplined poor who were not selfish became union organizers, communists, outlaws, or rebels of some other stripe. For these there were blacklists, prisons, and mercenary Pinkerton security forces with long rifles. But for those who lacked a critical analysis of class-based culture, being allowed to advance in the hierarchy was proof that they were better than other people. They rejoiced in their superiority, and climbed over each other to sign up as managers, cops, and conservative voters, volunteering to help oppress the great horde of filthy scum from which they had just emerged.

I ridicule the middle class for this mistake, but I should really be more sensitive. I can't imagine what it's like to come from a family that has been clawing towards the light at the end of the tunnel for generations, and then become the one who finally escapes into that light. It must be wonderful and disorienting all at the same time. I imagine I would hate my former peers, because I would have endured too much childhood trauma from their bullying and abuse to ever recover from. After a long struggle, they would finally be gone and I would be surrounded by sharp-dressed, important people telling me I made it and treating me like I was cool. And good God! Who even knew such delicious food existed!

I grew up in a family where my father was the one who beat the competition and made it to the end of the tunnel, and I mean to tell you he fed me so well I could never complain. I didn't know oppression even existed until I was a teen-ager and I never felt oppression myself until the first time I got locked in jail at age twenty-two. When he was younger, my father taught me that competition is needed to weed out the lazy people and the stupid people, and to this day he campaigns for industrial capitalism. There are many more like him and all this serves to cushion the slave-masters from the dangerous anger and political organizing among their wage-slaves. That's why the middle class is also described as the buffer class.

This tactic of creating a buffer class turned out to be a bit of a double-edged sword for the masters though. Perhaps no one thought to calculate that once the new middle class had children, they would shield their children from the terrible oppression that had scarred them so in their own youth. Lacking the emotional damage that would give them a competitive attitude, many of the new bourgeois children were not mean enough to make good cops or bosses. The parents wouldn't stand to see their children returning to work in factories and on farms, so more and more positions were created within the burgeoning bureaucracies of corporations and the government. If little Johnny wasn't tough enough to whip the slaves, he could still earn a living sitting at a desk shuffling papers. Thus the numbers of people who consumed without producing swelled into the millions. There was no historical precedent for such a huge middle-class anywhere on the planet. As the lives of so many millions became relatively free of oppression, America really did appear to be on the path to becoming a free society.

In many ways, this was more than just an appearance. As the temper of the middle-class softened, their function as a buffer started to work both ways, sometimes actually protecting the poor from the predations of the rich. By the early 1900's, unions were able to appeal to the gentle sentiments of middle-class voters and pass laws to make work conditions more humane. Politicians like Teddy Roosevelt found that they could bust a handful of corporations as a public relations stunt and gain wild popularity. 40 years later, after capitalist mismanagement was exposed as the cause of the Great Depression, popular sentiment in America had swung so far to the left that Franklin Roosevelt was forced to enact real socialist reforms.

Many of those reforms are still in effect today, but as it turns out, they have not changed the fundamental structure of class-stratification in our society, and many of them even strengthened it. For example, Franklin Roosevelt printed up millions of paper dollars and created jobs for thousands of poor Americans building the giant dams in the Pacific Northwest. The dams produced huge volumes of cheap electricity that brought new luxuries to the middle classes across the entire western third of our country. Those same dams also killed off the fish that were the food supply for many of the last free Indians, but that was never stated as a purpose for their construction.

FDR also started the mass-migration of Mexican "braceros" who were used to do the heaviest and dirtiest of the farm work. The Bracero program was a newly dressed version of the age-old migration to wage-slavery scam, but with a new twist. Instead of being able to stay and integrate with the ever-ascending American population, the Mexicans were brought in to the country only during certain agricultural seasons and then returned to Mexico in the off season. In this way they were kept hidden from the gentle sensitivities of the American middle-class.

To a great extent, Latin-American laborers are still used in this way. I have been lucky enough to work for one farmer who paid their foreign workers quite well, at least by farm standards, but I have also worked for a total scumbag who tricked Mexican migrants into working for free, and then called the border patrol on them when it came time for them to get paid. It's my understanding that exploitation and abuse of foreign farm-workers is still a rampant problem in our country.

For an enlightening project, try reading Upton Sinclair's book, *The Jungle*, and then watch the movie *Fast Food Nation*, (a docudrama about workers at a modern meat-packing plant.) Things have gotten a little better since the 1800's, but not as much as we would like to think.

After the "youth quake" of the 1960's, widespread overt oppression had to be seriously reduced here in the homeland. The middle-class Hippies and their liberal allies turned out to be an overwhelming majority of our voting population, so the captains of industry had to disguise their worst behavior in order to maintain the illusion of democracy.

Throughout the 1960's 70's, and 80's the CIA worked covertly to over-throw democratically elected governments in most of the nations of Latin America. Once the ruling class had their puppet governments set up, they could extract Latin America's abundant natural resources and farm products for a tiny fraction of their value, sell them cheaply here in the US, and still turn a massive profit.

American consumers were told that all this affordable luxury was the result of a technological utopia where machines did the grueling labor that used to plague humanity. Meanwhile south of the border, millions of subsistence farmers were forced into labor when their lands were confiscated by the government. They died by the thousands in mines, or on farms that pro-vided our sugar and fruits. Those that survived were kept in a constant state of anxiety by low wages, dangerous work, long hours, and inadequate food, shelter, and health care. Those that organized against the colonial take-over were imprisoned, tortured and executed. Just like Joseph Stalin, the dictators of Argentina, Chile, Brazil, and others rounded up tens of thousands of their political opponents and executed them.

Even in this modern era, the captains of industry are very good at con-trolling the flow of information across oceans and borders. Back here, we were told that "Free Trade" was bringing a similar level of affluence to the entire world. Anywhere that poor people were still suffering, it was because they had backwards governments that still hadn't made a genuine commit-ment to the mystical economic formulas of "Free Trade."

The once radical Hippies were mollified and took to consuming cheap imports as quickly as the business tycoons could ship them. The enslavement of Latin America brought such luxury to our nation that even poor Ameri-cans can get food stamps and welfare.

The illusion of a socialist utopia has gone even farther in the dominant nations of Western Europe. Over there, poor people can receive free food, shelter, and health care without working at all. The worst poverty has been all but eliminated in the First World nations. No one really even needs to work anymore in order to survive, and even those of us who have jobs rarely pro-duce anything that is essential to our lives. We have become whole nations of bureaucrats, middle-men, artists and entertainers. Meanwhile, the destitute masses in Africa, Latin America, Asia, and the Middle-East toil and die like slaves to provide our food, raw materials, and manufactured goods.

In the years just before I went walking, some of the larger nations in South America had broken free from our colonial domination. That's probably why the price of everything was inflating so much, and it may be why Bill Clinton was ordered to cut welfare. If all the Third World nations were to rise up and throw off their oppressors, much of the American middle class would be demoted to poverty, and the poor would be put back to work in that way that only the strongest could survive.

Our culture and economy are set up in a way that the luxury of the rich will be preserved at all costs, even if millions of other people have to sacrifice their freedom, health, or even their lives to preserve it. There is a certain type of "ruling class" people who believe it is their birthright to horde thousands of times more money and resources than they need, and they don't care how many people have to suffer for their luxury.

Honestly though, I think there are very few of those really sociopathic monsters left. Most modern rich people seem to be blissfully unaware of the harm they are causing. They are surrounded by an ass-kissing swarm of economists who have them convinced that they are actually helping the poor people of the world. It's still irresponsible for them to listen to their toadies and live in denial, but it's an improvement over the ruling class psychosis of previous generations. There is some hope that we might get through to some of those people and rehabilitate them. Some of them might even make powerful allies to help us fight the last of the real evil villains who would enslave us on purpose.

The cultural structure that forces most of us to toil in poverty so that a few can be ridiculously wealthy is called class stratification. It is the most dangerous problem we face as a culture, and we need to work together to find a way to change it. That's why I have digressed into this long summary of American labor history. I want to make sure you know how the pattern of oppression has endured and adapted for centuries. I want you to see how racism and language barriers have been used to pit us against each other. As Americans, we should have a better understanding of racism than any other people on the planet. We should be able to identify and debunk racism quickly, and we should be able to share this expertise with people all over the world. We could be the nation that figures out how to cure the sociopathic insanity of class stratification. We can create a culture of equality so beautiful that the master's own children fall in love with us and convert to our ways. I believe this, and that is why I write.

19. CROSSING THE DELAWARE

Late in the evening, I came to a larger town called Princeton. I knew there was an ivy-league college there with significant cultural influence, and I was really looking forward to distributing some zines. I had called and e-mailed in an attempt to arrange a meeting with some Princeton students, but no one had answered. I walked into town at a late-evening hour when all the cool students were sitting on café patios, buzzing with coffee and cigarettes. I was hungry, and feeling pretty close to broke, and people were discarding a lot of really good food right in front of me. At some point, I lost my manners and started eating out of the trash cans in front of horrified, gawking college students. I don't remember what all I found to eat, but I remember I scored a few bites of this and that at a couple different places. Then on the third try, I found a trash can completely empty of anything worth eating.

I got frustrated and lost my presence of mind. It doesn't make sense to dig deep into a garbage can looking for food, at least not in the era of this adventure. Even if you found food down there, it would be all cold and squished and maybe starting to rot. But for some reason I got frustrated and just kept digging. It was as if the lousy students who had been sitting at that particular store had eaten every last bite of the food they paid for, and it totally foiled my plan dammit! I got most of the way to the bottom of the can when a nice, Italian-looking kid in a blue t-shirt tapped me on the shoulder and handed me a plate of delicious food. He had been the next in line and he had bought an extra plate for me.

I was really grateful and suddenly I felt like an ass. I hadn't been begging, but I had stumbled pretty darn close. I tried to start a friendly conversation with the kid, but I got too political too fast. He thought I was an asshole and he left in a hurry. A small crowd of people had been watching, so I went into a group sales-pitch for my zine. No one was interested, and I felt really stupid. I gobbled up the rest of my meal in silence and slunk away. I should have offered a bow, or at least a belch for the worst performance of the night, but I didn't.

It was getting late, so I walked back down to the canal. I had been following the canal all day and I had seen a little stretch of forest that would be perfect to sleep in. I got there just as it got dark, set up the tent, and laid down for the night. I resolved to be more charming and make friends with Princeton in the morning. Then I drifted off to sleep.

That night I awoke to a strange sound that I couldn't identify right away. Back towards the college, there was some sort of amplified noise that was drifting all the way out to my forest hide-out. A light rain was falling, so the sound was totally distorted by the rain's soft whisper. There were drum beats, but they all seemed to be falling on top of each other without any sort of rhythm. Splashes of other sounds echoed off the trees and buildings, but it was hard to make out any details. It sounded like a rock concert. I had never been outside a rock concert before, but I have been several times since then, and it is really interesting how the sound distorts. I think what happens is that different sounds move at slightly different speeds, and over a great distance that adds up enough to make a song totally incomprehensible.

In spite of all that, every once in a while a few seconds of melody would come through all in order. Every time it did, I swore it sounded like Parliament funk songs. At first I thought it might just be someone covering Parliament, but then they went through all of Parliament's greatest hits and they tore the roof off with *We Want the Funk* for at least half an hour.

The show went late into the night, and I got tired, but alas I couldn't sleep until it was over. It was not loud, but it was a clearly audible sound that was just too weird to sleep through. It was ridiculous and at times I lay there giggling. There I was lying in my tent in the forest listening to a live funk show, horribly distorted by the laws of physics. I had been to plenty of rock shows and stood right in front of the speakers where the sounds all line up and sound awesome, but I never realized how silly it sounded from a half mile away.

I awoke at dawn and hurried back to the Princeton campus to make friends and sell zines. Unfortunately it was a Sunday and none of the students were up yet. I found a computer lab, but the doors were locked. Confused and frustrated, I just kept wandering around campus hoping to find someone. Within the hour, a number of students appeared, but they were all in a terrible hurry. No one had the time to stop and talk. It looked like maybe they were on their way to get some breakfast ready at a church or something. As the morning wore on, I found a few people to talk to, but still no one was interested in subscribing to my zine. I asked about the concert though, and one of the students confirmed that George Clinton had performed there last night. George Clinton was touring with a new band, but he had been the original front-man of Parliament, so I had been at least partly right in identifying the funk.

It was almost nine o'clock when I finally convinced a young woman to let me into the computer lab. I checked my e-mail to discover that I still hadn't gotten a response from any of the student activists I had tried to contact. After that I decided to give up on Princeton and continue on south. I hadn't distributed a single zine there, but it was already October and I had a long way to go before winter. I went back down to the canal and continued on towards Trenton.

I arrived in the outskirts of New Jersey's capital city around the middle of the afternoon. The canal path ended abruptly at a highway that was under construction, but it was Sunday, so no one was actually working there. I had to pick my way carefully between mud holes of unknown depth and heavy machinery, and I had to climb over several large cement barricades. I also had to wait in two places while long lines of traffic whizzed by and then sprint across the roadway as soon as there was a gap between cars. It took a while to traverse the industrial mess, but when I got to the other side, the canal continued on into town with a nice bike path beside it.

It had been cloudy and cold all day, but the afternoon sun came out and it was lovely. I sat down in a little urban park that the canal trail passed through. My feet were nasty and I wanted to wash them and change my socks before I walked into Trenton hoping to meet people. It had been too cold all morning, but now it was perfect. There were a few other people in the park, so I slunk down to an overgrown corner by the canal. For some reason I didn't want to be seen washing my feet, so I picked a spot where I was alone. I hung my slimy socks up to dry and washed my feet. They were pretty sore, so the water was refreshing. Then I sat in the sun to dry while I munched on peanuts and raisins.

Just then a couple of other guys showed up who were about my age. They had come to the same hiding place also hoping to be hidden. At first they were startled to see me, but they were friendly anyway. After glancing nervously at each other several times, they decided to stay and then they asked me if I would mind if they smoked a blunt.

"Hell no," I said. "I just walked here from Maine!"

They were relieved and also astonished to hear about what I had been

149

doing. One thing led to another and they ended up inviting me to smoke with them. I had never been to Trenton before and I had some concerns about walking into it balls-out stoned, but the guys were so friendly to offer, I couldn't say no. They rolled a blunt the size of my pinky finger, and we puffed on it for a while.

A blunt is a marijuana cigarette rolled in a tobacco leaf. Blunts are associated with inner-city poor folks. Stoned people love to talk about giant blunts, but the sad fact is that the weed they get in the inner city is usually so bad that you have to smoke an entire blunt to get high. Bags of leaf get shipped to the folks in the ghetto and sometimes they charge them the same price per weight as rich kids in the burbs get charged for buds. If you rolled a big urban-sized blunt of rich-kid buds, it would take you a week to smoke it and you'd be dysfunctional the entire time. Well, okay. I have friends who could prove that wrong, so I guess I'm bullshitting a little. *I* would be ruined if I tried to smoke a big blunt of Maine outdoor all in one sitting, but Trenton's finest wasn't too strong that fall. I got nice and stoned for the first time since July, but I didn't get so stoned as to be afraid of random things.

I don't really remember what we talked about, but we went on for a good while. I mostly just remember being glad that they were friends because one of them was a Polish immigrant and the other was Black. I couldn't help but think of the ARA guy in Lodi warning me about all the Polish Nazis. I was also really impressed with how fast the Polish guy had learned to speak English. It hadn't quite been two years since he moved from Poland, and he never learned a word of English until he got to New Jersey, but he already had most of the words and grammar down. He still had a bit of an accent, but it wasn't horrible, and I'm sure it's gone by now. It made me wonder how long it would take me to speak like a native Spanish-speaker if I moved to Latin America somewhere.

After a while the guys took off. They both signed up for zines and they left me with the roach end of the blunt as a gift. I stashed it in a little plastic container in my pack and thought about whether or not I was ready to walk into Trenton yet. It seemed like I didn't have much choice, so I put my shoes back on and hit the trail. Meeting strangers while under the influence of marijuana can be a harrowing experience, but I wasn't too stoned.

As it turned out, I didn't see anyone for about another hour anyway. The canal kept going right into the thick of an abandoned industrial district. I emerged from the forest into a landscape of old brick mill buildings and great works of steel. A few of the structures looked like they might still be used for something, but there were no humans in sight. Many of the parking lots and roofs had grown over with grass and ailanthus, and there were smokestacks that had sat idle for so long that the rain had washed them clean. The bike path beside the canal was still maintained with a little strip of green, mowed lawn next to it, but no one rode by on a bicycle the whole time I was there.

After a while I came into range of a disturbing sound. It started as a vague treble hissing and then developed into a far off cacophony of enraged voices. It sounded like thousands of angry voices screaming in tones so shrill that it made the hair on my neck stand up. I was frightened, but also drawn on by curiosity. After another few minutes I realized that I was hearing bird voices and not humans. That seemed a lot less frightening, but I was still really curious about what was going on.

Finally, I came to a giant steel structure literally swarming with angry crows. It looked like a five-story building had been stripped down to the steel frame. The steel itself had an odd texture. It looked like it had been splattered over with a thick layer of tar or something. I only called it steel because it was shaped into I-beams and bolted together like steel, but its surface looked like black mud that had dripped dry and then cracked all over. Every surface was also splattered with brown and white crow shit. The building was taller than it was wide, made for some industrial purpose that I couldn't imagine.

Everywhere on it that a crow could perch was covered with crows and there were more in the air around it. It was beautiful and terrifying all at the same time. Maybe I was just stoned, but it really sounded to me like most of the crows were vehemently angry.

I had to pass right by them on the trail and for a few hurried paces I was pretty worried about getting shat on. Once I had gotten a safe distance away, I turned back and watched the crow uproar for quite a while. At the time I remember thinking that they were protesting the abandonment of industrial sites with no cleanup effort. New ore is constantly being dug up and smelted into new steel while the stuff that has already been made is being left to rust into the Delaware. I felt lucky to be there since no other humans had even passed by to take note of the crows' complaint.

Looking back now, I imagine the crows must have been having a huge meeting. I have since learned that they are one of the most intelligent of all animal species. They fly over the land and see everything. Then sometimes they gather together from all over the continent and report to one another. I think they must also have to make important group decisions since many birds work cooperatively like that. I think the representatives of all the East-Coast crow tribes were sharing reports and then hammering out strategies that would involve the entire crow nation over the coming winter season. I just happened by at a time when tempers had flared and the meeting had broken down into chaos. They all seemed to be committed to the process, and I like to think they worked through it and came to a resolution. I certainly didn't see any factions give up and fly away while I was there. Maybe they weren't even angry, and I just got confused because I was high. There were literally thousands of them there. Maybe they just had to shout to be heard. Anyways, it was an amazing thing to behold. Whatever the explanation, I can tell you that the New Jersey crow nation was strong that year.

Right after I left the crows, I came to a place where the whole surface of the canal was covered with floating soda bottles and other plastic trash. The slight current in the canal had pushed them all up against a big screen. Just beyond that, there was a lock where the water level dropped about six feet. I knew I must be getting near the end of the canal, and I wondered if I could follow it all the way to the Delaware River. Once I got past the lock, I could see the canal disappear into a low concrete tunnel. The bike trail ended at a big street rushing with traffic and the towers of the city looming behind it.

At first I thought it was a good thing. It would be irresponsible for me to skip across all of Trenton on some abandoned industrial corridor. I needed to meet people.

A few paces later, I realized the first person I was about to meet was a police officer, and my mood changed dramatically. For some reason, a cop had his car parked on the edge of the road, blocking the entrance to the bike path. He was standing there, leaning back on his car with his arms crossed, gazing at the canal. I think he must have just been taking a break from work and admiring the view, but he sure made me nervous.

I had to walk right towards him for a couple blocks. I hadn't really gotten that stoned in the first place, and that had probably been an hour earlier anyways, but suddenly I felt paranoid as hell. Would I have to talk to him? What would I say? I still had a roach in my backpack. Could I get in trouble?

I kept hoping the cop would wander off, or at least get into his car, but he stayed right there. For the last half block, I kept feeling like I should smile or wave or something, and I think I did both several times. Finally I got close enough for a verbal greeting, and the cop started right out interrogating me. He asked all the usual sort of nosey cop questions, but it was terrifying because I was still a little bit stoned. He asked to see my ID, but he didn't take it to his car to check the computer. He asked me where I had been sleeping. When I told him I had slept in the woods down by the canal, he grew very suspicious. I started to get the impression that he wanted to bust me for vagrancy. He narrowed his angry eyes and asked me where I planned to sleep that night.

I blurted out, "Morrisville, sir." He looked my ID over some more. Then he handed it back and sent me on my way.

Morrisville is the first town in Pennsylvania across the river from Trenton. I was hoping to convince the cop that I would be out of his jurisdiction by nightfall, and thus not his problem. By the grace of something it seemed to have worked. I set off up a long hill and when I looked over my shoulder a few minutes later, the cop was just driving away. Just then a church up the block erupted in celebration with a loud-speaker blasting a tape of ringing bells. As I walked by the church's open door, I heard the voices of what sounded like a hundred joyous Black folk singing some hymn of celebration.

I didn't have a map of Trenton, but I soon found a major road headed right for the downtown district. I was still miles out from the center of the city though and first I walked through some old ghetto-like district. The houses were all tall, flat-faced rectangles, all pressed against each other like Philadelphia row houses. The change in architecture gave me the sense that I must have crossed into the Philadelphia region.

I ran out of water and I had to ask someone for help. Luckily I was in a Black neighborhood, so there were people all around. I came to an open doorway with four or five teenage boys standing on the stoop. I asked if there was a sink inside where I could fill my water bottle and a conversation ensued. One of the boys took my water bottle inside and filled it for me while the others asked questions about my voyage. I got my bottle back full and thanked them. Then suddenly one of them figured out how far I had come and blurted out, "Damn, you're gonna set a world record!"

Without thinking, I blurted back, "Shit, man. Your ancestors probably walked here from down South! I haven't gotten that far yet."

It was probably true, but it might have been a bit rude to throw the history of his people's oppression in his face at that moment. It definitely made the kid stop and think, but I felt like an asshole. He was just excited about my walk and I should have given him a zine. Instead I zapped him in the brain. Feeling awkward, I thanked them and hurried away.

Further down into the city a giant Black man slowed down and called to me from his car as he drove by. He was coming from behind me and when I heard him shout, "Hey kid!" When I turned to look, he stuck an arm the size of my leg out the window. His head was shaved and he was obviously a body-builder.

He gave me a big thumbs-up and made a hilarious mocking grin face. His head wobbled and his teeth twinkled like some cartoon kid from a commercial. He was obviously making fun of my "Love Earth" sign, but his joke was too funny to actually hurt my feelings. He was right! My sign was too cheesy. Somebody had to say something. In the last moment before his car rolled away, we both broke out into a hearty laugh and I kept chuckling for a while after that.

I decided I needed to sit down for a while and just then I spotted some benches. I was right near the New Jersey state capitol and the benches sat near the center of a large concrete plaza between government buildings. It was Sunday, so all the buildings were closed. The only other person there besides me was a Punk teen-ager riding his skateboard. He was really good. He jumped down stone staircases, slid down metal handrails, and even managed to bounce off the sides of the buildings. It seemed like his maneuvers were meant to disrespect and maybe even damage the government property. I was thoroughly amused and I stayed to watch the show for quite a while. Eventually he came over to meet me and I gave him a zine.

Just beyond the capitol I found a bridge and set out across the mighty Delaware River. I sighed, feeling certain I had escaped the Trenton Police. It was getting late and I would need to find a camping spot soon, but the river's mighty spirit caught hold of me and I stopped in the middle of the bridge to admire it for a while. It was flowing fast by the city, and small rocks broke the surface in many places forming white, foamy ripples. No large boat could ever have navigated it, and I guessed that Trenton was probably built at the highest point where ocean-going vessels could sail up the Delaware. The water had a strange, almost chlorinated smell to it, like all the water in New

Jersey and eastern Pennsylvania. I think that's why they call it "wootr."

The bridge I stood on was just downstream from the spot where George Washington crossed back over the Delaware to defeat the British at the Battle of Trenton. You know, that epic famous painting where George is standing in the front of a boat with his chest puffed out like a rooster while some peon soldiers row. He's crossing back over the river at night to surprise the British at daybreak. That's the Washington legend we are taught to be proud of and I don't doubt it's true.

It was also in Trenton, where George Washington had two Revolutionary War veterans executed by firing squad. All over the rebelling nation, soldiers had enlisted under the promise that they would be paid only if America won the war and gained independence. They knew they would not be paid if we lost, but their hearts were in it and they fought anyway. Some of them had been fighting for eight years. Once victory was ours, they expected to get paid, but Washington stiffed them.

As a result, there were small mutinies all over the country. Pennsylvania troops marched on Philadelphia which was the nation's capital at the time. Washington was holed up there and they moved to confront him directly. Old George didn't have the resources on hand to slaughter them, so he bullshitted and bargained with them. He ended up giving them three months' pay and they quieted down.

Soon after that a smaller group of soldiers broke off from the New Jersey militia and attempted a similar move on Trenton. Unfortunately, Washington was in a better position that time. He had a fresh company of new recruits who still believed they would soon be paid. They were well fed and well equipped, and they outnumbered the mutineers three to one. They disarmed the starving New Jersey veterans; then they put three ringleaders on trial for treason right there in the field. One was acquitted, and the other two were shot on the spot. Washington ordered the rebels' own friends to be the firing squad, and supposedly they wept as they fired. I have trouble imagining that not a single one of them had the courage to turn and fire on Washington himself. He must have been hiding somewhere and sending orders.

He was a ruthless motherfucker though. That's why they still put his face on dollars and quarters all these years later.

20. PHILLY

Morrisville Pennsylvania was not big enough to be much of a sister city to Trenton. I bought some junk food from a little market that doubled as a liquor store. Then I sat on the curb and ate. Just a few blocks further on, I came to a stretch of railroad tracks and decided to follow them. I didn't have a map of Bucks County, but I figured the tracks would make a straighter path to Philly than any road.

In less than a mile, I was out of town. The abandoned industrial mess just faded into a piney forest strewn with old junk. I climbed up an embankment, squeezed into a thicket of bushes and smoked what I could of the blunt roach. There wasn't enough left to get me high, and instead I just got paranoid. It was getting late and I had to find a camping spot, so I continued down the tracks.

The tracks passed by a shooting range where a steady stream of randomly-timed gunshots shook the air. As I approached the frightening noise, my paranoia peaked. Suddenly a train was upon me. I had plenty of time to get out of its way, but there was not enough time to hide and I saw the conductor look at me. At that point I had passed many "no trespassing" signs offering explicit legal threats.

Overcome by paranoia, I decided to hide in a little strip of forest right there and bed down for the night. Old tires, beer cans, and other rubble littered the forest floor, but the ground was level enough once I cleared some space. I could make out the shapes of ramshackle trailer homes through the trees, and an ATV trail passed right by my camping spot. Dogs barked in the nearby trailer-park and the shooting continued until hours after dark. Also, it turned out that I was walking down the Amtrak rails, so the trains came thundering by at alarmingly high speeds, and the interval between them was less than an hour.

At some point I did get some sleep, but the shooting resumed at the crack of dawn, so I got up early and rambled on. The trains' approach was so quiet and so fast that I was spotted twice more by conductors. After the second time I decided I better get off on the next road and quit trespassing. I kept looking for a gas station where I could steal some maps, but the first five stores I found were all Wawas, and they were all designed for total panoptic security. The tiny stores were set up so that the people working the counter could see into every last corner. There was literally no place for a person to hide and stick something in their pocket. They all had at least two people working the counter and at least one of them would watch me suspiciously the whole time I poked around their map-racks, so I left empty-handed each time.

Around noon I found my way to the Bristol Public Library and waited in line to check my e-mail. No one in Philadelphia had responded to my calls for help. My spirits fell. Back outside I needed to find a map, but hours of wandering proved fruitless. Finally I found a Rite-Aid pharmacy that was dimly-lit, and staffed entirely by teen-agers. I went on a fairly epic shop-lifting spree, filling my pockets with snacks and batteries for my flashlight. I got a map of Bucks County, a map of Philadelphia County and a map of Trenton, New Jersey. Even though I wasn't going back to Trenton, I figured I had earned a map of it. I bought one can of peanuts from the listless, acne-riddled cashier and celebrated outside.

This book is getting redundant with scenes of me wandering into ominous huge cities with no plans for my own accommodations and feeling nervous about it, but there I was on the verge of Philadelphia feeling the same way again.

My parents both grew up in Pennsylvania, and they felt a natural obligation to keep me and my sister safe from places like Philadelphia. Staggering numbers of poor people are all drawn or driven to the same cities to compete for very limited opportunities. Or they are just born there. Competition is fierce, and vast numbers of people live without adequate food or shelter. Crime is the natural result of this equation, and crime means danger. I was lucky to be isolated from such danger as a child, but I was also very ignorant. Once I got to high-school I could watch Spike Lee movies or rap videos on TV, but that didn't mean I understood anything about the Ghetto. In my senior year of high school, a friend and I started ditching class and sometimes we would drive down to check out the ghettos of Denver. We were mostly driven by our raw curiosity, but I think there was also some of that young male desire to prove our courage, because we always ended up parking his truck and walking around on foot. We never really talked to anyone though unless we were ordering food from some grease-pit restaurant. Probably the most meaningful interaction we ever had was the time a gang of White skinheads threw glass bottles at us.

After that I ended up in a small western college town for five years. It was a place specifically designed to maintain and solidify middle-class youths' ignorance of what life is like for the poor.

At age twenty-three I dropped out of college and took a job campaigning for liberal political reforms. My employer, a non-profit group called Green Corps, trained us how to campaign effectively for political causes and then contracted us out to various other non-profit groups who needed more organizers. My first assignment was to Philadelphia.

My employer was the World Wildlife Fund, (famous for their panda-logo handbags,) and they hired me to campaign for the United States to sign an international treaty called the Kyoto Protocol. Global Warming was a hot issue that many millions of people were concerned about, and the Kyoto Protocol was an attempt by world governments to address the issue. Unfortunately, it was also a blatant attempt to prevent Third World nations from gaining economic prosperity. Every nation was expected to cap carbon emissions at the levels they had reached by sometime in the 1990's. That meant that the US, Canada, Europe, and Japan could go on consuming gluttonous amounts of resources, while the rest of the world toiled to extract those resources and ship them to us. It was a pretty cynical deal but even so, American politicians refused to sign it. "Why should we limit our consumption if China won't limit theirs," they said.

The World Wildlife Fund hired me and eight others (who were sent to other prominent American cities) to campaign for the Kyoto deal, but we were prohibited from using any of the effective campaign strategies we had just learned in our training. Instead we were instructed to pour all our effort into gathering signatures for an e-mail petition. The goal was to get so many millions of signatures and then make a big deal out of it in the press. Unfortunately, an e-mail petition has no binding legal status, and there is little incentive for any politician to ever take such a petition seriously. This obvious flaw in the campaign strategy really bothered me and I followed through the motions of my job without any genuine enthusiasm. I didn't even know what was wrong with the Kyoto Protocol back then. I just knew that as long as I followed orders, we were not going to win the campaign. It felt like we were faking it, like we were helping the WWF pull off some kind of deception.

Looking back, I think we probably were. The WWF is an advertising company specializing in green-washing. Giant corporations like Ford and Kodak give the WWF "donations," and then the WWF spokespeople tell the media that those companies are doing right by the environment. It's a subtle kind of public relations, and it has to be done very carefully. The WWF has to maintain a branch of its organization that really does things to protect wildlife habitat, and some wildlife actually does benefit. I'm sure the majority of their employees believe they are working entirely for a good cause.

Global warming is one of the hottest political issues in modern times. The idea that our industrial lifestyle might change the composition of the atmosphere enough to disrupt the climate really is a legitimate thing to consider. People's instincts are telling them that we should not take so much from the Earth so fast. We have a sense that we are making a mistake and we fear the consequences of that mistake.

By posturing itself as a leader in the movement to avoid global warming, the WWF would take advantage of that fear, and increase its own credibility. The more they look like green superheroes saving the Earth, the more money they can charge to Fortune 500 corporations for their green endorsements. The tricky part is that if the WWF did anything that would actually hurt their customers' profits, it would hurt their profits too, so they hired us to create the illusion of a campaign. This is all just a theory that I can't prove. I just have to try to make some sense of the strange things I experienced back in the fall of 2000.

That all took place to the backdrop of the first real ghetto I had ever experienced in my life. My employers handed me a very tight schedule which left only a single day to find and secure a place to live. I was only contracted to live in Philly for three months and then I would be moving on, so I had to find an apartment that rented on a month-to-month basis. Despite the challenges, I did find an apartment in that one day, and it was surprisingly cheap. I moved onto Mount Vernon Street between 11th and 12th in the southern fringe of the vast ghetto region known as North Philadelphia. The office I worked in was only twelve blocks away, and I enjoyed walking, but I soon found myself riding the bus out of fear of my surroundings.

Several nights a week, I would see pairs or groups of men brawling with each other on the sidewalks. When I was walking I would sometimes have to cross the street, or loop around whole blocks to avoid violent street fights. I never heard any gunshots and sometimes there were whole crowds of other men cheering on the contenders in the fights. It occurred to me that maybe street-fighting was just a local pass-time, like some kind of amateur sport, but it was still way too hard-core for my little suburban sensibilities.

At night the sounds of the ghetto filled my room like a nightmare. There was more than one couple within earshot of my window who would reach extreme levels of domestic conflict almost every night. I overheard volumes of screaming verbal abuse in English and Spanish, and sometimes that was accompanied by the sound of things breaking. The mangy alley cats were constantly in heat and their banshee-yowling terrified me all night long, but I moved in at the beginning of September and for the first month it was too hot to even consider closing the window.

I think the scariest part of all was the police helicopter that would buzz the neighborhood at night. I guess its landing pad was somewhere nearby because it would rumble over just above my rooftop at least once every night. There was no sleeping through that even with the window closed. One night the "ghetto bird" stopped right in front of my apartment and hovered there for a long time. Overwhelmed by the noise, I went to the front door to see what was happening, but just then the burning white spotlight shone into the front window of the apartment and I ran back to my room in fear. All I could think about was stray bullets.

Very few of the traffic lights worked in my 'hood and most of them displayed all three colors at the same time. Some drivers dealt with this by stopping and looking both ways, while others would actually accelerate and blast through the intersection. There were a lot of collapsed buildings in the city, and every time it rained the news would report that more buildings had collapsed, sometimes killing their occupants. My neighborhood was peppered with big abandoned industrial buildings, and during one rain, a huge chunk fell off a building and destroyed three cars just a block east of where I lived. One block west of my house there was a car that someone had bashed to pieces with a sledge hammer (or something heavy) and then burned to a crisp. I don't know how long it had been there, but no one did anything to clean it up in the three months I lived there.

One night in November, I was walking home from work when the door to a building flew open beside me and a man was thrown out into the street. He was falling backwards and he would have tumbled into the street if not for the random coincidence that he ran right into me as I walked by. I hadn't really tried to help him, but as a result of our collision he was able to remain standing. He thanked me with a pat on the shoulder, and just as his one hand left my shoulder, the other one swung back and landed a punch on one of the men pursuing him out the door. I walked on quickening my pace and I didn't look back.

I observed all these and many other frightening scenes, but I had no time in my schedule to meet people in my neighborhood or learn anything about the ghetto. All I knew was that it was an awful place that I couldn't stand living in. I hated Philadelphia, and when I moved out that December I vowed never to return.

The following year, I got into Dead Prez, and read *No More Prisons*. I began to understand the modern American class structure and thus understand the function of ghettos in the geography of our homeland. When I walked to the Bronx in 2002, I came with an open mind, ready to learn, and hoping to help. My fear of the ghetto grew into an appreciation in New York, but Philadelphia was different. Philadelphia was the place where I first lost my bourgeois sense of innocence and I had not been back since. I knew it would be another big challenge that would take a lot of courage to pass, so I decided to pull up short and face the city at sunrise.

I ended up sleeping in Neshaminy Park in the southernmost corner of Bucks County just before you get to the Philadelphia city limits. The park was about a square mile of mostly serene forest with just a few roads and some picnic areas and sports fields in the center. The park's southern end was bounded by the mighty Delaware River and I sat most of the afternoon watching it ebb and flow. The lower Delaware is horribly polluted and teaming with motor-boats, but it was still a majestic sight. It's hard to describe, but the river smells of toxic industrial runoff and fresh fecundity all at the same time. I never realized the tide reached that far inland, but I learned that afternoon as I watched the water reach its lowest level and then slowly come back up. There was also a spot where you could look out over the water and see the distant towers of the city stabbing the sky like a pair of fat hypodermic needles.

I set up my tent and slept in the woods just above the river. The gentle lapping of the ripples and the paradoxical fragrance of the wootr soothed me to sleep.

Four gunshots rang out nearby sometime in the late night. I lay awake for a while wondering what had happened, but I was not afraid. My tent was well hidden and I had not slept in such a pleasantly dark place for days. I knew no one would find me unless they were using infrared goggles, so I soon drifted back into a long and peaceful sleep.

I got up at dawn feeling well rested and mentally prepared. I left the park and got a half mile down the road when a park cop pulled up beside me and rolled down his window. He told me sternly that overnight camping in the park was prohibited. He must have spotted me hiking out of the park, but I didn't admit to anything. I just promised him that I wouldn't ever try to camp there and smiled. He blinked a couple times and then drove away.

I came to northeast Philadelphia first, which is a middle to upper-class area that is technically part of the city, but looks more like a suburb. Before noon I found a payphone that worked and I actually got ahold of someone at one of the houses I had been trying to contact. They had not gotten any of the messages I had been leaving over the past week, but they thought I sounded cool and they gave me directions to their house. I would be spending the night at the Cocoa House on the west side of the city. I breathed a huge sigh of relief as I hung up the phone. I would still have to walk across most of the city in one day, but it was early yet and it was theoretically not too far.

Directly in my path lay North Philly, probably the largest continuous ghetto region on the East Coast- the place that had terrified me so just two years prior. I had never been north of Girard Boulevard, and I had always wondered about the jungle that lay beyond. Now I was crossing it, starting from the other side.

I walked through miles and miles of it. I saw hundreds of impoverished people crammed in to every block, block after block until their numbers spiraled into the tens and hundreds of thousands. They lived in decaying buildings, their alleys and yards festering with garbage, crawling with vermin. The whole region was stained with grease and tarnished by smog. The air stank, and it was pierced by police sirens every few minutes. Sadly, I heard that sound more often than the sound of boom boxes blasting hip-hop.

When I lived in Philly two years earlier I remember feeling distinctly like a target of racist hatred. When I would sit on the bus, Black people would scowl and refuse to sit next to me even if it meant they had to stand. I saw Black people glaring at me everywhere I went, and I felt lucky that no one ever did anything violent to me. It hurt to be hated for the color of my skin, but after I learned about the racist history of their city, I couldn't blame them.

In the 85 years between the Revolutionary War and the Civil War, Philadelphia was the first city north of the boundary between the slave states and the free states. It was essentially the gateway to freedom for any East Coast slave who was attempting to escape from the South, but that gate was guarded by the largest and most brutal squads of slave-catchers in the country. At first, private companies employed the slave-catchers, but when the city established its first municipal police force, it hired almost all of its personnel from those companies. Following that trajectory, the PPD has enforced centuries of brutal racist oppression against Black Americans. In a nation full of racist cops and institutions, Philadelphia manages to stand out as an extreme case, even in modern times.

In 1978, police attacked a communal house full of radical Black activists who called themselves MOVE. In a frenzy of shooting, police fired hundreds of rounds and accidentally killed one of their own officers. Nine MOVE members were then arrested and convicted for the murder of that one White officer who had actually been killed by his own co-workers.

In 1982, Mumia Abu Jamal was convicted of murdering a White Philadelphia cop and sentenced to death. As a journalist and radio broadcaster, Jamal had become a prominent leader in the city's Black liberation movement. In college he learned to imitate the vocabulary and dialect of White people very precisely, and that effectively disguised his race during radio broadcasts. Using this tactic, he reported on police brutality and advocated for Black liberation in a voice that White people could understand and relate to. His reporting was unprecedented in the way that it dragged the PPD's racist abuse into the light of day, and it made him a target of special police hatred.

When the officer was found dead, Jamal was found at the scene wounded by a bullet from the dead cop's gun. The situation was complicated and Jamal claimed innocence from the beginning, but it only took a few months for the courts to convict him and sentence him to death. The police never did a serious investigation to find out what actually happened. It was obvious that they cared more about nailing their powerful enemy than finding out what actually happened to their dead employee.

Today Mumia Abu Jamal is probably the most famous political prisoner in the United States. Because of his influence as a public speaker and his huge network of support outside the prison, his execution was delayed for decades. In 2012, he was finally taken off death row, but the state of Pennsylvania still intends to keep him in prison until he dies. He is now seventy years old having spent more than half of that time behind bars. Debate still rages as to whether or not he even committed the crime for which he is serving, but to me it doesn't even matter. I think if a Black person kills a Philadelphia cop in self-defense, or even in defense of someone else, that is a heroic act of bravery. I think whoever killed that cop back in 1981 is a hero, and I think Mumia Abu Jamal is a hero for speaking out against racist oppression in his radio broadcasts.

Not convinced? In 1985 Philadelphia Police dropped a bomb on the surviving members of the MOVE organization that had not been imprisoned back in '78. By all accounts, the MOVE activists were not good neighbors. They were known to broadcast obnoxious political sermons from a loudspeaker at all hours and their compost piles attracted vermin to the neighborhood. That said, they had committed no major violations of any law when police bombed their house from a helicopter and fired over 10,000 rounds of ammunition into it. Police chief Sambor refused to let firefighters intervene, and the resulting fire burned down sixty more homes leaving approximately 250 innocent people homeless. Six of the seven remaining MOVE activists were massacred either by fire or bullets along with five of their children. The one adult woman who survived was immediately put in prison. The one surviving child escaped with the help of a kind-hearted policeman who was then forced to resign under pressure from his racist peers. No police or city officials were ever charged with any wrongdoing in the case.

These are a few examples of what happens to "uppity" Black folks who organize and speak up for their rights in Philadelphia, but this is only the tip of the iceberg. There are probably more than a million poor Black people in the city, and all of them live in daily fear of police harassment, false convictions, and unfair sentencing. This is the legacy that makes them scowl when they see a White person walking down the streets of their city. It's a colossal racist mess that will take generations to heal.

Despite all of this, I didn't encounter much hostility walking across North Philly. Back in 2000, I was all dressed up to work in an office, walking around rigid and bug-eyed with fear. This time I was filthy as any bum, and my body language was much more relaxed. I stopped to talk to people here and there, and I even talked a gang of teen-age girls into receiving some free zines in the mail.

***

I'm not sure if I'm being insensitive to ghetto dwellers, but I have always loved the sight of ruined buildings growing over with plants. To me, a half-collapsed brick wall covered with ivy is a beautiful sight. It is a shrine to the beauty and strength of nature, and it breaks up the monotonous industrial structure of cities. These natural oases decorated almost every block of North Philly and they kept my spirits high. At one point I found an entire block of identical brick staircases leading up one flight and then stopping. The apartments that they once lead to were all collapsed forming a low plateau that had grown over with ailanthus, and all manner of grass and bushes. It looked like a red brick version of a Mayan ruin. It was beautiful and I stopped to take lots of pictures.

I know that most ghetto residents consider my shrines to be "blighted" areas that breed vermin and they frequently lobby city officials to "clean them up." To me this is yet another tragedy of the ghetto environment. Vermin are the only wildlife who have adapted to this new form of ecosystem, so the people's only contact with nature is disgusting and scary. Thus isolated from the more attractive and nurturing parts of the natural world, ghetto residents have very little chance of understanding themselves as one small part of the big, beautiful, interconnected web of life. The more we reject nature and try to separate ourselves from it, the more nature gives us vermin. That's just how it works.

***

Late in the afternoon I finally got down to the old neighborhood where I had lived. I was looking forward to taking pictures of some of the beautiful industrial ruins, but when I got there everything was different. All the old industrial buildings had been torn down and replaced with flimsy-looking condos. Not only that, but all the functional old houses had been torn down and replaced in the same way. The house that I had lived in was gone. The new condos looked like extremely cheap versions of the kind you would see lining major boulevards in cities out West. The characteristic Germanic architecture of Philadelphia was all gone, replaced by white vinyl siding and flimsy plastic porch-railings pretending to look like wood. Each condo was four or five stories tall and packed to the gills with the same kind of poor Black families who had inhabited that neighborhood before.

It was extremely disorienting, and for several minutes I thought I must have gotten lost. I stood there dumbfounded, staring at the street sign at the corner of 11th and Mount Vernon. Was this really the same street corner where I had lived only two years earlier? How could everything have changed so quickly?

As I stood there, head reeling, an angry pubescent boy charged up to me and hollered, "Yo man! Fuck the Earth!"

I was still wearing my cheesy "Love Earth" sign. I wanted to change it, but it would take me days to sew a new sign and I didn't even have any good ideas of what the new one should say. I blinked at the kid in bewilderment, so he repeated himself and moved closer as if he wanted to fight me. I mumbled something stupid and stumbled away, still totally disoriented by the half-assed attempt at "urban renewal" at 11th and Mount Vernon. It was like the ghetto had gotten a total make-over. She wasn't bad looking before, but they had done her all up with straight blond hair extensions, layers of make-up, and giant fake fingernails until she looked like a total zombie.

I walked through the skyscrapers of Center City without stopping to meet anyone. Then I crossed one of the many bridges over the Schuylkill River (pronounced Skookle) and passed by the University of Pennsylvania. Just beyond the university I came to another vast ghetto region known as West Philly, and it wasn't long before I found the house I had been directed to. No one answered the door just then, but after waiting on the front porch for an hour or so, I met one of the housemates coming home from work and they let me in.

I stayed at the Cocoa House for almost a week, but I cannot remember a single interesting adventure from the rest of my stay in Philadelphia. I guess it's lucky I had some stories from back in 2000 and some people's history to round out this chapter. Most of the residents at the Cocoa House were beautiful women, and I just remember flitting between them like a moth in a room full of light bulbs. After four or five days, it became obvious that none of them were going to kiss me and the chill of autumn reminded me that it was time to ramble on down the road.

21. THE GATES OF HELL

It took all morning to walk across the rest of Philadelphia proper. If North Philly is the largest ghetto region on the East Coast, I bet West Philly is the second largest. Then I was on to Delaware County where my day of walking ended fairly early in the afternoon. A friend from Maine had relocated to the suburb of Collingdale and I found his house not long after noon. His apartment was really small and I wanted to give him some privacy because he had just hooked up with a new girlfriend. Fortunately, the place had a nice back yard and the weather was nice, so I set up my tent out back and camped a couple nights.

When I left my friend's house, I didn't get going until mid-afternoon, so I didn't get very far that day. Delaware County, Pennsylvania is a thickly-populated swath of suburbs that's divided into many different, small municipalities, and there is one old industrial satellite city called Chester right in the middle. I ended up right in the middle of Chester when it was time to camp, but by random luck I stumbled into an easy camping spot without even trying. It appeared to be an old city park that had been abandoned and left to grow over. It was partially fenced-off, but it was easy enough to slip around the end of the fence.

The ex-park was a pretty strange place for a variety of reasons. The overgrown remains of pathways, benches and basketball courts gave it a bit of a haunted feel, and ever since its closure, the neighbors had been using it as a dump for old appliances, tires, and all sorts of random trash. I also found a large snake of some sort slithering down by the creek.

According to my map it was Chester creek that flowed through the steep little ravine and that creek was the weirdest thing of all. The industrial odor and foamy surface was nothing unusual for the Mid-Atlantic region, but for some reason the creek kept changing directions. At first I thought it must be going up and down with the tides, but then it changed every half-hour or so. The tide takes six hours to change. I couldn't think of any natural phenomenon that would cause a stream to flow back and forth like that, so I concluded that there must have been some industry downstream that was tampering with the wootr levels. But which way was downstream? I couldn't even tell.

The spirits of nature are the only true spirits I feel, and the spirits of rivers and streams are some of the most powerful grounding forces I know. To see a creek flowing back and forth like that was fundamentally disorienting to me, and it gave me a really uneasy feeling about the place. Alas, it was an oasis of abandoned darkness in the midst of miles of ghetto and suburbs, so I cleared away some trash and slept.

In the morning I turned southeast and walked down to the Delaware. At that point the river is a long narrow bay over a mile wide, and it might be the largest and filthiest industrial cesspool in North America. My first view of the bay was a spectacular panorama of industrial devastation. Vast fields of crushed concrete sprawled over sites where old factories had been torn down. The jagged surfaces were sprouting with hardy weeds, but it would be centuries before they would be smooth enough for humans to walk on. Looming in the distance were the blackened hulks of abandoned factories that had not yet been knocked down. Many more factories and power plants were still operating as demonstrated by the various colors of smoke and steam pouring from their smokestacks. The morning was cold and still and the clouds of toxic vapor hung heavy over the bay. Across on the New Jersey side, I could make out the silhouettes of countless more industrial structures. The bay itself was brown with sediment.

I walked through that scene all morning until my heart grew heavy. The entire shore of the Delaware Bay from Philadelphia all the way to Wilmington is one giant industrial zone. Factories, smokestacks, power plants, oil tanks and rubble stretch to the horizon and beyond. All this land is also peppered with crumbling brick row-homes full of the poorest of ghetto citizens. How anyone could survive in such a toxic environment is beyond my comprehension. Even if the air and water were not poisoned, I'm sure the ugliness of the scene would drive me to suicide in short time. All the buildings were stained grey by the air, and all horizontal surfaces were dusted with soot.

At lunch time, I decided to get away from the rushing traffic of the boulevard and find some peace and quiet. An abandoned building provided just such a refuge, and after lunch I spent about an hour exploring the place. It was nowhere near as interesting as the Kung Fu Castle, but it was about the same size, and I got a little taste of that frontier thrill exploring it. Someone had drawn quite a few swastikas on the walls with chalk, and I spent some time trying to scrape them off.

Back on the road I realized that I was approaching a horizon of small smokestacks shooting flames into the sky. It appeared that the road was going to take me through an active oil refinery. As I approached, I passed a sign indicating that I was entering the city of Marcus Hook, and then I was totally engulfed. For the next two miles, both sides of the road were lined with incredibly complex networks of pipes, oil tanks, and smokestacks. Some of the stacks appeared to be idle and some billowed with white, steamy-looking vapor. Still others were boiling with transparent vapor that distorted the light passing through it so the sky appeared to shimmer behind them.

Of course none of these were as impressive as the stacks that were billowing fire. Every few hundred paces I walked past a smokestack shooting great orange plumes of crackling flames. Sometimes I passed by close enough to feel their heat. Just when I thought the industrial nightmare of Delaware Bay couldn't get any worse, it had. I appeared to be at the very gates of hell, and I half expected to see Satan himself sitting at a checkpoint any minute.

Instead I passed a sign welcoming me to the great state of Delaware. Shortly after the state line, the oil refineries ended and I found myself back in a more garden-variety industrial zone. Once again I was wandering lost without a map and all the convenience stores were owned by the extremely security-conscious Wawa Corporation. After passing by several, I decided to case one out again. By a stroke of random luck, the store was slammed with customers. Each of the cashiers was busy waiting on a line of five or six people and at least a dozen more people were wandering around the little store shopping. Under the cover of such a crowd, it was easy enough to slip a map of Newcastle County into my pants and slip out the door.

Delaware has got to be the least interesting place on the East Coast, and quite possibly all of North America. They are very proud of the fact that they were the first state to ratify the Constitution, but it seems obvious to me that they had no other choice. The other states were large enough to support independent economies and distinct enough to have their own local cultures. For them the decision to lay down some of their sovereignty and join a new nation was something to consider very carefully. Delaware didn't need any time to think it over. They knew that they needed to join in something bigger and better if they were to have any chance of survival and I think that's why they became America's first state. Of course I am just being silly. I'm sure Delaware is rich with interesting history if only I took the time to look it up.

I am not exaggerating though when I tell you that modern Delaware is a

desperately bland place. In an effort to make their tiny state more economically significant, Delaware politicians have rewritten their state laws and tax
codes to be the most corporate-friendly in the nation. Corporations who
locate their headquarters in Delaware don't have to pay any taxes to the state
at all, and they are subject to very little if any oversight by the state government. For this reason, more corporations are headquartered in Delaware than
any other state, even though there are virtually no resources to be extracted
there and not many customers to sell anything to. Many of those companies
don't do a single dime's worth of business in Delaware. They are just headquartered there so that they don't have to pay taxes in the states where they
do make money.

If this strategy has done anything to help Delaware's economy, you wouldn't
know by looking at Wilmington. Walking in from the north, I traversed miles
of broke-down ghetto. The only thing I could see that would distinguish
North Wilmington from nearby West Philly was that the crumbling architecture was a bit less interesting.

Wilmington is Delaware's largest city with a metro area totaling about three
quarters of a million people. A little more than half a million of those people
live in Delaware, while the rest sprawl out into adjacent areas of New Jersey,
Pennsylvania, and Maryland. The only interesting fact I know about Wilmington is that Jamaican rock-star Bob Marley lived there for several years of
his childhood during the 1960's.

I made it to the downtown area in the late afternoon where I wandered
aimlessly looking for potential zine subscribers and allies who I might be
able to spend the night with. I don't remember meeting a single person. The
blocks of downtown were lined with countless corporate office towers, and
the resulting landscape was stiflingly monotonous. I've always found it interesting how much the homogenous landscapes created by corporate capitalism resemble the homogenous landscapes created by soviet communism.
Both are massive systems of centralized control that strive to crush diversity
and replace it with a homogenized lack of culture. The idea that the two systems are fundamentally different is more propaganda than reality.

By the time the sun set, I still hadn't met a single person, so I headed back
to a beautiful park I had seen along the shores of the Brandywine Creek.
To me the "creek" looked like a full-sized river, but streams have to get very
large in the Mid-Atlantic region before they earn that title. The banks of the

Brandywine were steep and high, and a thick forest had been left to grow on them. There were a few level spots in the valley bottom though, and I found a perfect place to set up my tent just as the last light of dusk faded into night. The gentle splashing of the creek helped to mute the sounds of the city somewhat and I slept easily. There was a light rain that night, but it only lasted a couple of hours.

The morning was grey and dreary. I made another attempt at downtown, but all I could find were businessmen in sharp suits. I spent most of the morning failing to distribute my zine in America's ultimate corporate stronghold. Then I headed west.

I had a place to stay in Newark, Delaware. A good friend of mine had a little brother who was attending the university there. Though I was barely acquainted with my friend's brother, I had managed to get in touch with him via e-mail, and he said I was welcome to stay at his apartment.

Looking at my map, I saw that the most efficient way to get to Newark was a long, straight road called the Kirkwood Highway. Unfortunately, the map gave no indication of just how much this route would numb my mind and suck my soul. If it had, I probably would have chosen a different path.

The Kirkwood Highway was a textbook example of "transportation corridor sprawl." Mile after mile of strip malls, fast-food chains, car dealerships and big-box stores lined both sides of the road. Behind them I could see many more miles of utterly homogenous suburbia, but the residential zone never came all the way out to the road. The roadsides were a solid strip of commercial zoning stretching all the way from Wilmington to Newark. It took me part of the morning and all afternoon to traverse it, and by the end of it I had seen some of the same chain stores repeated three or even four times. Here's another Walmart, a second Burger King, and a third McDonalds. Or was that the fourth? I couldn't keep track. All of this commercial landscape was designed to exclude pedestrians so I walked the whole way in the breakdown lane or in little modular strips of grass. The sky remained one dull shade of grey all day long. It was a quintessential Delaware experience.

The only reprieve from the desperate monotony was the sight of a Taco Bell that was in the process of being torn down. Some large machine had shattered the front half of the building into a thousand shards and flattened it to the ground. For some reason the process had then stalled, leaving the back half of the building intact until it gave way into a jagged pile of debris.

When I happened by, no workers or machines were present, and the mess was just sitting there for all to behold. Fast food franchises like Taco Bell have strict marketing policies that forbid the public from seeing any of their restaurants in any state of disrepair, so it must have been by some fluke that the demolition was started and then left unfinished. I'm sure it was only a matter of hours or days before the remains of the shattered store were swept away and a new one was constructed across the street or somewhere nearby. I considered myself very lucky to see such an anomaly and I took a picture. Perhaps I should not admit this in writing. I should not be surprised if spooks from the Yum! Corporation (which owns Taco Bell) show up at my door to make me and my photo disappear.

Around supper time, the monotony started to break up. First the sun started to come out and then there was a slight bend in the road. Then the commercial strip malls started to break up and I passed by a couple of farms. Then almost suddenly, I was in the dull college town of Newark.

I called my friend's brother and he answered the phone, but said he would be busy for several hours. He recommended a restaurant where I could wait, and said he would be there as soon as he could. The restaurant had a pleasant outdoor seating area and the weather was warm enough, so I ordered some food and sat outside.

Before long I had made friends with some random college students and a lively conversation ensued. Someone handed me a guitar and I started showing off my musical skills. One thing led to another and soon I had gathered a crowd of college students around me. The restaurant didn't mind the commotion because they were selling more coffee and snacks. I sold more than a dozen zine subscriptions and replenished my faltering supply of cash. I also felt like I had redeemed myself after failing to sign up anyone in Wilmington. It turned out Delaware would not be a complete waste of time after all.

Eventually my friend's brother showed up and we walked to a nearby bar with several of my new friends. We drank a few beers and then retired to my host's apartment where we drank a few more with his roommates. The building was not a dorm per se, but it was inhabited entirely by college students.

My friend's brother had gone to the University of Delaware specifically to study corporate finance. Through his high-school job as a golf caddy, he had made personal friends with the CEO of a massive credit card company. After some time kissing ass as the CEO's personal protégé, he went off to college to start his own career in the world of high-rolling finance. Needless to say, we had some fascinating conversations and I guess I was one of the first people he had ever met who really challenged his choice of careers. When I saw him again years later he had given up on the world of extreme capitalism, and he actually credited me as an important influence in his decision to change his life's course.

I stuck around for a few hours the next morning and helped my friend's brother with his job. For some reason, he was working in the university's experimental greenhouse. I guess most people just work wherever they can find a job, whether or not it lines up with their interests. Together we walked around to the various greenhouse buildings writing down temperatures and other random bits of data. Then I thanked him and said farewell, and within an hour I had reached the border of Maryland.

22. SUSQUEHANNA

Elkton, Maryland is essentially the southern tip of a giant swath of suburbia that stretches all the way north to the Pioneer Valley of Massachusetts. I had been submerged in urban and suburban landscapes for so long I had gotten used to it, but suddenly after Elkton, I was out in the country. There were a few suburban-style Mcmansions and a few farms, but mostly it was just wild forest. I recognized very few of the tree species. It was reassuring to see that many of them still had green leaves that had not yet turned their autumn colors, but it was still a cold day.

It was too cold for me to stop and admire the scenery at all, but the cold air was clean and when the rumble of passing cars faded away, all I could hear was the lovely chirping voices of the birds. Somehow I ended up on a less-traveled route for a stretch where thick hardwood forests pressed up to the road on both sides. I don't remember pausing even once from my hiking blitz, but the spirit of that forest found its way into my heart even so. That's when I remembered the story of Fredrick Douglass.

Fredrick Douglass was a Black slave who grew up on a plantation on the Eastern-Maryland shore of the Chesapeake Bay. He was born into the time period after the Revolution but before the Civil War when the North was a relatively safe haven for Blacks trying to escape slavery. Douglass spent his entire youth in servitude as a slave, but as an adult his will for freedom broke loose. He and three others stole a canoe in the darkest hours before dawn and paddled out into the estuary. They hid in wooded coves during daylight hours and paddled by moonlight until they reached the main trunk of the Chesapeake. The masters had deliberately kept them ignorant of American geography, but somehow, they knew to follow the North Star, and the great Chesapeake Bay took them most of the way to Pennsylvania.

After days of paddling, they arrived at the northern tip of the bay where they left the canoe and scrambled up into the very forest that I was walking through. On the bay they could catch fish to eat, but they had no food for the overland hike. Starving and running without shoes, they scrambled through the dense forests of northeastern Maryland for several more days before they reached the safety of the Mason/Dixon line.

Once they made it to the North, allies took the four refugees to Philadelphia where Douglass worked under the table for several years until he had saved up enough money to buy his own freedom. By then he had learned to read. He studied law voraciously and soon became a lawyer. He was adept at defending the rights of free Blacks and he became one of the loudest voices advocating for the freedom and equality of Black people in America.

I don't remember much about Fredrick Douglass's public career. I just remember the thrilling story of his escape from slavery. The story was made into a children's book that some teacher gave me to read in fourth or fifth grade. It captured my imagination and I remember the details to this day. What could be more romantic than an escaping slave? It was a thrilling adventure combined with a righteous struggle. It gave me goose-bumps. As a child, the story of Fredrick Douglass made me proud. I was proud to be from a country where such courageous people had fought against power and gained freedom. I was proud to be an American and I still am. If there was a flag that symbolized the struggle of people like Fredrick Douglass, I would hang one on my backpack.

Fredrick Douglass is only one of thousands of slaves who escaped through the Maryland woods. Together their stories weave an image of a world where the human urge to be free will always overpower the alien urge to oppress. Their stories remind us that we are a strong and righteous people. They remind us that the spirit of freedom will shine on even in the darkest hour.

***

I can't remember much about my camping spot that night, so it must not have been very interesting. I just remember waking up and walking through a raw and misty cold. I warmed up to some hot breakfast and coffee at a diner in Perryville and then it was time to cross the mighty Susquehanna.

The largest river on the East Coast of the United States, the Susquehanna begins in upstate New York and cuts right across the entire Appalachian Mountain Range of Pennsylvania. The geologic record suggests that the Susquehanna has maintained that same general course since eons before the Appalachians even existed. When the mountains began to rise, the river cut through them at a rate quick enough to avoid being diverted from its course. At their climax, the Appalachians were as tall as the modern day Himalayas, but that didn't stop the river from cutting right through them. In its time, the canyon of the Susquehanna must have been one of the geologic marvels of the planet.

Even now it is pretty cool to see the "gaps" where the mighty river cuts through the Seven Mountains of Pennsylvania, but that's nowhere near where I walked. I crossed the Susquehanna in its last mile before it empties into the north end of the Chesapeake Bay.

Perryville, Maryland sits on a steep bank high above the water, and the view was spectacular. Unfortunately I was in no mood to admire the view or soak up the spirit of the great river. The morning was frigid, and all I remember thinking about was the dilemma of how I was going to get across. The bridge I had been planning to walk was impossibly narrow and it was almost a mile long. There was barely enough room for the cars to cross without scraping their sides on the guardrail, and the stream of traffic was bumper-to-bumper. There was simply no way I could cross there without getting run over. There were train trestles on either side of the auto route, but they were both highly-trafficked as well. I couldn't imagine it would be much safer to cross on them.

After a moment of despair I gave up. It had been my intention to walk every step of the way to the West Coast, and it seemed very important on some spiritual level to follow through with that, but this just wasn't going to work. I walked back several blocks to a gas station and asked for a ride across the bridge. The first man I asked was happy to help. He was headed across the bridge anyway and no one was riding shotgun. He was driving a big work truck full of equipment and his rural Chesapeake accent was so thick that I could barely understand him. We had a brief conversation about how cold it was and then he dropped me off on the west bank of the river.

For the rest of the morning, I walked down the side of highway 40 shivering and cursing at the trucks that went by. For some reason there was a steady procession of those big square Peterbilt dump trucks headed east on route 40 that day, and each time one passed me, the icy gust of wind that it displaced would practically knock me off my feet.

I ate lunch in a little dive in the small military city of Aberdeen and then spent much of the afternoon walking past the perimeter of a large military base called the Aberdeen Proving Grounds. I had never seen so many porno stores in my life. I guess soldiers need to jack off a lot.

I was hoping to see some of the Chesapeake Bay, but there was only one little stretch of road with any view of the bay, and even then it was just a little finger of water. I walked down to the shore to try to admire the pathetic view and found the shoreline littered with garbage.

The cold weather spurred me to walk fast, and I kept walking late into the evening, trying to put many miles behind me. Unfortunately, I walked past many good camping spots in the afternoon and plunged ahead into the outer suburbs of Baltimore. Then when it was really time to bed down, all I could find were houses and lawns. Eventually, just before total darkness, I found a tiny chunk of forest and crawled in for the night. I could plainly see a big suburban house just up the hill from me, but I figured I had no other choices. I also figured that no one would see me anyway since it was already dark.

What I hadn't planned on was a massive barking fit from the hypersensitive dog that lived there. Even though it was closed inside the house, I could hear the damn thing crawling out of its skin with anxiety. Somehow it knew I was outside and it barked as if barking was the only thing that could save the world from total annihilation. After a while I could hear the voices of the people in the house worrying about what had gotten the dog so excited. Then they came to the front door and started shouting, "Hello?"

Needless to say, I didn't call back. I had refrained from setting up my tent for fear of being spotted and now I cowered deeper into the bushes. I could hear the damn little dog behind them screaming frantically, "He's out there! He's out there!"

They went back inside and commanded the dog to be quiet, but it would not relent. The frenzy of barking continued for hours and the dog owners came to the door twice more shouting into the yard. The third time they came out, they stood on the porch shining a flashlight beam all around the yard. I was hidden well enough to avoid the flashlight, but this was still a nerve-wracking development. Obviously the dog didn't behave like this on a regular basis. The people knew something was up and their methods of investigation were escalating. Were they going to call the police next? What if they simply let the dog outside to track down my scent?

To make matters worse, it was freezing out and I was shivering uncontrollably. I didn't feel secure enough to set up my tent at all, so I rolled up inside my tarp for what little insulation that offered. It made quite a bit of noise, but nothing was audible over the shrill barking of the dog anyway.

As the crisis wore on into the late night, there was a phase where the people in the house freaked out and screamed at their dog to be quiet. After quite a bit of that, I think they closed it in a room at the far and of the house from their bedroom and attempted to sleep. I also attempted to get some sleep then, but I didn't get much. I was frozen to the bone and I don't remember the dog ceasing to bark all night long. I remember wishing that the little bastard would tear its own vocal chords, but I have wished that fate on dogs many times and it never happens. I rose at the crack of dawn and walked on into the frosty landscape of northern Maryland.

I hadn't even been walking an hour when I came to a beautiful river called the Little Gunpowder Falls. Steep rapids squeezed between huge boulders for as far as I could see both upstream and down, and the sound of rushing water made my heart soar. I never realized there was such a steeply-flowing stream anywhere that close to the coast. The river was flanked on both sides by a broad swath of park land and I had to laugh when I realized that I had come up just short of such a beautiful camping spot the night before. I wanted to linger there and maybe take a nap, but I knew I couldn't afford to waste any time. Once again I was walking into a giant city without a place to stay or any plan of what to do. I hadn't even tried to contact anyone in Baltimore because no one had given me any contacts there. I wasn't really scared this time, but it did make sense to get there as early as possible so I would have enough time to improvise something.

Just a little ways further on I crossed the Big Gunpowder Falls which was also surrounded by a broad swath of beautiful park land. The river was not just bigger, but also slower and less rocky than the Little Gunpowder Falls. It was just as beautiful though and I stopped long enough to take a few deep breaths before plunging into the thick of Baltimore.

23. BAWLMR

Most of the day was another long trudge down a very straight road through miles of suburbs, strip malls, and light industry. When I reached Baltimore proper it was late in the afternoon. A long stretch of hospital buildings gave way to a mile or so of heavy industry and a complicated tangle of railroads. It was a small part of Baltimore's huge array of ocean port facilities. I never saw the water because I was on low, flat ground surrounded by darkly stained industrial buildings, but I could tell it was there because I could see the upper parts of dozens of huge ocean-going cargo ships and tankers.

Beyond that I came to a thickly-built ghetto. The rest of the afternoon disappeared behind the towering tenements and suddenly it felt late. Tough-looking men were everywhere, standing on porches, walking here and there, alone and in groups. Cars passed me with bass amps booming and electronic decorations flickering on their hub-caps. Some of the men glared at me. I got a few blocks into the ghetto and then decided to go back to the railroad tracks. I had seen several abandoned tracks there that were all grown over with young forest. Surely there would be a good place to sleep out there somewhere. I decided to get some food first and I had just walked past a greasy little Chinese take-out joint. I had a plan.

I turned back towards the restaurant and just then a kid somewhere in the range of twelve to fourteen years old came up came up and told me to give him a dollar. I declined as respectfully as I could and continued on my way, but he followed me, repeating his command. We walked together like that for a block until I reached the restaurant.

The place was tiny and gross. Soda coolers took up most of the waiting area and there was a little nook behind them where a hand full of people could stand while they waited for their order. The walls were all white plastic paneling, stained with dull brown and yellow grease, and there were no decorations anywhere. The top half of the front wall was all plexi-glass covered with menus, giving the impression that the place offered a huge variety of distinct entrees. You placed your order to a face you could barely see through a hole in the plexi-glass, and then passed money to a pair of hands through a little slot below the bottom edge of the plastic. After a short wait, a signal was hollered through the hole and a pair of hands would slide your meal through the lower slot, plated in a Styrofoam box.

The kid followed me into the Plastic Dragon and got right in my face. He poked me in the chest and demanded that I give him some money. He mustered the most menacing tone he could and it seemed like he was actually trying to rob me.

Fleeing without food had not been part of my plan, so I decided to cave in to his original demand. "Alright, you win," I said, and I handed him a dollar.

He took it quickly and for one instant I thought I saw a flicker of a smile on his face. Then he asked me for another dollar.

I lost my temper and said something loud and angry.

He countered with, "Give me five dollars."

A heated argument ensued for several rounds. Eventually I told the kid that he would have to be satisfied with the dollar I already gave him and he instantly denied that I had ever given him a dollar!

I blew my top and hollered, "fucking back off and give me a minute!"

The kid actually stopped for a moment while I picked something off the menu and paid. He waited right there though and as soon as I was done, he was back at it. I tried all manner of debate against him, but he never backed off from his strategy of direct commands and intimidating posture. The trouble was, he wasn't actually very intimidating. He wasn't a child anymore, but he still had a lot of growing left to do. If he had actually attacked me, I could have easily overpowered him. He didn't even have so much as a pocket knife for a weapon. He was just so annoying that I couldn't stand his presence.

I tried giving him another dollar if he promised to leave me alone. I held it above his head where he couldn't reach and went through a ridiculous process of negotiating a promise out of him. It was a dumb strategy. Finally, he made a promise, took my dollar and went right back to hassling me.

I only had about thirty dollars to my name at that point. I had not been hustling zines very effectively in the Mid-Atlantic region. I generally considered fifty dollars to be a minimum safe cushion to go travelling with, but I had been operating below that threshold for several days. I still had some of the money left from selling my car, but my parents couldn't send it to me unless I found a safe address to stay at for several days. At that point I didn't feel very confident that I would find such a place in Baltimore, so I wasn't about to let the damn kid rob me. I explained to him how broke I was, but he just shrugged.

Eventually I got my food- nasty fried chicken covered with sugary goo, served over salty rice that wasn't cooked enough. Perfect! I started eating while the kid continued to bother me. After a while I offered him a piece of chicken. He took it and ate it quickly, but he refused to say anything about it.

He escalated to demanding that I give him all my money, and at that point I finally found the words to really explain the situation to him.

"Are you actually trying to rob me? You're not big enough. You know? I'm not afraid of you. I mean, go get your big brother or something."

Finally the poor kid deflated. He cussed me out a little bit and then left with my two dollars.

As soon as he was gone I realized the air in the plastic box was making me sick. I stepped outside and ate a few more bites. Then I carried the rest back to the tracks where I sat on a pile of railroad ties and finished my greasy meal.

As I ate I was approached by a really haggard-looking bum who wanted to talk to me about a bottle of vodka. Due to his slurred speech and total lack of sanity, I couldn't even tell whether he was trying to explain something to me or ask me a question. This mess continued for a while after I finished eating and I became frustrated once again. I ended up trying to convince him there was a really awesome bottle of vodka downtown and he should go check it out. I kept pointing to the skyline of office towers in the distance and telling him to go there. By the end he seemed to be getting angry with me, but eventually he stumbled away.

I turned and climbed up the overgrown gravel causeway to an abandoned rail line. Almost immediately I was hidden in a sooty thicket of young trees, but there was nowhere flat to lie down. I walked south, away from the road and deeper into the industrial wasteland. After a short walk, I came to a clearing in the trees where I could see a broad panorama of the sunset with all of Baltimore in the foreground. The rusted old rails were elevated up on a causeway that gave me a slight vantage point over the foreground. From there I could see out over a broad swath of abandoned rail-yards all overgrown with weeds and strewn with old debris. Beyond it there was a mysterious and foreboding expanse of ghetto, and beyond that lay the silhouette of Baltimore's sprawling skyline. The left side of the picture was framed by a menagerie of giant cranes used to load and unload ships in the harbor.

I watched as the fiery orange sun sank from the smog-tainted sky. For several minutes as the sun slid behind the distant tenement roofs, a brighter orange light seemed to glow from all around. Baltimore suddenly became spectacularly beautiful, but gazing into the west, I felt the call of my western homeland. For an instant, my heart flew across the continent and basked in the heat of the Yakama Valley. I could see Patoh and smell the sage in the air. I knew I was going to make it, and I felt a renewed sense of determination to walk all the way there.

In the next moment, I smelled the rust and saw lights coming on in the towers.

The steep sides of the causeway were thickly bearded with saplings all interwoven with leafy vines. It seemed pointless to try to find a camping spot in that mess, so I settled for a spot right up on the tracks where a thick mat of fallen sticks, grass and dirt covered over some of the old ties. Out in the woods I would try to avoid sleeping on *any* sticks let alone a whole pile, but in Baltimore a pile of sticks felt like the coziest spot.

I had started to unpack my bag and bed down when a couple of guys came walking towards me out of the twilight gloom. They were a ways off, but I knew they could see me already. I was right in the middle of the tracks where they were walking, so I had to do something.

I decided to pack up and I had most of my stuff put away by the time they arrived. The two of them were drunk and they hollered a very friendly greeting from twenty paces off. One of them was shorter with a thin, blond beard growing down to his chest and long hair to match. He wore a long black trench coat with cowboy-style shoulder flaps and a blue bandana tied around his forehead. The taller one wore a leather jacket and leather pants that looked like they had survived more than one motorcycle accident. His hair was dark, curly, and shorter and he had his beard trimmed into a pirate's goatee. They were both White in terms of their ethnicity, but their skin was darker than most Mulattos. In fact, in the dusky light their faces and hands appeared to be covered with tattoos or maybe even scars. Maybe they were just dirty and my imagination was running wild.

They looked dangerous as hell anyways, but they were quite pleasant to meet. They were sharing a bottle of some hard liquor, and they each had a tall can of malt liquor hidden in their clothes that they were proud to show me. They said they were headed to a hobo jungle about a mile further down the tracks. There was going to be a party that night and they invited me to come.

I told them I was really tired, but I didn't say no outright so they kept trying to talk me into it. They told me about several exciting things they were anticipating. I don't remember what they were anymore, but the guys were convinced that it was going to be big night at the hobo jungle and they were pumped about it. I told them I didn't have any beer, but they just said, "Oh, somebody'll probably give you one!"

Finally I told them I would think about it, but I needed to rest some first. They agreed to that, toasted me with a gleeful swig off their bottle and tramped off into the darkness.

I did think about going to the hobo jungle for a minute. I tried to imagine what kind of debauched revelry I might experience at such a venue. Visions of people spitting fire and cheering on fist-fights danced through my brain. That might have been fun, but alas I couldn't imagine there was any chance that any women might be there, and that clinched my decision to stay and sleep. I looked around for a way to penetrate the steeply-sloped thicket, but found nothing handy.

Eventually I lay back down in the middle of the semi-public thoroughfare and slept. No one else came along that night. I know because I slept with one eye open and I awoke to the orange tint of the waning moon several times.

24. TEABAGGERS

Even first thing in the morning, the ghettos of Baltimore were pretty intimidating, but it didn't take me long to push through them. Then I made it to a gentrified area where the downtown met the harbor. I found some of the fingers of the inner harbor and at one point I saw a group of tourists being led around to some of Baltimore's best places to spend money.

I had all day to find some allies, so I fell back on the method that I had leaned on for most of my voyage. I had been to Baltimore once before to visit a friend who lived near the Johns Hopkins University. She had moved out of the city since then, but I figured if I went to her old neighborhood, I might meet other people with similar political beliefs to mine and then I would have a place to stay. I turned north and by lunch time I was in the John's Hopkins area.

I found some cool stencils denouncing Dick Cheney and some flyers for a protest that had already happened, but there was no contact information on them. I sold some zines to some cool-looking White kids and after a few hours I met a crew who was willing to take me in for the night. They didn't have any political views at all, but they were nice and they had space on their floor. They seemed to think of me more as a travelling artist than an activist and the idea of hosting such a person seemed very romantic to them.

I was taken back to an apartment where two women lived and both their boyfriends hung out to be social. After a night and a morning of dodging danger in the impoverished ghettos, it was relaxing to be sheltered under the wings of a bunch of privileged White kids.

It was awkward though. I felt obligated to entertain my hosts with interesting stories and perspectives, but they weren't interested in politics and my protest stories frightened them. They agreed with me that war was bad and President Bush was bad, but they didn't like to talk about it because it darkened their mood and highlighted their ignorance. I tried to adjust my tact to be a little less abrasive, but I didn't have much to say about arts and entertainment. I had trouble thinking of any stories to tell about my adventure that didn't lead to some deeper philosophical point.

I asked the woman who had been my most gracious host to describe Baltimore for me because I knew so little about their home. She proceeded to tell me all about John Waters' movies and how Baltimore is just like the movies. I was totally baffled by her descriptions. I have seen some of John Waters' movies, and I even thought *Pecker* was pretty good. I know he films all his movies in Baltimore and they are all ostensibly set there, but I couldn't imagine how a real place anywhere could have anything in common with them.

Almost all the characters are White with strange characteristics that are exaggerated to full on hyperbole. They dress in wardrobes that evoke a nightmare of Andy Warhol trying to do a caricature of 1950's fashion. The plots all center around awkward social situations that would never actually happen in real life. Waters' movies are art for art's sake and any resemblance to reality is methodically edited out. He doesn't even train the actors in his movies to speak in the signature Bawlmr accent. No one ever "gays dain to the ayshun," (goes down to the ocean,) and no scenes are ever filmed in front of the crumbling tenements that make up most of the city.

Nevertheless, my hostess claimed that her whole section of the city had filled with cool young people whose joy in life came from their mutual appreciation of John Waters' movies. They also bonded around a mutual effort to recreate his artistic styles in their real lives. That would explain why the woman had adorned herself in a bright polyester dress with a bold polka-dot pattern and horn-rimmed glasses of the brightest plastic. Even her hair was arranged in the style of the John Waters fantasy world. Clearly I had stumbled upon an enclave of highly orthodox hipsters.

I strained to be as polite as possible for the rest of the evening while the kids slurped on candy and coffee and chatted about vapid things. They fed me a decent supper and then the hostess baked chocolate-chip cookies.

***

In the morning there was a phone call followed by a great bustle of excitement. The kids had a friend who was a real live rock star and he had invited them out for breakfast. I was urged to get ready in a hurry so I did. I put on my shoes and a long-sleeve shirt as quickly as I could. Then I waited for fifteen minutes or so while the ladies dashed this way and that in a frenzy of preparation. Then we got in their car and drove to the downtown district to meet their friend at some classic diner.

The food was great. I had to order something really small because I was so broke, but everyone else fed me off of their plates and I got a delicious belly full.

Liam Burnell

The rock-star friend turned out to be a real asshole. He was the lead singer of some famous Punk band that I had never heard of and I don't remember his name. His band had been around since the eighties and he was in his forties, but he acted like a drunken teen-ager. He was drunk in fact, and he kept gulping from a bottle of liquor he had smuggled into the restaurant. He had been up all night partying and he intended to keep the party going. He was loud and rude and he insulted the other patrons. When it was time to leave, he gave his bill to the young hipsters who were all about half his age and they paid it. I was disgusted, but I kept my mouth shut.

After that he wanted them to drive his drunk ass around in their car, so they obliged. I piled in the back seat with two other people so he could ride shotgun. First we followed his demands that he be taken to a liquor store where he bought a six-pack of beer. Then he took one can, opened up the sun-roof and stood up so his upper half was sticking out of the top of the car. His hips pushed into the driver's shoulder and head so she had to bend to the left while driving. He kept poking her and shouting commands to turn in places and go faster. He hollered obnoxious jokes at pedestrians as we drove by and once he finished his beer, he threw the empty can at somebody. That act was followed by an immediate demand that we hand him another beer.

The hipsters were eager to follow his directions, but none of them could actually reach the beer since it was stashed on the passenger-side floor where the rock-star's feet should have been. The guy to my right tried to climb over the seat and the driver tried to reach all the way across the front of the car while driving. They couldn't reach though, and the resulting delay made the rock star angry. He shouted a burst of insults through the sun roof and then repeated his demand.

The guy next to me tried even harder to squeeze through the gap between the front seat and the ceiling and he let out a cry of pain as the head-rest pushed into his belly. Meanwhile the driver discovered her dignity and told the asshole to get his own beer. I don't think he heard her, but after another delay, he thought of the same idea on his own. Back inside the cab of the vehicle, he cussed us all for our incompetence.

Just then we stopped at a red light and the driver took a second to throw me a backwards glance. I could tell by the look on her face that the thrill of this encounter with a real live rock star had worn off. Just as quickly, the old man's smelly ass pushed her face back out of view behind the seat. After that

186

she drove straight to his apartment. Along the way, he drank another beer, threw the can at someone else and then slumped down into the passenger seat. He had almost passed out by the time we got to his home. One of the youngsters helped him inside and then returned alone just a moment later. While they were gone the driver apologized to me and explained that her rock-star friend "must have played an amazing show last night."

I had to admit that their lives really were kinda like a John Waters movie. Hippie physics seemed to be at work again.

***

It started raining that afternoon and it poured all night long. I wanted to leave in the morning, but it was still raining hard. It had become painfully obvious by that time that my hosts and I had nothing in common, so it was really awkward to linger in their apartment for so long. In the afternoon I walked down to a little store and bought some groceries so they wouldn't think I was trying to live off of them. I really can't remember how we passed the time. I just remember watching the gutters surging with oily runoff and the endless barrage of big cold raindrops.

That evening my hosts got invited to a party and they brought me along. We drove quite a ways out through the suburbs and ended up in a smaller town that I never caught the name of. I sold zine subscriptions to several people at the party and bummed drinks until I got fairly drunk. After that I felt like a real moocher, so when someone announced that they were going to the liquor store, I rode along. I spent most of the money I had just made on a fifth of some cheap whisky. Back at the party I passed the bottle around and drank quite a bit myself. The rain stopped and the moon came out and we all stood outside to admire its comforting glow.

In the morning I had a spectacular hangover. I had not been flexing my binge-drinking muscles lately so I far exceeded my tolerance. To make matters even worse, it started raining again in earnest, so I loitered around at the hipster pad for another awkward morning. By this time the kids had become visibly uncomfortable with me. Of course they were too passive aggressive to say anything, but I imagined they must be worrying that I might stay forever until they finally found the courage to kick me out.

Finally towards the later part of the afternoon, the rain let up a bit so I thanked the kids and bid them farewell. I walked about a mile west to the Druid Hill Park where I stopped to admire the view. According to one mythology, back in 1979 a group of young Black men invented the musical style we now know as hip-hop in that very park and their group was known as "Dru Hill."

Looking back from the grassy hilltop, downtown Baltimore looked like Gotham from the Batman movies. Little tufts of cloud drifted between the dark towers and several of the taller towers disappeared into the soft grey ceiling. The park itself had an eerie spirit that made me wonder how it came to be named after Druids.

I pushed on further west into the park. A light drizzle started up again so I spent some time sitting at a picnic table under a small pavilion waiting for it to stop. The evening's light began to fade before the rain stopped, so I trudged out in it to find a camping spot. There was quite a bit of overgrown forest in the western reaches of Druid Hill Park, so it didn't take me long to find a suitable spot. The eerie spirits had not followed me beyond the park's front entrance. Deep in the belly of the park the spirits were much more hospitable and there didn't seem to be any people around. The rain faded in and out several times throughout the night, but it wasn't enough to soak through the tent, so I stayed dry and I slept well.

25. WHEN THE RAIN COMES

I awoke the next morning to more steady rain so I decided to stay in the tent and wait it out. Just before noon the rain let up, so I packed up my wet tent and slogged ahead into the southwestern part of the city. The sun never came out and a light rain resumed falling shortly after I started out.

Baltimore is supposedly America's Blackest city with some estimates suggesting that as many as ninety percent of the city's inhabitants are Black. Certainly everyone I saw to the south and west of Druid Hill Park was Black, but their neighborhood was not as intimidating as the ones I had passed through in the eastern part of the city. Instead of towering brick tenements, the people there lived in one or two-story wooden homes with small lawns and big old trees in between them. Oppressive poverty was still apparent as all the windows were barred, and none of the houses were in very good shape. Some of them had actually collapsed and the streets were strewn with trash. Even so, the abundance of greenery and the relatively low population density made it a pleasant ghetto to walk through.

Before long I found my way to a long ribbon of park land following a stream called Gwynn's Falls. Normally a small creek, Gwynn's Falls was raging with brownish flood waters from all the recent rain. To my delight I found a trail along the stream and followed it down for miles until I was almost out of the city limits. The rain stopped for several hours but it kept dripping off the trees, so I continued to get wet anyway. After several miles, the creek flowed out of the park and into a coastal wetland that had been paved over with industry.

I got onto a major road headed south and almost immediately I came to the end of the Baltimore city limits. Just then, the sky opened up into a bone-soaking deluge of heavy rain. At first there were no real options of places to take shelter, so I just trudged through it. Then I came to a big, greasy-looking seafood restaurant in a building shaped like a barn. I left my backpack just inside the front door and took a seat at the bar. A puddle of water quickly formed underneath my stool, but the place was dumpy enough that no one seemed to mind. I ordered a heaping plate of awesome deep-fried Maryland shrimp and ate it slowly as the rain pounded on the roof. Most of the patrons at the seafood barn were captivated by a series of large television screens that were all tuned to a football game. I had no interest in the game, but it was easy enough to guess that the Ravens were losing. Every few minutes a great cry of despair would well up from the half-drunk crowd all wailing in thick Merlyn accents.

I lingered a long time waiting for the rain to stop or even slow down, but it just kept coming. I sat as close to the front entrance as I could so I could look out through the glass door and keep an eye on the weather. My waitress was sympathetic to my plight but after a couple hours we both started to feel a little awkward about it. I ordered a soda and sat at the bar for what felt like a couple more hours. The Ravens fans reached a collective rock bottom and went home. After that there was no competition for seats in the restaurant, so it really didn't matter if I stayed longer, but just then I realized it was getting dark outside. I was still deep within the thickly built suburban ring of the city with no map and no idea where I was going to hide for the night.

I thanked the waitress, tipped her as well as I could and resigned myself to an evening of slogging through the downpour. Night fell quickly and I found myself walking through miles of suburbs by the light of street lamps. I had always made a point of finding a place to camp before it actually got dark because it is just easier and safer to do it that way. The hedge in front of the church in Milford, Connecticut, and the dog-infested suburban yard in the northeastern suburbs of Baltimore stood out as prime examples of the terrible camping spots I would have to settle for if I let the sun set on me before settling down for the night.

Alas, there was not so much as a crevice for me to hide in anywhere in Baltimore's southern burbs, so I walked on into the wet night for hours. At first there were sidewalks, but then they ended and I had to stumble through the muck on the shoulders of the streets. One of the main reasons to avoid walking after dark is that passing motorists are no longer able to see you, so you are much more likely to get run over. On a rainy night, visibility is reduced even more. Luckily, I did manage to avoid getting hit by cars, and keeping that danger in mind made it easier to accept the relatively less dangerous fate of getting splashed every time the passing cars hit a puddle. I also came to appreciate the rain for its role in washing off the mud and oil that the cars would splash onto me.

Throughout this insanity, I kept my hope alive with a comforting idea. If I just kept going, I would eventually reach the Patapsco River. There would be a bridge and beneath that bridge I would at last be able to take shelter from the rain. Following that hope, I made it all the way across the sprawling suburb of Lansdowne. Then finally, I reached the Patapsco River only to have my hopes inexorably crushed. To my despair, I found the flooding torrent of the river had risen to within inches of the bottom of the bridge! There would be no shelter. Things could only have been worse if I were a Ravens fan.

Thankfully, the bridge was built with wide breakdown lanes and the traffic had slowed, so I was able to cross it safely. Just across the river was a large field of grass and tall weeds where nothing had been built. It didn't count as a legitimate hiding place because I could see directly to a gas station and a line of houses across the street, but no one was out on such a rainy night and at that point I just didn't care anymore.

Sheets of rain washed over me as I set up the tent. It was still wet from the night before, so it didn't matter anyway. I was already soaked, but at least the tent would keep the raindrops from hitting my face directly while I tried to sleep. I crawled inside, laid down and then wondered if I was far enough from the river to avoid being drowned by rising flood waters. It was a disturbing thought, but I was tired and I managed to sleep anyway.

At dawn the rain had slowed to a drizzle and the river had not yet inundated the field where I slept. My sleeping bag was soaked, but I had no choice but to pack it up along with all my other wet gear and trudge on.

I followed the south bank of the flooded Patapsco for several miles until it curved away to the northwest. After that I followed the valley of a smaller stream called the Deep Run which was also in a spectacular stage of flooding. I had maps of both Howard and Anne Arundel counties, so I was able to follow a network of smaller roads through the forested parkland around the stream. The rain stopped early on, and by mid-morning the sky had brightened considerably. Then as the sun started to appear, the valley of the flooded stream filled with patches of fog. The autumn leaves and the flooding stream made a beautiful scene viewed through the mysterious mist, and it was another treat to see the thick clumps of fog from the outside whenever I would emerge into the sun.

I came to the end of the parkland around noon and shortly after that I passed by a huge series of prisons. Seeing a place where hundreds or even thousands of people were locked up gave me a sad type of appreciation for my own freedom.

The landscape of central Maryland is a patchwork of sprawling, cookie-cutter suburbs, light industrial warehouses, and lush forested parklands. Along the winding route I walked, each of these three types of landscape were represented in just about equal parts. The only straight lines between Baltimore and Washington are giant, limited-access highways. Walking the back roads, I was forced to meander to the left and right constantly so it took me a long time to travel a relatively short distance.

Late in the afternoon I crossed the Patuxent River which had spread out to cover the entire width of its lush flood plain. Ordinarily a minor river, the Patuxent was at least a half a mile wide when I saw it. On the other side of the great chocolate-milk river I was in Prince George's County, where I was once again wandering without a map. I foolishly assumed that some major road would take me right into Washington and within a few miles I was hopelessly lost in a winding pattern of suburban lanes. A thick wall of clouds had covered over the afternoon sun making it more difficult to tell directions. A damp, cold wind whipped up threatening another round of rain. I asked some people standing in their driveway for directions and they got me back on track, but I got lost again within an hour. By then it had started raining again, so anyone I might ask for directions was safely hidden inside their homes and cars. I wandered in circles through the featureless maze of suburban streets for several more hours getting wetter and wetter until finally the daylight started to fade from the sky.

It would be the third consecutive night of camping in the rain and my spirits were reaching an all-time low. To make matters worse, this new round of rain was much colder than the previous one. It actually hadn't occurred to me how pleasantly warm the last rain had been until now when I had a real bone-chilling rain to compare it to. It was the third week of October. Cold rain was by no means inappropriate for the season.

In the waning light of the evening, I found a stretch of forest that was being bulldozed to make way for more suburbs. I had to cross a great muddy field of twisted stumps and slash piles to get to it. If I had arrived a few days later, there may not have been anything left, but by some stroke of random timing I arrived before all the forest had been cleared.

The last of the forest was located downhill from the new clearing, so every flat space where I might set up my tent was oozing with mud that had flowed down from the gaping new scar. I discovered this muddy mess by stepping in it and sinking up to my ankles. I cursed out loud at the real-estate developers for adding yet another layer of discomfort to my ordeal. I thrashed around in the wet bushes looking for some decent place to bed down until it was almost dark. I don't remember how many times I stepped in ankle-deep mud. I just remember that when I finally did pick a spot and set up camp, the process of taking my shoes off involved getting mud all over both my hands as well.

My camping spot was better than an open mud pit, but not by much. As the night wore on and the rain intensified, I found a stream of water seeping through the tent floor, adding to the wetness that was seeping through the roof.

I slept very little that night. The extreme discomfort, hypothermia, and hopelessness all scratched at my brain and kept me awake for all but a couple hours. It was another full night of heavy rain, and this time it was within a few degrees of freezing. I was already soaked to the bone and wrapped inside a dripping-wet sleeping bag. Within half an hour of bedding down, my heart rate slowed and genuine hypothermia set in. I spent most of the night shivering uncontrollably in the fetal position. I did manage to fall asleep for an hour or so at one point only to wake up from a disturbing nightmare.

I dreamt that I was hiding in the bushes alongside of some industrial warehouse in the suburbs of DC. It was a post-apocalyptic scenario and the police/military were hunting me down using helicopters and infrared sensors. Clearly my subconscious was expressing some anxiety about walking into our nation's capital. Walking through impoverished ghettos was old hat to me at that point, but what about walking through the enemy's official headquarters? To some extent I know that Washington DC is just a figurehead. The real powerful bad guys are located in secret compounds, mansions, and yachts all over the world, but there is still a lot of power concentrated right in DC. I'm pretty sure real diabolical arch villains do lurk inside the Pentagon, Langley, the FBI headquarters and other such buildings. After walking over a thousand miles, it would be cowardly and impractical for me to skirt around Washington DC. I wasn't about to chicken out, but I have to admit I was more than a little nervous.

The nights are considerably longer than the days in the second half of October. Unable to sleep, and feeling somewhat delirious from the hypothermia, I started to worry that the morning light would somehow never come. As I waited and shivered, my mind filled with horrible paranoid delusions. I imagined the world's economic overlords capturing me and torturing me for their sadistic pleasure. I wondered if I might freeze to death before I even had a chance to be captured. It occurs to me now as I write this that I may not have even showed up on an infrared sensor that night if some evil commandos had actually tried to hunt me down.

After what felt like a hundred nights of cold rain, I finally decided I had waited long enough. I decided the only hope for survival was to get up and start moving. Once my muscles started to work, my heart would start pumping my blood around and my body would find its warmth again. At least that was the plan.

It took me an excruciatingly long time to pack up because my fingers weren't really working. Even just turning my flashlight on was tricky, and anything with a zipper was an almost insurmountable challenge. I thought I was already at the limit of coldness, but once I got outside the tent, I discovered that it was even colder to feel the icy rain pelting right onto my skin and clothing. I did eventually get all my gear packed up though and then I managed to hoist my heavily water-logged pack up onto my shoulders.

Instead of backtracking though the deep mud of the new clear cut, I decided to wade right through the raging stream at the bottom of the hill and bushwhack through the forest on the other side. I'm not sure why I was possessed by such a crazy urge. I just remember feeling certain that the city lay in that direction and it didn't make sense to backtrack. I waded through the rushing thigh-deep water and emerged with all the mud washed off my shoes. Then I had to stumble up a steep slope with no trail by the dim light of my flashlight. The going was slow and treacherous. My feet kept sliding backwards on the saturated ground while I fought with both arms to push wet branches and vines out of the way.

If I had been in any significant stretch of woods, I probably would have expended myself quickly, collapsed and died. Luckily for me, the forest was tiny. Before long I popped out into someone's back yard, and by the time I got there I was already warming up from the exertion. I walked around their house and out onto the street where I started wandering in random directions. Once again I was hopelessly lost in the suburbs of DC, and now it was completely dark and everyone who might help me was asleep. At least I was moving.

Out on the roads the volume of traffic was steadily increasing, and after about an hour a faint glow of natural light started to trickle into the grey sky. At last, the longest night of my life was coming to an end. In my mind's eye, I envisioned a diner where I could sit under the shelter of a roof and order a hot breakfast. I set about wandering in all directions looking for it, but I never found my mythical diner.

For some reason it seemed like I wasn't in the suburbs anymore. Instead I was in a wide open region of forests and farms with random clusters of big ominous warehouses every so often. At one point I came upon a warehouse that looked disturbingly like the one in my recent paranoid nightmare. A sense of panic set in as I realized that I must have gotten turned around in the dark and wandered back out into the countryside. Was that even possible? The suburbs of DC stretch on for days and connect with the suburbs of Baltimore to form a true megalopolis. Surely it would take more than a few hours of wandering in the dark to find the real open spaces outside of the DC urban area.

Luckily I was too tired to really panic, so I just kept plodding along, sticking as close to one consistent direction as I could on the winding maze of roads. Eventually I came to a security checkpoint where a man in a little booth was screening every vehicle that came by. Apparently it was some kind of secure government area where the employees had to show their identification to gain entrance. One by one the vehicles would stop, show their ID, and then the gate-keeper would raise the red and white striped gate for their vehicle to pass under.

The weird thing was that I was already inside the secure area, so I had to approach the gate from the backside. For a minute I wondered if I would be in trouble for trespassing in a restricted area, but I was too cold, tired, and hungry to worry much about it. The man in the booth could tell me where I was and maybe even tell me where I could get breakfast. At the time, those considerations overrode all my paranoid fears of the government.

The gatekeeper turned out to be a friendly young guy and the land I had been wandering around was the National Agricultural Research Center. I told him I hadn't climbed any fences or snuck through any gates. I had just gotten lost and ended up there, but he wasn't too worried about me breaching security. He did check my ID and made a note of our encounter, but he said most of the back entrances to the NARC facility were not gated, so he didn't doubt that I had wandered in there by mistake. He pointed me towards the city, but he didn't know of any diners anywhere near where he worked. In consolation he gave me a granola bar out of his lunch box.

As the morning wore on, the rain slowed to a drizzle. I got some hot "food" at a gas station and ate under the shelter that covered the gas pumps. I spent the whole morning lost, looking for some place where I might steal a map. In the process I wandered through the suburbs of Beltsville, College Park, Greenbelt, and Berwyn Heights. If you look at a map you will notice that those places are not all in a straight line. I truly went on a grand walking tour of northern Prince George's County.

At long last I got a map from a Staples chain store and right after that the sun came out. Using the map, I found my way quickly to the University of Maryland campus and checked my e-mail. Having just dropped out of the liberal reform sector two years prior, I still had a lot of friends in Washington DC. Sure enough, several of them had responded to my e-mails and were eagerly awaiting my visit. That meant I would be sleeping in dry places for the next few nights. My spirits soared.

From the UM campus, I followed a bicycle trail through a beautiful park along the Northeast Branch of the Anacostia River. Before long the river widened into a tidal estuary surrounded by a broad swath of grassland. It was just past the middle of the afternoon and the sunshine felt so warm and pleasant that I sat down for a while to admire the view. I would be staying with an old friend in Northeast DC that night, and it was still a couple hours before she would be getting home from work. Since I needed to kill a couple of hours anyway, I unrolled some of my wet gear to dry in the grass and sat there soaking up the sun and the lovely view of the Anacostia River tidal flats.

26. APARTHEID

As it turned out, I was only able to spend one night at my friend's house because she was going through terrible drama with her husband at the time. He was out of town when I arrived, but he was coming home the next day, and I had to disappear before he returned. Not only that, but we had to pretend I had never been there at all or he would be suspicious and she would suffer. It was a sad situation to witness, but it was still great to see her and it was a blessing to get to use her dryer. After that I spent a couple days at an anarchist collective house in Northeast DC.

Washington DC is a relatively young and very unique city compared to its East Coast neighbors. It didn't grow up organically around some trade route like every other city in the region. It was actually designed by urban planners and built from scratch with the intention of being the nation's new capitol. The street plan was laid out all at once by an artist and it is far more artistic than functional. I have friends from the DC area who claim that the city is really easy to navigate, but they are crazy.

Beneath all the art, DC is just a big grid, and that would be functional if that's all there was to it. Unfortunately, then they added a thick, fractured pattern of diagonal streets with some radiating out from the capitol while others run at perpendicular angles, and still others run at totally random angles. Some of them transect the entire city while others are only a couple blocks long. As if that weren't complicated enough, then they put large, artistic traffic circles in most of the major intersections, designated many of the streets one-way, and put tree-filled islands down the middle of most of the two-way streets so you can never make a left turn into driveways or parking lots. It's a hillbilly's driving nightmare on par with Boston or Pittsburgh. Of course it wasn't so bad on foot, so I shouldn't complain.

I found the architecture in DC far more interesting than Baltimore or Philly where I had just come from. Unlike the flat-fronted tenements farther north, all the houses in DC seem to have some projecting feature like a hexagonal turret or a series of balconies with gorgeous wrought-iron railings. At the very least, they would have a three-sided column on the front with windows projecting out beyond the front of the building. Like Philly and Baltimore, most of the houses are made of brick, but in DC the bricks are all different colors, as if they have been sourced from a variety of different places. On any given block there aren't usually two houses the same color right in a row. Some houses are even made out of different colors of bricks with the different colors arranged in artistic patterns. Most of them have some sort of decorative brick-work along the top edges, and many even have beautiful tile mosaics inlaid on the front.

Some of the historic buildings have been torn down and replaced with ugly public housing projects, but even in the ghettos a lot of beautiful architecture remains. Most of the streets are shaded by big beautiful trees of all exotic breeds and the whole city is marbled with large and small patches of forested parkland. Obviously the urban planners who laid out the city had a sense that forested parkland improves the quality of life for urban dwellers. Their vision seems to have spread out from there because the Maryland suburbs are also full of big gorgeous parks.

In many ways, I'm sure the DC metro area is a wonderful place to live. It was built with more forethought and intention than any other city in the nation, and I'm sure that's due to its history of strategic significance.

Throughout the first half of the 1800's, the North and the South became increasingly hostile towards one another. The North held economic power over the South and they were also repeatedly accused of holding too much power over the government. The location of the old capitol in Philadelphia was seen as proof that the North had more access to government power. Eventually politicians decided to settle the matter by building a new capitol city in a more neutral location and they named it in honor of the recently deceased George Washington. The border of Virginia and Maryland was the most practical dividing line between North and South, so the federal government appropriated a ten-by-ten mile square of land spanning the Potomac River which forms that border. Only about a quarter of that land lay on the Virginia side of the river, but Virginia refused to cede the land, so now the District of Columbia has a Potomac River-shaped bite out of its southwestern edge.

In modern times the border is purely semantic as the Virginia side of the river is lined with countless government buildings including the Pentagon. That's the headquarters of US military which appears to be the most powerful head of the hydra (I mean, branch of the government.) I doubt the military pays any taxes to the state of Virginia for their giant cult-inspired building, but I guess it's neither here nor there. Most people in northern Virginia work for the government anyway along with most people in the adjacent region of Maryland. Four million people call the DC suburbs home and they are some of the most affluent suburbs anywhere in the country. Some commute into the city for work, but thousands more work at outlying military bases, bureaucratic offices, or other federal facilities like the National Agricultural Research Center.

According to the census, only about 600,000 people live inside the city of Washington, but the real number is probably much higher. When I walked through almost twenty years ago, the vast majority of DC citizens were poor. (Someone has to feed and clean up after all those bourgeois bureaucrats.) The city's servant class lived in a vast ghetto region that covered the whole eastern half of the district and a large swath of adjacent Prince Georges County.

The census has a long history of undercounting poor citizens. That demographic of people has been traumatized by routine police harassment and surveillance, so they are generally uncooperative with the census. They see it as just another way for the authorities to keep tabs on them, and in some cases they're probably right. They hide from census workers and refuse to answer questions even when they are found.

Meanwhile some racist or classist census workers know that if they undercount "minority" groups, the government can use those numbers to cut off funding to services like schools and fire departments in the poor districts. Put these two factors together and only a fraction of poor Americans get counted. It is an integral part of capitalist culture to pretend that prosperity is widespread and everyone is benefitting from it. When the census fails to count millions of poor people, it generates the statistics to prove that myth. I honestly believe there are far more peasants inside this empire than anyone realizes.

Certainly, there were more than half a million people in eastern DC in 2003, but I have to use the past tense, because the geography of the city has changed dramatically since then. In the last twenty years, the ghetto has been pushed all the way out of Northeast DC and into Prince Georges County, Maryland. I'm sure most of those poor folks have interesting stories to tell about the conditions that forced them to move out of the district, and I hope someone has made an effort to write some of them down.

I actually witnessed one such story unfolding back when I was there, and I want to share it with you, but I have to give this caveat first. The situation I'm about to describe resulted in legal procedures in court and I don't want my writing to be used in any way as testimony in that case. The only reason I feel comfortable sharing this story at all is because this all went down more than eighteen years ago, so it's safe to assume that the case has been closed for a long time. However, if for some reason the DCPD tries to use any of my writing as evidence, I want to make it clear that I am pulling all this from eighteen-year-old memories. If anything I say deviates at all from the official record, that would be the result of my memory deteriorating. I will also change the defendant's name for an added level of security.

The folks I stayed with in Northeast were young activists who had made friends with a number of their neighbors. One evening we were all sitting at the kitchen counter talking when one of the neighbors came to the door in an obvious state of distress and seeking help. His landlord had just evicted him under orders from the police. They had taken all his belongings and thrown them in a giant dumpster. He was a mechanic, well known for helping people fix their cars, and they had thrown some of his tools in there.

Right away one of my hosts realized that they should write down the story for use in his legal case. They went and got a notebook and asked him to repeat all the details he could think of, pausing between each one so they could write it down. The whole process took well over an hour. Once again, if anything I write here contradicts that transcript, then my account is the inaccurate one.

We'll say the man's name was Duyen and he was an immigrant from Jamaica. He was very dark-skinned and he still spoke with a thick accent, but he had been in that neighborhood of DC for many years and he had gone through all the processes to become a US citizen. He was a well-liked auto mechanic in his mid-fifties who had no record of criminal activity and no criminal inclinations. The trouble was, the cops were after Duyen's son and they couldn't find him. They tried to enlist Duyen to help them track down and catch his son, but he refused. He didn't believe that his son was guilty of any crime. He said he raised his son not to be intimidated by bullies and so the cops just hated him. Duyen said the police had been persecuting his son for years for no real reason other than to establish dominance over him. Duyen refused to cooperate with that and so they had taken up persecuting him.

Over the course of several days, their threats and tactics had been escalating to the point where they raided his house, took his gun and then took him into custody to charge him with illegal possession of firearms. They had also pulled some strings to get Duyen evicted and have his apartment emptied into a dumpster while he was in custody. After that, they released him and he returned to find his home destroyed. He kept the paperwork for his gun right with the gun in a special cupboard, but when he went to get it, he found the paperwork was gone. That was particularly distressing to Duyen and my hosts had to help soothe his emotions a bit before they could get a real concise testimony.

I got the impression that armed self-defense was a really significant part of Jamaican culture and that Duyen had submitted to really invasive levels of bureaucratic scrutiny and years of red tape to be allowed to own a gun. I'm sure it is a real bureaucratic ordeal for anyone to own a gun in the District of Columbia, let alone a Jamaican immigrant, but after years of effort, Duyen had finally jumped through enough hoops and demonstrated enough obedience to be allowed to own a gun in the city. The injustice of being charged with a crime for owning that very same gun was just too much. It seemed like he wanted to be furious about it but he couldn't because he was just too scared. Without his paperwork, he felt incredibly vulnerable and he kept asking my hosts if they thought he would be sent to prison.

I certainly wish I knew what happened to poor Duyen, but I never followed up on any of this. After his interview was fully transcribed, one person called a lawyer to start making arrangements and another person went with Duyen to explore the possibility of rescuing his things from the dumpster and storing them somewhere safe. No one asked me to help with anything, nor could I think of anything helpful I might do. I just sat there dumbfounded and bore witness. I was advised not to write about the incident in my zine, so I didn't even make a diary entry about it.

Even now, I still worry that I might be doing something wrong by sharing this story, but I think it's really important for stories like this to come out. The cops would never deal with a rich White person the way they dealt with Duyen. They follow a completely different code of conduct and pattern of behavior depending on the race and social class of the people they are dealing with. It is a glaring case of inequality and stark illustration of how the oppression of poor and non-White people is carried out by the police. I mean, maybe I randomly stumbled into an extraordinary situation like Forrest Gump, but I doubt it. I think I probably just witnessed an average day in Northeast DC. Probably the only thing extraordinary about Duyen's situation was that there was a nearby house full of more privileged people who were willing to help when he came to them in need.

The Apartheid government of South Africa was recognized worldwide as a flagrant violator of human rights and an inappropriately racist form of government that had to be changed. Basically, the government served as an institution to keep Black people separate from White people, and to impose a lower social status on the Black people. I have read that the defining characteristic of the Apartheid system was its enforcement of two completely separate codes of written law, one for Blacks and one for Whites.

Here in America, we only have one written code that supposedly applies to everyone equally, but if most of the police still follow an un-written code of conduct that treats Black people in a fundamentally different way than White people, are we not still living under an Apartheid system of government? The only difference I can see is that the South Africans were honest about it while we pretend it's not happening.

27. CAVE MAN TIMES

I had a best friend when I was a kid. Somebody nicknamed us Zog and Thang after the cavemen from the Far Side cartoon, so I will call him Zog now to hide his identity. Back in the desert when I fished with the cub scouts and we all listened to Christian tell fantastic stories, Zog was another tall kid who was really into maps just like me. Not many kids are interested in geography, so when two of us find each other, conversations can get spectacularly nerdy. We mostly studied geography in our own time and then talked about it when we'd see each other, but we did invent a couple board games that involved maps.

Mostly though, I remember riding bicycles through the desert with him. We had pedal-powered dirt bikes and we knew all the trails to all the secret corners of the undeveloped desert land beyond our little half-built suburb. There was an old quarry with dangerous high cliffs to climb on. There were abandoned old cabins to explore, mountains to climb, rocks to throw, and rusted old cars and appliances to throw them at. We often played games imagining that we were some kind of scouts on reconnaissance missions beyond the limits of safe territory. The desert became outer space and we were the last two dependable fighter pilots left on the good-guys team.

We were daring and mischievous and we often caused minor emergencies that we had to resolve ourselves or else face the anger of some adult. We each did our time being grounded and we each ended up in the hospital a couple times, but mostly we managed to solve our own problems and spare our parents from the emotional strain. Repeatedly we got ourselves out of dumb situations by using spontaneous clever ideas, heroic strength, or just by running like hell. It was through this process that I built up a level of trust and confidence in my best friend that I have never experienced since. When I hear rap songs about gangsters who know they can depend on their brothers, I think of my old best friend and it makes me miss him.

Unfortunately, we both had the kind of parents who move a lot. His family moved him to Europe the year before my family moved me to Maine. We did keep in touch for a while, but some time in college our communication trailed off. My parents kept in touch with his parents though and that is how I came to find Zog living in Washington DC.

He had a nice apartment on the top floor of a building on the edge of Georgetown, an expensive part of Northwest DC where most of the tenants are trendy young people. Georgetown was actually a pre-existing town that got swallowed up when the federal government created the District of Columbia, so its street pattern doesn't match the weird artistic design of the rest of the city. Zog's apartment was several stories above the ground, and it had an outdoor patio with a view of the Kennedy Performing Arts Center, the river, and Virginia beyond.

I arrived in the evening to find Zog cooking me supper and quite happy to see me. The feeling was mutual, but within ten minutes of catching up on our recent lives, we discovered a most bizarre twist of fate. Zog had studied economics in college, and then set out to right the world by fighting for something he called "corporate accountability." He worked for a non-profit that campaigned for better enforcement to make sure corporations didn't short the investors on their payments. His theory was that if shareholders weren't always getting ripped off by corrupt CEO's and state bureaucracy, then the wealth of corporations would flood the land with prosperity and all boats would rise. His understanding of economics was pure trickle-down so he was an outspoken advocate of globalized "Free Trade."

Here I was marching down the coast, waving my flag and trying to rally a revolution against the entrenched powers that were enforcing Free Trade on the people of the Earth. We were still two of the finest scouts, but we had joined enemy teams. I guess if you embark upon an odyssey, you should expect to face at least a few painful paradoxes and heart-wrenching moral dilemmas.

We sat down to eat and debate economics in earnest. Sparks flew and the debate raged on for most of the night. We managed to keep the discussion polite for the most part, but it was still an extremely emotional situation. Here were two people who had built up a profound amount of trust having their first serious disagreement ever. Feeling momentarily baffled, it took me several hours to accept that my enemies had really gotten Zog. I could tell he was feeling the exact same way. At one point, overwhelmed by frustration, he raised his voice and shouted, "I believe in the Free Market." That bold pronouncement burned into my brain and now, two decades later, it is the only fragment of actual dialogue I can remember from that night.

The actual theory of the Free Market is not a bad idea at all. The trouble is that the world's most diabolical villains have appropriated those words and used them as a new label for imperialism. Mercenary armies, enforcing the agenda of the Free Trade economy massacred tens of thousands of people across Latin America in the sixties, seventies and eighties. In Argentina, more than 30,000 people were "disappeared," and many of those people were high-school kids. In Indonesia, General Suharto slaughtered 100,000 people for the same agenda, and there were massacres in Africa and the Middle-East too. It was a world-wide, creed-based genocide, meaning people were singled out and executed based on their beliefs and their behavior. Basically anyone who stood up for equality, freedom for the poor, human rights or a healthy environment was hunted down and killed. Those people were identified by their ideological opposition to the Free Market agenda, and by their courage to stand up for their beliefs. Once the bravest people were eliminated, the rest of the people were much easier to control.

The victims of this genocide were people just like me. If I had lived in Argentina in the 1970's I would have been killed. But Zog didn't want me to be killed. He didn't mean me any harm at all. Clearly when he said the words "Free Market," he meant something totally different. This misunderstanding originates from the study of economics. To explain the significance of economics, I have to go all the way back to prehistoric times, so make yourself comfortable.

Let's talk about old Zog and Thang back in cave-man times, communicating in grunts and holding fish over the fire with their bare hands. Before we invented technology, humans were stupid right? We lived short, brutal lives, always struggling just to survive. The human population remained small for eons because life was so difficult that most of us died before we reached breeding age. Anyone who didn't get eaten by a large predator or starve to death was doomed to die in violent competition with other humans for scarce resources. That's the popular understanding of where we came from as a species, but I'm pretty sure it's completely false.

Recent fossil discoveries suggest that the earliest humans appeared about 240,000 years ago. The size of our skulls has not changed since then, so it makes sense to assume that the brains inside them were just as complex and effective as our modern brains. It is actually stupid to believe that ancient humans were stupid. They definitely didn't spend any time staring at electrified screens like we do. Nor did they spend any time trying to figure out ways to make money and get ahead of their competitors.

In fact, mountains of anthropological data suggest that ancient people cooperated with each other a great deal more than they competed. Times of drought or other food shortages probably did bring ancient tribes into violent conflict with one another once in a while, but there is no evidence that they spent very much time preparing for such conflicts. Weapons that were specifically designed for fighting other humans didn't appear until very recently in our history. There are also no pyramids or any other big monuments that would indicate the existence of kings or other authority figures having power over large numbers of people. The first weapons of war, and the first mega-monuments don't start to appear until about 6,000 years ago. That implies that for the vast majority of human history, people lived in relatively egalitarian cultures, cooperating with each other, and making decisions as a group.

The artifacts that we do see from the long prehistoric period are mostly just tools that facilitated an easy lifestyle, children's toys, and artwork that appears to have been made for spiritual purposes. Ancient humans were very spiritual. Many were polytheistic, worshipping gods in the forms of animals, plants, mountains, the moon, the sun, and other natural phenomena. It was also very common to perceive God as a loving mother, generously nurturing humans and all the other species of life. Nature provided everything that ancient humans needed to live comfortable lives, and expressions of gratitude and appreciation for nature were the central theme of all the ancient religions.

By cooperating and sharing nature's bounty, ancient human cultures assured a high standard of living for everyone, not just for a privileged fraction. Many modern people assume that the ancient people failed to develop higher levels of technology because they weren't smart enough, but that is not the only possible explanation. I think it's more likely that ancient humans had no motivation to develop higher technology because their lifestyles gave them so little to be dissatisfied about. In the absence of competition and selfish hoarding, there was almost always plenty of food to go around.

We have only found evidence of long, neat rows of planted crops intentionally isolated from the rest of the ecosystem in the last 10,000 years, but that's a very narrow definition of agriculture. It's hard to imagine that ancient humans weren't planting the forests full of extra fruit and nut trees, burning off grasslands to keep them open for large herds of wild game, and practicing a myriad of other less obvious methods to increase their food supply. With food and other resources so abundant to come by, many anthropologists have theorized that the average ancient human experienced a great deal more leisure time than the average modern human does now.

These concepts make perfect sense to me, but I can imagine a skeptical person would have two major questions. Firstly, if ancient humans were so smart, and they had so much free time, but they didn't use their big brains to develop high technology, then what did they do with all that free time? Wouldn't they have developed technology out of sheer boredom?

Well, I don't think so. Ancient humans lived in harmony with nature. Their complex brains were perfectly adapted to absorb huge volumes of information about all the wild plants, animals, insects and fungi around them, as well as weather patterns, and all the other relevant Earth sciences. Our modern myriad of technological devices is probably roughly equivalent to the myriad of techniques that ancient people developed for interacting with nature, not only for utilitarian purposes, but for entertainment as well. Just to give one example, the Bedouin people named every single star in the sky, including some that we can only see with the use of a telescope.

Beyond that, humans developed spoken language very early, leading to infinite conversations, storytelling, and all the other benefits of a highly satisfying and stimulating social life. Surely, they also developed whole cultures of music, dance, art, games, spiritual rituals, and complex cuisines. Perhaps most importantly, ancient people spent a great deal more time raising their children than we do now. Ancient children got so much attention from the adults in their lives, that they were fully grown and ready to function as adults themselves by the time they reached sexual maturity in their early teens.

This discussion of child-rearing leads to the second obvious question that my skeptic should be bound to ask. If life was so easy, why didn't the human population explode into the massive size that we see nowadays?

Well, it's not likely that men were any less horny back then than we are now, but ancient women understood the value of small families. They knew that they would not be able to give each child enough attention if they had too many, so they learned which wild plants and fungi they could use as contraceptives and abortifacients, and they kept the size of their families small on purpose.

I suspect a lot of skeptics might find this idea hard to believe, so I want to digress just a little bit here and cite some of the sources of information that have led me to draw this conclusion. My most significant printed source is a textbook called, *Saharasia: The 4,000BCE Origins of Child Abuse, Sex Repression, Warfare and Social Violence*. While this is just one book, it contains work from literally hundreds of different anthropologists, and it was compiled by a fairly large group of editors.

There is also a great book on this subject called *The Old Way*, by Elizabeth Marshall Thomas. While Thomas' book is largely about her study of an indigenous African culture in the mid 1900's, it demonstrates emphatically that we can learn a great deal about the ancient cultures who no longer exist by asking people from the remnants of tribal cultures that still exist today. The San people, who Thomas studied, claimed to be living the same way that their ancestors lived since the dawn of time, and the anthropological record supports their claim.

North America is home to hundreds of ancient cultures who survived until very recent times. It has not really been feasible to practice their cultural methods since the European and American empires conquered them in the last several centuries, but there are still thousands of people who have been raised with detailed descriptions of these cultures passed down from their elders.

The oral testimony of these surviving native people has honestly been the main source of information that has led me to my understanding of ancient cultures. Literally every surviving Indian tribe I know of has a strong faction who insist that their ancestral methods of survival were easier and more fulfilling than our modern, high-tech, hierarchal methods. It is less common to talk about sexual habits, but I have also heard from a wide range of different tribes that women were allowed to control their own reproductive processes. Every region had its own types of medicinal plants, or other methods of birth control. That is what kept the human population small and stable, and the quality of life for the average individual so high.

It turns out that almost every region of the planet has the remains of ancient cultures who followed this same pattern. There have been more than a thousand different tribes from all corners of the globe who have tried to explain these same basic concepts to our anthropologists. It's hard to imagine that they have conspired with each other to trick us since they speak more than a thousand different languages and they are too geographically isolated to even make contact with each other. Their message has failed to work its way into our public consciousness only because we have a willfully ignorant culture.

Ancient humans lived easier and more fulfilling lives than most of us can even imagine, but something went dreadfully wrong about 6,000 years ago. That's when male warlords took over and invented the culture of rigid hierarchy. Rather than producing its own resources, this culture gained a large percentage of what it needed by raiding other tribes and stealing theirs. As soon as one tribe went down this path, all of its neighbors had to develop their own hierarchy of warriors or else be conquered and enslaved, so the warlike culture quickly spread across the entire planet.

The majority of women opposed this cultural shift because they didn't want to see their children exposed to the dangers of war any more often than was absolutely necessary. Because of their opposition, women were removed from all leadership roles and demoted to the bottom of the hierarchy. The warlords wanted to breed as many children as they could to replace the soldiers they lost on the battlefield, so they outlawed the use of birth-control techniques. Women who tried to maintain knowledge and practice of those techniques were labelled witches and executed, so the knowledge died out. That's when the runaway growth of the human population began.

As the number of mouths to feed suddenly multiplied, the traditional food sources were quickly used up. The Garden of Eden was literally devoured. The ensuing famines led to a sudden flourish of advances in agricultural techniques and the technologies to support them. The health of the average human plummeted at the same time that our numbers grew and became concentrated in cities. This made us ripe targets for contagious diseases in a way that our species had never known, and of course, that inspired us to take a much more serious interest in medical science.

As if the natural austerity caused by overpopulation wasn't enough, the new hierarchal culture imposed all sorts of additional, unnecessary austerity on everyone. A pecking-order was established, and it became the cultural norm for anyone with any rank to pass on violent abuse to the people in the ranks below them. Of course, women and children bore the worst of this abuse.

Maniacal, self-obsessed emperors would horde generations worth of wealth that they could never even use themselves, and they would keep those resources under lock and key even as millions of their own people starved. Many emperors would refuse to relinquish control of their horded wealth even after they died. Instead, they would force armies of slaves to build great monuments where the resources would be buried with the dead emperors and never be used. The Egyptian Pyramids and other such monuments may be the "Wonders of the World," but they are also monuments to the lowest levels of mental and cultural illness our species has ever sunk to.

Life became a relentless nightmare for almost everyone living inside the empires. This situation would not have lasted very long if it were not accompanied by a system of myths and philosophies that made it seen natural and unavoidable.

The original warlords were the most competent and dominant men on the battlefield, but most of them probably weren't clever enough to create the mythology and philosophical framework that would justify their domination. Luckily for them, a very clever class of sycophantic ass-kissers stepped forward to volunteer for that task. The warlords and emperors saw the value of these men's contribution and rewarded them with power and luxury second only to the rulers themselves. These inventors of mythology became the original clergymen, and their ideas laid the framework for the original patriarchal religions.

Suddenly God became an angry, jealous, and dominant man, punishing all those who disobeyed him, favoring a chosen people over all others, and rewarding the obedient only after they died. All the behaviors that a person would have to live by to earn this reward contributed directly to the agenda of the emperor. At the same time, nature lost its divinity, and became an enemy to be mistrusted, dominated, and modified as much as possible for the progress of human civilization. The same famines and diseases that were actually brought about by the change in human culture could be blamed on nature and used to justify this new world-view. This was also the origin of the myth that ancient humans were stupid, lived in caves, and struggled to survive.

Each successive empire used up its available resources too quickly and collapsed in very short spans of time. Unfortunately, the patriarchal philosophy survived, so basically every time the forest grew back, a new empire would emerge to make use of it.

At present, human culture is still stuck in this cycle of rising and falling empires, characterized by a hierarchal class structure where a powerful few horde excess resources and wield control over a huge, suffering majority. However, the structure of the hierarchy, and the philosophy that justify it have both evolved a little bit in the last 500 years. A new philosophy called science has pushed ahead of patriarchal religion, and a new economic system called capitalism has come to replace battlefield dominance as the method by which emperors are chosen.

For several millennia, the emperors would pass their crowns on to their own male children, but it was rare for any of these men to produce a son who was as competent or as dominant as he was. For these weakening dynasties to be overthrown, a new competitor would literally have to defeat the emperor's army on the battlefield, and kill the emperor.

Capitalism made it possible to transfer wealth and power smoothly to the most competitive person of the time, regardless of what family they were born into. A billionaire can still pass their wealth onto their heirs, but if those heirs are not competitive enough, they will lose their money and power and descend in rank. Capitalism makes every rank within the hierarchy subject to this competition, so in theory, anyone who is competitive enough can ascend in rank and improve their lot in life. This system has actually created considerably more freedom for a large number of people who used to be hopelessly stuck among the oppressed masses. At the same time, Capitalism has strengthened the basic hierarchal structure of our culture by ensuring that the weak and incompetent leaders are quickly replaced.

Science maintained the view of nature as a mistrustful force to be modified for the progress of human culture, but it dealt a significant blow to the concept of a dominant male god who would punish disobedient humans. Without this component of the philosophy, there is nothing to justify hierarchy. This development left open the possibility for humans to question hierarchy and to consider equality as an alternative.

Unfortunately, the same type of clever sycophants still exist in modern times, and they have come forward with a new philosophy that justifies inequality. The business tycoons at the top of the social pyramid have recognized the value of their contribution, and they have elevated these ass-kissing philosophers to the rank of clergy. The new religion is called economics. The priests whose job is to control the way we think are called economists, and

God has been renamed "The Economy." Strict obedience to the Economy will be rewarded with prosperity at some vague time in the future, and only the economists are qualified to tell us what the Economy really needs. As it turns out, every single one of the behaviors that the economists recommend are precisely in line with the agenda of the most powerful business tycoons.

One of the main functions of the religion of economics is to justify the hierarchal class structure that allows those business tycoons to horde more wealth than they could ever use by exploiting the work of lower-class people. Some economists will insist that it's literally impossible to structure a society any other way, and even if it were possible, it would cause a landslide of ruinous negative consequences. Other economists claim that the ability for strong competitors to gain rank within the hierarchy is essentially the same thing as equality. There is also a faction who acknowledge that equality is actually desirable, but they argue that it can not be achieved until the poorest classes of people make the necessary sacrifices. The day that we transition to an equal society always remains out of reach in the future, and we can't ever seem to get there because the poor are always demanding higher wages, more welfare, and the like.

If a lay person like me were to suggest that no one needs to be rich or poor, and that we could all be equal instead, it is the economist's job to explain why I am wrong. In his explanation, the economist should reference obscure theories and speak in incomprehensible jargon that only other economists can understand. That way I will understand that he is the expert and I am just an idealistic fool.

My friend Zog was a firm believer in the principles of the "Free Market." This concept was first described by an English philosopher in the 1600's named Adam Smith, but the most eloquent spokesman for Free Trade was an American economist in the 1900's named Milton Friedman. His vision was that if every human were allowed to compete and work exclusively for their own self-interest, we could eventually bring about something close to a utopia. No one is obligated to buy anything they don't want, or work for anyone they don't want to work for, because so many other alternatives exist. Employers could not mistreat their workers because of competition from other employers who would treat the workers better. As Friedman said, "No exchange will take place unless both parties do benefit from it. Cooperation is thereby achieved without coercion." He argued that government was only necessary to stop people from breaking the contracts that they entered into voluntarily with other people, and to protect us from crimes like murder, theft, and so on. Any other interference from government would reduce the freedom of the individual and bring about undesirable consequences.

Friedman was in the prime of his career during the Cold War when the United States was trying to block the spread of communism around the world. The stated goal of communism is to bring about equality among humans, but the proposed method is to use government power to force that equality on the citizens. All that freedom to choose the course of your own life goes out the window in communism. The way I think of equality, it essentially means freedom for everyone, not just for a percentage of people who are lucky enough to win the competition. In theory, maybe communism could bring about a form of equality where no one has freedom, but why would we strive for that? Despite its claims of enforcing equality, communism is still a system of centralized control with a ruling class of powerful decision makers.

The more control government takes over people's lives, the more mistakes it makes. First of all, in any hierarchy, capitalist, communist, or otherwise, it is usually the worst people with the worst intentions who work the hardest to get themselves into the positions of power. Even if good people with the best of intentions were in charge of the government, it would be impossible for them to anticipate all the unique situations that come up in people's lives, so any important choices they make for disempowered citizens are going to bring about unintended, harmful consequences. As Friedman says, "The characteristic feature of action through political channels is that it tends to require or enforce substantial conformity. The great advantage of the market, on the other hand, is that it permits wide diversity." I agree with Friedman on this point and on the points that I quoted and paraphrased above. I think capitalism is a highly flawed economic system that we should strive to improve upon, but it probably stands a better chance of improving the human condition than communism. Socialism is just a hybrid of the two.

Unfortunately, the U.S. State Department latched onto Friedman's ideas as a mandate to overthrow democratically-elected governments all over the Third World and replace them with puppet dictators, usually called "presidents." They started by targeting governments that showed communist or socialist tendencies, but once they got on a roll, they went on to overthrow almost every Third World government who prioritized the needs of their own people above the agenda of First World corporations.

First World corporations wanted free metals, free sugar, fruit, drugs, free labor, and free petroleum. If they couldn't get these things for free, they would pay, but they were never willing to pay a fair price. Everything had to be cheap enough that they could sell it cheaply to First World consumers and still make enormous profits. They needed dictators to oppress their citizens so thoroughly that the people couldn't stop their resources from being stolen. And they got what they wanted throughout the second half of the twentieth century.

The United States empire stopped conquering and annexing the territory of other nations after Hawaii, but it installed dozens of puppet dictators who functioned exactly like colonial governors, oppressing the local people, and exporting as many discount resources as possible to the heart of the empire. Many of these regimes are still functioning that way to this day. That's why most Third World countries are still so poor and underdeveloped, and that's why so many people are trying to migrate here.

None of this was reported in the US media, because our media is all owned by the same companies that are profiting from it. The official story has always been that Free Trade is spreading freedom to the entire world. When we buy our coffee or our bananas, we are told that some of that money makes it all the way to the Third World workers who grew it and harvested it. It might not be much, but it's more money than they had before, and every little bit will help them catch up to our standard of living.

What we don't hear is that the Third World workers were all set with a nice standard of living until our puppet dictator drove them off of their land at gunpoint to make way for a banana plantation. They grew their own food and never owed rent to anyone before, but now they live in the city, so they need money. Some of them can get jobs exporting food, or manufacturing technological toys for First World consumers. The work is grueling and dangerous, and the pay is always just barely enough to survive, but it beats starvation. There are never enough jobs for everyone, so the weakest competitors do starve.

Most of the money our government sends away in "foreign aid" goes to build infrastructure specifically designed for First World corporations to export resources to the First World. That way they don't have to use their own capital to build the infrastructure, so they can make even higher profits.

The rest of the foreign aid money covers the dictators' expenses for weapons, ammunition, and mercenary soldiers.

Nothing about this situation resembles Milton Friedman's Free Market in any way. Friedman was always in favor of freedom above everything else. He would certainly try to persuade people not to choose communism over capitalism, but ultimately, he would prefer to let countries make their own mistakes and learn from them. He would never argue that any country should have their economy forcibly controlled by a foreign, colonial power. At least, that would not be consistent with his stated philosophy.

In practice, Milton Friedman was a loyal economist. He supported the First World imperial expansion by never uttering a word about it and he went to his grave pretending it wasn't happening.

Every Third World country has its class of people who see that they can gain rank in the hierarchy by kissing up to the economists and saying things that validate the party line. These people learn to speak English and volunteer themselves to preach the gospel of Free Trade. When American tourists travel to Third World countries, it is this type of person who they are most likely to meet. In this way, the truth can be hidden without even a conscious conspiracy to hide it. Opponents of the neo-colonial system have to be very careful what they say to strangers, because they are hunted by their own governments.

I realize this probably sounds like a crazy conspiracy theory to anyone who is unfamiliar with the subject. There are a lot of books and independent media sources you can look up to research this situation on your own. I recommend *The Shock Doctrine* by Naomi Klein, *Harvest of Empire* by Juan Gonzales, and *The CIA's Greatest Hits*, by John Zerzan. For a more succinct, and eloquent explanation than I could ever deliver, look up the song *Open Your Eyes* by Immortal Technique. There are many more good sources of information, but I don't need to recommend them all. There are millions of voices clamoring for this situation to be understood and resolved. As a First World citizen, you are unlikely to come across any of them by random chance, but they are pretty easy to find if you actually look for them.

If we could ever get control of our government, our top priority should be to fire all the people who think it's their business to control what people in other countries do. The Republicans are all freaked out about immigrants. If we let the Third World countries develop stable and prosperous economies, the immigrants will stop coming. The Democrats are all freaked out about global warming. How about if we produce things locally and stop shipping God-sized quantities of resources here from the far corners of the planet.

After sixty years of being clubbed by the shit end of the capitalist stick, it's reasonable to assume that a lot of Third World countries will want to give communism or socialism a try. We need to let them elect whatever kind of government they want. Every attempt at communism doesn't have to fail as badly as the Soviet Union did.

In 1978, the Nicaraguan Sandinistas overthrew their country's Spanish dictator, and attempted to set up the most liberatory form of government in modern history. They called themselves communists, but they developed such radical methods of decentralizing government power, and put so much faith in their average citizens that they clearly evolved far beyond the classic definition of communism. Unfortunately, we never got to see how the San-dinista experiment would have turned out. Communist or not, they didn't play pattycake with American business interests, so Reagan shut them down right away. The Sandinistas were only in power for five years, and they had to spend the last three of those years totally focused on defending themselves from Reagan's mercenaries.

Here in the United States, I think it makes more sense to try to evolve capi-talism into a more egalitarian system. Our economy was set up for capitalism right from the beginning and that's what everyone here is used to. Friedman's idea of cooperation being achieved through purely voluntary exchange that benefits both parties has a lot of promise.

As I see it, the big weakness of capitalism is that it depends on compe-tition, and competition necessarily divides the human race into a class of winners and a class of losers. The winning class gets a lot of freedom, but it comes at the expense of freedom for the losing class. The winning class has grown to include a much larger number of people in recent years, but it can't possibly include everyone, or even a very large majority of everyone. I know the economists disagree. They insist that poor people just need to keep faith-fully working their butts off for low pay, and eventually it will pay off. But the economists are dishonest people who are going to say whatever they can think of to persuade us to accept, or even strengthen the hierarchal structure of our society. They should be ignored, ridiculed, and forced to learn what it's like to earn a living through actual work.

I think capitalism gives us a lot of the building blocks we will need to create a free and equal society. I want to team up with Zog and work to build a utopian Free Market. All exchange between human beings *should* be voluntary, just like that old MF said. But if some people have to sacrifice their freedom so that others can have an excess of freedom, that's not good enough. That's exactly what we have now, and it's a terrible mess. Capitalism will have to change a great deal before it can bring freedom to all people. And make no mistake. I will not hesitate to switch my allegiance to whatever system makes true freedom available to everyone. If a freer and more equal method comes along, I will be there to help it put capitalism in the loser column.

I wish I could offer my own ingenious new way to restructure the economy, but as one individual, I can't even come close. That will take a giant group effort. I mean, I have loads of ideas that seem clever to me, but I don't want to publish them until I have talked about them with a lot more people. For now, I just hope to convince as many people as possible to start thinking about it and working on it. Freedom for everyone is totally possible, totally worthwhile, and we need to go for it now. We needed to go for it yesterday! I'm ready to help.

28. BREEDING LIKE BEECH TREES

In chapter two, I mentioned that I would leave out a lot of stories to protect the security and anonymity of a lot of my fellow radicals. I also claimed that I would not so much as hint that they were happening, but I am going to give you a hint right here. During my nine days in our nation's capitol, I got to observe people implementing some of the most inspirational strategies to bring about radical social change I have ever witnessed in all my years as a rebel. Their ideas were so brilliant, and so potentially effective that I have felt more confident in our movement's potential for success ever since I met them. I am also honored and very grateful that they trusted me enough to tell me what they were up to. There were two different groups, working on more than two different projects. If I wrote it all down, I think it would add two more chapters to the book, and they would likely be the two most inspiring chapters of the entire American Odyssey.

Alas, I am not going to. It has been almost twenty years since I first walked through Washington DC and I have not kept in touch with any of those people, but I think there is a strong chance that their operations are still on track, and I am not going to risk blowing up their secrets.

Sorry to tantalize you like this and then leave you hanging. Even though I can't share any details, I still want you to know that the world is full of little bands of brilliant and fearless people committed to the cause of spreading equality and freedom. Some of them are operating inside the beltway, right under the nose of one of the world's most terrifying systems of surveillance.

As the reader, this is where I urge you to use your imagination- not just to ponder what secrets I might be withholding here, but also to think about what new strategies you and your friends might use to defeat the power structure. It's true that the empire has almost limitless resources to hire smart people who can help advance its cutting-edge strategies to maintain power. But at the root of things, it is a more intelligent lifestyle choice to cooperate as equals in a community than to compete and be selfish. It is inevitable that those of us who understand equality will eventually outsmart the selfish ones, show them the error of their ways, and heal humanity. Our situation is infinitely complex and constantly changing, so opportunities for new strategies and tactics are popping up all the time. As long as you understand that you are an intelligent and potent person, then you will be able to seize some of these opportunities and make a real difference. Let's go!

***

I spent the last couple days of my DC tour on a fund-raising campaign. I knew that I would soon be crossing a major cultural boundary, leaving the Mid-Atlantic region, and entering the South. I lived in Alabama for four years as a child, and I had recently spent another two months there as an adult, so I wasn't handicapped by the usual fears and prejudices that most Yankees seem to feel toward the South. At the very least, I knew Alabama was a nice place and I looked forward to learning about all the other Southern states I would be walking through on my way there.

Even so, I knew I could never pass for anything but the Yankee that I am. At best, I would still stick out like a sore thumb because of my accent. I also knew of a number of other cultural behaviors that were different between North and South, and I figured there might be more that I wasn't even aware of yet. It seemed likely that I might make the random strangers I was about to meet feel more uncomfortable than I had up North, and I might even offend some people. I felt less confident about expressing my political ideas, and less confident that I would be able to make any money selling zines. I had also almost completely run out of money by the time I got to DC, so I paused there at the southern tip of Yankee land and took a couple days to build up my finances a bit.

My strategy was about as cynical and irreverent as you can imagine. Before I found my way to the radical end of the political spectrum, I had spent three years working in the liberal non-profit sector campaigning for reforms to be passed through government policy. I spent the majority of that time as a fund-raiser, and in three years I raked in tens of thousands of dollars for nine different NGOs. I burnt out and got fired before I even found out just how corrupt and disingenuous most of the groups I was working for really were, but by the time I went walking, I had learned a lot more.

Firstly, I had come to an understanding that government-mandated reforms were not an effective way to achieve the kind of cultural change that we really need. Secondly, I learned that less than half the money I had raised even went into the reform campaigns. Most of it just provided for my bosses to fly all over the country on airplanes, stay in expensive hotels, attend high-class parties, and drink absurd quantities of the most expensive alcohol. So when

I got to DC I decided it was time to try to take some money back from the ridiculous farce that I had worked so hard to finance just a few years prior.

Almost all the major NGOs are headquartered in the capitol for obvious reasons, and an old friend had given me a fairly comprehensive list of them, complete with their addresses. The NGOs had trained me to weasel and nag money out of people much like Lawrence the hustler, so I figured it was time to turn those skills back on them. In a few cases, I actually called in advance and made appointments, but mostly I just showed up at their front doors and did my best to persuade the secretaries to let me talk to someone important.

The first group I ever raised funds for was the Sierra Club. They are the nation's oldest, largest, and quite likely most corrupt environmentalist non-profit. I called in advance, and they were good enough to give me an appointment the following day. I showed up a few minutes early, so I made friendly conversation with the secretary and told her about my project while I waited. Then I actually got to make a brief sales-pitch to a group of five or six Sierra Club employees, some of whom may have actually been important executives. It only took me about five minutes to say my piece, and it only took them about five seconds to reject me and send me on my way. Fortunately, on the way out, the secretary asked me how it went. When I told her they had stiffed me, she said, "Oh no! I think your project sounds really cool!" Then she promptly fished a twenty out of her wallet and gave it to me.

The biggest score by far came from the Greenpeace building. I had never actually worked for Greenpeace, so I didn't feel like they owed me anything, but I had an old friend who was working there, and he got me an interview within a few hours of when I called. He set it up so that I was pitching to him and one of his bosses. After I gave a brief spiel, they both asked questions and listened to my answers for about twenty minutes. My friend asked most of the questions, and he obviously set them up so I could give answers that would make me sound awesome. He helped me out in a big way, and I really appreciated it. After a certain point, the boss seemed satisfied. With that, he whipped out a checkbook and sliced me off a hundred dollars. He left right away, and as soon as he was gone, my friend got his wallet out and gave me another hundred dollars of his own money. That ended up being about half the money I made in my two days of canvassing non-profit groups.

I probably hit up about two dozen different organizations and made about $400. Most of them sent me away with nothing, but that's how canvassing always works. Overall, I think the effort was worth it. I knew I could make that money last a long time, and I felt a lot more confident about jumping off the diving board into Dixieland. I barely remember any details from any of the other NGOs I canvassed, and even if I did, they would be too boring to print. However, the very last office I visited provided me with an unforgettable story, as well as a springboard into another important philosophical rant.

The organization was called the Zero Population-Growth Network (ZPGN). I had never heard of them before, but my first impression of them was good. It was a small, cheaply-rented office space of the third story of an old building that housed several other small businesses. It was a far cry from the glitzy office towers housing the likes of Greenpeace and the Sierra Club. The whole organization fit into just one dimly-lit room with semi-organized stacks of paper covering every horizontal surface including much of the floor. Of the nine non-profit groups for whom I worked, there are two who I still really respect and consider to be legitimate, cutting-edge forces for social change. This cramped, cluttered office reminded me very much of one of those, and I immediately felt comfortable.

I did not have to talk my way through a secretary to get to the people in charge. The entire staff consisted of two guys. One of them answered the door when I knocked and they both stopped what they were doing immediately in order to give me an audience. They were both about the same age as I was, and they looked like they were auditioning for the video to the Weird Al Yankovic song "White and Nerdy." They took a box of files off of a spare chair so I could sit down, and cleared some of the stuff off of a small table so we could all sit together and talk. I went first and told them about my walk for a few minutes. Then they started explaining to me what their group was all about, and that's when everything went to hell.

The ZPGN was very concerned that the consumptive lifestyle of First-World nations was depleting the Earth's resources too quickly, and causing irreparable damage to fragile and important ecosystems. (OK. That sounded about right.) The population of these countries was growing at an alarming rate, and we had to do something to slow them down. (OK, maybe…) So, the solution was to close the borders and block all Third World immigrants from coming here. (What!?) Their data showed that it took the average immigrant less than five years to achieve a First World level of resource consumption after arriving in the United States. If the tide of immigration could not be

stemmed, then it would only take x number of years before the US population hit x many hundreds of millions of people, some specific number that
their group had calculated would irrevocably destroy the planet and all hope
for the future, so we had to act fast.

All the comfort I had felt upon seeing their cozy little office vanished the
second I realized what I was hearing. I waited and listened as patiently as I
could to their ideas. Clearly, they were nice guys with good intentions who
were much more genuinely happy to pay attention to me than any of the
other people I had canvassed over the last few days. Still, I felt my blood
boiling hotter with each word they said. There are few things I find more
offensive than to hear White Americans- directly descended from the only
really dangerous wave of immigrants our nation has ever known- trying to
block the migrations of other people. To hear my most sacred environmentalist principles being used to justify that racist Republican border policy was
just too much.

To be fair, it was not the first time I had heard the concept. At that point,
it had only been six or seven years since the grand old Sierra Club had come
very close to taking a similar stance on immigration for the same reason.
The proposal was voted down by a slim majority of their members, but it
still created a huge scandal and alienated a lot of people. When I went door-
to-door raising money for the Sierra Club, quite a few people refused to
donate because of that scandal, and that's how I found out. Still, none of
the disturbingly-large minority of bigots within the club had ever expressed
their anti-immigrant ideas to me, so this was the first time I had ever received
this next-level offensive bullshit right to my face. I could tell that these nice,
nerdy boys were not evil. They were just ignorant, but I was quick to anger
back then, and it probably took less than two minutes before I boiled over.

I interrupted the boy who was talking in an attempt to debate him, but my
voice came out louder and more shrilly than I had expected, and my point
came out far less articulate than I had intended. He rallied, and a very brief
debate ensued, but I realized I needed to leave almost immediately. Not only
was I too angry to express myself effectively. I also looked like an asshole
because they had welcomed me into their space with far more hospitality
than any of the dozens of liberals I had just approached, and here I was
yelling at them.

I got up and hurried out the door, yelling over my shoulder that what they really needed to do was send the White people back to Europe. I heard one of them shout after me "It's too late for that!" and then I was gone. I hit the down button on the elevator in the lobby, but then realized I couldn't wait. With a few quick glances, I found the door to the stairwell and ran away. It was getting late and I was too frazzled after that to do any more canvassing, so that ended up being my last attempt to hustle money out of a non-profit group.

It's true that there are a lot more people on our planet now than there ever were in the history of our species, and it's true that most ecosystems have changed as a result of that. It's true that the First World lifestyle has used up resources too quickly and damaged the ecosystem too much, even though only a small percentage of the Earth's vast human population lives that way. It's true that if all humans were to live that way, it would throw the Earth's ecosystem and climate into a dangerous chaos. It might not even be possible for all of us to live like cheeseburgers in paradise. To try would be a very dangerous experiment. I don't think it's worth the risk, and I hope we can convince humanity as a whole not to do it. Up to that point, I think I'm right on the same page with the Zero Population-Growth Network.

Blocking immigration however, is not a strategy that would work, or even an ethical strategy to consider. Although the ZPGN boys did not state this overtly, their proposal to limit First World consumption by blocking immigration implicitly suggests that we continue to block Third World nations from using their ow resources to develop their own prosperous economies. If we didn't, the people of those countries would quickly achieve a First World level of consumption without even having to leave home.

We can't keep hoarding all the wealth for an elite minority of people anymore, because that's actually what's causing the population to grow so much. I explained in the last chapter how Third World countries get bullied out of their resources. People are forced into an oppressive economic system. Whole nations become impoverished because they have to send such a large percent of their natural resources and work output to the First World.

Poverty and oppression cause people to breed faster. In every case where a culture of class-stratification causes significant hardship for its lower classes, the people in those lower classes produce larger families in shorter generational intervals. Here in the First World, a much higher percentage of us belong to the middle and upper classes, but the poorest among us still have the largest families and the shortest generations. It is logical to assume that if wealthy people were suddenly subjected to oppression, they would start having lots of babies too. It's not an uncommon phenomenon in nature.

There is a disease that kills almost all North American Beech trees. Some manage to live with it for two or three decades, but you will very rarely find a big old Beech tree like our ancestors got to see. One might worry that the Beech is in danger of extinction, but in fact, the northeastern forests are thick with them. Millions and billions of thin little babies grow strong even in the shade of taller trees. Or they grow in giant thickets so dense that there is no room for any other trees, and it's hard for a human to push through. The disease threatens their species, so they have learned how to breed young and produce a lot of offspring.

Mice, rabbits, insects, fish, and all the other species of animals who most commonly get eaten are all fast breeders. When we prune pieces off of fruit trees every year, they produce more fruit in an effort to breed faster. Of course, it is also possible to cut off too many limbs at once and get less fruit.

In a similar way, it is not uncommon for conquering empire cultures to commit genocide, consciously attempting to eliminate other groups of people, or at least reduce their numbers. I think genocide and oppression are both symptoms of the same cultural sickness, but they are two very different things. Genocide reduces the population of the targeted group, while oppression increases it. Genocide is obviously perpetrated intentionally. I don't know if diabolical villains are intentionally stimulating poor people to breed faster so they will have more slaves, or if it's an unconscious mistake.

The English economist Thomas Malthus theorized that the human population will always grow to exceed its food supply, so that a percentage of us will always be starving. He actually claimed that starvation was the only thing limiting human population growth, but his theory has been disproven by every single group of people who have ever achieved freedom from oppression. Middle and upper-class people have enough food to support enormous families. The freedom from oppression gives them much more time to have sex and raise kids, yet they consistently breed at a slow and reasonable rate. Middle and upper-class people use a combination of birth control and family planning strategies to avoid having large numbers of children. Many First World countries have slowed their birth-rate so much that their populations would shrink if not for a steady stream of immigration from the poorer countries.

Our dogma tells us that the ever-increasing number of humans is a sign of progress, a proud cultural accomplishment to be celebrated. But if the majority of those people are suffering short, austere, unfulfilled lives, then I disagree. Before the rise of the empire cultures, the total amount of human suffering on the planet was negligible. The number of people who live free, comfortable lives probably isn't much bigger today than it ever was. All that oppression has really accomplished is to add billions more suffering humans whose lives that are mostly characterized by heartbreaking struggle. We have to admit that this unprecedented amount of human suffering is an indication of total cultural failure, and it outweighs any of the benefits our species has gained from its hierarchal structure.

Class-stratification is a cultural sickness that is the root cause of all our other major problems. Overpopulation is just one symptom of this sickness, and it will continue until we address the root cause. Take away the disease of oppression, and the population will stabilize. Degradation of the environment is an enormous problem, but we cannot restore ecosystems first, and then deal with oppression. As long as oppression and inequality endure, the ecosystem will continue to suffer.

We can be certain that the suffering masses will keep trying to increase their standard of living. As long as First World culture continues to model massive resource consumption and technological extravagance as the most fulfilling way to live, then the oppressed masses will mostly follow our lead, and the ecosystem will continue to destabilize. I think it is our responsibility to grow out of this selfish and gluttonous phase, and set a better example for the rest of the world.

We need to open our minds to the wisdom of the traditional egalitarian cultures. They keep trying to tell us that technology and gluttonous consumption are not the path to true happiness or fulfillment. All we really need is freedom! Middle and upper-class people here in the first world already have a relatively high level of freedom. We are free to wallow in selfishness if we so choose, but how fulfilling is that really? We are also free to develop ways to share our freedom with all of humanity, cure the global cultural sickness, stop our runaway population growth, and bring about a golden age. Come on now, let's go!

29. DC NOUEMENT

When I got back to Zog's and told him about my day, he decided to help me. Not only did he help me convert all the checks I had received to usable cash, but then he gave me a hundred dollars of his own money as well. It was very sweet of him considering that he knew I would spend it on my mission to directly oppose the economic philosophy he had devoted his life to. I got back on the road the next day, but I didn't actually get going until mid-afternoon. I'd like to tell you what the cause was for the late departure, but I can't honestly remember.

My first order of business was to get rid of a half-empty bottle of whisky that was left over from the teabagger's party. Without thinking, I had carried it with me all the way from Baltimore. Finally, it had occurred to me that it was silly to carry all that extra weight, so I decided to give it away.

Washington DC has the densest population of homeless panhandlers I've ever seen anywhere, and I assumed that almost all of them would be thrilled to be gifted a half a bottle of hard alcohol. Everyone knows that's why they beg for change, but I literally tried to hand the bottle to five or six different guys and every single one of them refused. What's more, they all acted like they were really offended. There's no conceivable way I randomly met six street bums in a row who were not desperate alcoholics. I could only imagine that they must have been pretending to be straight, and it was more important to maintain the show than to score some free whisky. After I saw the pattern, I just ended up sitting it on the sidewalk beneath a highway over pass in a place where it looked like someone would notice it and be able to pick it up discreetly.

After that I went to the National Mall and made a spectacle of myself wandering around with my backpack on. I stopped in front of the Capitol Building, and on a whim, I took a picture of my left hand giving the finger to the US capitol. That felt satisfying, so I backtracked a few blocks to the Supreme Court building and took a picture of old Lefty flipping it off too. I had to pee pretty badly, so I wandered back down the Mall to the back gate of the White House.

Over the last year, I had developed a real skill for peeing in public without being noticed. I would discreetly open my fly, pull out just the very tip, and then put my hands on my hips or hang them by my side while I looked around nonchalantly and peed. I emptied a whole bladder worth onto the fence that encloses the back yard of the White House like that, and got away with it. Safely back in my pants, I flipped off the executive branch and took a picture for posterity. Then I turned an about face and did the same to the ever-symbolic Washington Phallus. I lingered on the Mall for a couple hours trying and failing to sell zines, and then I moved on. I crossed the bridge into Arlington, Virginia, and took one last picture of my hand giving the bird to the Pentagon. I had done my best to show the federal government the error of their ways. If that didn't teach them a lesson, then nothing ever would.

It was evening by then, and I needed a place to camp. I turned left to follow the Potomac downstream. In less than two miles, I found a considerable buffer of forest surrounding the security fence around the Reagan International Airport. The forest was a bit swampy, but there were enough dry spaces, that I found a suitable tent site without too much trouble. I could also see the security fence from my campsite and that made me a bit nervous. Surely, just fourteen months after the hijackings, *all* airports would be on high alert, let alone the Reagan Airport which had actually been targeted by the terrorists. I laid awake worrying about that for quite a while, but if anyone watching the surveillance cameras noticed me, they didn't care to react. Of course, the sound of jets taking off and landing didn't help me sleep either, but eventually the airport closed, and the noise stopped. It was a pleasantly warm night for the first week of November.

In the morning, I followed the river south into the city of Alexandria. I sat down to have breakfast in a nice park right on the waterfront. The river was much wider there and after a moment, I realized it was flowing upstream as the tide was coming in. Then I realized this would most likely be the last time I would see any part of the ocean until I reached California. That gave me a reverent feeling, so after I finished eating, I went right down to the water and stuck my hands into it. I prayed goodbye to the great, world-wide spirit of the ocean, and prayed that I would greet it again in a few years when I reached the West Coast.

Then I decided to turn west and head for the Appalachian Mountains. It would have been wiser to keep walking south the way I had been headed. If I had, it would have only taken a few days to reach the city of Richmond, and after that, it would have been maybe a week and a half to Durham, North

Carolina, where my friends would shelter me for the winter. Unfortunately, wisdom frequently eluded me at that age.

I just couldn't stand the thought of walking through another city so soon. I had just been through a dozen major urban areas, and I needed a break. I felt like I had earned some vacation time, and I decided to take a stroll through the beautiful countryside. I had never heard anything interesting about Richmond, Virginia, and I figured it would be okay to skip a city once in a while. I thought it would be nice to see the autumn leaves on the Appalachians. The days were growing short, and I needed to turn the intensity level of my life down a notch. First, I had to get out of DC.

I cut back across the entire length of the city of Arlington. The boundary of Arlington is shaped to be the missing piece of the District of Columbia that Virginia never ceded. Put together with DC it makes a perfect diamond on the map. I left the river behind and took a more westerly tack through a long stretch of giant residential apartment buildings. Lots of people were out on the sidewalks or in the parks in that neighborhood, and I assume many more were inside the densely-packed residential units. Almost everyone I saw there looked like they had migrated from a wide variety of foreign countries, but they did not look poor, and the whole neighborhood was very tidy. That must have been where city planners put the immigrants who achieved First World consumption levels within five years.

Late in the morning, I found a deep ravine that had been preserved as a forested park. A bike path followed the little brook at the bottom of the ravine, and it was coming more or less from the west, so I followed it. I felt a little irresponsible dodging away from people when I should have been trying to distribute zines, but it was a pleasant trail and I followed it all through the middle of the day. Part way in, I discovered that I was on the route of a bicycle race that was in progress. That was stressful at first because the riders were coming from behind me and I didn't want to block their way. The fastest ones came first, but after those first few, I realized it wasn't really a very competitive race. Most of the riders were not in particularly good shape, and they were all wearing the same yellow t-shirts with some charity logo on it. There were lots of other people out walking on the trail too, and the racers didn't seem to mind, so my tension eased. Yellow-clad cyclists kept passing me for hours, but the intervals between them were long enough that it wasn't really any trouble to stay out of their way. It was one long gradual climb, and the brook got smaller and smaller as we neared the top. As I approached the very top of the ravine, the trail got a bit steeper. Right in that little stretch, a pair of bike-racers actually stopped to talk to me, and I ended up selling them a zine subscription.

Moments later, the trail popped me back out onto a loud and busy city street. I followed that west through the city of Falls Church and into the desolate suburban wastelands of Fairfax County. In a nation of soul-sucking suburbs, Fairfax County, Virginia is a uniquely wretched place. In the years since my walk, I have made friends with three different people who grew up there, and I am basing this opinion on their testimony. I know everyone says things like that about their home town, but I have reasons to take these people more seriously than most.

Apparently, it is one of the most affluent suburban regions in the country, and people make a large percentage of that money doing unethical things for the government. Not all government jobs are unethical of course, but enough are that it brings the average per capita karma of the region to a record low. It should come as no surprise that the youth of Fairfax County suffer some of the nation's highest rates of depression and all sorts of other mental illness.

One of my friends claims to have dated no less the two guys with the exact same combination of mental illnesses: agoraphobia and anorexia. Agoraphobia is the fear of going out in public. She claims that both of these guys hid inside their parents' houses for years, surviving off their parents' efforts, and choosing to interact with the outside world only through their computers. Apparently, they were also so ashamed of themselves that they basically stopped eating and turned into living stick figures. How she ever met these guys is a mystery, let alone how she found them attractive. I guess you have to lower the bar a few notches when you grow up in Fairfax County, but that's beside the point. If those two guys really exist, how many more people like that are hiding out in those big suburban houses? Do they vote on things that affect all of our lives? I shudder to think!

I walked along a major through-route towards the city of Fairfax, so I don't remember seeing any big houses at all. All I remember were miles of smaller, glass-front office buildings, strip malls, and endless parking lots. At least there was a sidewalk. When I look at a map now, I can see that the whole area is marbled with forested parks of all sizes, but I didn't have a map then and

I managed to miss all of them. Sunset caught me right in the middle of the city of Fairfax. I blundered along blindly stabbing for a place to sleep until it was almost dark. Then I just crawled under a hedge in a strip of landscaping between the main road and a huge strip-mall parking lot. I was just across a narrow lane of asphalt from a corporate pizza chain, so I was frequently tantalized by the smell of pizza. I couldn't set up a tent in the narrow space, but I gambled that it wouldn't rain anyway.

A very cold wind blew in that night, and I spent more time shivering than sleeping. The wind finally stopped, but the cold stuck around, and I crawled from the bushes the next morning to find a heavy frost coating everything. If it had tried to rain it would have snowed.

I walked along US Highway 29 through more hours of monotonous suburbs that don't deserve to be described. Then I turned south on route 28 towards the city of Manassas. It was a bit of a detour, but I wanted to see Manassas. It was the site of a major Civil War battle, so I expected it to be an interesting place. I was sorely disappointed. I got a decent sandwich at a deli there for lunch, and I managed to sell a couple of subscriptions at a coffee shop, but I have nothing interesting to report to you about Manassas Virginia.

I turned back west after that and the suburbs finally started to thin out a bit. As the day got late, I spent a couple hours walking past a large piece of land surrounded by a huge security fence that was really more like a wall. A narrow strip of forest lined the inside of the fence, but I could see that the land was mostly clear behind the visual screen. It stretched on for several miles, but I never could figure out what was going on inside. I couldn't tell if it was some corporate or government facility, or just someone's heavily-fortified private ranch.

I made it back to route 29 just as the sun went down behind the first ridge of the Appalachian foothills. The road ran atop a plateau which was covered in farm fields, cow pastures, and a handful of big suburban mansions, but I could see a deep, forested ravine ahead on the left, and it didn't take me long to reach the shelter of the forest. I set up in the most secure camping spot I could remember in a long time, but the night was uncomfortably cold again. I got a little more insulation from the bubble of air that my tent trapped around me, so I slept better than the night before, but I awoke to discover a new problem.

I usually like to start my first waking moments with a big, healthy drink of water, but that morning it took me a couple minutes to figure out how. My water bottle was one of those Camelback models where the water stays in a big bladder that can ride in your backpack while you suck the water out through a tube that you can run over your shoulder. The water in the tube had frozen solid, and there was a good bit of ice in the big bladder as well. I ended up unscrewing the big filler valve, puckering my lips, and sucking water awkwardly off the surface. It took a couple hours before I could use the bottle the way it was intended. I also got a couple hours of really chilly walking in before the day warmed to a more comfortable temperature.

I thought I had escaped into the countryside, but by mid-morning, the suburban sprawl was thickening again. Then in the late morning, I found myself in a large town called Warrenton. By a stroke of luck, I found a good-looking diner. Feeling flush with money and chilled in that way that can only be cured by a hot meal, I went for it. The restaurant was a big building with a lot of seating, but it was packed with so many customers that there was only one place left for me to sit. I don't remember what day it was, but it must have been a weekend. It was that time of day when you could choose from the breakfast menu or the lunch menu. That complicated things for me a little bit, but I eventually settled on some sort of omelet. It was a good meal, and I felt better after that.

After Warrenton, the scenery got very pretty. The foothills were growing larger all around me with every mile I walked. There was one larger mountain off to the right, and the great high wall of the Blue Ridge mountains was now clearly looming above the western horizon.

Just then, a huge old, dark-brown-painted El Camino pulled up beside me and stopped. Two young men and a young woman were inside, and they were dressed a bit like Hippies. After a brief, friendly conversation, they told me I was welcome to stay at their house. If I took a right just about a mile ahead, I would find it just a short ways up the side road. I got directions, thanked them, and they drove off, but I ended up deciding to walk on by. It was barely afternoon yet, and I just felt like I should put more miles behind me that day.

An hour or two later I reached the bottom of a great hill and came to a bridge over the lovely Rappahannock River. I stopped to admire the swift little river, and it occurred to me that I had not passed anymore suburban sprawl for several hours. After almost a year and a half of slogging through the largest and densest cluster of cities on our continent, I had finally escaped into the country. My heart surged with excitement and relief.

As if on cue, a loud pickup truck came up behind me on the road. The truck crossed the bridge, and then had to slow down considerably to go around a tight corner right where I was standing. As it slowed, one of the two men inside threw a half-full can of soda at me and they both hollered something hostile that I couldn't understand. The can missed, but it still managed to communicate an additional level of hostility above and beyond whatever they were yelling. As the truck pulled away, I saw a confederate flag displayed on a sticker on the back bumper. In my reverie to finally escape the city, I had forgotten my trepidations about leaving behind the land of the Yankees. Apparently, the spirits had sent those two men to remind me, and to welcome me to the South.

30. DOGS AND VULTURES

A wind picked up that afternoon, and big heavy, cotton-ball clouds began to appear out of the west. The clouds didn't cover the entire sky, and the sun managed to keep shining between them most of the time. As the sun dipped towards the west, and the shadows grew long, the usual dull orange-brown color of the autumn oak leaves lit up like fire. The grass of the many cow pastures glowed better than emeralds, and the contrast between the brightly-lit ground and the dark bottoms of the clouds made a spectacular scene, unabashedly revealing the magic of autumn. The clouds looked so heavy, it was hard to imagine how they could stay afloat up in the sky, and before long, I could see that some of the larger ones were starting to rain out some of their weight.

I had just come to a little town called Amissville when one of those clouds blew directly overhead. The wind, which had already been blowing for hours, increased to a gale. Then a cold squall of rain came down in droplets that were small, but numerous enough to get me wet pretty fast. I only had to walk through it for about a block though before I came to a cozy-looking little general store, so I ducked inside for shelter.

I sat my pack down and stood out of the way near the front windows. The staff and the clientele all looked like friendly rural people, so I gave everyone my friendliest smiles and said hello to anyone who came within range. I was hoping to make friends, sell zines, and maybe even find a place to stay, but no one was up for conversation, and I thought I noticed a hint of suspicion in many of the looks I was getting. I realized I had sat my pack down in such a way as to display the big green and black sign that said "Love Earth." Was this the wrong message for the South? Could it be part of the reason why Rednecks were throwing things at me and friendly-looking people were not being friendly to me? I had felt awkward about the sign since the first day I put it on display, and I decided right then that it was time to put my freak flag away for a while.

It only took a few minutes to wait out the rain, and then I was back on the road. The sun came back out. Everything was glistening wet, and now bright sunset colors were beginning to appear in the sky. I thought the limits of scenic grandeur had already been reached before the rain, but I was wrong.

About a mile after Amissville, the sky darkened, and I could see that I was about to receive a second round of rain. I ducked into a patch of forest on the left, cleared the acorns off of a patch of ground, and set up my tent without hesitation. I got my shelter up just in time to escape the rain which came down harder this time and for a longer duration. It was still evening when the rain ended though, so I came back out of my tent to look around.

The forest was composed of big old hardwoods, spaced far apart with very little undergrowth to hide my tent. I was only about fifteen paces from the edge of a large cow pasture, and I could see several homes on the far side of it. I wasn't very well hidden by rural standards. I had a lot less space to myself than I had the previous night, but it was still a lot more than I was used to, after living for so long in the megalopolis. The sky had filled with sunset colors again after the second rain, but I resisted the urge to walk to the edge of the pasture for a better view, because I did not want to be seen. Instead, I took a minute to unfasten the safety pins that attached the Love Earth sign to my pack, rolled it up and stashed it away. I spent the next few weeks brainstorming a better sign, but I walked the rest of the way to my winter destination without one.

I don't think it rained any more after that, but the world was still all wet the next morning. As I continued west along route 211, the landscape changed quickly from hilly to mountainous. Large mountains blocked off portions of my western view, but between them I could always see portions of the great Blue Ridge looming ever higher to the west. The Blue Ridge Mountains are essentially one long, narrow ridge that stretches all the way across Virginia, and beyond. The summit of the ridge ranges from an elevation of 3,000 to just over 4,000 feet. From a distance, the top of the ridge appears quite level without any higher peaks or lower notches to break its continuity. Coming from the east, it is the first really high mountain in the Appalachians, and you can see it from many miles out on the Piedmont Plateau. From that direction it looks like a giant wall spanning the entire western horizon. It is a beautiful spectacle of mountain geology, and a foreboding gateway to the Appalachians all at the same time.

Before long, I was surrounded on all sides by the smaller mountains leading up to the Blue Ridge. Then, by late morning, I came to a larger town called Washington that sat right at the foot of the mighty ridge. From that perspective, the ridge looked less like a wall, and more like a range of mountains with distinct peaks and notches between them. I will try to use words to describe the beauty of the scene, but if you really want to understand, you will just have to go there and see for yourself.

I had always thought of the Appalachians as a bunch of smooth, rounded hills, covered in forest, so I was surprised to see cliffs and pinnacles of rock sticking out through the forest canopy all over. Some of the mountain tops were smooth and rounded, but many more were quite jagged, and they were much too tall to describe as hills. I had to crane my neck to look up at them. Wet-looking clouds still peppered the sky, and ragged pieces of them stuck to the sides and tops of the mountains, swirling and tearing apart as I watched. It was breathtaking. Also, that section of the Blue Ridge is protected inside the Shenandoah National Park, so there were none of the radio towers, trophy mansions, or clear-cuts that would normally detract from such a view.

The highway turned south in Washington so it could continue on parallel to the bottom of the Blue Ridge. Shortly after that, another little rain shower caught up with me. I ducked under some trees and put on my poncho, but the rain was over quickly, so I had to stop again right away to take it off. I reached another little town called Sperryville in time for lunch. There were a couple of nice-looking places to eat, but on closer inspection, they were both too expensive for me. Gift shops, motels, and other signs of a tourism-based economy lined the roadside, and that made sense just outside of a major national park. It also made sense that the restaurants would jack up their prices to take advantage of the affluent tourists. Luckily, I had brought some groceries with me from the city, so I sat down on the roadside and made myself a sandwich.

After Sperryville, route 211 turned west and climbed its way up to a pass over the mountains, so I turned off onto a smaller route called 231 that continued south along the bottom of the ridge. A couple of hours passed uneventfully until I realized my pocket knife was missing. I use my pocket knife for some purpose or other every few hours. It's more useful than most of my fingers, so its disappearance caused a moment of panic. I checked all my pockets three or four times, and all the pouches of my backpack, but alas, it was gone. I checked my memory and realized I had just used it to make my sandwich at lunch time. I must have left it on the ground back there where I ate. I had already walked several miles from Sperryville, up and down some large, steep hills, and I hated the idea of walking all the way back. I had also just been warned by someone back in DC that it's illegal to hitch-hike in Virginia. I sat down to weigh my options for a few minutes and then decided that the risk was minimal. I hid my pack in some nearby bushes, crossed over to the north-bound side of the road, and put up my thumb.

It didn't take long to get a ride, and when I got back to the spot where I had eaten lunch, I spotted my knife right away, laying on a bed of pine needles with the blade still open. I was so happy to find it I did a little jig. I folded the blade back in, returned it to its rightful home in my pocket, and got back to hitch-hiking in less than a minute.

It took a while longer to catch a ride the second time, and while I was waiting, a cop drove by. I had been gawking at the mountains and I didn't notice him until he was almost on top of me. When I finally did notice, my adrenaline spiked, and I jerked my hand down conspicuously. It was far too late to disguise what I was doing, but the cop just drove by and never came back. I guess the no hitch-hiking law is usually just enforced around the DC metro area, not in rural parts of Virginia where hitch-hiking is a fairly normal behavior.

I did eventually get a ride back to my pack and resumed walking. Just about then, the sun went behind the mighty wall of the Blue Ridge and made me want to start looking for a camping spot. The high ridge to the west made for an artificially early sunset, so I knew it would continue to be light for several hours. Still, I was worried that it might be a real challenge to find a camping spot because of an unexpected new problem: dogs!

I had walked well beyond the limits of the suburbs, but the rural homes were still fairly close together along the highways, and almost every single one of them had a dog that would bark at me as I walked past. Usually, before I would get far enough away from the dog I had already passed for it to stop barking, I would trigger the next dog I was approaching to start barking, so I had spent most of the day walking to the sound of multiple barking dogs.

What was worse, many of them would run right up to me, and that was a real problem. I am really handicapped when it comes to making friends with dogs. Even so-called "friendly" dogs bark at me hysterically, and I have been bitten enough times that the sight of a barking dog charging towards me always frightens me, regardless of how much its tail is wagging, or how much its owner is yelling to me that it's "friendly." The dogs can sense my fear, of course, and that's all the proof they need to confirm that I am a dangerous enemy. They then feel duty-bound to report the danger to their owner over and over at top volume until I am gone out of earshot.

At least a dozen times that day I had to do my defensive dog dance, first walking sideways, and then backwards so as to keep facing a menacing dog while continuing in the direction I was trying to go. I would open my knife blade and then clutch it behind my butt, hoping that no nearby humans would see it. My adrenaline would surge as I prepared myself to kick or stab in self-defense the instant the dog jumped at me. Luckily, that day I only had to dish out a couple of minor kicks. I also encountered quite a few dog-owners who came out to investigate the commotion and call their pets into the house. A few of these people shouted brief apologies to me, or the standard "he's friendly" line, but of course no actual conversations resulted from those encounters because no one can hear another person talking over the sound of a screaming dog.

Now I had to find a place to sleep. Presumably, the forested hillsides beyond people's back yards would not be the territory of any particular dog, but to get there, I would somehow have to cross the unbroken chain of canine alarm systems lining both sides of the road. I kept walking without finding a single gap that I might squeeze through until the sky turned the colors of sunset. I reached the top of a small ridge, and miraculously found myself in a place where I couldn't hear any dogs barking or see a single house. To the left of the road was all pasture, but a forest of pines came right down to the road on the right. I waited for a passing truck to disappear out of sight, climbed over a barbed-wire fence as quickly as I could, and hurried into the woods.

I had another sandwich for supper, and it wasn't long before I heard doors closing and other human sounds coming from somewhere nearby to the south. There must have been another house there that I hadn't seen yet because I stopped before I got to it. At least their dog wasn't barking. After supper, I carried my stuff a little further back into the woods and hid my tent in a thicket of young trees. The forest ended just a little ways down the hill to the north, so after I had my camp se up, I walked to the edge to admire the view.

I was at the top of a long stripe of pastures and farm fields filling the narrow bottom of the valley I had just walked through. Rounded hills and mountains were stacked in a panorama as far as the eye could see. Each distant layer was a little more faded into the blue haze than the one before it, and it was easy to imagine that infinitely more were hidden in the haze beyond the last one I could make out. The last colors of the sunset faded from the sky as I sat there in reverie.

The next day was sunny and much warmer than it had recently been. By late morning it was so warm that I decided to walk for a while with my shirt off. The warmth of the sun felt nice on my skin. The mountain scenery was as beautiful as ever, and my heart soared.

I don't remember how far I made it like that, but all at once I came over a slight rise in the road and came face-to-face with an enormous vulture. It was perched on top of a fence-post right beside the road, and it was looking me right in the eye. As I got closer, I realized there was another vulture on top of the next fence post, and the next and the next. The fence they were sitting on was pressed up to the edge of a narrow ditch right off the edge of the road. My walking trajectory was about to take me disturbingly close to the giant birds, and I assumed they would fly away when I got too close. But as I came abreast of the first one, it just sat there staring me down. From the look in its eyes, I could tell it didn't give so much as a fraction of a shit.

From the tip of its tail to the top of its ugly head had to be almost three quarters the length of my whole body. The added height of the fence post meant I had to look up to see its face. My heart thundered and my palms were sweaty. I knew that vultures were saprophytes, meaning they never kill living animals. They invariably wait until we are already dead and eat our carcasses. I kept reminding myself of that, but I still couldn't calm down. I felt so vulnerable walking bare-chested past all those huge beaks and talons that were specifically designed to tear flesh. If for some reason they had chosen to violate the saprophyte code of ethics and attack me, it probably would've only taken three of them to overpower me. And there were a lot more than three of them.

I glanced up ahead and noticed that the vultures continued on fence-posts as far as I could see. At that point I actually had the presence of mind to start counting them. Their heads were covered with ugly red flesh that was a little bit asymmetrical. Their feathers were mostly black or dark brown, but with plenty of lighter brown, grey, and even white ones mixed in. They were all facing towards me, so I couldn't see their backs, but the coloration of feathers on their breasts appeared to have no organized pattern to it at all. They just looked mangey, and to emphasize that look, many of their feathers appeared to be falling out, and hanging loosely. Some of them had their wings tucked, but others were posing with them partly open. I don't know if they were soaking up extra warmth from the sun or what, but the open-winged pose made those ones look even more intimidating. None of them moved, and all of them gave me that same intimidating stare. It was about five or six paces between each fence post, and it took me several eternal minutes to walk the whole gauntlet. Finally, I passed the last one and counted 47.

47 enormous vultures! In a row! Wow!

I walked until the vultures were out of sight behind me. Then I stopped and put my shirt back on. There was no real reason to, but I just needed to feel that comforting layer of cotton between me and the big scary world again.

The rest of the day passed without incident. I just kept on south with the spectacular scenery of the Blue ridge Mountains on my right, and the lovely smaller mountains on my left. Late in the afternoon, I came to a little town called Banco, and stopped to get some groceries in a store that looked like it had originally been a barn. I lingered a while there, and met a few people. One of them warned me that a late-season tropical storm was moving up the coast and I should make sure to find a good shelter that night.

After Banco, the road veered away from the Blue Ridge and back out towards the Piedmont. I kept walking until it started to get dark, and pulled up suddenly as I realized I was coming into the town of Madison. I set up camp in a thick patch of woods behind a small church. By that time, the clouds had rolled in and the wind was blowing. For the next couple hours, the wind kept increasing. A warm rain blew in and came down heavily at times. It certainly did appear to be the tropical storm I had been warned about. At times the wind blew so fiercely that I worried about tree branches falling on me, but none ever did. Towards the end of the night, I finally got some sleep.

31. GET OUT OF TOWN

By morning, the storm was over and the sky was clear, but the wind remained as fierce as it had been all night. I walked through the little town of Madison and out onto route 29 headed towards Charlottesville. It was the only time on my whole voyage that I ever remember walking through wind so strong that it actually made walking difficult. It was a steady westerly, not particularly warm or cold, with periodic gusts that threatened to knock me right off the shoulder and into the ditch. As the land dried out, occasional drifts of autumn leaves would wash across the highway and rattle around my ankles like ocean waves on a shallow beach.

Highway 29 made a very straight line for many miles across the flat surface of the Piedmont Plateau. The whole day passed without any notable events, but I never got bored of the continuous, gorgeous view of the Blue Ridge off to the right. I was further from it there, and from that perspective out on the Piedmont, it went back to looking like an imposing blue wall with no gaps that one might pass through, and no visible end in either direction.

The wind finally started to let up around mid-afternoon, and by early evening, it was almost calm. It was right around then that I walked into some newly-built suburbia and realized I was nearing the city of Charlottesville. I could have made it right into the heart of the city before nightfall, but with no place lined up to stay, it made more sense to pull up short for the night. The pattern of new suburban sprawl was disrupted by a deep, forested ravine, so I climbed down in there to camp. The banks of the ravine were so steep that I lost my footing and slid part of the way down on my butt. When I came to a stop, both my shoes were filled with dirt, and bits of autumn leaves and forest duff were stuck all over me, but I was otherwise unharmed. An enchanting little river flowed through the bottom, surrounded by a flat, sandy floodplain that made for very comfortable camping. Looking at a map now, I am pretty sure it was the South Fork of the Rivanna River. Many of the trees down in my sheltered nook still had green leaves on them, and it gave me a sense that I still had plenty of nice autumn days left to get to North Carolina.

Charlottesville, Virginia is home to about 150,000 people, and about 25,000 of them are students. It's a big college town, and it's strikingly similar to all the big American college towns. The city was brimming with awesome little take-out restaurants, coffee-shops, bicycle shops, and any other businesses you can imagine that would appeal to college students. Everywhere I went, the city looked clean and new, and hip. Beat-up old cars plastered with way too many liberal bumper stickers were everywhere. There probably was a ghetto district somewhere, but I never wandered into it. The whole west-central part of the city was taken up by the sprawling University of Virginia campus.

By mid-morning, I found my way into a computer lab there and eagerly checked my email. Back in Alexandria, when I had decided to change course and dodge Richmond, I had stopped in a library and emailed my whole rebel network asking for contacts in Charlottesville. In a town with such a large college scene, it was reasonable to expect there would be some activists who I could stay with. Maybe I could even help them with some projects or get into some adventures with them. Alas, no one had responded to my emails in the five days since I had reached out. I was on my own.

I did get one very exciting message though from my friend Jen up in Maine. I had seen her the previous summer while I was back in Maine on vacation. We had exchanged email addresses, and I had been sending her periodic updates on my adventures ever since then in an attempt to convince her to come hike with me. This was the first time she had responded to any of my overtures, and she wrote to tell me she was actually considering coming out to join me. You will read a lot more about Jen in a later chapter, so I won't go into it here, but I have to tell you, that email was a really big deal to me. My heart did cartwheels for the rest of the day.

Charlottesville was a great place to sell zines and I must have signed up at least a dozen people for subscriptions. The owner of a coffee/ice cream shop bought one with plans to display it in the customer seating area with the other magazines. That seemed really cool. In the afternoon, all the parks filled up with groups of young Hippies lounging in the grass, or kicking hacky-sacks. I had a lot of good interactions, but no one came close to offering me a place to spend the night.

In one particularly hip part of town, the sidewalks were very wide, and shaded by big beautiful hardwoods that grew out of dirt islands in the paving stones. One of these tree trunks was surrounded by a whole tribe of Punks sitting or laying on the ground. They were all dressed in the same complex style of black leather clothing. The leatherwork was so unique, I could only guess they must have made their own clothing. I couldn't imagine anything like that being sold in stores. I counted seven of them, and all of them also had the exact same style of tattoos covering their faces. I can't think of many words to describe their tattoos other than "tribal." Most of them had a lot of ink on their faces. It made them look very dark, and maybe just a little bit dangerous. Some of them were female. Others were male, and at least one was too ambiguous for me to guess.

To my aesthetic taste, they looked strikingly beautiful, and I was drawn right to them. I walked right up and greeted them with even more than my usual warmth. To my shock, one of the males snarled a stream of curses at me in response. Straight black bangs hung down over his face, so I couldn't really make eye contact. One of the females who appeared to have been sleeping opened her eyes and looked up curiously. Then the spokesman put on his meanest Chuck Norris voice and said, "You've got 'til nightfall to get out of town… (dramatic pause) Or you're DEAD!"

It wasn't a very scary threat. None of the Punks got up off the ground, or even did so much as move. Three of them hadn't even turned their heads to look at me. But it hurt my feelings! I was so stunned I didn't even leave right away. I looked over at one of the males whose eyes I could see. Big nasty blond dreadlocks dangled out from under his weird leather hat and he was glaring at me. His eyes narrowed when I looked his way. It probably only took a few seconds, but I eventually granted their wishes and left them alone without saying another word. I had been so attracted to them. They were so neat looking, I had just wanted to be their friend, but they automatically hated me. I wasn't the least bit scared that they would actually do anything to hurt my body, but I spent the whole next hour feeling rejected and sad. It ended up being one of the best reminders I've ever gotten to not judge a book by its cover.

A couple hours later, it actually was time to "get out of town." No one had offered me a place to stay and it was getting late. It didn't take me long to find a nice camping spot. Just beyond the western beltway there was a golf course surrounded by quite a bit of lovely forest. I hiked a ways back into the forest until I got to a spot where I couldn't hear the rushing of traffic so loudly. I set up camp there, and slept well.

I was camped right beside one of the greens. When I awoke the next morning, I strolled out onto it and realized that I couldn't see any houses or other buildings. Ever the class-war hooligan, I followed a sudden whim to squat and do my morning business right there on the neatly-mowed grass of the golf course. Just so there would be no mistaking my mess for that of a wild animal, I left a wad of toilet paper right beside it. If I had walked a few more paces I could've scored a hole-in-one. When I told this story to my rebel friends, they howled with laughter, thinking how much funnier it would have been if I had pooped right into the cup. Alas, I am committed not to exaggerate the story that much. I just wasn't feeling that rude or that gutsy on that particular morning.

Ever since I changed course in Alexandria, I had been dreaming of walking a stretch of the Appalachian Trail. The iconic trail follows the Blue Ridge across most of Virginia. Today was the day I planned to climb up onto the mighty ridge and leave the roads behind. I had almost a full day of walking left to get across the last of the Piedmont, and work my way through the foothills to get back to the mighty ridge. I had looked at a map the day before and found a route made of smaller roads that I could take so as to avoid the rushing traffic of US route 250. I followed the Dick Woods Road (no joke) all morning, and then turned right on the Plank Road in the afternoon. To some extent, I was just trading the bummer of rushing traffic for the bummer of barking dogs, but there weren't as many dogs as there had been a couple days earlier.

Late in the afternoon, I merged back on to highway 250 for the long ascent up to Rockfish Gap. One of the rare, low gaps in the Blue Ridge, Rockfish Gap makes an excellent pass between Charlottesville and Waynesboro. Both 250 and Interstate 64 squeeze through the gap. At an elevation of 1,903 feet, the gap is only about half as high as the rest of the ridge, but it was still many times higher than any other hill I had climbed in my year-and-a-half of walking up to that point. It took me quite a while to reach the top, and I was sore and tired when I got there.

The summit gave me a beautiful view of the Shenandoah Valley to the west, all aglow with early evening light and deeply contrasting shadows. Unfortunately, a cold wind was howling through the gap, so I couldn't stay and admire the view for long. Right at the summit was a big dirt parking lot with a maze of hiking trails leading out from it in all directions. After a few minutes of probing around, I found one of those iconic AT signs where the

"A" sits on top of the "T" such that the top of the "T" and the bar across the middle of the "A" are formed by the same horizontal line. That was it. I had found the Appalachian Trail. Goodbye roads!

I followed the trail that the sign seemed to be indicating down into the woods. At first, it descended from the parking lot back down the same eastern side of the ridge that I had just come up. Then it cut across the slope of the mountain so that the slope rose steeply to my right, and dropped off steeply to my left. The trail kept up like that for quite a while, but it also kept descending gradually, so I was losing a lot of the elevation I had just gained climbing up to the pass. After a mile or so, I noticed that I had been stepping over quite a few fallen logs. That seemed odd because I had assumed that professional or volunteer trail crews would have cleared fallen logs off the trail on a regular basis. Then I came to a spot where a large fallen tree had come to rest against the cut bank above the trail at such an angle that it was difficult to pass. I either had to climb up onto the low side and go over, or get down on all fours to crawl under the high side. It seemed like quite an obstruction to be left in the middle of America's most popular long-distance hiking trail. Something wasn't right.

After that I thought to examine the actual trail. It was not swept clean as if hundreds of human feet had been going that way. Instead, it was covered with a thick coat of autumn leaves that weren't even packed down. I pressed on, but my thoughts filled with a growing urge to turn back. It just felt like such a huge setback to have to backtrack up that hill that I kept going for what must have been almost another mile. Eventually, I came to another large fallen tree that had completely blocked the trail, and that was enough to get me to finally stop. This just couldn't be the Appalachian Trail.

I sat my pack down and took a rest while I contemplated my strategy. I just couldn't stand the thought of hiking all that way back up the long hill I had just come down. I was tired, and my legs and shoulders felt terribly sore. I had been walking along the shady side of the mountain ever since I left the parking lot, but just then I realized that it was getting even darker. Night was falling, so I decided I might as well camp right there. There was nothing but precipitous steep slopes on either side of the trail, but the trail itself was graded nice and level, and it was plenty wide enough for my tent. The ground there was nicely padded with fresh autumn leaves, and it certainly didn't seem like I was going to be in anyone's way, so I pitched my tent right in the middle of the abandoned trail, ate some supper, and went to bed.

Sometime after the last daylight faded, I was laying there waiting for sleep to overtake me when all at once, the spirits of the mountains came out to greet me. Some nights, my own spirit reflects off the inside of the tent fabric and fills up that little space around me enough to drown out whatever might be going on outside. Other nights, the ambient, local spirits gush right through that flimsy nylon like a river, right through my skull and into the core of my consciousness.

The spirits of the Blue Ridge were as powerful as any such energy I've ever felt, and it gave me goose bumps. I lay there terrified for a solid chunk of time before I realized that nothing bad was going to happen. I just wasn't used to such a high level of spiritual energy. I had gotten little whiffs of spirits in those forested gaps between the cities, and even in the Druid Hill Park, but I hadn't been that far out into the wilderness for a couple years. Those wild mountain spirits were much stronger than anything I had felt for quite a while.

Eventually, I got used to the feeling and managed to calm down. I decided that they must not have meant to scare me. Their voice was just so massive and powerful that there was no way to turn it down. I decided that they must be offering their greetings, and welcoming me to the mountains. The thought made me smile. I spoke an audible "Thank you" into the night, and then I slept.

32. INTO THE WILD

When I awoke the next morning, I still couldn't stand the idea of backtracking over miles of terrain I had already covered. By the same token, it was obvious that I couldn't continue on the abandoned trail I had been following. I had already lost a lot of elevation. If the trail continued at that rate, I would end up back at the bottom of the Blue Ridge in short order. With those two choices crossed off, the only course of action left was to bushwhack straight up the steep slope. Normally, it would be foolish, verging on suicidal to wander off trail into the wilderness, but in this case, I reasoned that there was a fairly dependable safety net.

A scenic road called the Blue Ridge Parkway runs along the top of the Blue Ridge all the way from Front Royal, Virginia to Asheville, North Carolina. Built by the National Park Service in the mid 1900's, it is a narrow, two-lane road with a pleasantly low speed limit. Given the rugged mountain topography, the road rarely follows the actual crest of the ridge, but it usually follows that crest as closely as it can within the limits of reasonable engineering. I figured if I just kept going up, I would eventually run into the BRP, the real Appalachian Trail, or the crest of the ridge. If I reached the crest of the ridge before crossing the BRP or the AT, I reasoned that I could just follow the ridgetop south until it intersected with one of those human routes.

Needless to say, it was a tough climb, and I had to take it slow. Going off trail meant that I had to push through, or detour around large patches of underbrush, and the loose soil and leaves slid backwards under me feet so that a single step would sometimes only gain me a few inches of forward progress. I slipped on the damp leaves and fell frequently, but falling forward onto the steep slope wasn't that dramatic or dangerous. All the leaves had fallen from the trees, so they provided very little shade. The east facing slope soaked up all the heat from the morning sun, and before long I was dripping with sweat.

I must have carried on like that for about an hour when I noticed a clearing in the forest canopy directly ahead of me up the hill. The slope got even steeper leading up to the clearing, and I actually had to scramble up it on all four limbs. It looked like a place where humans had filled in dirt and rocks to create a level space up above. It seemed likely that I would encounter some sort of human structure when I reached the clearing at the top, but that idea didn't deter me.

Sure enough, when I reached the top of the steeply-filled slope, I found myself in the backyard of a mid-sized suburban-style house. I had expected some kind of human development, but I was surprised to find a regular old house. It was awkward to be in someone's back yard, but I wasn't about to go back to bushwhacking. Surely a house would have a road leading to its front side, so I strolled quickly and easily around the house through the nice, level yard.

There was indeed a driveway on that side, and in the driveway was a man unloading something from his minivan. We were both surprised to encounter one another in that setting, but we were both friendly people, so the tension eased quickly. When I explained how I came to be there in his remote driveway, he was very sympathetic. He told me that the people who maintain the Appalachian Trail had just changed its route a few years prior, and the abandoned trail I had been following down the hill was the old route. He said that if I followed his driveway out to the main road, I would see the new route leading up the hill to the left, just beyond where his driveway reached the road. Then he offered to fill my water bottle, and it just so happened that I was almost out of water. What a nice guy!

I followed his driveway north for about a half mile until it came out at the main road. I was dismayed to find myself back at Rockfish Gap, in the same dirt parking lot where I had stood the previous evening. I had wasted about a half a day being lost, and that was frustrating. I also realized that I actually could have kept following the abandoned trail. If it really was the old route of the AT, then at some point it would have climbed back up the hill and rejoined the current route. Oh well. I got on the new AT, and it wasn't long before I found a milage sign reassuring me that I was on the right track this time. The weather was pleasant. The scenery was gorgeous, and my frustration wore off quickly.

The trail cut across the slope on the east flank of the ridge for several hours, dropped down into a ravine, and then ascended up the ravine very steeply for what seemed like an impossibly long distance. I had thought that I was already very high up, so it was a surprise to find that there was still so much mountain above me. The sky clouded over part way through the afternoon, so I lost track of time. It seemed like the people who built the Appalachian Trail couldn't stand the idea of following a level contour. I was either climbing a steep slope, or descending a steep slope at all times. Over all, there was definitely a lot more climbing than descending, and I found myself walking through more and more stands of spruce and fir trees, the kind of trees you would find in colder climates much further north.

Eventually, the daylight gave out and I made camp. Down in the land of human settlement, there was always at least some amount of challenge in finding a place to sleep, so it's not too hard for me to remember each one of those situations. In contrast, it was no challenge at all to find a good camping spot in the wilderness of the Blue Ridge. I know that I spent twelve nights in total up on the AT, but as I write this, eighteen years later, I can only remember specific details from about half of the places that I must have camped. I can't remember anything about my camping spot that first night. I must have just noticed it was getting dark, wandered off the trail a little bit, found a level spot and camped. No big deal.

I had been hiking the AT since late morning, and in that time, I had noticed a couple of unexpected patterns. First of all, I had expected to see lots of other hikers on the trail. The Appalachian Trail is the most popular backpacking trail in the country. More than 100,000 people attempt to walk the whole length of it every year, and even more people hike sections of it. Yet I hadn't seen a single other person since I left Rockfish Gap. I was literally all alone out there.

Also, I had come to the mountains expecting to see a dazzling display of autumn foliage, but when I got there, all the leaves were already on the ground. Whenever I got to a grand viewpoint, I could still see some fall colors down in the valleys below, but up at the high elevations where I was hiking, all the deciduous trees had already let their leaves drop. I had arrived too late.

I awoke to a cold rain and an incredible stiff soreness in my legs and butt. I was in great shape for walking along graded roadways, but I had done more steep climbing in the last two days than I had in the rest of my trip combined, and my muscles were feeling it. I lingered in the tent for several hours that morning hoping the rain would stop, but eventually boredom overcame laziness and I got myself moving. It was only a light drizzle anyway.

At some point that morning, it came time to fill my water bottle again. I had carried along one of those backpacking pump-filters for my entire trip, and I had used it many times already to drink water out of streams that would have otherwise made me desperately sick. I came to a tiny stream and started pumping, but then I was overcome by an urge to drink the water directly out of the stream without filtering it. It's a bad idea to drink out of any stream anywhere because giardia spreads through deer feces.

If you don't know, giardia is a bacteria that causes infected humans to suffer two to three weeks of diarrhea so severe that many people would die without medical intervention. Even after surviving that initial blast, many giardia patients will continue to suffer from digestive difficulties for years. So it was a foolish idea to drink unfiltered water, but for some reason, I just couldn't help myself. I was only a few hundred feet from the top of the mountain, and the little steam looked so perfectly pure. It was as if the spirit of the little brook seduced me.

After that, I filled my whole bottle with unfiltered water and continued on my way. Over the next eleven days, I routinely drank unfiltered water from enchanted little streams in the highest reaches of the Blue Ridge, and I never got sick at all. I don't understand how I got away with this. For the record, I strongly discourage anyone who reads this from doing what I did. As a child, I drank water from a full-sized river in the Washington Cascades numerous times before my parents found out and made me stop, so maybe I had built up an immunity to giardia. Who knows?

The morning was cold, with frequent intervals of thick fog. The drizzle came and went, but it never came down hard enough to get me very wet. At some point, the trail crossed over to the west side of the ridge and the parkway. Not long after that, a spur trail forked up to the left with a sign saying it was only a few tenths of a mile to a lookout. I had passed by a number of similar spurs and side trails already, but this time I decided to check it out. I had been walking the AT for more than a full day, and I had not yet seen a single view off the west side of the ridge. Also, the drizzle and the fog had cleared out, at least temporarily, so there was some hope that I might actually see something. I sat my pack down and climbed the short distance up to a spot where a rocky crag stuck out above the forest canopy. It really was a spectacular view even though portions of it were still hidden behind cloud and clumps of wet fog. To the right, I could see a large portion of the vast and fertile Shenandoah Valley with clumps of fog settled into many of its lowest notches. To the left, the more southern reaches of the valley were hidden behind a series of huge, nearby ridges.

As I sat there eating a snack, I was at first startled, and then excited to hear the sound of quite a few human children approaching. They were climbing up to the same viewpoint as me, and they were accompanied by a woman who looked to be about the same age as me. She was a school teacher in the nearby town of Waynesboro, and she had just led eight or nine third-graders on a hike all the way up from the bottom of the ridge. The kids kept her too busy to have much of a conversation, but it was still very nice to meet someone. It had only been about 24 hours since the last time I had seen other people, but somehow it felt like it had been weeks.

I only got one more little rain shower that day. It cleared up gradually throughout the afternoon, and then the sun came out that evening, making it the warmest part of the whole day. It was warm enough for long enough that the ground was dry by the time I set up my tent.

Right about sunset, the trail descended into a pass where it crossed a dirt road. After so many miles of steep, forested terrain, I was surprised to find myself in a broad meadow in a level valley. It was the lowest gap I had seen in a day and a half of walking the ridge top, and it was the first road to cross the mountains since Rockfish Gap. When I got down to the road crossing, there was a sign for the AT hikers to tell us this was Reed's Gap.

The meadow made for open views, but all I could see to the west was the top of a nearby ravine. The view to the east was amazing though, so I walked down the road a short distance that way to take in more of it. Everything in the countryside down below was so dark under the shadow of the mountain that I could only make out vague details. But off in the distance, where the mountain's shadow hadn't reached yet, a stripe of the Piedmont was still in the sun. It was too far away to make out any details, and in the next moment, it went dark too.

Level land and a meadow of soft grass made an irresistible camping spot, but did I really want to camp that close to a road? It seemed silly to hike so far through the wilderness and then camp right next to a road, but I was tired and the sun was about to set, so I went for it. I had been there for twenty minutes, and I hadn't seen a car go by yet, so I figured it wasn't such a busy road that it would bother me.

I got about halfway through setting up my tent when a jeep drove by. It took a long time to go by because the road was too bumpy for it to go very fast. Suddenly I felt very awkward. I couldn't disguise what I was doing, so I just continued setting up my tent and kept my back to the jeep. Finally, it went down over the east side and out of sight. After that, I relocated my tent. I was pretty sure it was legal to camp there, but I wasn't 100% sure. I was in the George Washington National Forest. Growing up out West, it had always been legal to camp just about anywhere in a national forest as long as you didn't make it a permanent residence. I compromised and just went behind the first layer of trees. The land was still level there and the ground was still soft. I had a great night of sleep, and no more vehicles came by until after I left the next morning.

The next day was quite warm. By mid-morning, the trail left the crest of the Blue Ridge and led me out along the crest of an even taller ridge that spurred off to the east. The trail went up, up, up to the summit of a peak that had to be the highest point I had reached yet on the trail. When I got to the top, a sign said the mountain's name was Three Ridges. The trail followed the very crest of the mountain with steep slopes dropping away on both sides. After quite a distance like that, the ridge suddenly ended in a great eastern promontory, capped in a cliff. The trail brought me right to the top of a cliff where I marveled at a more amazing view than I could ever imagine. At this point, there were a great many more mountains out to the east of the Blue Ridge. None of them were quite as tall as the mountain I was on, and none of them made a continuous high ridge like the Blue Ridge, but there were so many of them standing alone or in clumps that I could barely catch a glimpse of the Piedmont out behind them. There was a little more flatland off to the south. Out there I could see several plumes of steam rising from some sort of industrial smokestacks.

The mountain I was on stood out to the east, in front of the actual crest of the Blue Ridge. To the southwest, across a great gaping valley, was another spectacular huge mountain standing out in front of the range. It was shaped roughly like an enormous pyramid, but more complex, with great buttresses sweeping off in several directions. Several other people had climbed up to the Three Ridges viewpoint for day hikes, and one of them told me that the mountain across the way was called The Priest. They said it was the highest mountain in that whole part of Virginia, and they told me the AT would take me all the way to the bottom of the valley, and then all the way to the summit of The Priest.

I looked down. The bottom of the valley was so far down that I couldn't actually see it from where I stood. Over the next week or so, I would learn that the Appalachian Trail can in no way pass as a legitimate transportation route. In every situation where there is a choice between an easy way and a hard way, the AT chooses the hard way. As I have already mentioned, the crest of the Blue Ridge is relatively level for hundreds of miles. It would be possible to build a fairly level trail along this crest that would allow a hiker to go many miles in a short time. The Blue Ridge Parkway stays fairly close to this ideal because it is built for automobiles. In contrast, the AT goes way down over one side of the ridge or the other every few miles, like a drunk person trying to walk a balance beam. Sometimes there is some rhyme or reason for the route, such as a waterfall or a scenic viewpoint that the trail is detouring to look at, but more often than not, there is no discernable reason for the detour. Sometimes the trail climbs a thousand feet to the summit of a mountain, only to find out there is no viewpoint at the top. The hiker who desires a better view is welcome to put their pack down and shimmy up a tree. No one in their right mind would take the Appalachian Trail as a means to get from one place to another. Hiking it is a purely recreational experience for athletic people with a lot of time to kill.

Sure enough, the trail went right over the edge and down the steep south flank of the Three Ridges. Down, down, down I went until my sides ached fiercely. Going down is the easy part and yet it still must have taken me almost three hours to get to the bottom. Two thirds of the way down, I passed a beautiful little waterfall. At the bottom, a lovely little river called the Tye rushed over a bed of rounded rocks. Down there, the sun had already set, but I knew there were several hours of daylight left, so I cranked my ass into low gear, and started up The Priest.

Up, up, up I climbed. The trail was ridiculously steep, just as it had been coming down the north side of the same valley. Evidently, the technique of using switchbacks to decrease the steepness of walking trails was not widely practiced way back when the AT was built. I was feeling strong though, and I must have made it at least two thirds of the way to the top before it came time to make camp. I vaguely remember my campsite that night. Right where one of the buttressing ridges made contact with the main bulk of the mountain, there was a narrow shoulder of level land. I set my tent on that, just below, and in sight of the trail.

I awoke in the middle of the night when the rain started, and it was raining cold and hard by the time dawn arrived. It had actually rained so hard already, that my tent had started to leak and I was fairly wet. Something told me this rain wasn't going to let up any time soon, so I ignored the urge to wait. I got right into my poncho, put my tent away sopping wet, and got moving. I still had a long climb to the top of The Priest. The rain just poured on me, but the exertion of carrying my ass and my big backpack up such a steep hill kept me warm enough. I finally reached the summit which was marked with a sign that read, "The Priest, 4,063ft." I couldn't even see the trees at the edge of the clearing, let alone the view beyond. From there, the trail veered back west towards the crest of the Blue Ridge.

Being the AT, there were no level spots, but for most of the day, I switched between up and down frequently, so I never lost too much of the elevation I had gained climbing The Priest. The rain did let up a few times, but never for very long. Despite how unpleasant that was, I couldn't help notice the beauty of the rare alpine forest I was hiking through. Spruce/fir taiga is no big deal in Canada or northern Maine, but when it's isolated on the highest peaks of the central Appalachians, it feels quite magical, even in the rain.

I had no way of telling time, but it must have been about mid-afternoon when I came to a shelter. The Appalachian Mountain club builds wooden shelters about every ten miles along the trail for hikers to sleep in. I had already passed several of them since I got on the trail, but they didn't make sense as places to sleep. The floor was made of solid wood boards, far less comfortable than the duff of the forest floor. Anyway, I had always passed by them in the middle of the day when it wouldn't have made any sense to stop. This time it made a lot more sense. It was pouring rain hard enough to drown a frog and I was soaked to the bone.

I changed into the driest clothes I could find and hung the rest up on the rafters. As far as I can remember, the rest of the day went by in a flash and then I was trying to sleep on the uncomfortable wooden slabs. If the rain let up at all during the night I certainly didn't notice. When daylight came, it was raining as hard as ever. None of my hanging clothes had dried at all. At that point, it made the most sense to keep waiting.

I stayed in that trail shelter for a whole day. I swear to you, in all my life, I've never seen it rain so hard for so long. I've seen it rain harder a few times, mostly in Florida, but I've never seen it rain for a whole day in Florida. Anyway, Florida rain is warm. This Appalachian Winter Rain was cold! It would have been suicidal to go out in it.

I read all the names carved into the wood of the little hut. There were very few places that had not been carved over with the names of hikers. There were lots of names that sounded like names a mother would give, but many others sounded like nicknames that the hikers had given themselves. I recognized many of the names from the previous shelters that I had stopped and inspected. AT shelters also tended to have diaries made of paper closed inside a hinged metal box with some combination of pens and pencils. I had read quite a few interesting diary entries from random AT hikers in the shelters I had already passed, and I had gotten a sense that there was a hiker sub-culture and I might have made lots of friends if I had come during the right season.

Unfortunately, the shelter I got stuck in didn't have any paper diary, or pencils, or anything. All it had was a bucket full of wax with a candlewick sticking out of it. I never felt any need for the candle, so I never lit it. I wished there was a diary, because I wanted to write in it. I wished I could say, "Mid-November, 2002. Rained so hard for so long, it reminded me of Noah's Ark, and I felt lucky to be on a mountain top." It really must have been flooding badly down below.

I slept a second night on the hard wooden boards, and awoke at dawn to an interesting situation. It was still too foggy to see the trees on the far side of the trail, but the epic rain had finally stopped. I reached for some breakfast, and it wasn't there.

When I left Charlottesville, I had my pack loaded heavily with all sorts of food. I would tell you the details if I could remember, but I *do* remember that I believed I had enough food to make it all the way to Roanoke. That was before I knew how difficult the AT was, before I knew how cold I would get, and before I knew I could get stuck in one place for more than 24 hours waiting for the flood waters to subside. It was also before I knew that wild animals could rob me of all my remaining food.

By my second night in the AT shelter, the only food I had left was a bag of peanuts and raisins, but I wasn't worried, because I had several *pounds* of peanuts and raisins. It was plenty of food to get me to the next road-crossing where I could set down my pack, walk down the mountain, find a town, and get some groceries. It hadn't seemed like a problem, until that morning when

The End Never Comes

I woke up and found that all my food was gone.

It has been explained to me since then, that the Appalachian Trail shelters are infested with elite new species of mice and rats, and I'm sure that's who robbed me. The zipper to the food pouch on my backpack was open just a couple inches. Either I had neglected to close it all the way the night before, or the rodents had figured out how to work it open. The thing is, there's no way the rodents who robbed me ate all those nuts in one night. I had a lot! It would have taken hundreds of them to eat that all up in one night, and that would've woken me up. No. A small number of rodents did lap after lap hauling my food out of my pack and stashing it somewhere nearby. Or they all lined up and passed my nuts down the line like a bucket brigade and stashed them somewhere nearby.

I would still walk to the next road crossing, go down over the side, and find a grocery store, but now I would do it on an empty stomach.

33. REAL MOUNTAINS

It had been too cold and humid for any of my clothing to dry out. All that wet cotton kept my pack heavy even without any weight in the food compartment. I was already quite hungry by the time I got packed up and set out that morning. I didn't know how far I would have to walk before I got to the next road, so I was craving to look at a map almost as much as I was craving to eat something.

I hiked out into pea-soup fog that morning, but before long it got very bright, and I could tell there were no more clouds above the one I was engulfed in. By mid-morning, the fog was burning off and land started the slow process of drying out. I couldn't stop thinking about how much I wanted to eat something. It felt like a merciful miracle when I came to a couple of places where the AT actually stayed on a level course for a while without climbing or descending any slopes. It ended up being a beautiful, sunny day, but I can't remember any details beyond how hungry I felt.

Early in the afternoon, I happened upon a much greater miracle of mercy. A small dirt road crossed the trail at a place that turned out to be called Salt Log Gap. A sizeable stretch of meadow surrounded the road, and a hunter had set up an elaborate camp there, right beside the trail where the forest service had placed a picnic table. The man was hospitable as all git-out, so I followed his suggestion to take a seat at the table.

A dead deer was hanging by its back legs from a nearby tree. It had finished bleeding out, but the hunter had not yet begun the work of gutting it, so his hands were still clean. I caught myself hoping that there was some venison meat already prepared somewhere and I would be offered a sample. I swear I didn't say a word to indicate that I was starving, but I didn't have to. Maybe he could tell I was hungry by the way I kept staring at his deer, or maybe he was just raised with the custom of feeding strangers. Whatever it was, it only took him a couple minutes to dig some ingredients out of a cooler and fix me a turkey and cheese sandwich with mayo on a burger bun. He presented this amazing gift to me along with a can of cheap beer!

I did my best not to woof it down like a wild dog, but it was the best damn turkey and cheese sandwich I've ever had in my life. I also did my best to make friendly conversation, but there was a bit of a language barrier between us. His hillbilly accent was so thick that I could literally only understand about a third of the words coming out of his mouth. I kept having to ask him to repeat himself, and I felt like an idiot.

He kept referring to himself as "we," and I realized that there must be another hunter who wasn't there at the moment. There certainly was enough gear there to accommodate more than one person. The campsite was cluttered with far too many man-made objects for me to observe all of them, or remember the details. The hood and roof of the nearby pickup were piled high with gear. It's quite likely that the man actually told me where his buddy had gone and I just didn't catch what he said.

I did manage to glean some critical information from him about how to best get to the nearest town. He said I should skip right over the little road there at Salt Log Gap, and the next little dirt road that I would encounter just a few miles beyond. Neither of them would lead me anywhere worthwhile, and I was unlikely to encounter enough traffic on either one to even hitchhike. After that, I would reach some place called the "Hog Camp Meadows," and beyond that, I would come to Highway 60. He advised taking that highway west into Buena Vista, (pronounced Byoona Vista by Virginians.) There I would find some good groceries.

The turkey sandwich had only filled a fraction of the hole in my belly, and it sounded like I still had a pretty long way to go, but at least now I had some idea what to expect. The friendly hunter sent me off with one of those trapezoidal metal cans of compressed corned beef- the kind where you peel the top open by twisting it around a little, key-shaped metal tool that comes attached to the package. I thanked him as much as I could and set off with a renewed sense of hope.

It took a few hours to climb over another viewless mountain top, and then down into the next gap, where I crossed another very small dirt road, just as the hunter had foretold. This one was called Hog Camp Gap. It couldn't have been more than an hour of climbing up the next hill before I came out into a broad area of meadows right on the broad summit of a mountain. A sign confirmed that I was in the Hog Camp Meadows. The view was breathtaking in the late-afternoon sun. I could see so many successive layers of mountains to the west that I wondered if I was looking all the way to West Virginia. Most of the mountains were shaped like long, level-topped ridges just like the Blue Ridge.

I still had maybe an hour until sunset, so I could have made it a couple more miles before I really had to set up camp, but the meadow was so beautiful, I decided to hold up and make camp there. I hung my clothing up on some little trees to start drying, and went to look for a source of water. There were no cows there at the moment, but I saw significant evidence that people brought cows up there to graze sometimes. That made me feel nervous about drinking the water, so when I did find a trickling little stream, I used my filter for the first time in days. I sat and watched another glorious sunset, opened my can of corned beef, and ate about half of it. My whole supper consisted of about three ounces of extra-salty meat byproduct, and I saved the other half for breakfast the next morning.

It was almost noon before I finally reached route 60. The AT took another one of its detours down over the east side of the ridge, and I had descended to a very low elevation before I actually got to the road crossing. I stashed my pack in the bushes and put my thumb up for the west-bound traffic.

Hitch-hiking is always a gamble. You never know how long it's going to take to get a ride. That day, for whatever reason, it took a long, long time before anyone stopped to pick me up. By the time I got to Buena Vista, I was ready to try chewing up acorns, and my ride didn't drop me off right in front of a store. I still had to walk around town for a while searching for food.

Eventually, I happened upon the filthiest little restaurant in Virginia. It was so dimly lit inside that it took a couple minutes before my eyes adjusted enough to see anything, and it smelled like recently-smoked cigarettes. I don't remember what kind of sandwich I ended up ordering, but I remember it was awesome. I was still hungry after I finished it, so I got a large order of onion rings and they were awesome too. I got directions to the town's lone grocery store which was a Giant Eagle, (pronounced "Giant Iggle" in Appalachia.)

It's a fact that the industrial food system distributes a lower quality of products to grocery stores in areas where only poor people live. The Giant Eagle in Buena Vista was one of my first experiences with that phenomenon, so it surprised me that I couldn't find any of the products I was used to. Once again, I can't remember many details about which food items I picked out, but I gathered a goodly load, and once again I was convinced that I had enough food to last me to Roanoke. Most notably, I bought a huge box of dehydrated potato flakes. I had never tried potato flakes at all, let alone as a trail food, but my friend Jen (the one who sent me the exciting email) had suggested it. When I ran into her up in Maine the previous summer, she had just returned from hiking the Pacific Crest Trail. She said that dehydrated potatoes had been a staple of her diet on the trail, so I gave it a try. The box took up so much space that I figured it would cover most of my needs for starch, so I bought very little else in the way of carbohydrates.

Hitch-hiking back over the Blue Ridge, I noticed a spectacular series of huge rock outcrops towering over the town. Layer after layer of sedimentary deposits had been turned metamorphic, tipped up at a steep diagonal angle, and then broken off along jagged edges. It was the kind of rock formation that people often call "flatirons."

It was evening by the time I got back to my pack and resumed hiking. The trail just kept descending beyond the highway crossing, and before long, I stopped and camped in another wilderness location that I can't remember at all.

In the morning, the trail finally reached the bottom of the valley where it came alongside a larger creek and followed it downstream. It was lovely to walk with the sound of rushing water, but it was also quite cold. The creek had carved a deep valley, and it would still be hours before the sun would shine down into it.

I was still in that early morning shade when I came to the site of an historic settlement called Brownstown. A sign there explained that sometime in the mid 1700's, a group of African slaves escaped from a plantation in the lowlands and set up a village there at the foot of the Blue Ridge. Escaping to the North wasn't even an option before the Revolutionary War, and in those days, the western frontier was much closer anyway. Very few European settlers had moved up into the Appalachian Mountains, so there were vast stretches of territory where escaped slaves could hide, provided they could master the skills to survive in the wilderness.

Apparently, a large and diverse enough group of people escaped to Brownstown to form a breeding population. Historians and archaeologists speculate that at least one generation of free people were born and lived partial lifetimes there until the secret town was eventually discovered and re-enslaved in the 1790's. It was a fascinating and inspiring story. That valley really was a shady little nook in the mountains that was not on the way to anywhere. It was not hard to imagine how a band of cautious refugees could stay hidden there for decades.

Below Brownstown, the trail wrapped around the shore of a mid-sized reservoir that supplied water to the nearby city of Lynchburg. The sun finally came up above the ridge to the east, but I was still in the shade for much of the way, because I was down at such a low elevation that many of the Oak trees were still holding onto their brown-orange leaves. Below the dam, the trail crossed an even larger stream called the Pedlar River on a charming wooden bridge. I stopped and had lunch there, and then began the long, grueling climb back up to the crest of the Blue Ridge. By afternoon, the weather had warmed, and I was sweating hard from the workout. I think I made it all the way to the top before setting up camp that night, but once again, I can't remember the details.

It was getting towards noon the next day when I saw another hiker approaching. I was walking down a long, gradual descent without any curves, so I could see him from a long way off. I had been on the trail for eight days, and this was the first time I had seen another person with a backpack who was obviously hiking on the AT for multiple days. I hadn't seen a single other human being since I got dropped off after my hitch into Buena Vista two days prior, so I was really excited to make a new friend. I picked a nice flat rock to sit down on, took my pack off and waited for him to arrive.

When he got close enough, I shouted a friendly greeting. He reached up to pull and earbud speaker out of his ear and said, "What?" I repeated my greeting and then asked how his hike had been going. By then he had reached the rock where I was sitting, so he stopped. He said he had gotten on the trail somewhere in North Carolina, and he had a few days left to get to his destination at Rockfish Gap. He said he had made really good time yesterday, but he was hoping to break his record that day, and with that, he promptly left.

I felt confused and rejected. Being alone in the wilderness for days on end made me want someone to talk to badly. I thought AT through hikers would be interesting people who I would have lots in common with, but this was not what I experienced. Over the next few days, I met two other backpackers heading north, and they both treated me the same way. They were all really focused on getting their trail-hiking experience over with as quickly as possible, so they didn't have any time for social pleasantries. The trail was designed to be a scenic route, leading us through some of the most beautiful places I had ever seen. Why in the hell would a person want to stick speakers in their ears and hurry through it as quickly as they could? I really didn't understand,

and it bummed me out.

The trail stayed up at high elevation all day long, and I got to see beautiful views off both sides of the ridge every few minutes. The afternoon shadows were just beginning to grow long when I came to the most spectacular view of all. The James River is Virginia's largest river, and it cuts right through the Blue Ridge from west to east. The resulting canyon is called the James River Face, and it is truly one of the great scenic wonders of the Appalachians. Approaching from the northeast on the AT, you catch your first view of the canyon from several miles away. I had not studied the map enough to know that I would come across such a spectacular place, so the amazing view stopped me dead in my tracks.

I had only sat down for a minute before another man came along the trail, but instead of a backpack, this one was carrying a rifle. In my prejudiced mind, I still assumed that thru-hikers would be my kind of people, while hunters would not. I gave the man a polite nod, but then I was surprised when he strolled right up to me and started a friendly conversation. He looked to be in his mid-thirties, and is accent was not nearly as difficult to understand as the last hunter I had met. We must have talked for at least twenty minutes until my need for human interaction was thoroughly satisfied. He told me it was illegal to use the AT for hunting access, and I was impressed that he would put so much trust in me not to rat him out. When we parted ways, he gave me a can of some product called "potted meat."

I ended up being really glad that there were so many hunters out there breaking the rules. I only met those two, but they both gave me food at times when I really needed it. I saw four or five more hunters from a distance in my time up on the trail and all of them gave me friendly waves. In my experience, hunters on the Appalachian Trail are much friendlier than thru-hikers.

The James River Face is one case where it isn't even an option for the trail or the Blue Ridge Parkway to stick to a level contour. Both of them have to drop down to just a few hundred feet above sea level to get across the mighty river. As the trail descended into the great canyon, and the afternoon shadows grew longer, the view in front of me just kept getting more and more spectacular. For at least an hour, the trail kept popping out onto big bald stretches of rock where there were no trees to block my line of sight. If you are reading this at a time when the internet is still working, I actually recommend a quick search for images of the James River Face here to enhance your reading experience. You will see some really pretty pictures.

I made it most of the way to the bottom before night fell and I camped in another place that I can't remember. Even at that low elevation, it got bitterly cold overnight, and I had a hard time sleeping through it. I don't remember finding any ice in my water bottle the next morning, but once I got moving, I do remember seeing an occasional puddle with a thin layer of ice over the top.

The trail meandered around the lowlands for an hour or more, crossed a mid-sized highway, and then brought me to a grand metal bridge built specifically for pedestrians hiking the AT. It was an impressive structure spanning the river that was hundreds of feet wide. I stopped out over the middle to admire the view as clouds of my own breath swirled around my head. The river was wide, but not very deep, and it made a beautiful rushing sound as it hurried its way down over the trillions of big round rocks. What a river!

Then it was time to start the long climb back up onto the Blue Ridge. It was sunny that day, but the orientation of the trail on the mountain kept me in the shade all morning, and as far as I could tell, the weather never warmed up more than a few degrees. Even the exertion of walking up a steep hill for hours was not enough to warm my body. As I got up higher, there were some pretty cool views of the river, but I was so uncomfortably cold that I couldn't really enjoy the scenery. I also got so hungry that I had to stop for an extra meal in between breakfast and lunch, and it was then that I realized something was dreadfully wrong.

It was only two and a half days since my last stop at a grocery store, and I had already eaten through most of my food. I had brought well over two pounds of pepperoni sticks with me, but I scarfed down the end of the last one there in the cold shade of the James River Face, and it wasn't even time for lunch yet. I had been eating huge meals, but never really feeling satisfied.

For the last two days, I had been ignoring a growing suspicion that there was something wrong with my box of potato flakes. I didn't seem to be gaining any energy or strength from eating them. A whole belly full would only leave me feeling hungrier than before I ate it. I was shivering hard that morning as I choked down another bowl of the cold, flavorless mush, and I finally faced up to the dire truth of the matter in my conscious mind. Even if there were some calories to be gleaned from the dehydrated potatoes, my body was failing to glean them.

I wondered how Jen could have made it through hundreds of miles of wilderness in the Sierra Nevada while eating that shit. Did she add some other ingredient that she hadn't told me about? Was she using some cheese enzyme to help her body unlock its nutritional potential? It occurred to me that her skin had been stretched very tightly over her skeleton when I had last seen her a few months prior. I also couldn't help but wonder if these "potato" flakes were made of real potatoes at all, or if they were just some industrial by-product intended to give poor people the sensation of a full belly. It reminded me of Jurgis trying to sustain his family on sausage meat diluted with sawdust in Upton Sinclair's book, *The Jungle*.

I was still hungry, and very cold when I finished my brunch and continued up the mountain, and morose thoughts clouded my mind for most of the day. I skipped lunch that day in an effort to ration the small amount of food I had left. For a couple hours in the afternoon, the trail took me through an area that was not shaded by any higher ridges, and my mood brightened a little bit. At one point, I stopped to lay on my back in a bowl of soft grass that was angled directly toward the sun. It was the first time I had felt comfortably warm all day. By late afternoon, I was back on the crest of the ridge, and I made it a couple miles along the top before camping in another spot that has faded from my memory. Needless to say, it was another cold night.

By morning, a layer of high clouds had rolled in and it wasn't quite as cold. It was that morning when two more thru-hikers blew me off as they hurried by on their way north. Within a few hours of hiking, I made it to a very high summit called Thunder Ridge. Ordinarily, the view would have been inspiring, but that morning, it was just ominous. The clouds had lowered and darkened, and it looked like it was about to rain. Sure enough, within the next couple hours it started to sprinkle, and before long, it was pouring. It wasn't the coldest rain I had ever walked through, but it was tied with the rest for wettest. There was no choice but to just keep walking, so that's what I did.

It was hard to tell time without the sun, but it seemed like it must be getting late when I came to another wooden shelter, so I stopped. It was perfect timing. I had only been there about half an hour when it started to get dark. By some miracle, the clothing inside my backpack had remained mostly dry, and it felt like the pinnacle of luxury to change into almost-dry clothes. This shelter had a diary and pencils, but my fingers were too cold to function, so I could not write my own entry in the diary. I read the others though. Then

I ate a small ration of supper and crashed out hard. The solid wooden floor of the shelter didn't bother me one bit. I became one of the floorboards that night.

In the morning I had to assess my situation. I was pretty sure I didn't have too much further to go to get to Roanoke, but I was almost out of food. I downed my last ration of potato flakes, for whatever that was worth, and topped it off with a couple spoons full of corned beef. Ever since that first hunter rescued me from starvation at Salt Log Gap, I had developed a taste for the trapezoid cans of salty corned beef, so I had bought several more in Buena Vista. Now it was almost all that remained of my food supply. I had one can of the stuff left, minus the two bites I had eaten for breakfast, plus the smaller can of potted meat that the second hunter had given me. It was still raining hard as ever, but it made no sense to stay in the shelter where I would quickly run out of food.

It also didn't make sense to stay on the Appalachian Trail. I reasoned that the Blue Ridge Parkway would make a much straighter line, with a lot less up and down. I preferred trail hiking to road hiking, but there wouldn't be many tourists out for a scenic drive in the pouring winter rain. The trail and the parkway had crossed each other several times the previous day, and I knew that I would find the road just a short distance through the woods to my left. Reluctantly, I saddled up and set off into the pouring rain. As I recall, there was a little branch of trail connecting the AT shelter to a parking lot on the side of the BRP, so I found it without difficulty.

The rain seemed to have gotten colder overnight. My poncho kept my upper torso relatively dry for the first couple hours, but overall, it was a sadly ineffective set-up. By mid-day, I was soaked to the bone, freezing cold, and halfway to insanity with hunger. There were no such thing as regular meal times that day. I would just stop and eat another couple bites of corned-beef every time I felt like I couldn't stand the hunger anymore.

I think it was still morning when I came to a building called the Peaks of Otter Visitor Center. The Peaks of Otter are a pair of very pointy, high mountains that draw in tourists as a scenic attraction along the BRP. I learned that information by looking it up years later. The day I was there, I could only see a few hundred feet through the rain and fog. There was a little gift shop right inside the front door of the building, and my heart and stomach both surged with hope that it might have some food.

The End Never Comes

As it turned out, all they had were about a dozen little bags of incredibly expensive trail mix. You got about four ounces for eight dollars, but I grabbed one bag and eagerly went to pay. The cashier was an elderly woman with a big, complex Deep-South haircut, thick layers of makeup, gaudy metal earrings, and fake fingernails. She gave me a look of horror and disdain, but she sold me the trail mix.

I headed back towards the front door, but within a few steps I realized that my fingers were too cold to open the plastic package. I looked around for someone who might help me, but the old cashier was the only other person there. I took a deep breath and sheepishly returned to her counter to ask for help. She never stopped looking at me like I was the scum of the Earth, but she was willing to help. Her old fingers were also too weak to open the package, but she had a pair of scissors in a drawer that did the trick.

The visitor's center was one big room, and it had a couple of benches in it. Rather than go back out in the rain, I decided to sit on one of the benches to eat. In that position, my back was turned to the cashier. I turned around to glance at her one time and she gave me a look that made me wonder if she was considering calling the police. A puddle was forming on the ground underneath my bench.

The trail mix was not much of a food source. When I make my own mixtures, I prefer a ratio of about three quarters nuts to about one quarte dried fruit. That gives me the perfect balance of protein and carbohydrates with a nice little kick of sugar to keep me going until the protein kicks in. The trail mix I got at the Peaks of Otter was almost all dried fruit with extra sugar added, and just a few precious nuts. It was typical of most pre-mixed trail mixes you can buy, but it was about three times as expensive. I thought about buying more bags of the stuff and decided against it. The potential of a brief sugar high followed by an even more ravenous hunger seemed even more unpleasant, and maybe even more dangerous than regular starvation. I finished my sugar snack quickly and made for the door before the old lady could kick me out.

The Blue Ridge Parkway twisted and turned, and went up and down a few big hills after the Peaks of Otter. Then it levelled out into a long stretch of relatively straight road where I was able to put a lot of miles behind me pretty quickly. I remembered from the maps that the BRP doesn't go directly into Roanoke. Instead, it swings quite a few miles off its normal course in order to skirt around the southeast side of the city. Looking at a map now, I can see that I was mistaken, but at the time, I though the AT would take me much closer to the city, so I decided to get back on the trail. The rain had been slowing down for hours, and it had almost stopped by the time I found another crossing with the AT.

A mile or so out on the trail, the rain finally stopped completely, so I decided to sit down and celebrate. I felt certain that this would be my last night up in the mountains, so I got out the little can of potted meat, pried it open with my pocket knife, and gobbled it down. It was not salty like the corned beef, and it was much more gelatinous. It reminded me of the canned cat food that our family used to feed to our cat when I was growing up. I imagined that the floor of the slaughter house must need to be squeegeed clean fairly often, and whatever material they came up with that was unfit to make into hot dogs must get made into potted meat. Under ordinary circumstances I would not be able to put such a foul substance into my mouth without gagging, but that evening, it honestly tased like pure heaven. I felt so much gratitude for the friendly hunter who had given it to me that I actually cried a little bit.

It was getting dark, but I couldn't stop walking right there because the trail was cutting across a very steep slope. There were no level spots anywhere, and the trail itself was a jumble of rocks where I could not possibly bed down. I got out my flashlight and hiked through the dark. A little while later, a dim stripe of sunset appeared in the west where the edge of the cloud was moving away to reveal the last little bit of daylight. I felt even more reassured that the rain was finally over, but as the cloud moved out, the temperature was dropping quickly.

I kept going for maybe an hour after dark when I finally came to a broad saddle with a lot of level ground. It was a great place for camping and there were obvious signs that other people camped there frequently. By then, I could see some stars through ragged holes in the last of the cloud, and it was distressingly cold. I wedged my flashlight into a notch in a tree and fumbled to set up my tent with frozen fingers. By the time I crawled in to sleep, I was shivering so hard I was on the verge of panic. The clothes I was wearing were soaked, and I didn't have a single dry thing to change into. My tent was wet. My sleeping bag was wet. Even my hair was wet.

I had carried one of those ultra-light "emergency" blankets with me all the way from Maine. I had never used it before, but I remembered it that night. I fumbled for a few minutes to get it out of the package, and then slowly unfolded it and wrapped it as best as I could around the outside of my sleeping bag. It was made from some paper-thin material that looked like reflective foil, but it was the texture of plastic. It took a lot of fussing, but I finally got it all wrapped around my body and tucked it in underneath. Then I lay there in a tight, fetal ball shivering and waiting for the reflective blanket to make me feel warm.

It never did. I don't know if I was supposed to strip naked and wrap the blanket around my bare skin. Maybe there were just too many layers of wet fabric between me and the emergency blanket for it to work. Maybe it was another one of those bullshit products that doesn't really work at all, or maybe it was just enough to keep me alive and you wouldn't be reading this now if I hadn't used it. All I know is that I never did feel any warmer that night. I was too cold to get any sleep. I spent the whole night clutching my knees to my chest shivering, waiting, and praying for dawn. The nights are long in the third week of November, and they seem almost endless when you are freezing to death.

I was a bit delirious by the time the first birds started chirping, so I didn't really trust my senses to tell me what I was hearing right away. My body had stiffened so much that it took quite an effort to pull the blanket off my face, but I eventually got my eyes uncovered. It really did appear that the long night was finally coming to an end. Not only was my whole body incredibly stiff, but my sleeping bag was stiff with ice. Packing up my camp was a monumentally slow ordeal, and it was full daylight by the time I was all packed and ready to go. Alas, I was on the west side of the ridge, so it would still be hours before the sun would actually shine on me. I was thirsty as hell, but my water bottle was a solid lump of ice. I had actually come close to dying of hypothermia once already a few years before, but this was the first time I had ever been starving, dehydrated, and hypothermic all at the same time. What an adventure!

My legs still worked well enough to walk at an almost normal pace, so without further adieu, I set off again. It couldn't have been half an hour before I came to a flowing stream that cured my dehydration. It seemed like I had gotten so used to being hungry and cold that it didn't even bother me anymore. I felt like my body was already 90% dead, and I was making my way through the mountains as a detached spirit. The scenery was beautiful that morning, and I remember feeling fairly euphoric to be there. Thinking back to that morning, I literally can't remember feeling any physical discomfort at all. At least, not after I quenched my thirst.

A couple hours later, the sun finally came up above the eastern ridge, and almost immediately after that, I came to an intersection with a small forest service road. I had no idea where the little road would take me, but I turned down it on pure faith that it would take me to the right place. It plunged steeply down the west side of the ridge, and before long I was on the bottom of the valley, walking through farm fields. The sunshine was so pleasantly warm, that I stripped down to my t-shirt. Then, after a couple miles of that, I came to the intersection of a major highway rushing with traffic. Straight across the highway from my little side road was a big, barn-shaped building that had been converted into a country store. Surely, they would have something to eat. I waited for a break in the traffic, and crossed the highway. As soon as I opened the front door, I could smell food cooking, and right in front of me was a row of stools at a counter. I made it!

I ordered a burger. The woman at the counter told me that it was still breakfast time, but then she did a double-take and decided to make me a burger anyway. She was a friendly rural person, a little older than middle-aged, but not quite elderly yet, and she came over to talk to me every time she had a minute in between her work duties. I regaled her with adventure stories, and we became good friends in that temporary way that you do with service workers who you're never going to see again. I had an ambition to eat two burgers, or three, or maybe seven, but my stomach had shriveled so much that I could barely finish my first one. I tipped the cook, and headed off down what turned out to be route 11 towards Roanoke.

I had survived twelve nights in the high Virginia Blue Ridge, and I had learned a valuable lesson that I want to share with you now. Growing up out West, I was surrounded by snowcapped mountains complete with glaciers. From that perspective, I never thought of the Appalachians as real mountains. Peaks topping out at 4,000 feet? Not impressive. South of New York state, you wouldn't even find any alpine tundra in the Appalachians. They were just some quaint little forested hills. I figured it would be lovely to see the autumn leaves in those quaint little hills. I figured if October was peak leaf season up North, the November would be the month to see it down South.

The End Never Comes

As it turned out, mid-November was already fully winter time in the central Appalachians. The autumn leaves were all gone, and the weather was dangerously cold. Winter is a bad time to go up into the mountains unless you know what to expect, and you are really well prepared. That's why I encountered so few other thru-hikers up there, and that's why I quite nearly froze to death.

I am not one to learn a lesson any other way but the hard way. That's how I learned that the Appalachians are indeed *real* mountains. I have been convinced ever since, and I will never doubt them again. Any Westerners who don't believe me are welcome to find out for themselves.

34. ROANOKE

I passed through the small town of Troutville, and then I got one last look at the Appalachian Trail where it crosses route 11 and jogs to the west to avoid the city of Roanoke. Across the whole state of Virginia, there is only one really significant gap in the otherwise unbroken wall of the Blue Ridge. For a stretch of about six miles, the Ridge just peters out completely, and then starts up again on the other side. In the early years of our nation's history, this gap was the obvious route for hundreds of thousands of migrants on their way to settle the western frontiers. The main carriage trails leading to both the Cumberland Gap, and the fertile Tennessee Valley passed through this gap, so the city of Roanoke grew up right there as an important supply station along those trails. The modern city of Roanoke fills the entire gap, and most of the broad valley that opens up to the west of it. Home to about a quarter million people, it is Virginia's fourth largest metropolitan area.

I ended up approaching the city from the north through several hours of strip malls and suburban sprawl. I was passing an older, much more run-down strip mall further down into the city when I encountered an elder woman dressed like a Hippy. I didn't have any clue where I might be spending the night, so I asked her for suggestions. She gave me directions to a homeless shelter, and then implored me to meet her back at that same strip mall the next morning. She couldn't offer me a place to sleep, but she was very interested in my walking project, and she wanted to help. I thanked her, and found my way to the shelter which was several miles further down the road near the few small skyscrapers that make up Roanoke's modest downtown district. It was evening by the time I arrived, and I ended up being right in time for check-in.

The shelter was operated by the Salvation Army. It was nowhere near as hostile as the last homeless shelter where I had stayed back in New Haven, but there were still plenty of silly rules. We would be locked in from 7pm until 7am, but I didn't have anywhere else I needed to be, so that was fine. We were separated by sex at intake, and I was led to a room where I was given the upper deck of a bunk bed for my night's accommodation. I would be sharing the room with about twenty other men, but we weren't packed in too tightly, and all the guys who were already there seemed to be quiet and polite. There was a television set in the room, but it was not overly large, and the volume was not overly loud. Best of all, it was down on a table top where we could reach it, and I saw no reason to suspect that we would not be allowed to shut it off when it came time to sleep. The only condition of the place that I found unreasonable was that the heat was turned up so high. I was already sweating uncomfortably by the time I had finished with the intake process, and it was even hotter back in our communal bedroom. I asked the worker if it was possible to turn the heat down a notch or two. All I got was a brief, blank look.

It took about an hour for the whole crew who would be staying there that night to be processed in, and then we were fed supper. It was a pretty good meal. The dining room was large enough to fit a lot of people, but it had a comfortable, almost home-like feel. The whole shelter was lit by incandescent lights, so it was much easier on the eyes than the harsh fluorescents that tend to be used in public buildings. There were couches along the wall, another television, and a book shelf with a fairly large selection of Jesus-themed literature. Doors led into two more bunk rooms the same size as the one I was staying in, so altogether the place could reasonably accommodate about sixty guys. It was not filled to capacity that night, and everyone there was either friendly and polite, or just silent.

After supper, we were given a choice. We could either stay in our rooms, or we could go to a classroom down the hall for two hours of Bible study. Almost everyone chose to go to class, so I hung back in the bunk room with about three of my roommates. I wasn't able to make any friends though, because I was so preoccupied by the stifling heat. I was so uncomfortable that I felt mildly claustrophobic, and it almost seemed like a struggle to draw breath. I complained to several people and inquired about the possibility of turning the heat down, but it didn't take me long to notice that I was the only one suffering. There must have been about fifty of us there that night, and no one else was at all uncomfortable. Most of the other guys were wearing sweatshirts and hats, and behaving like everything was normal. I realized that I looked like some kind of crazy drug-addict, so I decided to shut up and deal with my discomfort alone.

I could only guess that something must have shifted in my metabolism when I almost froze to death the night before. There was a window right next to my bed. There was no way to open it, but when all but one of my companions left the room at the same time, I snuck over to it, lifted up my shirt, and pressed my bare belly and chest against the cold glass. It was such a relief that I held that pose for quite a while, even after the other guys came back. They must have thought I was a total tweeker, but everyone kept their judgments to themselves.

After that, I crawled up onto my bunk and stripped down to my boxer shorts. It was a slightly indecent thing to do, especially in a place that put so much emphasis on Christian morality, but once again, no one said anything to me about it. Not long after that, the crowd came back from Bible class, and it was time to turn the lights off and go to sleep. I hadn't slept at all the night before, so I was tired enough to pass right out in spite of my discomfort. My metabolism must have readjusted overnight, because I was back to normal when I awoke the next morning.

The Salvation Army fed me a nice breakfast, and then I spent the first half of the morning hiking back out to the strip mall to meet up with the elder Hippy. I found her right where she told me she would be. About half the storefronts in the old strip mall were abandoned, and several of them were boarded over. One of the biggest ones had bee repurposed to house a large flea market divided into dozens of small stalls, each occupied by different vendors. The market was open, but the vendors greatly outnumbered the handful of customers who had come to shop there. The woman who had invited me had a stall there, and I found her right away. Her stall was a chaotic mess that no customer would feel comfortable entering. She said she was in the process of reorganizing, and she asked if I would be willing to help.

I was glad to oblige, but it only took a few minutes for me to sense that something was wrong with the situation. None of the things she asked me to do made any sense, and as time went on, the mess only got worse. She was doing all the talking, and her diatribe was growing weirder by the minute. She struck me as the kind of woman who probably lives with at least twenty cats, and come to think of it, she was giving off a strange and unpleasant odor. It took me about a half an hour to fully understand that I had been latched onto by a real live crazy person. That was the moment I realized I needed to get away, but it took me much longer to actually extract myself from the situation.

I have already explained what a struggle it is for me to get along with dogs. Well, one of my other real handicaps is that certain types of crazy people can just latch onto me and hijack my attention for hours at a time. I treat everyone as my equal, and I see the value in all people. I feel particularly sympathetic towards crazy people who get ignored and left behind, and often times when I meet those people, they appreciate my attention so much that they never want to let me go. Usually, it isn't too hard to get away, but every once in a while, I meet someone who has just the right verbal skills to keep me trapped in a never-ending interaction. To call it a conversation would not be quite accurate. It's more like a filibuster where the crazy person just goes on and on. Sometimes they may ask questions and listen to my responses, but they never allow the exchange to reach a logical stopping point where I might leave without hurting their feelings. While I hurt people's feelings by accident on a regular basis, something prevents me from ever doing it on purpose, so I end up getting hopelessly stuck.

The woman at the flea market in Roanoke was more effective at dominating me in this way than anyone I have ever met before or since. I forgot her name right away, and for years I have just remembered her as the Roanoke Tar Pit. I am embarrassed to admit it, but she hijacked me for almost an entire day. Eventually, I just broke through my chains of politeness and fled. Unfortunately, I had my big backpack with me, so I couldn't go very fast. The Tar Pit actually pursued me most of the way across the vast parking lot before I broke into a fast-enough jog to actually ditch her. What a nightmare. It must have been about four o'clock by the time I finally escaped.

I had wasted the whole day. I hadn't even met anyone worth talking to, let alone anyone who might let me sleep on their couch. Lacking any other ideas, I started walking back towards the Salvation Army shelter.

I only made it a couple of blocks before a car pulled over on the city street, and the man driving offered me a ride. It was one of those giant old Buicks with a hood so large and flat that I could lay down on it comfortably. The driver seemed friendly enough, so I got in and told him where I was headed. He was a middle-aged guy named Sandy, and it only took a couple minutes of us getting to know each other before he started hitting on me. At first, I assumed he was joking, so I laughed and changed the subject. A few minutes later, he was back at it and he was getting less subtle by the minute. He stopped short of saying that he had picked me up specifically hoping that I would have sex with him, but he spelled it out to me more clearly than anyone else ever had using very obvious euphemisms.

Now I have been mistaken for gay, and hit on by gay guys plenty of times. It doesn't really bother me, so I gave him a polite, "no thanks," and continued talking about other things. I figured that was all there was to it, but a few minutes later when we got to the intersection where I needed to stop, Sandy just kept driving. At first, I thought he had made a mistake, so I said something like, "Oh! Whoa man! That was my stop. Could you pull over on the next block and let me out?"

He didn't respond right away, and suddenly things got really tense. "Sandy?" I said, and then he responded with something along the lines of, "Come on man. Wouldn't it be nice to come back to my house? I could make you a nice supper and then we could…. You know?" He raised his eyebrows and made a perverted facial expression. I looked out the windshield and rode along for about another block while I thought about how I was going to handle the situation. I had never met a gay man who wouldn't take no for an answer before, so I wasn't sure how to behave, but I eventually realized that this was not a situation where I felt any obligation to be polite whatsoever. With that I leaned halfway across the spacious front seat towards him and yelled in a very loud and angry voice, "I said, LET ME OUT OF THE FUCKING CAR!"

Sandy leaned away from me. His eyes went wide, and this time his eyebrows raised up in an expression that suggested he thought I was being really unreasonable, but he pulled over and let me out right there. I grabbed my pack, slammed the door and walked away quickly without looking back. After about a half a block, I looked back and he was gone. At that point I stopped to let myself calm down and ponder what had just happened. I had been listening to homophobes rant about the danger of sexually-aggressive gay men all my life, but I always thought that was something they had just dreamed up in their paranoid imaginations. I still doubt that there are very many. To this day, Sandy is the only one I have ever met, but he did actually exist. Not only was he gay and sleazy, but he was also Black!

I burst into a moment of hysterical laughter when I realized what had just happened. I had survived the conservative bigot's ultimate nightmare—an encounter with a real live, sexually aggressive, GAY Black man! I had emerged unscathed, and all I had to do was raise my voice. Ha! I snickered all the way down the block as I imagined the bigots being too paralyzed with fear and curiosity to escape the way I had. They would be trapped and become Sandy's sex slaves for the rest of their lives. He probably had a bunch of them chained up in his basement already!

I had met two creepy people in one day, but my luck was about to change. I only had a short ways to walk to the homeless shelter, and I was waiting on a street corner for the lights to change, when an attractive young woman struck up a conversation with me. She was waiting to cross the street too, and she asked me if I had been hiking on the AT. The traffic stopped so we could cross, but it turned out we were going the same way, so we walked together and continued to make friends.

She had just gotten out of work and was walking home. It only took a couple minutes to reach the front door of the homeless shelter. It was almost check-in time, and people had begun to accumulate out front waiting to be let in. I saw some familiar faces from the night before and waved a greeting to them. To my surprise, the beautiful young lady was not done talking to me yet, so she actually stopped right there in the cluster of homeless people with me and continued our conversation. We must have talked for another fifteen minutes before it occurred to her that I didn't have to spend another night in the shelter. At that point, she took out a cell phone and called up her roommates to ask if they would mind if she put up a travelling stranger on the couch that night. They quickly gave her the green light, and then we were off.

Her home was not near her workplace at all. We must have walked together for at least 45 minutes, and it was dark by the time we got there. She shared a nice big city house with four other people, two men and two more women. I don't remember any of their names, but they were all in their twenties, and they were definitely the Hippy-type, so I made friends with all of them easily. They fed me supper, gave me a beer, and smoked me up. We stayed up late talking about all manner of things, and then I slept gratefully on their luxurious old leather couch.

The next day was Thanksgiving, and the Hippies didn't have to twist my arm to convince me to kick it with them for a whole day of resting and feasting. None of them had to work that day, plus a whole crowd of additional cool people came over that afternoon to celebrate at their house. No one gave me much money, but literally all of them signed up to receive zines, so Roanoke ended up being my largest cluster of subscribers since New York City.

We ended up having the most unique Thanksgiving feast I can ever remember. There was no turkey, or any other meat for that matter, but we still made a wide variety of delicious entrees and side-dishes. The main entrée was a giant vegetable frittata. When I say "giant," I mean I literally remember a pan about as wide as my arm is long, filled at least two inches deep with all colors and shapes of savory, sliced vegetables and mushrooms, cooked to perfection, and mixed together in a matrix of scrambled eggs. I am not the biggest frittata fan, but that one was to die for. I can't imagine how many eggs it must have used up, but there was plenty for everyone.

After the feast, we all had as many beers as we wanted, and partied on into the evening. At some point, someone suggested that we go for a walk, and six or seven of us came along. The city was almost abandoned at that late hour on a holiday. It was a chilly night, but it was so nice to be out walking with my new, short-term friends that I didn't mind the cold. It felt like we discovered all the great truths of life that night, the way drunk people are want to do when they wander around cities together at night. And of course, we forgot all of it by the next morning. I just remember thinking that there was no danger of getting lost at night in Roanoke, because the city had built a giant star made of lights on a nearby mountainside, and it seemed like no matter where we went, we could always see that electric star. I slept on the same couch as I had the night before.

I decided to spend one more day in Roanoke, but I didn't want to wear out my welcome, so I arranged to spend my final night at the home of someone else I met at the Thanksgiving party. I spent the whole day walking around the city, and I even walked out to downtown Salem, a smaller city just to the west. At the time, I reasoned that I was trying to sell more zines, but in hindsight, that rationale doesn't make much sense. Honestly, I think I was just really enjoying staying indoors with people who liked me, and I wasn't quite ready to give up that luxury yet. On my way back from Salem, I walked along a charming stretch of the Roanoke River. By the time it reaches the ocean, the Roanoke is another one of the East Coast's mighty rivers, but up there where I saw it, so close to its headwaters, it looked like it was just a little bit too big to wade across.

I stopped back by my first hosts' house to pick up my backpack late in the afternoon. My new hosts were located in a suburb called Vinton, out to the east of town. I had failed to understand just how far it was to their house, and it ended up taking me until after dark to walk there. It was the home of a couple high-school kids, a brother and sister, and they assured me that their parents were not the type who would care at all about a stranger spending the night. They lived in a mid-sized suburban home, positioned on a hill so that it appeared to be just one story from the front, but when you went around back, you could see there was another level downstairs with a sliding glass door leading into it. The downstairs turned out to be sort of an autonomous kid zone, where the kids could do whatever they wanted without any interference from the adults. Eventually, I talked them into taking me upstairs to meet their dad, just so I could feel reassured that nothing weird was going on. He was a nice guy, and he confirmed that his parenting strategy was very hands-off.

The kids showed me the couch that was to be my bed, but it would be many hours before I could sleep. Several of the adults who I met at the Thanksgiving party showed up, and they brought with them a dangerous amount of alcohol. A bunch more high-school kids showed up too, and another night of partying ensued. I got to be the center of attention for hours, regaling wide-eyed kids with my heroic adventure stories, and I signed up even more subscribers for my zine. High-school kids are not good at sensing when it's time to stop partying, so I had to stay up very late before the couch cleared off enough for me to sleep on it. I drank too much myself, so I got going a little late the next day, and my head was a bit muzzy all morning.

35. DOGS AND GEESE

For the sake of simplicity, I have been talking about the Blue Ridge running from "north to south" across Virginia, and the AT going down over the "east" side or the "west." To be more accurate though, the ridge actually runs from northeast to southwest, so by the time I got to Roanoke, I was quite a ways west of Durham North Carolina, where I needed to get to before I could stop hiking for the winter. On a grand scale, I needed to hang a 90-degree left in Roanoke. This route would take me down out of the mountains and many miles out onto the Piedmont Plateau. I would not have to go up and down so many steep hills, and I also felt hopeful that I might leave some of that cold mountain weather behind. A quick look at the map revealed that there was no route going southeast out of Roanoke, so I settled on a plan to follow US 220 south to the smaller city of Martinsville, and then turn east.

There was no real shortcut to get from where I was to that highway, so I had to walk all the way across the city one more time. As I mentioned, I got started late, and I had to walk pretty slowly at first, nursing a hangover. It was already lunchtime by the time I found route 220, and then I actually had to walk uphill for most of the afternoon while the road made its way up to a gap between two large mountains. I made it to the gap right at sunset, and just a little ways down the other side before it was time to set up camp. A pretty little creek ran parallel to the highway, so I climbed down to it, hopped across it on rocks, and set up camp in a pleasant, level spot concealed by dense, riparian undergrowth. I could hear dogs barking, and I wondered if I was the one setting them off, but they weren't close enough to really worry about. It was uncomfortably cold that night, but I was still up in the mountains. I told myself that things would get better once I got down onto the Piedmont.

A high shelf of clouds blocked out the sun and kept things chilly for most of the next morning. At one point, a large flock of geese flew overhead, honking urgently, and I mused that they were honking at me.

"Hurry up! Winter is coming!" They said.

I turned my head to the sky and hollered, "Wait up! I'm going as fast as I can!" The geese were right. Winter was coming more inevitably than anything ever, and it was almost upon us. I had never really noticed the urgent emotion in the voices of migrating geese before, but that morning I was feeling the exact same emotion, so I heard them loud and clear. I felt like I was one with the geese, at least for a couple minutes until they flew past me. Then I felt like the migration was leaving me behind. That gave me an even greater sense of urgency, so I quickened my pace even more.

This scene kept repeating five or six times a day, all the way to my winter destination. I didn't shout back at every single flock of geese that passed by, but I did sometimes, and I felt that same urgent connection every time. I walked harder and faster than ever before on that last leg of the year, and I'm convinced that I gained some energy from the encouragement that the geese gave me. It was like I was running with a football, and the geese played the role of my coach yelling, "GO! GO! GO!"

After several hours, I came to the town of Rocky Mount. Here the highway divided between a limited-access bypass and a business route, so of course, I took the slow route through town. It was a pleasant little town, and I enjoyed it all the more because the sun finally came out, so I felt warm enough for the first time all day.

I was still on the business route, exiting the south end of the town when I passed a boy who was out playing in his front yard. Most kids didn't even notice me going by, and the ones who did usually just gave me weird looks, but this one hollered out, "Hey Mister! Where you goin'?"

When I told him I was walking across the country, that led to more questions, so I stopped and made a friend.

His name was Pete and he was nine years old. He was full of questions, and we must have talked for almost fifteen minutes. He seemed like he was about ready to adopt me, but I was still feeling hurried by the geese and the changing season. I also worried about how his parents might react if they looked out the window and saw him talking to a strange vagabond on the side of the road, so I cut the conversation short. I told him I would send him zines to read, and I took down his name and address. I have always wondered what his rural Virginia parents must have thought when their little boy received his shipment of radical rebel writings.

Back on the main trunk of highway 220, I walked through some amazing scenery. Technically, I was out on the Piedmont Plateau now, but the terrain was nothing like the flat surface you would imagine when you hear the word "plateau." It was all ridges and deep ravines without any level space to be found anywhere. In addition to that, small and medium-sized mountains sat at random intervals in all directions of the compass. I might have even called some of the mountains large, but I could still see the truly grand mountains of the Blue Ridge in the distance to my right, and that kept the nearby mountains in perspective.

When it came time to set up camp, I encountered a familiar problem. Once again, I was stuck on the wrong side of an impenetrable wall of dog territories. I must have stopped to check out half a dozen nice little patches of forest, but every one of them was guarded by at least one dog who screamed a continuous alarm until after I left. Route 220 was too new and large to have very many driveways fronting onto it, but the backroads provided access to the homes of a population that was fairly dense by rural standards. All the neighbors had plenty of acreage to themselves, but there was never quite enough for there to be any gaps between the ranges where their dogs would notice me.

It was past sunset and almost dark by the time I finally settled on a camping spot. At that point, the highway ran along the top edge of a slope that dropped steeply for about a hundred feet before levelling out at the bottom. I could see the lights of several houses down below, and two different dogs struck up a round of their relentless and irritating song before I even stopped walking. There was just a little bit of level ground between the highway guardrail and the top of the steep slope, and I found a little clear spot there that was just big enough to set up my tent. I reasoned that the dog owners would not be motivated to climb up that steep slope in the dark to investigate why their pets were making such a racket.

It was a terrible camping spot. The speed limit on route 220 was 65 miles per hour, and a vehicle going that speed makes a very loud noise. I had never camped that close to the side of a major highway before, and I found the noise of the cars almost as unbearable as the sound of the dogs. As the night grew late, the traffic thinned out, but occasional vehicles still happened by all night long, and their noise made a shocking contrast to the quieter intervals in between. I was also plainly visible from the road. That was a clear violation of protocol and common sense, but it was already dark enough by the time I got there that all the cars had their headlights on, and within a few minutes it was fully dark. That late in the fall, it was dark most of the time. I reasoned that I needed to spend every minute of daylight walking fast, so I was glad

I had pushed it right up to the brink of night. The way I remember it, the damn dogs kept barking down below all night long, but no one came looking for me, and I did eventually get some sleep.

It was another frigid night. I packed up at the first hint of dawn, before anyone would see my obvious camping spot. I was on the road for less than an hour before the sky started to drizzle. The rain seemed too cold to be coming down in liquid form, but at least it was not raining very hard.

It was still early when I reached a large, ugly town called Collinsville. I was very cold and gradually getting more and more damp, so I decided this would be the perfect place to stop into a diner and get a nice hot meal. Unfortunately, the diner of my fantasies did not actually exist in Collinsville, at least not on the main drag. It took most of the morning to walk across the town, and at the far end, I finally gave up and settled for a Hardees.

I have made a point of boycotting fast-food chains my whole adult life, but it had been several years since I had slipped up on my boycott, so I figured it was okay. I also hadn't seen a Hardees since I was a small child living in Alabama, so it gave me a sense of nostalgia. Back then, my dad had a tradition of taking me out to Hardees for breakfast biscuits once a week. Biscuits were still on the menu twenty years later, so I got one for old time's sake. The drizzle finally stopped after my late breakfast, and the clouds cleared out shortly after that.

Collinsville is one of several towns clustered around the small city of Martinsville, Virginia. Together, they make up a metro area of more than 50,000 people. The city is draped over a nearly impossible topography of high ridges and deep, steep ravines. It's not a reasonable place to build a city. The steep hills force the streets into a tangled maze, and there is no direct way to get anywhere. Naturally, I was lost within minutes of arriving there. One strange mountain sits off in the distance to the south, and I would see it every time I came to the top of a ridge. It wasn't a particularly large mountain, but it was distinctly pimple-shaped, and I kept thinking it was odd to see one mountain, all by itself, without any others around.

Sometime in the early afternoon, I happened by a nice little café and stopped in for lunch. It was kind of a fancy place, and I spent a little too much for my sandwich. Nobody there was interested in my zine, but someone was nice enough to give me directions to Route 58 East. I ended up leaving Martinsville without signing up a single zine subscriber, but I really didn't care. It had gotten back around to that time of year when my warrior spirit fades out. All I really wanted was to get to a safe place for the winter and relax with my friends.

Heading east from Martinsville, the highway was very straight and a lot less hilly than the previous day. I knocked down a lot of miles that afternoon, and I noticed by the end of the day that I couldn't see the Blue Ridge on the western horizon anymore. When it came time to camp, I happened upon a brand-new road that had just been punched into the forest on the north side of the highway. I followed it back a short ways to a cul-de-sac where half a dozen house lots had been cleared, but nothing had been built yet, and the road surface was still dirt waiting to be paved. There was no one around and no barking dogs within ear-shot. What a lovely place to camp! I slipped into the woods behind the embryotic subdivision and slept awesomely. It didn't even get very cold that night.

I was cruising right along the next morning, trying to keep up with the geese, when I started to notice an odd sensation. The paved shoulder of the highway was comfortably wide, so I could walk along the edge of it without getting dangerously close to the passing cars. Of course, there were countless little bits of gravel spread randomly over the pavement. Little rocks covered the edge of every road I had walked along all the way from Maine, and I was used to the feeling of little lumps under my feet almost every other step. But that morning, little by little, I noticed that the lumps felt slightly different. They felt just a little bit sharper than I was used to.

Finally, after contemplating the feeling for several miles, I stopped and sat my pack down. I grabbed my left foot with both hands and twisted it so I could see the bottom. Holy shit! I could see most of the ball of my foot through a huge hole in the front half of my shoe! I hopped onto my left foot and found an almost identical hole in the sole of my right shoe. These were big holes. They hadn't just formed overnight. The rubber had worn away under that whole front portion of both feet where all my body weight pushes off as I propel myself forward. For the last couple of days, I had noticed that all my socks had developed big holes in the same place, but it hadn't occurred to me to check for holes in my shoes.

My feet had grown so tough that I hadn't even noticed I was walking partially barefoot across all manner of surfaces. What a badass! I made a mental note to look for a new pair of shoes the next time I happened by a thrift store, but I also felt a huge surge of pride to discover just how tough my body had gotten. I felt like I was basically indestructible.

The day was November 30th, the third anniversary of the day we shut down the WTO meeting in Seattle. The success of that protest gave the rebel army a real taste for shutting down big trade summits. Several such events took place every year, and the good guys kept bringing huge crowds of protestors to all of them, always hoping to disrupt the agenda of the international financial warlords. Seattle was the only time we ever really caught the police off guard though, so none of the successive protests ever had much on an effect. In fact, while our protest tactics evolved very little, the police seemed to be learning and dealing with us more effectively each time. I kept telling my allies that we needed to abandon the giant protest tactic for a few years, and develop some new strategy that would catch the cops off guard, but I couldn't seem to persuade anyone.

That fall, the call went out for mobs of protestors to converge on Miami and try to stop a meeting of big business gangsters who were getting together to set up the administration of the newly-formed Free Trade Area of the Americas (FTAA.) During Clinton times, the overlords had enacted the North American Free Trade Agreement (NAFTA.) It was designed to bankrupt millions of Mexican farmers so they would be freed up to work in sweatshops. Then the businessmen would be able to reap massive profits by laying off millions of well-paid American factory workers and moving production to the Mexican sweatshops. The FTAA was the next stage in the that plan.

I had been heavily recruited to come join the protest, but I declined to go, and I warned all my friends that it was not going to work. Miami had just hired John Timony, a police chief who had been moving from city to city ahead of the big protests, training all those police forces to deal with our tactics.

I was up on the Blue Ridge, hiking the Appalachian Trail the day that the protest actually went down. The Miami police increased the level of brutality a couple notches above anything our crew had ever experienced before. Not only did they fail to stop the FTAA meeting. Most of them also went home covered with bruises and other wounds. One of my friends actually lost an eye in the battle. Miami police fired an unprecedented number and variety of "non-lethal" projectiles into the crowd. While the projectile that took out my friend's eye lived up to its promise of being non-lethal, it certainly did change the rest of his life. I knew the Miami protest wouldn't be worth attending, but I have still always felt guilty that I wasn't there with my crew. It ended up being the last time a large number of protestors assembled to try to block the meetings of the international financial overlords.

By noon, I had made it to the outskirts of Danville. At one point in American history, the city of Danville reached a population of 100,000 people. Similar to Lewiston Maine, Danville was a powerhouse of textiles manufacturing. In this case, the mills were powered by the rushing waters of the mighty Dan River, which joins the Roanoke further down and doubles the size of the Roanoke. Also like Lewiston, Danville fell on hard times in the 1980's when the global Free Market exported all its manufacturing jobs to Third World countries. The census shows that Danville has recently started growing again, but when I got there in 2003, its population had shrunk to 85,000, and the city was gutted.

Windows were broken or boarded over. Parking lots were empty. Trash accumulated along the sides of the streets, and even the structures that weren't abandoned looked dirty. The red brick architecture was charming, but the city felt empty, or hollow somehow. So few people were out and about, I could walk five blocks without passing another pedestrian. It felt a little unsettling to walk past so many large buildings and see so few people.

I walked around the city all afternoon. I had one brief conversation with a very poor-looking woman who I encountered coming out of a dollar store, and she became my only zine subscriber in the entire city. I didn't charge her anything for the subscription. At one point, I happened by a thrift store, but it didn't have any shoes that fit me. At least the river was nice.

I also got a fabulous dinner at a very modest, home-style restaurant that looked like one of the last businesses left in the old downtown district. It was one of those places where you get an entrée, and then you get to pick out side-dishes from a big long list. Normally, in a place like that, you get to pick out one or two side-dishes, but that place gave me three. Then they brought me the bill and it was just under ten dollars for the whole meal. What a deal!

After supper, I found my way to route 86 and headed south out of Danville. I realized that I had lingered in town much too late. I feared that I might have to keep walking for a while after dark before I got far enough out of the city to find a decent camping spot, but my fear was unfounded. The sun had set, but there was still plenty of daylight left when I came to the bottom of a hill and found a nice, forested park lining either side of a large creek. It made for a perfect camping spot, and I slept well.

Danville is right near the southern border of Virginia. I had only been walking for about twenty minutes the next morning when I came to the state line. A metal sign on the side of the road displayed the NC state flag and said, "Welcome to North Carolina."

36. TWO DAYS LATE

The road was straight as an arrow for many miles, and the morning passed without incident. The day started out bright and sunny, but as the hours went by, the sky had gradually filled with clouds until it was completely overcast. I reached the town of Yanceyville just in time for lunch. I didn't spot any promising restaurants, so I settled for some hot junk food from a gas station. It was there that I overheard the radio crackling with urgent warnings of an incoming winter storm. I asked the man and the woman working the registers if they had any more details, and they confirmed that everyone was expecting a bad one. There was potential for sleet, or maybe even a few inches of snow. Frozen precipitation sends Southerners into a state of emergency, so the convenience store was packed with customers hurrying to stockpile milk, eggs, beer, and whatever other supplies they would need to hunker down and ride out the storm.

Needless to say, I was stressed out too. I needed to be done walking before the first winter snow. That was a hard deadline. I am a very skinny person who is very vulnerable to the cold, and the idea of being stuck out in a winter storm frightens me deeply. On the other hand, I am a very stubborn person who was committed to walking the whole way, so I couldn't cheat for so much as a mile. I knew I couldn't be more than three days out from Durham by then, but I never even considered hitch-hiking. All I could think to do was hurry.

I left the gas station and set off walking with the remains of my lunch in my hand, taking bites and chewing as I went. I got on Route 158 East and walked for all I was worth. The landscape of northernmost North Carolina was interesting. A series of large creeks made their way north to the Roanoke River. Each one cut a broad, deep valley into the Piedmont, and the highway ran perpendicular to the valleys. The hills never got very steep, but each valley was several hundred feet deep, and there were some really expansive views from the ridgetops. Each valley took more than an hour to walk across, so I made it through maybe four of them all afternoon.

I had almost reached the bottom of the first valley when I saw a strange object in the grass beside the road, and I picked it up to examine it. Two hot-pink spheres about the size of baseballs were sealed in a plastic package.

The wrapper said they were "Snowballs," but on closer analysis, they were actually made of some substance resembling marshmallows, with pink sprinkles stuck all over the outside. I realized then that it was some kind of snack designed to take advantage of sugar addicts, and I devoured them without hesitation. Normally, I have no taste for that kind of sugar-crack, but at that point in my life, I had no steady source of income, and I was burning about a million calories a day, so any source of free calories was welcome.

There were an amazing number of abandoned wooden structures lining both sides of the highway. Some appeared to have been small human homes, while others looked like they had just been sheds or small barns. Some were completely or partially collapsed, while others were still in pretty good shape. There were plenty of new homes that were obviously still inhabited too, and of course almost all of them had barking dogs. More abandoned structures kept popping up every few minutes though, and many of them were nicely secluded in places where they couldn't be seen from any houses, nor be smelled by any dogs.

It would have been wise to duck into one of these places and take shelter for the night. Indeed, a voice in the back of my head kept making that suggestion every time I saw another abandoned shack, but for some reason, I kept ignoring it. My conscious mind kept telling me that it wasn't really going to snow at all. Weather forecasters can't resist the temptation to sensationalize their predictions, and I figured the good people of rural North Carolina were taking them way to seriously.

I was convinced of that right up until the moment it started snowing. The storm didn't ease its way in either. Within five minutes of the first flurry, it was snowing in earnest. I was just coming into a somewhat denser cluster of houses than I had been walking through, so there would be no hiding places any time soon. I had blundered into just about the worst scenario I could imagine.

A few minutes later, I came to a small cluster of buildings. There was a church on either side of the road. The one on the left had a small post office next to it, and a tiny little town office with a sign that said, "Leesburg, NC." It wasn't a big enough town to have side-streets, but the houses were clustered along both sides of the highway, close enough together that there were no gaps between them for me to hide in. That pattern continued for as far ahead as I could see. My heart sank and I cursed myself for skipping past all those luxurious abandoned cabins.

Suddenly, across on the south side of the road, I saw a house that looked abandoned. It wasn't a quaint wooden shack, but a modern, two-story house with vinyl siding and the works. I can't point to any details to explain why I felt so sure it was abandoned. I just had a weird feeling. I crossed the road just before I reached the house. I was walking fast, and I only had a few seconds to make up my mind. I could clearly see the next house up ahead and across on the side of the road I had just come from. If anyone in that house was looking out the window, they would have a clear view of me trespassing, but what were they odds someone would be looking out the window right then? There were no cars passing by on the road at the time, so at the last second, I decided to go for it. The house wasn't set back very far from the road, so it only took about ten paces before I got around behind it and out of sight. There was already enough snow on the ground to make an obvious line of tracks where I had walked across the yard, but the snow was still coming down hard, so I had reason to hope my tracks would be buried quickly.

Out back, there was a modest concrete slab that served as a porch, and a sliding glass door opened from the house onto it. I tried the door, and it was unlocked. One quick glance inside confirmed that the house was indeed abandoned, but it wasn't a very reassuring sight. It looked like the house had been abandoned in the wake of some violent domestic disturbance. I slipped in quickly and closed the door so as to be fully hidden. Then I sat my pack down and surveyed the scene.

The floor was piled with random things. Everything made of glass or pottery had been smashed. The sheetrock on the walls had big holes in it where things had been thrown against it violently. Much of the furniture was overturned, and some of the wooden legs were ripped off. The kitchen cupboards had been emptied onto the floor. There were no spray-painted pot leaves or crude images of male genitalia, such as would be left by teen-agers who would vandalize a place for kicks. This scene looked distinctly like the result of a violent and furious adult-sized tantrum. It gave me a really uneasy feeling, but there was no going back. It would make a suitable shelter during the snowstorm. I clearly didn't have any better options.

I didn't feel much like exploring, but I did need to find a suitable place to bed down. The staircase led up to a big open room that took up much of the second story. That room was also full of disturbing wreckage, but in the

The End Never Comes

far corner, there were four or five queen-sized mattresses that hadn't been damaged and they were all arranged in a neat stack. I brought my backpack upstairs and set it down near the mattresses in such a way that it would blend in with the rest of the mess.

I was still extremely nervous about the potential that I had been seen sneaking in, so after that, I went to peek out the front of the house. A couple of bedrooms faced out to the street on the second story, and one of them had one of those thin, opaque curtains over the window, so I could look out without fear of being seen. I knelt there for quite a while watching the snow fall. I felt more reassured every minute that passed without any cops or neighbors showing interest in the house where I was hiding. It was already starting to get dark, so I ate a couple cans of food, and prepared for bedtime.

I was more than adequately sheltered from the snow, but it wasn't any warmer inside the abandoned house than it was outside, and I still hadn't gathered enough warm clothing for that time of year. I probably could have gathered a nice pile of blankets and slept comfortably on top of the stack of mattresses, but I was too frightened to search the house at all.

I have not had much experience with ghosts in my life, and I'm not even totally convinced that they exist, but I figured that house was the most likely place to meet a ghost of anywhere I had ever slept. The bad vibes were so thick there, I could probably convince myself there was a ghost even if there really wasn't. I also wanted a good hiding place in case the cops showed up and searched the place. Just because they hadn't arrived yet didn't mean they weren't coming. I was way out in the country. It might take the police hours to respond to a call out there.

I decided to lift up the top mattress and crawl in underneath it. I positioned my head near the edge facing the wall so that my breathing hole would not be visible from the rest of the room. As a hiding place, it was ridiculous. I was hoping my body would sink down into the mattresses below me enough to avoid making a giant, obvious bulge in the one on top of me, but it probably would have still been really obvious to anyone searching the room that something very large was hidden between the mattresses. It was also very uncomfortable and difficult to sleep with all that weight pressing down on top of me.

There were two perks to the setup though. The mattress provided lots of insulation, so I ended up being warmer that night than I had on most of the

289

previous nights when it wasn't snowing. And it gave me a purely psychological sense of security, so I could stop freaking out about how creepy the place was.

The storm had ended by the next morning. I left my garbage from dinner in with the rest of the mess and packed up. I opened the sliding door to the backyard and paused for a long moment. Three solid inches of snow covered the ground. I would have to leave an obvious set of tracks originating from that door, and proceeding out to the roadside. No new snow would cover them, and they would stay there until all the snow melted. There was no way around it, so eventually I just went for it, and got away with it as usual.

I was still wearing those same old low-topped skateboarder shoes with the gaping holes in the bottom, so my feet were soaked within a minute of walking down the slush-covered shoulder, but I was tough, so it didn't really matter.

I had one terrifying standoff with a dog that morning. Some giant beast resembling a Saint Bernard, only bigger, met me at the end of a long driveway and tried to block me from walking down the public highway past its house. It growled and drooled, and reared up on hind-legs so its enormous face was almost level with mine. It was the closest I ever came to actually stabbing someone's dog with my pocket knife. I retreated to the other side of the road, but the beast just followed me without hesitation. Halfway through the process, a man came out of the house to see what all the barking was about. I hoped he would call his dog inside, but I feared he might freak out at the sight of me brandishing my knife. Strangely, he did neither. He just stood there and watched without reacting the whole time as I gingerly side-stepped, and then backed away. Public roads are open to all vehicles, but in some parts of the country, domestic dogs effectively close many of them to pedestrians.

I made it to a large town called Roxboro around mid-day, and turned south on highway 501. From that point on, the signs counted down the miles to Durham. I don't remember the exact number, but I could tell I would only have to camp out one more night before I reached my destination.

It had been four days since I left the mountains, so I was surprised when another small mountain appeared, standing alone on the southeastern horizon. I found out later that its name is Red Mountain. The highway brought me quite a bit closer to it, and I was right alongside it when it came time to make camp.

It was another one of those stretches where each dog territory overlaps the next, but after a mile or more, I just gave up. I picked a spot where I couldn't see any houses, and walked in a good ways off the highway. I could tell right where the house was, because it was distinctly marked by the obnoxious sound of a frantically barking dog, but there were enough tree trunks in between that I couldn't see any part of a human structure. A thin layer of slushy snow still covered the ground almost everywhere underneath the shade of the trees, and I ended up having to pitch my tent on top of it.

There was still a fair amount of daylight left, and I had just crawled in and laid down when a gunshot rang out from the house. It was disturbingly loud and close, and it scared the crap out of me. I felt certain that the shot was intended to frighten off whatever animal was making the dog bark. That meant me. I didn't leave, and the dog kept barking. I wondered if the paranoid human would come out searching for me. I wasn't particularly well-hidden. A few minutes later they fired another shot, and I jumped again. It was almost dark by then, but the dog kept barking, and my chest was still heaving with adrenaline.

Right about the time it got completely dark, they fired one more shot and this time it made me angry. How had our culture gotten so messed up that we had to shoot at people before we even knew who they were? In a healthy culture, I could have made friends with that guy and slept on his couch. Instead, he was hiding in his house, watching his television, and learning that all strangers were dangerous psychopaths. The only way to keep his family safe was to shoot first, and ask questions later. I hate that mentality. There were no more gunshots that night, and eventually they let the dog inside, but I was too upset to sleep for a long time. It was also too cold, and it didn't take long for the wetness of the ground to seep up through the floor of my tent.

It was just a little after noon the next day when I reached the first strip mall on the northern outskirts of Durham. I found a payphone to call my friends, and felt a wave of relief when they actually answered. I hadn't talked to them since June. They asked me to describe my location, and after a few of those questions, they told me to hold tight. They would be out to pick me up soon. I said I would prefer to just walk to their house and asked if I could get directions. For some reason, they vetoed that idea, so we hung up and I commenced to wait where I was. I was two days late to beat the deadline of winter weather, but I had walked all the way to the city limits of Durham,

North Carolina. It was okay to compromise a little bit.

38. SHELTER

Hours passed while I waited for my ride, my frustration building the entire time. Why couldn't I have just walked? I would probably be home already if they had just given me directions. I had visited them there two winters prior, but I had been delivered in a car, and I had no idea what part of the city their house was in.

The house was a large rectangular box of red brick that they had lovingly named, "The Stronghold." At least a dozen crusty rebel Punks lived there, and they were the ones who had given me my nickname, Leroy. We were all drinking 40-ounce beers on the porch one afternoon, when one of them forgot my actual name. The closest thing he could think of was Leroy, so he just called me that, and it stuck for about the next twelve years. Eventually, I started introducing myself to new people as Leroy, and by the time I got back to Durham two years later, most people I knew thought that was my real name.

It was about time for supper when my friends finally showed up in their nasty white minivan. I said something about The Stronghold right away and they all laughed. It turned out they had been evicted from that house more than a year ago at that point, and they had lived in several other places since then. They still kept in touch with the whole cast from The Stronghold though, and they gave me everyone's update as we rode along.

We ended up driving for almost two hours. They took me all the way across Durham, all the way across the next city of Chapel Hill, out into the country, and through a small town called Pittsboro. A couple miles beyond Pittsboro, we finally came to a stop at a remote little shack on the top corner of a sloped cornfield that had been plowed under for the winter. No wonder they didn't want me to walk. It would have taken me two more full days to reach that location, and that's assuming I didn't get mixed up in any business in Durham or Chapel Hill.

The place was a dump. There were about three light bulbs in the whole house, and one electric space-heater was the only source of heat in the entire place. There were a couple really cold nights when we turned on the oven, opened its door, and all sat around it in a circle to stay warm. There was no furniture, and all four of us slept on mats on the floor of the one big bedroom behind the kitchen. That room had a rear exit, and the door had been ripped off the hinges and leaned up against the hole it was supposed to cover. Needless to say, the place was draughty. They had named their house "Pitlachia," a cross between Pittsboro and Appalachia in an attempt to make light of the squalid conditions. They assured me it was a temporary situation, and we would soon find a better place to live.

The first thing I did upon arrival was to get desperately sick. I rarely ever get sick, but when it does happen, it's usually timed perfectly to make a bad impression on a new group of people who I am about to depend on for a place to stay. This one was a doozy. It was as if I had gathered germs from all the cities and towns I had passed through on my way there, but they couldn't get me down because the athletic exertion of walking kept them at bay. As soon as I stopped working my body so hard and sat still for a few days, they all pounced, and I was down for the count.

I literally couldn't get up except to go to the bathroom for about a week. It felt like someone had positioned the end of a baseball bat right between my eyebrows, and was leaning on it with all their weight. The guys gathered some extra blankets for me, and mostly left me alone. Most days, they would all go out together to work on various projects or gather resources, and sometimes they wouldn't get home until late at night. One of them was convinced that the cabin was haunted and it worried him to leave me there alone and helpless. I was too sick to notice any ghosts though. Towards the end of the ordeal, another one of my friends actually brought me to his mother's house in town, where I convalesced on the couch for two or three days.

My friends were a tight little squad of direct-action heroes who I originally met at a protest to block an industrial development out West. For months leading up to my walk, I continued to meet up with them all over the country and run with their team, militantly protesting everything from American neo-Nazis to the invasion of Palestine. Each one of them is an epic character worthy of his own series of books, and I met a much larger gang of similarly awesome characters that winter.

Unfortunately, they have forbidden me to write about any of them. It's frustrating because their characters and stories would really enhance this book. I never witnessed them, or even heard them talk about committing any crime serious enough that the authorities would still want to bust them for it eighteen years later as I write this. Nor did any of them share any schemes with me to overthrow the government or cause any serious property damage. If the spooks were to interrogate me, they would be very disappointed, because I just don't have anything really incriminating to hide. Nonetheless, I intend to follow through and respect my friends' wishes. I haven't kept in touch with any of them, so I don't even know where they are living anymore, but I still hope we will cross paths again someday. If that happens, I don't want to have to tell them that I broke my promise to keep their identities a secret. I don't actually believe they are in any danger, but they do, and they would not be pleased if they thought I had compromised their safety.

Nothing much happened in December. My cousin and his wife had recently moved to the outskirts of Charlotte, so I hitchhiked out to visit them for a couple days at Christmas time. They had an adorable baby daughter who was not quite one-and-a-half years old, and I thoroughly enjoyed playing with her as she crawled around on the carpet and drooled on everything.

Charlotte is pretty far west of the region where I spent the winter, so it took all day, and six or seven rides to get there. The return trip was very similar, and I was surprised to find that more than half of the people who stopped to pick me up were immigrants from Mexico. I had no idea there were so many Mexicans in North Carolina. Once again, I found reason to be glad I had spent so much time and effort learning to speak Spanish.

After I got back, I found out that one of my new friends there had also hitchhiked to Charlotte to visit his family for Christmas. He was by far the comedian of the group. Any story he told would make people laugh until their bellies were sore. His story of hitchhiking back from Charlotte was automatically funny though, because his parents actually gave him an axe as a Christmas gift. Any male person who has ever hitched anywhere knows that the vast majority of people drive past and look at you as if you were an axe murderer, but this guy actually got to carry a real axe with him while hitchhiking!

My friends spent most of the final week of the year negotiating with a man in Chapel Hill to rent his cabin. They brought me along with them a couple of times, but I mostly just sat there in confused silence while the rest of them chatted endlessly about everything they could think of other than renting the man's cabin. He was an intimidating guy, probably fifteen years older than us, but still very robust in the prime of his life. He was a karate instructor, and at one point, he identified himself as a "hick." He was friendly enough though, and at one point, he told us a story that I'll never forget.

Back in his twenties, he got the dumb idea to try to paddle his canoe out into the ocean so he could go fishing out there. He tied it to the top of his truck, and drove to the Outer Banks off the coast of North Carolina. Miraculously, he managed to point the nose of his canoe right into the incoming breakers and paddle out through them. He was a strong guy, but even so, it was a monumental effort. It must have taken him almost an hour to get out past the breaking point. Once he got there, he had to rest up for a few minutes before he had enough energy to start fishing.

It only took a few casts before he hooked a large fish that pulled so hard it tipped his canoe over immediately. He lost all his fishing gear before he could do anything about it, but he was determined to save the canoe, so he swam as hard as he could with two legs and one arm while dragging the swamped canoe beside him with the other arm. He made it back to the breaking point where the crashing waves pushed the canoe to the bottom, but he still refused to give up. He was a poor man and he loved his canoe. At that point, the water was not much deeper than the height of his body, so in the troughs between waves, he swam down, tugged the canoe a few feet forward, and then surfaced, gasping for air and preparing for the next dive. After what felt like an hour, he finally got to the point where he could stand on the bottom between waves without his head going under. The going should have gotten easier at that point, but by then he was already so exhausted and half-drowned, that it took him almost as long again to drag the canoe the rest of the way to shore.

Towards the end of the ordeal, he could see that a woman and her child were standing on the beach watching him with looks of great concern on their faces. When he finally dragged his body and boat far enough out of the water to rest, he didn't have a single drop of strength left in him. He just flopped down on his back and lay there panting, contemplating the lesson he had just learned, and feeling grateful to be alive. At that point the woman and child ran to him. They stood looking down on him and asked if he was okay, and at that moment, he actually had the presence of mind to fake a French accent. Through gasping breaths, he said, "I come (gasp gasp) from France (gasp gasp) Please tell me (gasp gasp) What land is dis?"

The first time I came along to visit, we must have stayed for an hour and a half, but then we left without ever discussing the rental deal. The second time, we had been there for more than two hours, and still no one had brought it up. I was really confused. It was the second-to-last day of December, and we had to be out of Pitlachia by New Years. We had about 36 hours until we would be homeless, but all three of my friends seemed to be too timid to ask the guy about renting his cabin.

Finally, I just went for it. There was a brief pause in the conversation, so I changed the subject, and asked how much money he would want and how soon we might be able to move in. All three of my friends, as well as our prospective landlord all looked at me like I had just said something really offensive. A couple of awkward seconds passed while the man just looked at me with his brows furrowed, but then he answered my question, and we all ended up negotiating a very reasonable rent deal.

I was relieved, but as soon as we got back to our vehicle, two of my friends laid into me with an angry lecture. They had the situation under control, and I was way out of line bringing up the topic of renting the cabin. I needed to understand that I was down South now, and you don't just cut to the chase in business dealings the way I just had. You have to get to know a person really well, and even then, you still had to beat around the bush and follow a very delicate code of conduct when talking business. I needed to stop acting like such a damn Yankee or I was going to screw things up for all of us.

I apologized and resolved to stop being such a Yankee, but inside I wondered if I would even be able to figure out how to make such a change. I hadn't even known about the cultural rule I had just broken until it was too late. How many other rules might be waiting to surprise me?

***

The cabin was located at the very end of a dirt road, about six miles outside of Chapel Hill. Six acres of beautiful forest came with it, but the woods kept going, and there was no telling where our property actually ended. The land was high and flat without any water. The cabin had been built in the near corner to the road, which put us awkwardly close to the neighbors. It would have taken me some effort to throw a stone all the way to their house, but there was a clear line of sight to it because our landlord had cut down all the trees in that direction. The neighbors never waved, or even looked at us, so we ignored them in similar fashion.

Our yard was piled with every type of junk you can imagine. As the story went, our landlord had built the cabin to prepare for the end of the world on Y2K, and he had stockpiled everything he could get his hands on that might be useful in a survival situation. Unfortunately, he had left it all outside to get ruined by rain and disappear in the weeds. It's even more unfortunate that I never went around with a notebook to write down a list of the items in the yard. It would make a great couple paragraphs now, but I can't actually remember a single detail.

The cabin itself was epic. In many ways, it was even more squalid than the place we had just come from, but at least the door was still attached and there was a woodstove to provide heat. There was a nice pile of firewood in the yard to heat with too.

The walls of the ground floor were made of cordwood, with cement as the mortar to fill the gaps between them. When I say "cordwood," I mean foot-long logs, stacked up just like a pile of firewood, but held in place by cement, so the walls looked like they were covered with big wood-colored polka-dots. Many of the logs had dried and shrunk since the cabin was built, so thin crescents of light would shine in around their edges. There were no windows downstairs, so it was almost pitch dark inside. On warm days, we would leave the front door open just to shed some light on the situation inside without using up flashlight batteries. The front of the cabin faced roughly southwest toward the afternoon sun which shone through the gap where the trees had been cut down. There was a nice cement porch along the entire front of the house with a shed roof that was up high enough to let the winter sun in, and a couple big chairs. When the weather permitted, that porch was the nicest place on the whole property to hang out.

While the walls of the ground floor looked virtually bomb-proof, the second floor was just a thin layer of plywood nailed onto a frame of two-by-fours, without a scrap of insulation. The whole thing was covered by a solid metal roof.

The upstairs was divided into three bedrooms and a smaller room that must have been intended to be a bathroom. The whole southeastern end of the second floor was a master bedroom, and there was a smaller bedroom in the middle. Another large bedroom took up the westernmost corner, and the little bathroom was in the northernmost corner. All four rooms were connected by a hallway against the back wall, and the staircase ascended to that hallway. The woodstove sat directly under the staircase in the middle of the back wall, and vented through a masonry chimney that sat most of the way outside the back wall. There was also a fantastic antique wood cookstove to the right of the heating stove, and it was plugged into the same chimney.

The upstairs was generally much more pleasant than the downstairs, because it had windows to let in some daylight. Unfortunately, it was a catastrophic mess, so we all had to sleep downstairs until it could be cleaned up. The idea was that our landlord would come over and clean it, but after a week of waiting and sleeping on the floor, I initiated the cleanup effort.

I only planned to stay through the end of February, so my housemates offered me the master bedroom. That room was cluttered with personal items, mixed together with cigarette butts, empty whisky bottles, and beer cans. The guy had obviously suffered through a rough stretch of depression the last time he was living there. My housemates would not have wanted me to touch that situation with a ten-foot pole, but they all went away to Washington DC one weekend, and left me alone with my motivated attitude.

I made a meticulous effort to separate anything that looked like it might have any value from the trash. I arranged everything for keeping on top of the two dressers, and along the northeastern wall where there was extra space that I would not need. I never even looked in the dresser drawers, or inside any boxes or other containers. All the garbage actually fit into one large barrel that I found in the yard. The effort only took a few hours, and I moved in promptly that same night. My room had a window in each of its three walls, and a nice double bed on a metal frame that raised it up off the floor.

When my housemates returned home to find me living in the landlord's old room, they called him and he came over immediately. He was so furious with me that his face turned red and he quivered when he spoke, but he managed to keep his voice calm and avoid saying anything really crazy. No one said as much, but I think I had just pulled another unacceptable Yankee move. I just felt like it was unfair for us to pay rent for a whole structure that we could only use half of.

He emptied my entire garbage barrel onto the porch and spent the next hour or so going through it piece by piece. When he found that I had not thrown away a single item of value, he went upstairs to take inventory of his old bedroom. The guy was a real-live, kung-fu Redneck, a veteran of the Marine Corps, with a dangerous reputation. I spent that afternoon bracing myself to be beaten to a pulp while my housemates gave me the silent treatment and looked at me like I would deserve whatever happened. Eventually, he came down with a small box of stuff, and he had calmed down.

"Well Leroy, you did a pretty good job. I guess… I guess you saved me a lot of trouble in the long run."

With that, he shook my hand, gathered all the trash from the porch back into the barrel, and left. He was obviously really embarrassed that I had waded so deeply into his personal mess, but I honestly never felt any judgement towards the man. I had dealt with much worse messes than that before, and I knew what it was like to waste years of my life crippled by depression. I just hope my efforts helped erase some of the record of that episode of his life.

After my cleaning incident, we got the green light to clean the rest of the upstairs ourselves. The small, middle room was just cluttered with valueless junk, so it didn't take that long, and the bathroom was a similar situation. Unfortunately, the other large room in the western corner was piled from wall to wall with a tangled mass of junk so deep that it almost reached the ceiling. Between all four of us and the landlord, there was not enough motivation to tackle that project, so we all decided that it could wait for a better time. We actually ended up shoving all the crap from the middle room and the bathroom into the two feet of space that was left up by the ceiling of that room. One of my friends moved into the middle room, while another slept on the couch downstairs. The third one left after a few days to work on some project in a different state, and I only ended up seeing him a couple more times all winter.

I made one more big mistake in regards to our living space, and this one brought about the most dire consequences. The cabin had sat abandoned for almost two years after our landlord moved into town, and in that time, a family of grey squirrels made it into their home. They had a nest somewhere in that deepest pile of junk in the western bedroom, and that gave us another reason to put off dealing with the mess. The squirrels were amazingly tolerant of us moving into their home at first. I guess it was more space than they needed all to themselves, and they might have thought of us as a potential benefit too, since we would be bringing in a food supply that they might be able to share. We saw them often, but they didn't really bother us. They didn't poop inside the house like rats or mice would do, and they went to bed as soon as it got dark.

They rose at the crack of dawn though, and I often awoke to the sounds of one or more large squirrels scurrying around in my bedroom. The door to my room had obviously been shut when the house was abandoned, because the squirrels had chewed a hole through the wall up by the peak of the roof to gain access.

After about a week, I decided it would be nice to keep the squirrels out of my room, so I salvaged some nails and a board from the yard and boarded over their entrance. That was the wrong move. Somehow, I had crossed an unacceptable line in squirrel etiquette. Maybe they thought I was an insufferable Yankee too. From that moment on, we were at war with the squirrels.

One of their main tactics was to ransack our food supply. We would gather all sorts of food and store it in the kitchen, but we all had active lives, so it was fairly common for all three of us to be gone from the cabin at the same time. Usually, whenever there were no humans home to guard the food, the squirrels would dump out any containers and spread our food all over the counters and the floor. I'm sure they ate some of it too, but it was clear from their methods that their primary goal was to render the food inedible to us.

Even worse was their behavior in the bathroom. The cabin had no running water or plumbing. (We filled up tanks of drinking water in town.) Within the first week, we built a bucket toilet and placed it in the small room in the northern corner upstairs. My friends then set up a barrel outside with the intention of making our poop into compost for a future garden. This system worked just fine until the squirrel hostilities commenced.

After that, anytime someone went to use the bucket, all four of the squirrels would notice and rush in to disrupt them. They would wait until their victim had their pants down and was seated on the throne. Then they would enter the room, clinging to the top of the walls up by the ceiling where they were safely out of reach, and let loose a continuous, loud barrage of aggressive, chattering squirrel profanity until the human left the room. It was so stressful that I could never relax my sphincter enough to actually poop. I don't know what my housemates did about it, but I just ended up hiking out into the woods with my own roll of toilet paper when it was time to do my business. The only times I ever tried to face the squirrels were when it was pouring rain out, and even then, sometimes I just couldn't follow through.

It was clear to all of us that the animals were actually trying to drive us out of their home, and we were at a loss for what to do about it. None of us were the kind of people who felt like we were superior to wild animals, and we knew it had been their home for a long time before we moved in. None of us had any inclination to try to kill them. In hindsight, I probably should have tried taking the board down and letting them back into my room. At the time it just seemed like there was no going back. We all learned a valuable lesson from the experience though: Don't ever start a conflict with squirrels unless you are prepared to actually kill them.

The squirrel war was not resolved by the time I left that spring, and I never heard how it ended up. I did hear one amazing update about the cabin several years later though. When I lived there, one entire exterior wall of the cabin had grown over with a thick mat of poison ivy that stretched from the ground, all the way to the peak of the roof. It was the northwestern wall that made the back wall of the bathroom and the room full of junk that we never attempted to clean. Apparently, the roots of the poison ivy slowly broke apart the concrete and weakened its integrity. Then, about two years after I left, the entire wall collapsed into the yard, followed by an avalanche of junk that had never been removed from the upstairs room.

38. FOOD SUPPLY

I have grown to really enjoy working on farms. I like the feeling of being responsible for everyone's food supply. The work keeps my body strong and healthy. It keeps my attitude positive and my conscience clean. I avoid going into debt, and I enjoy paying for things with cash that I earned. But in my mid-twenties, the goal was to avoid working for money at all costs. Corporate capitalism is a broken system that limits our freedom and exacerbates inequality. I'm still convinced of that, and I'm still looking for ways to fix it, but at the time of my big walk, all I could think to do was slack off. The idea was that if I could free up my own time by not working, then I would be in a better position to liberate everyone else. Both of my homies were living the same lifestyle that winter I spent in North Carolina. At one point, one of them made $750 by letting medical scientists do experiments on him, but I'm pretty sure that was the total combined income for our entire household that winter.

That made the normally mundane task of feeding ourselves into an adventure. It was a six-mile trek from our cabin to the near edge of Chapel Hill, and the first thing we would come to when we arrived in town was a shopping plaza with a Food Lion grocery store in it. The dumpster behind it was almost always full of things we could eat, so we checked on that as often as we could. Dumpsters are always a good source of food, but winter is the best time of year for dumpstering because the cold weather keeps the food fresher. Further into town, there was a whole circuit of other dumpsters we would check on a regular basis.

For the first whole month, it seemed like the Food Lion was being terribly overstocked with blueberry pies. Any time we checked the dumpster, there would be at least one, and sometimes we got a whole stack of them. I remember all of us speculating that it might not be healthy to live on a diet of mostly blueberry pie. Maybe natural blueberry pie made of flour, sugar, butter, and blueberries would be okay, but the list of ingredients printed on the packaging of the free pies we scored from the dumpster was an entire paragraph of obscure chemicals that we couldn't even pronounce. That's what life is like though for a penniless scavenger. You eat whatever the dumpster gods see fit to provide.

The other item from the Food Lion that really stands out in my memory was fish. We didn't find fish quite as often, but sometimes when we did, there would be a huge load of it. I would estimate there were eight or ten times that winter when we really hit the fish jackpot, and a lot of it was really high-quality stuff too. The price tags were still stuck on the packaging, and there were a couple times when the value of our harvest exceeded $100. We all got a good laugh one time from a very expensive package that was labeled, "The *Elusive* Arctic Char." Of course, fish goes bad faster than almost anything, even in the winter chill, so we had to eat it up fast. This led to incredible binging feasts. We would literally eat fish until we were so full, we would have to take naps. Then we would repeat the cycle every three or four hours until the fish was all gone, or until we lost the rest to rot.

After the first couple major fish events, I decided we needed some sort of refrigeration system at the cabin. I found a blue plastic barrel in the yard that had the top half cut off, so it was only about knee-deep, and easy to reach into. I put it out behind the house, right up against the back wall where the sun never shone, and I filled it up halfway with rainwater that I collected from the roof. It only took a few days for a layer of ice to form in there thick enough to support the weight of any perishable food items we might bring home. I sat a piece of plywood over the top to keep the warm daytime air out, and I sat a couple of heavy cinder blocks on top of that to keep raccoons and other critters out. After that, we could make our big fish scores last for days, and I gained back some of the points I had lost with my friends by being such a relentless Yankee.

Besides the dumpsters, our other best source of food was the Lenoire Dining Hall at the University of North Carolina. I have snuck into college cafeterias all up and down the East Coast. I've sampled the fare at such prestigious institutions as Yale and Tufts, and none of them come close to the quality available at Lenoire Hall. Not only did it offer the best food, it was also the most porous college cafeteria I've ever encountered. There were three easy methods to get inside.

Firstly, we could come in through the exit. This method involved a little bit of physical exertion because we had to run up an escalator that was slowly pushing us backwards. It made sense to wait until no one else was riding the escalator down, because it was especially awkward and challenging to squeeze by another person on an escalator at a running pace. Of course, when we were looking up from the bottom, we couldn't tell if someone was approaching the escalator, about to step on. We just had to go for it, and apologize if we ended up bothering anyone. I only tried that method one time. I got away with it, but it felt like I was making a dramatic spectacle of myself. When I finally popped up into the big dining room, huffing and panting, dozens of heads turned to glance at me. No one cared enough to rat me out, but I still preferred a more subtle method.

The next method took advantage of the factor that none of the employees gave a single shit about their workplace. Literally everyone who worked there was Black, and they all wore the same look of a mistreated, underpaid, disgruntled employee on their faces. If we went around to the backside of the kitchen, there would always be someone outside on a cigarette break. All it took was a couple minutes of friendly conversation to convince the employees to let us in through the kitchen. I tried that method a few times, and it worked every time, but I didn't like the feeling that I was taking advantage of exploited workers who might get in trouble for helping me.

The easiest method was simply to ask students to swipe us in. The official entrance to the dining hall was guarded by an obese woman with a magnetic card reader. Each student had a card which they would swipe to gain access to the building. They each got a set number of meals per week, and every time they swiped their card, the computer would subtract one meal from their total. Like most colleges, UNC offered a variety of meal plans. Some of the students got just enough meals every week to meet their own needs, while others got many extra meals that they would never use. During peak hours, there would often be a whole line of students shuffling slowly towards the checkpoint, so we didn't even have to slow them down to ask them for a favor. We could just walk down the line, politely asking each kid if they had any extra meals that week and if they would be willing to hook us up. It only ever took five or ten tries before someone would say yes. All the students had to do was tell the guard that we were their guest and swipe their card twice.

Once inside, we were free as birds to pick up a tray and load it up with any of the dozens of choices of scrumptious, nutritious grub. The entrees and side-dishes were arranged in a smorgasbord with serving tools pointed out towards us, so there was literally no limit to the amount we could eat short of the capacity of our bellies. Whenever they served lasagna or breaded catfish, I would put the capacity of my belly to the test. The Lenoire Hall's catfish fry was seriously to die for.

All the Punks in town dined there, so after my tray was loaded up, it made sense to look around before choosing a seat. Usually, someone else I knew would already be there, and then we could eat together. Sometimes we would end up with a whole table full of filthy, outrageously-dressed Punks with heavily-heaped trays all festering up the college cafeteria together. One of my housemates would refer to these gatherings as, "the whole Fraggle army."

We would also wear our backpacks, so after we were done with supper, we could fill them up with fruit and bagels to take home. My fondest memory of that winter comes from all the time we spent sitting around the woodstove, toasting bagels, and telling stories.

Given the total lack of insulation in our cabin, it only ever got comfortably warm in a tight little circle around the heating stove. The stove itself was incredibly half-assed by northern standards. It was essentially just six pieces of heavy sheet-metal welded together with legs on the bottom and a hinged door on the front, but the smooth top was perfect for toasting bagels. We would cut them in half, butter them up and sit them right on the top of the woodstove without even a skillet in between. We'd pull our three chairs right up close to the stove to stay warm and pass the long winter nights listening to each other's epic adventure stories.

I'm not even supposed to describe any characteristics of my homies to you, but I'm going to break the rules just enough to tell you that one of them was a phenomenal storyteller. I would say that his style and delivery were a notch or two better than mine, and his repertoire of crazy experiences was an order of magnitude bigger than mine. He loved hearing my stories too, and sometimes the third guy would contribute a crazy story as well. We probably didn't spend every night like that, but that's the way I remember it now.

The last piece of the food supply puzzle came from shoplifting. Only one of us actually had the guts to be very good at shoplifting, but once every two weeks or so, he would herd the other two of us into some big corporate store or other to practice our skills. We were nervous and cold-footed, but we never did get caught. That was how we kept butter stocked for the bagels, and there were a number of other products we needed that generally weren't to be found in dumpsters or at the college cafeteria- things like spices, cheese, cooking oil, and the like.

***

We never even came close to going hungry, and I thought our diet was very healthy considering it was 100% free, but I had more problems with my digestive system that winter than ever before or since. Now to be fair, I have always had more trouble digesting food than the average person. Maybe it's because of that river I drank out of when I was a kid, but my dad and my sister both suffer from identical issues to mine, so it may be a hereditary thing. None of us have ever figured out anything we can do to alleviate our symptoms, so we just live with it. Compared to other people's handicaps, it's really pretty mild.

I tried limiting my diet in all sorts of ways throughout my twenties, but every different diet I tried only made the situation worse. I don't even worry about it anymore, and that seems to be working better than anything else I ever tried. The only sense I can make of it is that it might correspond to my mental health. When I was younger, I was always distressed about something. Whether it was politics, the environment, my failed love-life, or whatever, I could rarely go a whole day without getting really upset about something. In my old age, I have simply lost the capacity to worry so much all the time, and it may or may not be a coincidence that I am finally starting to be able to adequately digest the things I eat.

Age 26 was rock bottom for me. My guts worked well enough while I was out walking and exerting myself, but I couldn't poop right at all while I was sitting out the winter in North Carolina. Sometimes I'd be clogged up for days. Other times I'd have to run outside with my toilet paper twelve times in one morning. There were some other nitty gritty details too, but I won't trouble you with all of them. I worried that I might be infected with worms or some other kind of parasite. I thought it would be a good idea to see a doctor, so when someone told me the university's medical school offered a free clinic on Wednesday evenings, I jumped on it.

I followed directions to a building on the north side of town where I asked a staff person about the clinic. They led me to a waiting room full of Mexican people who were all sniffling or looking uncomfortable, or holding sniffling, uncomfortable children. I was the only gringo, and for some reason, I worried that my race might disqualify me from receiving free medical care. After ten minutes or so, a nurse opened up a door to look into the waiting room. As soon as she spotted me, she said, "Oh, woops!" Then she waved her arm motioning for me to come with her. I got up and followed her into an adjacent waiting room full of White kids who looked like college students.

"We had you in the wrong place," she said, "Sorry about that!" And she left.

This was confusing. The kids in the White-people's waiting room didn't look sick at all. After a few minutes, I asked one of them to explain what was going on. It took a little back and forth for them to understand just what I was asking and for me to understand what they were telling me, but eventually we sorted it out. Patients at the clinic did not receive treatment from actual medical professionals. They received treatment from UNC medical students in their final year of college. The clinic was intended more for the purpose of training the students than healing the patients, and that's why the service was free. I also realized that I had been taken to a room full of medical students who were waiting to practice their skills. Because of my race, I had been mistaken for a student. The next time a nurse came by, I let her know about the mistake and had myself put back in with the Mexicans where I belonged. I was one of the last people to show up, so I waited late into the evening while all the other patients went first.

When it was finally my turn, I was led to an examination room where I was weighed and measured. A student took my pulse and my blood pressure and wrote down their findings on a chart. They shined a light into my mouth and looked at my throat, and then they pressed a stethoscope in various places all over my chest and back and listened while I breathed. They finished up by hammering below my kneecaps to check my reflexes. At no point did they ask what my reason was for coming to the clinic, so I brought it up myself. They said that was not their area of study, so I would have to see someone different.

After that, I was left to wait for a few minutes until another student came in and repeated the exact same process as the first one. They were not a gastro-intestinal specialist either. After some more waiting, I was led to a different room where I was given a vision test and got my eyes examined. At some point I realized I was going serve as a practice dummy for every single student in attendance. Rather than examine me for anything relevant to my symptoms, they were going to examine whichever part of my body they were training to work on. I can't honestly remember all the different tests I went through that night, but at least I didn't have to get any blood drawn.

Things got really weird when the social worker-in-training took his crack at me. He asked me a long series of questions about my living situation, and I just answered him honestly. At that age, I had no idea how much trouble you can get into by telling the truth to a social worker. It wasn't like I went on and on, embellishing about all the details of my ramshackle cabin like I did in the last chapter of this book. I answered each question pretty succinctly. He just got really worried about me and kept asking more and more questions until he had most of the same details that you now have.

He couldn't have been more than a couple of years younger than me, but he obviously hadn't met any travel Punks before. He mistook my lifestyle choices for a crisis. He didn't understand that I wasn't depressed. Becoming a homeless rebel with only a few possessions was the move that finally got me out of a decade of depression. I was having the adventure of my life. But he thought I was going down the tubes and he wanted to save me. He got so upset that the tenor of his voice changed, and it seemed like he was about to cry. I had half a dozen friends in town who would let me use their shower any time I wanted, so I volunteered that detail in hopes that I could console him, but he was just overwhelmed.

He ended up calling his teacher who was somewhere in the building that night. While we waited for him to come, I kept trying to convince the kid that I wasn't having any mental or emotional problems. I had just come in hoping I could get tested for worms or get some attempt at a diagnosis for my gut problems. The trouble was, I had just told him about eating out of dumpsters. In his mind, it was obvious why I was having digestive problems.

When the teacher showed up, he turned out to be a full-grown, licensed social worker. That was when I realized I had really screwed up, and I was in danger of getting myself and my two buddies in trouble. I politely declined to answer any of his questions. I repeated the story about the actual medical situation involving my intestines, and then expressed frustration that I couldn't see a gastro-intestinal specialist about it. I had been called in from the waiting room at eight o'clock. Now it was ten o'clock, and I still hadn't met a single person who was qualified, or even *willing* to address my real-life situation. I had spent two hours being used as a mannequin for people who were playing pretend.

My point finally got through, and the social worker left to get the program director. She told me they didn't have any students who were studying the digestive system, but she would try to get me in to see one of the actual doctors who was on duty that night. After another half hour, I got taken to an exam room in a different wing of the building where I met with a young doctor who was working the late shift. He also assumed that dumpster food would not be clean inside plastic packages and must be the vector for any one of a hundred intestinal pathogens. I didn't even tell him I had been eating out of dumpsters, but I guess the social workers must have told everyone about my interview. He agreed to help me get my stool tested for worms, but I was the one who had to suggest it. He gave me a little kit with a little plastic container, explained how to use it, and told me where to drop it off in the morning.

When I got back to the clinic, the distressed little social worker pup was waiting for me, and he was literally wringing his hands. He had called a taxi so I wouldn't have to walk six miles back home so late. It was a really nice touch, so I shook his hand and thanked him. It was probably his teacher who thought of it, but that didn't matter. It only took a couple minutes for the cabbie to get there, and that was the end of my adventure at the free medical clinic.

My stool test came back negative for worms a couple weeks later. At first, I thought maybe I had eaten a few too many synthetic blueberry pies. Then I thought maybe I had just stretched myself out by gorging too much. The catfish fry was so good at Lenoire, and I never knew when they were going to serve it. They served it less often than some of the other dishes, so it was really a treat. I probably only got to eat it four or five times in all, but each time I did, I ate WAY too much. I'm talkin' like seven to ten whole fish, all covered with fry-batter. And I wasn't burning a million calories a day hiking. I think that just overwhelmed my system which was already odd to begin with. I don't think I will ever really know. I have seen enough doctors now to know that they aren't going to help. My symptoms got better when I took off walking again in the spring, and they have been getting better ever since.

39. TRANSPORTATION

My one friend who took off for the winter was technically the owner of the minivan, so when he left, that vehicle went with him. One of the guys who remained had a large motorcycle that he lovingly referred to as "The Bastard," but he spent a lot more time trying to fix it than he spent riding it. Both of my homies had bicycles, and after a few trips to town on foot, I decided I needed one too.

The town had a big enough radical scene to have a "Recycle-a-Bike" program. A team of volunteers would gather up old bicycles that were being thrown away and repair them, or at least scavenge parts of them to repair other bikes. They would give the bikes away for free to anyone who needed one, but they would not actually do the repairs until the recipient of the bike was there to watch and help. They would open up shop in the garage and driveway of someone's private home every Saturday afternoon. To receive a free bike, you had to show up during those hours and pick one out from their extensive supply of broken old models. Then the volunteers would let you use their tools while explaining and guiding you through the process of repairing your own bike. If you really needed help, they would do something for you, but their goal was to encourage self-sufficiency. After that, you were welcome to come back any Saturday to borrow tools or ask advice as needed.

The bike I got was pretty old and beat up, but I liked it because it had a big wire basket attached to the front of the handle bars, so I could bring home a lot of food or other resources I found on my scavenging runs. I still chose to walk into town fairly often. At that point in my life, a six mile walk twice in one day wasn't really a big deal. It seemed like I needed a totally different set of muscles to pedal a bicycle than the ones I had built up for walking. Hills that felt like nothing on foot felt torturous on my bike, and it always made my crotch hurt. It was nice to have the option though, and I brought home many loads of good stuff in my fancy basket.

It ended up being the coldest, snowiest winter North Carolina had seen in many years. It snowed six times, including the one that caught me in Leesville two nights before I arrived. One storm at the beginning of February dumped half a foot, and it took three days for all the snow to melt away. That was more of an emergency for the locals than a hurricane. I had no particular schedule that winter, so anytime it snowed, I would just stay where I was until it was over. I had several friends in town who didn't mind me sleeping on their couches, so if a snow or rain hit while I was in town, I would just spend the night there. But I was home when the big snow hit, and I couldn't wait three days to go into town, or I would have run out of food.

It was about a half mile down to the bottom of our narrow, pitted little road. Then you would turn onto a much larger dirt road for all of about 200 yards before reaching the highway. The next five and a half miles were a nicely graded, newly paved highway with wide shoulders to walk or ride on all the way to the edge of town.

I decided to ride my bike into town the afternoon of the second day after the big snow. By then, the drive lanes had mostly melted off. There were no snowplows in that part of the state, but enough people had driven over the snow, and packed it down enough that the sunshine could warm the blacktop underneath and melt it. Very few people were out driving, so I could mostly use the clear drive lanes. When a car did need to use my lane, I would pull off and wait on the slushy shoulder.

I was amazed to see how many people had slid off the road and then abandoned their cars. There had to have been at least fifty of them in that little stretch of highway between our dirt road and town, all spun off at different random angles. Luckily, none of them had collided with each other. They were all right-side up, and there were very few places along that stretch of road with steep banks or deep ditches, so I imagine it wasn't too hard to get them all back on the road. Many of them probably made it without even needing to be towed. I didn't stick around to watch the cleanup, but all the vehicles were gone a couple days after the last of the big snow melted. Well, almost all of them. One car and one pickup truck got left behind for the rest of the winter. For all I know, they might still be there.

***

One of my homies liked to team up on dumpstering missions, so we often worked together. On one bitterly cold and frozen night we were looking through the dumpster behind a Panera bakery when we heard the metal door open up on the back of the building just a few feet away. We shut off our flashlights right away, but there was no time to climb out of the dumpster and get away. We just crouched down still and silent and tried to blend in with the garbage. Seconds later, a big black plastic bag full of trash came flying in over the side and bounced off my buddy's back and shoulders. He may have been startled or even hurt, but he managed to hold his silence.

After taking out the trash, the Panera employee stayed outside to smoke a cigarette, and he took his time. After a while, another employee came out and they got into a whole conversation. It was the night of the big basketball rivalry game between UNC and Duke, and one of them was really pissed that he had to work instead of going to the game. They chatted for so long, they must have each smoked at least two cigarettes. By the time they finally went back in the store, my friend and I had been holding still for so long that we were frozen to the bone. We hadn't gathered much food yet, but we decided to call it a night after that, and we rode our bicycles home.

It was just a few nights later when I was riding home from another mission with that same guy. It was not so cold that night, so we had stayed in town pretty late and gathered a good load of food. The highway was all but deserted at that hour, and the waxing crescent moon had set hours earlier. There were only a couple of places where little stretches of the road were illuminated by lights from someone's house, and right at the halfway point, there was one big church beside the road that was lit up like a baseball stadium. Other than that, we pedaled through the pitch darkness.

That may sound terrifying, but it was actually pretty fun. All the stars were out, and there was an obvious line on either side of us where the stars disappeared behind the trees. We just stuck to the middle of the stripe of stars above us and everything worked out fine. Two or three cars came along the entire time, and we just pulled over out of the way to let them pass.

We had made it about two thirds of the way home, and we were coasting down a long hill. I can't even guess how fast we were going, but I can tell you we were really cruising. It was exhilarating to feel the wind in my face while navigating by the stars above. All of a sudden, BAM! I collided with something! The front of my bike lifted off the ground, and I shouted in surprise. I felt a couple items from my basket bounce off my chest and face, and my back tire rolled over some large, rigid object causing my seat to pound me in the crotch and send a crunch the whole way up my spine. Luckily, I had been going so fast that the centrifugal force of my spinning tires kept me upright. I decelerated very quickly though because my front tire was no longer shaped like a circle. I instinctively steered towards the right shoulder in the few seconds it took me to thump to a stop.

My friend was screeching to a halt down ahead of me, braking as fast as he could, and hollering out, "Whoa! What happened? Are you alright?" As soon as he could, he came running back up the hill with his flashlight on hollering words of concern. I was very startled and surging with adrenaline, and my crotch hurt a bit, but after a quick assessment, I decided I was okay.

Now I'm going to break the rules again and tell you that my buddy grew up in the deepest, darkest, most isolated holler in all of Appalachia, so he spoke with a Duck Dynasty accent times ten. When I told him I was okay, he shouted in response, "I thought you was gonna DIE!" Then he kept repeating that phrase every few minutes, loudly and full of emotion, like it was helping him to process his own feelings about my accident.

I got out my flashlight and we walked back up the hill to figure out what I had collided with. There, right in the middle of the westbound lane, was a large dining room table, flipped upside-down with its legs pointed up to the sky. The underside was reinforced with a sturdy wooden rim about four inches wide that was turned perpendicular to the table's flat surface. It didn't even show any signs of damage where my bike tires had run into it. Food from my basket was scattered all over the road, so we took a moment to gather it back up. Then we dragged the table out of the road and moved on to assess my bicycle.

The front tire had popped, and the rim of the wheel was bent so badly that I couldn't even push it along the road. Even the back tire had a considerable dent in it, but at least the tire was still inflated. My friend's bike had a basket on the handlebars too, and we were able to cram all the food from my basket in on top of the food that was already in his. Then I was able to stand my bike up on its back tire and walk it home, keeping it balanced with one hand on the handlebars and one hand on the seat. My friend didn't want to leave me behind, so he walked his bike home too. Every few minutes, he kept repeating his line, "I thought you was gonna die!" in his very emphatic, emotional tone and his crazy backwoods accent. For weeks afterward, every time we would tell the story to someone new, he would tell them several times, "I thought he was gonna DIE!"

The following Saturday, I ended up taking both the wheels off my bike, and I walked into town to the Recycle-a-Bike workshop carrying a wheel in each hand. When I showed the volunteers, they were astonished at how badly I had fucked up my bike, and they all needed to hear the story too. They didn't even think it was worth trying to fix the rear wheel let alone the front one. Unfortunately, they didn't have any spare wheels they could give me right then. I missed the next couple Saturdays, and then I left town, so the dining room table incident turned out to be the end of the bicycling stage of my adventure.

40. HONORARY TAR HEEL

The University of North Carolina was a good resource for more than just food. It also had a public computer lab that I didn't even need a password to access, so as soon as we moved within range, I started to work on episode two of my zine. I found out about a student group that was dedicated to opposing the neo-colonial Free Market, and reached out to them. They met once every two weeks, so I went every time, and chimed in once in a while encouraging them to try more radical tactics. I don't think I actually persuaded anyone along those lines, but I did make several new friends and signed up about a dozen more zine subscribers. Sometimes I would schedule meals with my student friends at the cafeteria so I didn't have to canvass the whole line, and one kid let me sleep in his dorm room a couple times.

They also showed me the student activities building where there was a nice lounge in the basement featuring a kitchen where I could heat up leftovers or fill my water bottle, and several couches to sleep on. I had to be inside the building by nine o'clock when the staff locked the doors, but that was really the only issue. I rode out a couple of snowstorms sleeping on those couches, and I stayed there four or five other times when I had stayed up late working on my zine and felt too tired, or just too lazy to commute back to our country cabin. One time a janitor came in, turned the lights on, and vacuumed all around my couch. That was a little bit stressful, but he never said anything to me. Nor was there any evidence that he told anyone else about me sleeping there. Other than that, I rarely even encountered any students down in that basement lounge.

I spent a lot of time on the college campus. I would imagine some people there got used to seeing my face and just assumed I was another student. I didn't dress or style my hair like a crusty Punk, although I truly was one in my heart and in my lifestyle.

One night, I decided to sleep in the enormous library on campus. It wasn't necessary. I had lots of better places to sleep. It was more of a stunt that I wanted to do so I could feel cool about it, like sleeping out in Prospect Park where KRS-1 slept. As I recall, the library was six stories tall. Initially, I went up to the fourth floor, and just laid down on the floor in a tight aisle between two shelves of books. I didn't bring a sleeping bag or anything, just my winter coat and hat that I had bought at a thrift shop. At first, I used my coat to pad the hard floor, but then I got chilly, so I just put it on the way it was designed to be worn.

Within a few minutes, announcements came over the intercom to let everyone know the library was closing and we all had to be out. Then it closed, and the lights went down to a dimmer setting. I felt too exposed and nervous to sleep. After about an hour, I heard a vacuum cleaner start up on my level and realized that I was certain to be discovered there. By then, it was too late to get into the student activities building, or to solicit a night on the couch at any of my friends' houses. I snuck away from the vacuum cleaner sound, and snuck around until I found a wall with a whole line of doors leading into small study rooms. I went into one of those and closed the door. Eventually, the vacuum cleaner came right by the outside of my door, but the janitor never opened it up to clean inside. It was nice and dark inside the little study room, so after the vacuuming ended, I was finally able to sleep.

I finished episode two of my zine right around the beginning of February, and then it was time to print it out and mail it. I was particularly proud of the back cover. I cut out pictures from cologne ads and made a whole collage of ridiculously hot models all oiled up and dressed in skimpy clothing. At the top, I wrote, "Tired of advertisements using your most precious dreams to sell you crap you don't need?" Then below, I gave one of the bimbo faces a speech-bubble that said, "Then you need… The Beginning Is Near- a bold new gimmick, by Leroy Walker."

Once again, someone had a photocopy scam at a nearby corporate office-supply store that I could use to get free copies. The store was in a shopping plaza all the way over near Durham. In fact, it might have actually been in Durham, so I parked my bike in Chapel Hill and rode the Triangle Transit bus out to the plaza. Just like the previous winter's photocopy scam, this one involved a code, but in this case, I had to make all my copies first. Then I would type in the code, and it would erase the charge for the copies.

I ended up staying in the store and hogging one of the self-serve copy machines all afternoon. I had well over 300 subscribers at that point. Roughly half of them had already received episode one, but they still needed episode two. The more recent half of my subscribers needed both episodes, so I had a *lot* of copies to make. I loaded several new reems of paper into the machine. I'm lucky I didn't have to change the ink cartridge, because I would have needed an employee to help me with that. My backpack was heavy with warm paper by the time I finally finished.

By then, my total had climbed up to a number just shy of $700. I typed in the code, and nothing changed. The charge on the screen was supposed to drop back down to zero after I entered the code, but it wasn't working. I tried it two or three more times and got the same result. That was stressful. I had about fifteen dollars and a bus transfer in my wallet. What the hell was I going to do? I couldn't just keep standing there looking nervous. I decided I was just going to have to walk out and then run if anyone gave chase.

The closest cashier to me was a young-ish, somewhat overweight woman. No one was in her line, so I walked up, gave her a really nice smile, and just kept on going. She smiled back and wished me a nice evening. All the employees there recognized me as the guy who had been at the self-serve photocopier all afternoon, and the normal procedure was to pay for self-serve copies by swiping a credit card at the machine, so I guess my behavior looked totally normal. I sure was nervous though. There was a little bit of forest behind the store, so I walked around the building as quickly as I could and hid in the woods. I stayed there, watching to see if the cops would show up until I got very cold and it looked like the sun was about to set. The cops never came, and I finally crawled back out of the woods and caught the bus back to Chapel Hill.

I spent what felt like a small fortune on envelopes and postage over the next few days. As I recall, it took me three whole days to collate and staple all the zines together, address all the envelopes, and take them to the post office.

I realized that I couldn't keep doing the zine that way. By the time episode three came out, I would have hundreds more subscribers. It was only a matter of time before I got caught doing some multi-hundred-dollar photocopy scam. Hell, it was only a matter of time before the self-serve copy machine caught on fire from me using it so excessively.

Luckily, there was an alternative. Back then, the Crimethinc publishing collective was headquartered in North Carolina. I got to hang out with various writers and artists who worked for the collective a number of times, and they thought my project was pretty cool. They told me about a newspaper printing company in a nearby town called Benson where I could get my zine mass-produced for an incredibly good price. I asked if a local business would be willing to publish material with such radical content, and they said, "Oh yeah. No problem." They had been working with that guy for years, and they had published all sorts of crazy stuff. They said he couldn't care less about the content of my writing as long as I paid.

It turned out to be a bit of a saga to get to Benson and back. The city of Raleigh NC is by far the largest of the three Triangle cities, and it sat directly between me and Benson. It is very difficult to hitchhike through cities, so I opted to ride the Triangle Transit across Raleigh. It was already afternoon by the time I reached the end of the southeastern bus line, and then I had to hitchhike. One of the people who picked me up was a virulent racist who couldn't stop spewing his hatred for Black people the entire half hour I was in his car. I don't look the slightest bit Black, but it still made me really uncomfortable, and I was very relieved when it was finally time to get out of his car.

The guy at the printing shop was easy to work with, and he did give me an excellent deal. The trouble was, he was not willing to set up his machine to make any fewer than 3,000 copies of anything. That seemed like a lot more than I would need, but he only charged me $200, so I went for it.

Hitchhiking was slow that day, and the sun set before I made it back to Raleigh. A saintly woman picked me up in the waning light of dusk, and said she would take me to the outermost bus stop, but not before she got some supper. She then drove me to her house, which was only a few miles away. She and her husband shared their supper with me. Then we got back in her car, and she drove me about fifteen miles out of her way to the edge of Raleigh. I had to ride that bus line into the downtown terminal and then get on a different bus out to Chapel Hill. The Triangle Transit closes for the night at a certain hour, and I literally caught the last bus to Chapel Hill by less than a minute.

A week later, I had to go and pick up my 6,000 zines. I enlisted the help of a friend who had a large car. I also enlisted the help of my parents to store all the extra zines at their house out in Colorado. From then on, when I signed up new subscribers, I would email their address to my mother who would mail the zines out to them. She wasn't thrilled about the idea, but she agreed to help me.

When we got to Benson, it turned out that boxes weren't part of the cheap printing deal. The guy had just tied them into stacks of 200 with one string wrapped around them horizontally and a second one wrapped vertically. We just barely got all of them into my friend's car. The big trunk was stuffed to capacity. The back seat was piled all the way to the ceiling, and I had to put the last few stacks on the floor below my feet. The car sagged low on its shocks the whole way back.

The original plan was to take them straight from the print shop to the post office, but I couldn't ship them without boxes, so we ended up storing them out in the cabin for a few days. The zines were printed on 8½ by 11 paper, so two stacks of 200 fit just right into a paper box. I spent the next few days knocking on office doors at the university, asking professors and graduate students for their empty paper boxes, and piling up my scores in the basement lounge at the student activities building. Once I had enough, I called in my friend with the car to help again. All the zines had fit in his car before, but the dimensions of the boxes made that impossible, so we had to make two trips to the post office. Even at the media mail rate, it was several hundred dollars more to ship them all to Colorado. By the time the zine project was finished, I had spent all the money I made in Washington D.C. plus all but about $200 of the money I had started out with two years prior. I was almost broke and it was pretty stressful.

As it turned out, I only signed up about 90 more zine subscribers after that. As far as I know, my mom followed through and sent them their zines. The other 5,820 zines sat there cluttering up my parents' basement for the next sixteen years until they finally took them to the recycling center.

41. JANET JACKSON

Here in the United States, we pay incredibly cheap prices for food. The economy has been set up that way for generations, so most people don't even realize how valuable food actually is. It takes a lot of work to produce food, or any agricultural product, and that work is what makes it valuable. Our modern religion teaches us that machines and chemicals do most of the work to produce our food supply, and that's what makes it possible to provide food at such cheap prices.

In truth, farm chemicals and machinery are so expensive that they have put most small farmers out of business. Giant trans-national corporations are the only businesses with enough money to afford those machines without going into massive debt, but even they don't use machines as much as they would like us to believe.

It's probably fair to say that commodity grains like wheat and corn are produced mostly by machines and chemicals, but human labor is still, as it has always been, the engine that produces most of the other things we eat. Human labor is valuable, but food remains cheap because the big agricultural companies exploit their workers, meaning they only pay the workers a small fraction of what their labor is actually worth. Very few American workers would tolerate a high level of exploitation, which is why so few of us work on farms. The millions of workers who toil to produce our food supply come from Third World countries, and they are willing to accept being exploited because poverty in their home countries is so extreme that they will do almost anything to make a buck.

Much of our food gets shipped here all the way from the Third World, but I'm proud to report that the US still gets the bigger half of our food supply from within our own territory. It takes a lot of field work, harvest work, and processing work to tend America's vast farmlands, and most of that work is done by people from other countries to our south. A worker can make a lot more money on a farm here in the US than they can at a farm or a sweatshop back home. It's really worth it to anyone who can make it, and they compete like football players. The difference is, a football game lasts a few hours, once or twice a week. Farm workers go hard all summer and through the fall without weekends. Some jobs pay hourly and some pay piece rate, but either way, no one wants to take any time off. Often times they'll start at dawn and work until dark. They are rescuing their families. The trouble is, getting here to the United States difficult and dangerous.

Our borders are highly restricted, so anyone who migrates here without citizenship or at least a green card is under constant threat of deportation. The process to gain citizenship is expensive and very time consuming. Most people aren't even interested in moving here permanently anyway, but the bar to achieve citizenship is set so high that it serves as an additional deterrent to anyone who might consider it.

Even to get a green card takes time, and a considerable amount of money by Third World standards. Big companies that depend on migrant laborers collaborate with Mexican drug cartels to sneak people across the border and avoid the difficult legal process. Once those people are here, they have to remain hidden at all costs, so their employers are free to exploit them as much as they want. If anyone sticks their head up to complain about low pay or dangerous working conditions, they will be instantly fired and deported.

Many others do get green cards, so they can be here legally for a limited amount of time, but their jobs are still very vulnerable. If they try to demand better pay or safer conditions, they can simply be fired and replaced from the almost bottomless reservoir of desperate Third World people. The same fate awaits any worker who gets sick, injured, or pregnant. If you strain to listen to these people's cautiously whispered complaints, one of the most common things you will hear is that they have no access to any kind of medical care whatsoever. That's why Mexicans were the only ones besides me who were willing to put up with all that bullshit at the UNC free medical clinic.

To make matters worse, most of the migrants who come here end up taking shelter in employee housing on the same farms where they work. It's common practice to charge tenants exorbitant rates for their housing, so much of the money from their paychecks goes right back into the company they work for. Much of this housing is utterly squalid by First World standards, and workers are often packed together as densely as they would be in any urban barrio south of the border. Even people with legal paperwork have a hard time finding other options for housing. It's very rare for them to get an opportunity to learn any English, so they are almost always trapped behind the language barrier. Also, many of them are simply afraid of us, because so many of us are racist and hostile towards the people who feed us.

This system is not technically called slavery, because the workers do make money, and they make an autonomous choice to come here and work rather than being captured. Still, on a spectrum, their jobs are much closer to slavery than they are to freedom. At any given time, millions or even tens of millions of foreign workers are here in our country enduring these situations, but they are so isolated from us that most of us don't even realized they exist.

For decades, the Mount Olive Pickle company took advantage of foreign workers in this way, keeping them hidden on cucumber plantations around the flat coastal plains of eastern North Carolina. Then in 1999, some of those workers were lucky enough to make contact with some labor organizers in the Triangle cities.

Labor unions succeeded in protecting American workers from that kind of exploitation all the way back in the 1890's and early 1900's, so the organizers were amazed and appalled to hear about the conditions at the Mount Olive plantations. They wanted to help the pickle workers, but it was too dangerous to organize them into a union because of the circumstances I described above. Instead, they settled on the strategy of a boycott. The plan was to publicize the fact that Mount Olive was exploiting their workers in all the places where their pickles were sold, and convince the customers to stop buying Mount Olive products. If they could convince enough people to boycott the company, they could squeeze its profit margin, and then they would be able to put pressure on the executives to change the way they treated their employees. When I got to North Carolina, the boycott had been going for four years, and it was starting to gain some traction.

Now I have to change the subject here, but you will soon understand how this all ties together. When I was a kid out in eastern Washington, my parents were good friends with another couple who had two kids. I will call the kids Bo and Joe to hide their identities. Bo was about the same age as me, and Joe was about the same age as my sister, so whenever our parents got together, the four of us would play together. Bo wasn't the kind of friend who I would have made time to play with on purpose, but we saw each other pretty often, and we got along well enough.

As soon as my parents found out I was spending the winter in the Chapel Hill area, they wanted me to know that Bo was there too, and they passed his phone number on to me from his parents. It took me a few weeks to actually reach out to him, but when I did, I was pleasantly surprised. We weren't very good friends as children, but we really hit it off as adults. He had grown up to be a union organizer. He had taken a job with a union called the Farm Labor Organizing Committee, and they had sent him to Chapel Hill a few years earlier to be one of the main organizers of the Mount Olive Pickle Boycott. Obviously, we had a lot in common, and a lot to talk about. It was another one of those too-good-to-be-true coincidences that seemed to characterize my whole walking adventure.

Both of my housemates were straight edge, which means they would never consume any alcohol or any other drugs, but Bo was always down for a beer or two. I couldn't afford much beer that winter, but whenever I could, I would go over and kick it with Bo. The floor of his apartment was covered with a thick, shaggy rug that was very comfortable to sleep on, and I probably used the shower there more than anywhere else.

One day I was walking home from town on foot. I had made it just about halfway when I noticed something in the ditch wrapped in cellophane. I unwrapped it to discover it was a small stack of brownies, and a quick sniff suggested that they had not yet begun to rot. I ate one right on the spot and stuck the rest in my backpack to take home. It was a nice warm afternoon, and my spirits soared as I neared the cabin. When I got there, I sat down on one of the chairs on the porch and just reveled in the beauty of life. Something amazing was happening. I could just feel it. I am a very spiritual guy, and sometimes I can sense good or bad energy just from the vibes in the air. I had never felt a vibe that good before though. All I could think of was that some world-wide positive breakthrough had just happened. Maybe there had been a revolution and Bush had been overthrown. The wars were over and the troops were coming home! I got really excited imagining all the possibilities.

Then I realized I was just high. I had eaten a pot brownie. Someone had probably gotten scared when they saw a cop, and thrown their brownies out the window of their car. I hadn't smoked, or even thought about pot for months, so it took me a long time to figure out what was going on.

I saw Bo the next day, and he got really excited when I told him about the brownies. He hadn't had any weed in a long time either, and he really wanted to try one. We got in his car that evening and drove out to my house to grab them out of our refrigerator barrel. Back at his apartment, we each ate a brownie, and proceeded to get rip-stavin' stoned. We giggled and grinned our way through the evening until it was bed time. He went into his room, and

I laid down on the nice soft floor, but I was too stoned to sleep for hours. I had only been there for about a half an hour when I heard Bo run into his bathroom and puke his guts out. The sound was dramatic, loud and awful. It sounded like it really hurt, and it went on for so long that I went in to check on him. He didn't blame me for getting him sick, but he did regret eating the brownie.

The situation gave me pause to think. I had wondered before if my stomach had built up a resistance to various bacteria because I had been eating out of trash cans and dumpsters so much, but I never had another person to compare myself to before. Here was a guy who never ate discarded food, and he became violently ill after eating one little brownie that had sat on the side of the road for a while. I had eaten two identical brownies, and I never got so much as a cramp. If you've never lived off the waste stream, but you want to give it a try, I guess I would recommend starting with baby steps. Make sure you build up some immunity and toughness before you move on to eating pot brownies off the side of the road. I threw the rest of the brownies away after that.

Bo was also a huge fan of the Carolina Panthers football team. They were one of the new expansion teams. They had only been around for a few years, but that winter, they made it to their first Super Bowl. Bo was beside himself with excitement. He invited me, and a whole gang of his other friends to go out to a sports bar and watch the game on the big screen. We got a table right under the giant TV, and Bo paid for my dinner and drinks. I don't remember who was playing against the Panthers, and I don't remember who won the game, but I do remember one thing.

Super Bowl halftime shows are some of the weirdest and most overly-extravagant entertainment stunts in the history of humanity. Watching them is one of the worst ways ever for a person to spend their time, but for some reason, I caught myself watching the halftime show. I don't expose myself to very much television, so I am really sensitive to it. That means when I do see one, the flickering images can really capture my attention and mesmerize me. I had taken the seat with my back to the TV for that very reason, but somehow, I still ended up twisting all the way around in my seat and watching the halftime show.

Janet Jackson was performing. She was singing and dancing in some ridiculous complex costume with about a hundred backup dancers and pyrotechnic displays exploding behind them. Then on the final beat, at the very end of the song, she reached up in time to her last dance move and ripped open a little door on her costume that was shaped just right to let one whole breast pop out. It was obviously planned. Her highly energetic dance routine ended right on that move so that she suddenly went perfectly still, holding that pose, with one breast hanging out. The editors switched to a commercial as soon as they saw it. I would guess that I probably only got to see it for about 1.7 seconds, but it was a timeless moment. When the commercial break ended, the announcers apologized for Janet's "wardrobe malfunction," but I could tell that her wardrobe had functioned exactly the way she meant for it to.

It was awesome! I- the guy who never watches TV- got to witness, live, one of the most significant moments in television history- and football history! My life was changed forever. Where were you when Janet Jackson flashed her titty at the Super Bowl?

I also think its important for everyone to know that Janet Jackson and I have the same birthday. I didn't know that back then, but I found out a few years later. I was actually born on Janet's eleventh birthday. As a person who's trying to be heard and spread my philosophy to the world, I think that lends me a lot of credibility. So listen up!

Janet, if you ever read this: I'm a Taurus too, and you know what they say about us Tauruses!

42. HATEBEAK

There used to be a Punk band called Hatebeak. The band was made up of several humans, a parrot, and a pig. They would hang a microphone in front of the parrot's perch; strap another one to the pig's head, and plug them into the amplifier to add backup vocals as they performed. They came to play a show in Raleigh that winter, and someone with a car drove out to get all three of us ramshackle cabin-dwellers and bring us to the show.

Hatebeak was awesome. The pig doesn't understand human rhythm, so it belts out these big, long screams that don't really fit into the song. They put so many effects on it's mic though, that it sounds like some terrifying monster shrieking, so it still sounds awesome in the context. The parrot actually gets into the rhythm and chatters along like a beatbox addition to the drummer, but with mechanical precision, and its voice is all distorted by effects too. It was a pretty fun show.

There were one or two warmup bands, so there was at least one break where one band put away their stuff while the other band set up. During the break, much of the crowd went outside to smoke cigarettes, or just get a breath of fresh winter air. I went out because I really needed to find a place to pee. There must have been at least 40 young Punks lining the sidewalk, and it took me a minute to pick my way politely through the crowd.

We were right in the city, and there was some kind of club right across the street. Making my way through the crowd, I realized that an enormous stretch-limousine version of a Hummer was parked right out in front of the club. Some of the Punks were glaring at it and making rude comments.

Bush's wars were probably the only thing that all of us radicals were unanimously against back then, and Hummers were kind of a symbol of the pro-war assholes. A stretch-Hummer limo was probably about the most offensive symbol a person could wave in the face of a crowd of people like us.

Suddenly, it seemed obvious what I had to do. These kids wanted to dress like class warriors? I was gonna show 'em how it's done. I walked across the street, right to the back of the Hummer, unzipped, and started peeing all over the bumper. I really had to go, so I peed for quite a while.

I knew at least some of the kids across the street would see me, so I looked back to see what kind of a reaction I was getting. I was expecting lots of grins, affirmative nods, and maybe some thumbs up. Instead, most of them looked worried or even frightened, and some of them just looked totally baffled. Something was wrong. They all knew something that I didn't know yet.

I looked all around, and after a few seconds, I saw it. The driver of the limo was right there leaning with his back against the driver's-side door. He was a ridiculously huge body-builder, with a shiny shaved head, dressed in a sharp suit, sunglasses, and a wire in his ear. I definitely would not have had the guts to piss on his car if I had noticed him before I started, but there I was pissing on his car, and I still had a ways to go.

He hadn't noticed me yet either, and the Hummer was so damn long, he really wasn't that close to me. Still, it was hard to imagine that he would not make the effort to chase me down and beat me savagely if he did notice what I was up to. I was about 90 degrees to the left of the direction he was facing. He probably would have noticed me in his peripheral vision if he hadn't been wearing sunglasses. It took forever to finish peeing, but he just kept staring straight ahead. Finally, I finished my business, zipped up, and walked back across the street grinning. The Punks were duly impressed.

43. RUN NAZIS RUN!

I don't know who sounded the alarm, but the call came in early February. The Nazis were coming to town, and all courageous Fraggles were needed to fight them off. My housemates and I signed up without hesitation. We had already run together against Nazis a handful of times, and I felt like it was really important to keep taking that stand. Over the years, I had been approached too many times by White racists who would try to recruit me to their cause. They seemed to assume they could trust me simply because my skin was White too.

Most Nazis and other White power creeps believe that we are approaching an apocalyptic war which they call the "Race War." Many of them have been gathering weapons and networking with each other in preparation. In their fantasy, White people will be pitted against all the other races of people on the planet, and White people will inevitably prevail because they are the superior race. Key to this belief is the idea that most other White people would side with the Nazis. This is delusional, of course. If such a war did break out, most White people would hide like cowards, and another large percentage of us would join in the army of diverse races fighting against the racists.

In the years since my big walk, antifascist organizing has increased dramatically in the United States. I assume the American White power movement has had to accept the fact that vast numbers of White people oppose them, and are ready, willing, and even eager to kick their asses. Back in 2004, they had not yet received their reality check. Every White racist I met made the same mistake of dramatically overestimating how many other White people had their backs.

I reasoned that they were far too confident, and in that state, they were much more likely to try to initiate their Race War themselves. I reasoned that they were also more likely to commit hate crimes if they thought they had popular support for it. What they really needed was to see large, angry mobs of White-skinned people jeering them, throwing things at them, and trying to do them harm. Maybe then they would go back to hiding in their rural compounds and inbreeding themselves into obscurity.

They had scheduled a hate speech on the steps of the state capitol building in nearby Raleigh. The Nazis would be driving down from their headquarters in Minnesota, and standing in solidarity with members of the local Ku Klux Klan. That was interesting because those two groups usually don't get along. Klansmen tend to be country boys who oppose all forms of government beyond a racist police department, while Nazis are technically socialists who advocate government control over almost everything. Apparently in this case, they were willing to put their differences aside for the greater goal of White supremacy.

I asked why Nazis would come all the way from Minnesota to make a speech in North Carolina, and I got an interesting answer. My friends told me that the movement for organized racism had been in decline for decades in the southern states, but it was still going strong in the Midwest. Of course, they didn't know for sure, but their best guess was that the Midwestern Nazis wanted to make some appearances down South to try to breathe some life back into the region's dying White power movement. We couldn't let that happen.

We got a couple weeks advance notice, so we had some time to prepare. We went to two planning meetings where we joined a crew of about 40 other people who were down to take militant, illegal action against the Nazis.

The first meeting was not much more than a pointless paranoia-fest. I was one of a small handful of people who were unknown to the majority of the group, and there were several people there who were totally overwhelmed by the fear that we might be spies or infiltrators. In theory, they were willing to break the law, but only if there was zero chance that they would get in trouble. I had a number of trusted gangsters vouching for me, and so did all the other new people, but it still took quite a while to convince the chickens. I wondered how they were ever going to build their movement if they were not willing to work with new people. Maybe they thought they already had enough people to succeed. We did finally get down to business by the end of the meeting, and we came to 100% consensus that we wanted to beat up the racists. It was the beginning of a plan.

The second meeting was much more productive. Someone had figured out where the racists would have to park in order to get to the capitol. The streets made a perfect grid in that part of the city. The capitol building and its lawns took up two whole city blocks, and the closest parking lot took up most of another city block. The parking lot was located diagonally to the northeast of the capitol, so the Nazis would have to cross the intersection at the northeast

330

corner of the state capitol. Our plan was to get into that intersection ahead of time and block the Nazis from attending their own event.

One person updated us that we would be joined by hundreds of students coming out from all the local colleges to protest. Unfortunately, their plan was to stand with their backs to the Nazis and be silent. We worried that such a pathetic display of liberal weakness might actually encourage our foes. After all, German liberals took a similar approach to dealing with the original Nazis and everyone remembers how effective that was. I agreed with a number of people who said we should make an effort on the day of the protest to inspire a mob mentality in that much larger group. Our scout said it was a good idea, but there was a potential problem. The leader of the student group who had planned the silent protest was Black, so confused, liberal students might worry that they were being racist themselves if they disobeyed his wishes. Oh well. We resolved to do our best and take advantage of whatever situation unfolded in the moment.

Someone else suggested that we make enormous protest signs out of plywood, tie them together, and use them as a defensive barricade to keep the police from separating us. They had tried it at another protest and it had worked well. The whole group agreed to try it, and we set up a smaller committee to make the banner/shield. The only other detail that I remember from that meeting was that we split up into small units called affinity groups. It was basically like the buddy system except you got more than one buddy. My two housemates and I made an obvious group, and we were joined by one more of their old friends who they had done all kinds of crazy shit with. Each one of us was responsible for keeping track of the other three and making sure we were all present and healthy.

The big day came, and we rolled into Raleigh. Each affinity team arrived in a separate vehicle coming from all different directions. We all parked in different places and got out walking. We came dressed in identical black clothing, and in the last block before we reached the rendezvous point, we all pulled identical black ski-masks over our faces. This tactic would make it harder for police, Nazis, or other witnesses to identify us as individuals. Someone had arranged for a pickup truck to deliver our giant protest signs, and we all converged on it at about the same time. It was parked along the street that made the southern boundary of the strategic parking lot, and it left as soon as we had the big boards unloaded.

I had not been on the team that made the signs, so I was amazed at how big they were. I guess they were just regular 4x8 plywood, but they looked really impressive. The wood was old and weathered, and fairly thin, so it had a good bit of flex to it. The front sides of them were all painted up with anti-Nazi and pro-diversity slogans, but I never got a good look at them, because I was behind them most of the time. Multiple handles were attached to the backsides so we could hold them up, and two holes were drilled out near the edges of the short sides so we could wire them all together. As quickly as we could, we arranged them all end-to-end, ran some heavy-duty wire through the holes and twisted it tight.

We had barely started this process when a police helicopter appeared over-head. I assume that meant that someone in our group had informed the police in advance, because there was no other way the chopper could have gotten there so quickly. It didn't make much difference though. In about two minutes we had a giant, flexible wooden shield to protect us. The helicopter only stayed for a couple of minutes, and then it never came back for the rest of the day.

We only had a half a block to go, so without further adieu, we picked up our big crazy shield and went for it. The cops were waiting for us right there in the intersection where the informant must have told them we would be trying to go. They left us alone right until the edge of the sidewalk, but as soon as we stepped onto the blacktop, they charged us like the defensive line of a football team. We outnumbered the cops by a few people, but most of them were heavier than most of us, so it was a pretty even match. We pushed for all we were worth, and we had them backing up for a while. We made it out to about the middle of the intersection when they finally got the better of us. Then they pushed us backwards for a few minutes. The push-of-war must have gone on for at least fifteen minutes. Eventually, everyone on both sides ran out of steam and we just stopped pushing. At that point, we were still out in the street, but only by a few feet.

We had showed up an hour before the Nazis were supposed to arrive so as to be in place by the time they got there. That meant we got to spend quite a bit of time facing off with the police at very close range. They hadn't worn their riot gear, so we could see their faces and interact with them like human beings. My teammates hurled a lot of accusations at them about supporting their Aryan brothers and that really made some of the cops angry. Not everyone on the police force was White, and it was obvious that some of them, including some of the White ones, really didn't appreciate having to work so hard to help White supremacists.

When the first Nazi arrived, a pair of cops escorted him down the sidewalk across the street from us. A wooden fence prevented them from taking a route any further away from us than that. We had failed to completely close off their access, but we had created a pinch point, so the racists had to run a bit of a gauntlet to get to their party. As the first guy went by, we assailed him with the most aggressive roar of curses and threats I had ever heard. I was surprised and impressed by the level of anger in my own voice.

As the man reached the closest point to us, one of our people hurled a small, but heavy projectile at him. I couldn't tell if it was a rock or a lump of metal. It only missed the man's head by inches and it made an intimidating bang when it hit the wooden fence just behind him. None of us had broken any laws up until that point, but that was an attempted assault. The cop who was closest to the assailant reached across our barricade and grabbed them by the shirt collar. It only took a second for another cop to follow his lead, and then they were trying to pull the kid up and over the plywood shield. As soon as the good guys noticed, a whole gang of us grabbed the kid's shoulders and pulled them back in, while others pulled on the cops' arms and wrenched them away from our teammate. It proved very easy to save our fellow from being arrested. The wooden barricade was obviously a good idea.

A couple more early Nazis ran the gauntlet, but no one else threw anything at them. Then the police brought in four or five large vans and parked them bumper to bumper right in front of us, so the fascists had a little bit of a wall to hide behind as they walked past.

It was right around that time that we heard a loud roar of angry jeers erupt from the south side of the capitol building. An assortment of hedges and ornamental trees blocked our view across the capitol lawn, but our ears told us there was a much larger crowd of anti-racist people just a block away, and they were by no means holding silent. This was encouraging, so we sent a scout to check it out. They came back in just a few minutes to report that there were at least 300 people of all different ages and races gathered there, screaming with rage at the villains, and some of them were even throwing things. After a minute of discussion, we decided that our plan A had failed, so we might as well go join that group.

We made our way south along the sidewalk, and our compliment of police came along, ready to push back if we made any advance towards the capitol grounds. We turned west at the street corner, and quickly added our strength to the larger crowd, significantly expanding and strengthening its eastern flank. A cheer of approval went up from the crowd when they saw that the "Black Bloc" had arrived. The police had built their own barricade there out of orange and white striped boards in the shape of saw-horses that looked like they had been borrowed form the Department of Transportation. We slid our barricade in behind theirs and surveyed the scene.

The White power coalition was assembling behind a podium up on the capitol steps, and it looked like they were about ready to get started. I counted nine Nazis who were actually dressed up in what appeared to be vintage Hitler costumes, and four guys were dressed up in ghostly white Ku Klux Klan outfits with the pointy white hoods and all. I felt an intense emotional reaction deep in my guts when I saw them. This was the fourth time I had come out to try and disrupt a White power rally, but I had never seen anyone dressed up like that before. The Klan is not very powerful anymore, but they are indisputably the most dangerous terrorist organization in our nation's history. The Nazis rank among the most effective perpetrators of genocide in world history. To see people dressed up in costume celebrating those traditions was overwhelming. Before that moment, I never even knew that I had the potential to feel such hatred and disgust in my heart. I also have to admit that it frightened me considerably to see people dressed like that. Over the course of the afternoon, I screamed enough blood-curdling venom at them that my voice was hoarse for the next week.

About half of the guys in the Nazi uniforms were quite old and frail, and even the younger ones looked like weaselly little bureaucrats. It would have been really satisfying to take them on in a fight. There was no way to tell what shape the Klansmen were in because they were so thoroughly disguised, but the robes and hoods would have seriously impeded their mobility and vision. Those two groups were also joined by six very large White men with shaved heads and lots of tattoos, but otherwise, no ridiculous costumes. That must have been the warrior caste of the racist hierarchy. Each one of those guys looked like he could probably take on two or more of us, but we still outnumbered them by enough people that it would have been fun.

I do believe in the freedom of speech. I don't want the government to block anyone from expressing themselves, and I'm glad they gave the Nazis their permit to speak. I just think that as private citizens who are not employed by the government, we should be allowed to work out our disagreement with them face-to-face. The Bill of Rights simply says that, "The government shall make no law abridging the people's freedom of speech." It says nothing about what private citizens can and can't do.

Someone had come out the night before the rally and exercised their freedom of expression in a most beautiful way. The exterior of the North Carolina state capitol building was whitewashed like a lot of government buildings, but it sat on a thick foundation of dull grey stone that reached up to about the height of my belly button. Just to the right of the grand staircase where the White supremacists set up to speak, someone had spray-painted "FUCK NAZIS" in huge, black letters on the exposed front of the building's foundation. The lettering was big, bold, and very neat. It must have taken quite a bit of time to empty all that spray-paint onto the stone, but the phrase was complete right to the last "S," suggesting that whoever did it actually got away with it.

A couple of the Nazis and one of the Klansmen made speeches. The roar of anger from the crowd was already so loud that we couldn't make out what they were saying, but as soon as the first amplified voice came through the public address speakers, the jeering and cursing suddenly increased by many more decibels. It was literally so loud that I couldn't hear the PA system at all, let alone what the haters were saying. The crowd of anti-racists kept swelling as time went on, and I would guess that we grew to well over 500 people.

Right at the front and center of the crowd, there were seven or eight college students standing silently with their backs turned to the Nazis. They must have set up some kind of platform to stand on because they were elevated a couple feet above the rest of the crowd. Several of them scowled in disapproval at the much larger crowd for refusing to join them in their silent "protest."

Their behavior made a very interesting statement. Nineteen White supremacists stood in formation on the capitol steps facing south and making hate speeches. Down below, seven or eight liberals stood in formation, also facing south. I don't know what thoughts were going through their minds, but their behavior certainly gave the impression that they were on the same side as the White supremacists. In contrast, everyone else faced north, loudly expressing their opposition to the hate speech. Liberals will certainly vote against racist policies if they are stated overtly enough, and they will always make sure to be heard saying the right words about diversity and racism. But they will not lift a finger to stop the victims of genocide from being massacred, and at times, they will even stand in formation with the people who are committing genocide.

I was growing increasingly frustrated that we couldn't do anything about the Nazis. At one point, I found a rock on the sidewalk and hurled it at them with all my strength. I have a good throwing arm, but the cops had us pinned down much too far away from the targets, and the stone landed harmlessly on the ground down below them. For the most part, everyone in our group just shouted whatever curses we could think of as individuals, but there were several times when we got organized chants going. The best one was simply an endless repetition of the refrain, "Come over here! Come over here!" I loved that one, and I helped keep it going for a long time. We also did quite a few rounds of, "North Kakalakie ain't nothin' to fuck with," to the beat of the notorious Wu Tang Clan rap.

At one point, one of our people tried to throw a smoke bomb. The word "bomb" sounds pretty intense, but it was really just a little ball, available at any fireworks stand that gives off a couple minutes worth of thick, colorful smoke reeking of Sulphur. Unfortunately, the kid didn't have the guts to stand up and give it a real throw. Even though his face was covered with a mask, he still crouched down where the cops couldn't see him, and swung his arm with a kind of sky hook motion. The smoke bomb bounced off the inside of our wooden barricade and landed in the middle of our Black Bloc. For a moment, we were surrounded by a thick cloud of stinky, yellow smoke. Then someone succeeded in kicking the little firework out under our sign and into the swarm of cops directly in front of us. It took the cops several more seconds to kick it back behind their line where it pointlessly expended the rest of its fuel. Then the cops made fun of us.

After what felt like a couple hours of accomplishing nothing, I was fed up. I had been circulating around our whole group of 40, insisting to everyone that we try harder to take some sort of tangible action. There was one other affinity group made up of four young guys who agreed with me wholeheartedly, so I ditched my affinity group and joined theirs. There was also a young Black woman who had come over from the larger group in hopes of finding something more militant to join in with, so we added her to our team also. She had no mask, and she looked very obviously different from the rest of us. There would be no way to conceal her identity, but she didn't care. She was ready and eager to throw down, so we were happy to have her on the team.

We split off from the main group and headed east, making it look like we were leaving the protest. After one block, we turned north, circling back towards the lot where the Nazis' cars were parked. Our plan was to find their cars and vandalize them. All four of my new male teammates had brought blunt weapons for bludgeoning, and our new female friend had a long tube sock with a pound or so of nuts and bolts in the bottom. All I had was a pocket knife, but I figured that would be great for slashing tires. Then the cars would have to be towed, and that would cost even more money.

Unfortunately, when we got to the parking lot, there were hundreds of cars there, most of which must have belonged to innocent people. The Nazis had been clever enough not to put swastika stickers on their bumpers, and we didn't spot any Minnesota license plates right off the bat. Two police officers had been left behind to guard the parking lot. They spotted us from a distance, and started strolling slowly towards us as we angled our way northwesterly across the field of asphalt and parked cars. We had all been really excited to split off from the stagnant group and do something more proactive, but suddenly, our hearts all sank back into frustration and disappointment. Here we were within range of our targets, and there were nowhere near enough cops to stop us from striking, but alas, we couldn't figure out which vehicles to strike.

Just then, we met with a stroke of lucky timing. For some reason, one of the big, modestly-dressed skinhead warriors was leaving the rally early, and we spotted him walking across the intersection to the southwest corner of the parking lot. We changed our direction to intercept him. The two cops immediately figured out what was going on, and moved into a defensive formation between us and the Nazi. His car turned out to be right near that corner of the lot. He unlocked his door, got in, closed the door, started the engine, and rolled down the driver's side window. The car was facing south, so we were approaching from the driver's side.

As we closed the distance, both cops started giving us orders to stop our advance. They were at a serious disadvantage, being just two cops against the six of us, and you could hear the distress in their voices. The cop on the left was a young, healthy-looking White guy, but the cop on the right was an overweight Black man who looked to be in his fifties. As we approached the cops, I reached into my right pants pocket, oriented my knife in the right direction and clutched it tightly, keeping my hand concealed in the pocket for the last few steps. We had been walking quickly, and all at once, the moment for action was upon us.

Without even thinking, I burst into a sprint directly towards the old, fat cop. He threw his arms out in a blocking position and shouted, "No!" but his voice sounded weak and defeated, and I was much too quick for him. I faked right, then darted around his left side and left him flat-footed. At that point I was running at a dead sprint, and there were only about four paces between me and Nazi seated in his car. He bared his clenched teeth like a growling dog, and I could see the fear in his eyes. By then, my right hand was out of my pocket, but my knife blade was still closed. The Nazi was in a very vulnerable position. I could have easily flipped my blade open and stabbed him in his ugly face, but my instincts told me that wasn't the plan. I didn't know who that guy was or if he even deserved to be stabbed. I also didn't want to do years behind bars for assault with a deadly weapon.

I changed course slightly and dashed around the backside of his car, flicking open my knife blade as I ran. With the quickness of a striking snake, I plunged my blade into the sidewall of his right rear tire, and immediately heard the satisfying sound of the air gushing out.

Three more things all happened in that same instant. A huge roar of excitement rose up from a crowd of protestors on the sidewalk across the street from the south edge of the parking lot. That was surprising, because I hadn't even noticed anyone was there. Also in that moment, I heard the rapid slap of footfalls running up from behind me and I knew without looking that it was the young, healthy cop coming to catch me. The Nazi also hit the gas pedal in that moment, and his car started to move. The car was old and heavy though, so it was slow to accelerate. In two more strides, I had caught up to the front tire, and I bent quickly and stabbed at that one too.

By then, the footfalls were almost on top of me, so I stood up and bolted towards the crowd on the sidewalk, which happened to be the direction I was already going. The Nazi had to make a 90-degree left to get into the drive lane, and I heard his tires squealing as he accelerated into the turn. I could tell exactly what was happening from the sound of the footfalls behind me, so I didn't waste any energy turning my head back to look. Nonetheless, the cop caught up to me about halfway to my destination. I was wearing a small backpack that was mostly empty, and I suddenly felt my shoulders tug backwards as he caught ahold of it with one hand and pulled.

At that point, the cop made a critical mistake. If he had wrapped me up in a two-armed tackle, he would have had me right there. Instead, he pulled me back by the backpack with one arm, while he reached in front of my head with the other and sprayed me in the face with pepper spray. My mouth and nose were covered by my ski-mask, but my eyes were exposed, and he hit me directly in both eyes. The pepper spray was intended to subdue me, but instead, it gave me one of the wildest jolts of adrenaline I have ever experienced. With super-human strength, I tore free from his grip, backpack and all, and resumed running towards the crowd of cheering supporters.

The pepper spray had blinded all of my peripheral vision, so I could only see a small circle directly in front of me. The rest of my vision had gone black, so I felt like I was looking through a tube. I still heard the footfalls of the cop who was chasing me, but his pepper spray had given me turbo speed, so I could hear his steps falling further and further behind me as I ran. The crew in front of me had not brought the wooden barricade with them, but they were positioned behind a dense hedge of plants that was roughly the same height and would serve roughly the same function. On my final step, I launched into the air and dove, head-first over the hedge. People did their best to break my fall, and I ended up laying on my back on the sidewalk without any injuries.

For a minute or two, that last little circle of vision went black and I couldn't see anything. Immediately, I heard the voices of my other three original team members offering me praise and asking me if I was okay. Someone poured water into my eyes in an attempt to flush them out. After a couple minutes, my vision came back, and I stood up to look around. As soon as my head popped up, a cluster of nearby cops pointed at me and started advancing, but a large crowd had gathered around me, so I was safe for the time being.

My friends told me that when they saw the six of us stomp away to the east, they all knew where we were headed, so they took the shorter route, straight north where they had just arrived back in roughly the same place where we had all pushed against the cops that morning. They hadn't brought our wooden barricade, but most of the original Black Bloc had come along, followed by 20 or 30 more people from the bigger protest. Only five cops were there yet, so the crowd of people between me and them locked arms and refused to let them pass.

My team told me I needed to get back to the even bigger group to the south of the capitol. That made sense, so I let them guide me. Most of the group came with us to continue making a barrier between me and the cops. The going was slow, and the cops kept right up with us. They kept pointing at me and shouting at me as if they were trying to get my attention. I was dressed in the same black clothing and black ski mask as most of the others, but I was the tallest out of the whole group, and I assume that my eyes and all the skin around them was probably glowing red from the pepper spray.

We made it about halfway back to the main body of protesters when a sixth cop joined the gang. Then we saw another five or six cops hurrying across the capitol lawn towards us. With that many people, they would probably be able to break through my human shield and get to me. My third team-mate- the one who I didn't live with and didn't know as well- had a really big heart, and he decided in that moment to try to save me. He could tell that I hadn't regained my wits since being pepper-sprayed, so he crouched down in a squat, and pulled me down with him. He said, "Come with me buddy! I'm gonna get you on a bus."

Then he moved in a crab-walk across the sidewalk and into the mouth of an alley that was conveniently right behind us. I followed him into the alley. By staying low, we had kept ourselves hidden behind the thick mass of other protesters. Once inside the alleyway, we were hidden behind the corner of the building, so we stood up and ran like hell. Glancing over our shoulders, we could see there were no cops pursuing us, and no cops standing in a position to look down the alley.

We had almost made it to the other end when our luck ran out. In the last five paces before the end, I glanced back one more time to see a whole gang of cops pouring into the far end of the alley. Apparently, they had finally broken through the human shield and made the logical assumption that we had ducked into the alley. Three more seconds and we would have turned another corner without them seeing which direction we had gone, and our chances of escape probably would have doubled. Alas, they got there just in time to see us hang a right out of the alley.

As soon as we turned the corner, my friend had me stop for a few seconds while we changed our look. We pulled our ski masks and black, long-sleeved shirts off to reveal the much more normal-looking clothes underneath. We stuffed our Black Bloc layers into a bush, and took of running south. In half a block, we reached the central bus terminal for the Triangle Transit and dashed inside through one of the big openings where the buses enter and exit. Our herd of pursuing officers had not yet cleared the end of the alleyway, so they didn't see us duck into the bus station. The plan was to jump on whatever bus was leaving at that moment and ride away to wherever it was going. Luck was against us though. We had arrived at an odd moment when there weren't any buses loading up to leave. My buddy grabbed a newspaper out of a trash can, took a seat on a bench and motioned for me to sit next to him. As soon as I was seated, he opened the newspaper up and held it in front of both of our faces.

The bus station was a large building that took up an entire city block. There were several stories above us, and I have no idea what was up there. The ground floor was built like a giant cave with a road through it for the buses to drive on. The road entered from the east, the way we had come in, turned a 90-degree left under the building and exited to the south. It was lined with broad sidewalks and plenty of benches for people to sit on while they waited for their bus. When we arrived, the station was quite full of people waiting. We got one of the last seats on a bench, and there were plenty of people standing up too, so there was some hope that we might be able to blend in. The trouble was, the pepper spray had done something to my brain. I couldn't think straight. All I could think to do was run like a panicked wild animal.

We couldn't have been in there for half a minute when a police car came roaring in on the road that was supposed to be for the buses, lights flashing and sirens wailing. I should have sat still and hid behind the newspaper, but instead, I got up and ran. I looked back to see my buddy starting to stand up, holding up his hand and yelling. "Wait! No!" Then I rounded the corner and ran for the southern exit. Another squealing squad car pulled into the station from that direction. The driver jumped out and hollered at me to stop, I blew right past him only feet away, and he gave chase. He was a hefty cop. Normally, a guy like that should not be able to catch me, but I had already run for several blocks and I was getting tired, while his legs were fresh.

I made it out of the bus station, and almost all the way across the street when he caught up to me. This cop was smarter than the last one, and he went for a full-on tackle. I let my weight drop, and tried to spin out of his grip as I fell. It almost worked, but not quite. He managed to hang on, so my falling weight pulled him forward. In the same instant, I accidentally stepped on one of his feet, so he couldn't step forward to stay upright. As a result, I fell down, and the extra-large cop fell right on top of me. My head and my left shoulder landed up on the sidewalk, and the rest of my body landed in the street. As the cop's big body landed right across my abdomen, I felt a strange sensation in my guts. It felt like he had literally squished the poop out of me.

The cop took a couple of seconds to catch his breath, and then he asked me in a very composed voice if I intended to keep struggling. I said, "No. You got me," and he said, "Good." He handcuffed me and then helped me to my feet.

As soon as I stood up, I looked back and realized that my buddy had chased after me. He had made it right to the exit of the bus station where he was now on his knees with his hands held high in the air. Two cops were pointing guns at him. I realized immediately that there was no good reason for him to be in trouble. He was only getting busted because he had tried to help me, and I had screwed up. The emotion was overwhelming, and I started to cry, but something about the tears mixing with the pepper spray stung so badly that I had to choke them back down.

The cop recited my Miranda Rights as he led me to his cruiser and put me in the back seat. As I walked, I felt a warm, squishy mass between my butt cheeks that definitely didn't belong there. I also felt a savage pain from my left shoulder down to the upper left side of my chest. I had made it to the age of 26 without ever experiencing a broken bone, but something told me that was exactly what it felt like.

After another moment, they loaded my buddy into the seat beside me. I felt awful that he was suffering for my mistakes. I kept trying to apologize to him, but he kept telling me everything was going to be fine. I also kept feeling the urge to cry, but every time I would start, my eyes would sting so badly that I had to choke the tears back down. My arresting officer got into the driver's seat and I immediately informed him that I thought my shoulder was broken. He gave me a snort of laughter and ignored me. I whispered to my buddy beside me about my shoulder, and I also whispered to him that I thought I had shit my pants. He was sympathetic, but I don't remember exactly what he said.

It was only a few blocks ride to the police station. I remember the intake process at the jail being really quick and efficient. I don't think it even took us a half an hour to get processed in. At some point I was informed that I was being charged with resisting arrest and destruction of property. I complained to everyone I could that I thought my collar bone was broken, but they all ignored me. I had not told anyone about the poop in my pants, but at the very end of intake, I decided I had to say something.

I said, "Excuse me," to the guard who was leading me at that point. When he looked, I made a face to indicate that I had a secret to tell him. He leaned in close, and I whispered to him that when my arresting officer landed on top of me, it had squeezed some poop out of me. It was gross and uncomfortable, and I wanted to know if there was anything we could do about it.

The guard had a good laugh, and he did not ignore me the way everyone else had ignored me about my broken bone. Maybe he could smell that I was telling the truth. We changed course and he took me to a large, empty holding cell. He let me into the cell, pointed to a sink in the corner, and said, "There. Clean yourself up man." The he undid my handcuffs and locked me into the room by myself.

Something was definitely wrong with my left collar bone. It hurt so badly, I could barely move my left arm, so it took a long time to get my shoes and my pants off. There was definitely poop in my pants. Miraculously, it was contained pretty well inside my boxer shorts. My outer layer of jeans wasn't too bad, so I separated out the boxers and washed them out thoroughly under the running water. My butt crack was packed right full, and I scooped a whole dollop out with my right hand. It was too much to go down the sink drain in one lump, so I had to keep poking at it with my fingers for a couple minutes until the running water made it all disappear. Then came the matter of cleaning off my backside.

The sink was much too tall for this to be a simple process. Somehow, I had to figure out a way to climb up onto it backwards, and without the use of my left arm. I really can't find the words to explain how I accomplished this, so you will just have to use your imagination. It took a while, but I eventually got myself sitting with my bare ass in the bowl of the sink, facing out into the room with my feet dangling well above the ground. I did end up having to use my left arm quite a bit, and the pain was almost unbearable. The running faucet poked right into my tailbone, so then it was just a matter of reaching between my legs, cupping handfuls of water, and rubbing them over and over the messy spots until I was as clean as I could get.

I was in the middle of that process when the guard poked his head back in to ask what was taking so long. He wasn't even done asking before he saw me and started laughing again. I told him I needed a couple more minutes, and he understood. It took me even longer to get my pants and shoes back on. I wrung out my wet underpants as best as I could and stuffed them into my pocket. Once I was all dressed, I took a moment to examine my collar bone. Feeling with my right hand, I found several lumps the size of brussels sprouts that didn't belong there. I looked in the mirror above the sink I had just christened. My left collar bone was all lumpy and misshapen, and that whole shoulder was swollen up much larger than the other one. That couldn't be good.

I don't know if my guard stood there and waited through my whole cleanup ordeal, but as soon as I put my face up to the small glass window, I saw him standing outside. He refastened my handcuffs, and I told him about my collar bone. He had taken my poopy pants seriously, so I hoped he would take my broken bone seriously too, but he ignored that like the rest of them.

We rounded a corner, and there on a bench in the hallway were three of the other guys who had come with me when we went to attack the Nazis. They all wore the dejected looks of people who had just been busted, but they smiled and gave me warm greetings when they saw me. As soon as I saw them, I started crying again, and once again I had to stop right away as the tears stung my eyes horribly. I stopped to talk to them, and my guard actually waited for me for about a minute.

They told me that the fierce young woman who joined us at the protest had been picked up too, but they made no mention of their fourth friend. It was implied that he had gotten away, so I didn't ask about him. One out of six of us had gotten away, and he was replaced by my heroic friend who had only tried to help me escape. I realized quickly that there wasn't much we could discuss with the guard right there, so we exchanged wishes of strength and good luck, and the guard led me away.

For some reason he brought me right to the front lobby of the police station where I could see out onto the street through a glass door. A group of six cops were standing there chatting, and when they saw me coming, one of them got a big smile and shouted out, "Hey! It's the runner!" One of the others said, "Why you wanna run? Haven't you seen the Cops show on TV? Don't you know we always catch the bad guy?" The chiding continued for a couple minutes, and I wondered if the guard had brought me to the front lobby specifically so those guys could pick on me. I noticed my arresting officer was with them, but I don't remember him saying anything.

After the jokes subsided, the sergeant on duty got very serious and asked me why I had been running. I looked at my arresting officer and said I was running because he was chasing me. The sergeant asked why he was chasing me, and I told him it was because I was running. We went through several more cycles of that nonsense before he understood that I was not going to cooperate with his investigation. Finally he said, "Alright, alright," and he ordered the guard to take me to a cell. At that point I leaned in close to the sergeant who was quite a bit shorter than me, looked him right in the eyes, and said in my most serious tone, "Sir, my collar bone is broken. It hurts like hell. I need medical attention." He told me he would get the jail's doctor to look at it, and he sent me off to my cell.

It didn't take long for the doctor to get there, but I doubt she was actually a doctor. She was dressed in the same kind of police uniform as the rest of them, and she was incredibly angry at me for wasting her time. I don't actually remember any of her dialogue, but it was pure verbal abuse. She was convinced that I was lying and being a big baby before she even looked at my shoulder. She examined me for all of about five seconds before she stormed out without telling me her diagnosis.

About ten minutes later, my arresting officer unlocked my cell and told me to come with him. I asked where we were going, but he ignored me. He led me out to the parking lot and put me back into his cruiser. Once we were inside the car, he told me he was taking me to the hospital.

We drove to the Wake Medical Center where we entered through a subterranean parking garage. I noticed that the door between the garage and the interior of the hospital locked behind us. The door led into a hallway, but we only walked a few paces down it before the cop led me into the very first room on the right. It was an examination room. Someone from the hospital staff took down some information about me from the cop, and then left. After that, the cop indicated for me to sit up on the examination table while he took a chair in the corner.

He said I was in line to be seen in the emergency room, and he would have to stay there to guard me since I was a prisoner. He wasn't the kind of guy who could sit there in silence, so he struck up a conversation. He started by telling me that he didn't know what I had done and he didn't really care. He didn't like Nazis, and he was frustrated that they had come from out of state to cause trouble in his hometown. He thought their position was totally unreasonable, but he also thought my position was totally unreasonable. He felt like had to be the adult in the situation and keep us crazy kids from hurting each other.

I disagreed with him, of course, but I found his opinion far less offensive than most of the opinions I've ever heard cops express. He said he hadn't meant to hurt me and he even said that he was really sorry if I turned out to have a broken bone. I knew he was telling the truth. I had been the victim of intentional police brutality plenty of times before, and I could tell that this situation had just been an accident.

For the first long portion of our conversation, the guy gave me a very paternalistic attitude, like I was a criminal who had gone down the wrong path in life, but maybe he could help straighten me out with his well-worded advice. Finally, he hit a point where he ran out of energy to rehabilitate me. In closing he asked me, "So you're not going to come back to Raleigh anymore right?" I hadn't told him I was from out of town, but he was a local boy, so I guess he could just tell.

I was supposed to say something like, "Yes sir! You'll never see me around here again!" But I didn't. I refused to play the part of the bad guy who deserved his negative judgement. Instead, I gave him a thoughtful look for a couple seconds and then said, "I don't know. This seems like a pretty nice town. I'm kinda looking forward to checking it out someday when there aren't a bunch of out-of-state Nazis around." That actually got through to him. We stopped talking for a while, but when we started up again, he dropped the paternal act and treated me more as an equal.

His name was Hoolan, and he was born and raised there in Raleigh NC. He had joined the police force right out of high-school, and it was the only job he had held as an adult. At that point, he had been on the force for more than twenty years. He was what they call a "beat cop," meaning that he always patrolled the same neighborhood. He hadn't even been assigned to watch over the Nazi rally. He was just working his usual shift right around the bus station when he got a call that there was a suspect on the run there.

He had been working the same beat for nine years, and he hoped he would be allowed to stay there for the rest of his career. He had made friends with every single business owner in his area, and as many of the residents as he could. He said that getting to know everybody on his beat made it much easier to understand the situations that his job got him into. That made it easier for him to make split-second decisions, and it made him more effective as an emergency responder. Before he settled onto that beat, he had been transferred all over the city, but he hated the feeling of confusion he got from always having to deal with strangers.

I really appreciated Hoolan's attitude. I would rather live in a world where we all deal with emergencies instead of leaving them to a professional class of hardened police who quickly loose track of the humanity of the people they have to deal with. Still, at this point in history, we are nowhere near being able to abolish the police department. As long as we still have to live with cops, I think we should really try to staff their departments with people who understand things the way officer Hoolan did. For a cop, he really seemed amazingly honest and good-hearted. How ironic that I got myself injured by that guy. I guess maybe I was lucky. I truly had resisted arrest with all my effort. A more aggressive cop might have really beaten me up or even shot me.

After a couple hours, I asked officer Hoolan if he had any idea how long I might have to wait to see a doctor. He told me that people who were under arrest were given the lowest priority in that hospital. Any free people who checked into the emergency room would automatically be able to cut in front of me in the line. I would only be seen if the stream of new patients slowed down enough to give the doctors a moment of spare time. Maybe if I was in critical condition they would make an exception, but I obviously wasn't about to die. I couldn't help but think the basement of the Wake Medical Center resembled a dungeon much more than a place of healing.

Hoolan ended up sitting with me for six whole hours. At 10pm, his shift finally ended, and he was replaced by a young guy who looked like he was straight out of the marines. He was tall and buff with a military-style buzz-cut, and his head was literally shaped like a jar. I was in a friendly mood after spending six hours with officer Hoolan, so I immediately tried to strike up a conversation with my new guard. He just gave me a look of hatred and disgust, and then proceeded to ignore me. We sat in tense silence for almost another hour. Without anyone to talk to, all I could think about was the intense throbbing ache that had taken over the whole upper left quarter of my body. It actually made me miss the guy who had broken my bone.

At long last, a doctor came and led us to an elevator where we rode several stories up out of the hospital's secret basement dungeon. We skipped the examination rooms and went straight to the x-ray lab. As soon as I took my shirt off, the doctor glanced at me from halfway across the room and said, "Oh yeah. You've got a broken collar bone." I got x-rayed, and a ghastly printout came back a few minutes later. My left clavicle (collar bone) was broken clean through in two places. Both ends were still connected to my other bones the way they should have been, but a segment in the middle, about an inch and a half long, was completely broken off, and turned almost 40 degrees out of line with the rest of the bone. No wonder it hurt so damn much. I asked if they would do anything to try to twist the broken piece of bone back into place, and he said no. He said that would only cause me a bunch more pain, and the bone would heal up fine anyway. I was skeptical, but I had no other choice than to take his word for it.

A nurse came in and set my left arm in a cheap-looking sling. He said there was no real way to immobilize a broken clavicle. I would just have to wear the sling, be careful, and wait for it to heal. With that, we went back down to the dungeon, out to the police car, and back to the jail.

They put me in a large, clean cell with three other guys. It was almost midnight by then, so the lights had been dimmed for quiet time. One of my cellmates was already asleep on one of the two benches in the cell. When the other two guys saw what condition I was in, they moved off the other bench and offered it to me. I tried to decline modestly at first, but they just sat down on the floor and told me it was no problem. They said I should try to get some sleep, so I thanked them sincerely and gave it a shot. The bench was not at all comfortable, but I was exhausted, and I actually did manage to fall asleep for a while.

It was only about an hour later when the guards came in to rouse me and tell me I was being bailed out. One of my cellmates was still awake, and he exclaimed, "Oh you lucky dog!" It made me feel guilty in spite of everything. I had to go through a ten or fifteen-minute process which involved talking to a bail bandsman over the telephone. Then I was released. I expected to see my housemates, but instead I was being picked up by one of my new friends from the student group at UNC. Not only had he driven to Raleigh at one in the morning, but he had also borrowed enough money from his parents to pay for about three quarters of my bail. I asked about the other five people who had been arrested at the protest, and he said they had been bailed out hours ago. I was the last one left because I had been stuck in the hospital all night. He drove me back to his dorm room where he slept on the floor so he could give me the bed.

***

Along with the entire Bug Food book, I also have to dedicate this chapter to Amber and Eden. They had me retell this story so many times that I could never forget a single detail. Every time I got to the part where I had to clean up my butt, they would howl and giggle, and make me tell it again.

44. WHITE POWER

It turns out that central North Carolina was one of the best places in the country to get busted for fighting White supremacists. Why? There was an aging civil rights lawyer there who took on all of our cases for free. Within a few days of our arrest, I was summoned to his office for consultation, along with the guy who had tried to help me escape. It turned out that he lived in Chapel Hill, and his office was just the front room of his house. The house was very small and modest. It didn't seem like the kind of place I would expect to find a lawyer living at all. The guy was very friendly and interesting. We covered everything we needed to discuss about our cases, but we spent considerably more time chatting and making friends. His wife brought us tea around mid-afternoon, and when we were still there at dinner time, they went ahead and fed us dinner.

The man had started his law career in the 1960's, and he had provided legal defense for many of the civil rights activists of that era. He took on just enough paying customers to pay his bills, but he spent the majority of his time working for free. Not only did he volunteer to defend every single anti-racist he could. He also brought charges against all the local White supremacist organizers he could, and prosecuted them. Over the years, he had taken millions of dollars in court settlements from the North Carolina branch of the KKK, and he had stripped them of millions of dollars more worth of land and other assets. He donated that money to legal defense for political prisoners. He was too modest to toot his own horn, but I got the impression that he was one of the major factors causing the pattern of long-term decline in the state's racist movement.

Our court appearance was scheduled about a quarter of the way into the month of March. I had originally planned to leave before that, but it's usually best not to skip court dates, and I couldn't carry a backpack on my busted shoulder anyway.

The courtroom was large, and packed to the gills with other people who had been busted for a whole range of offenses. Everyone seemed to be chatting with one another, and at times, it was actually hard to hear the judge over the murmur of other voices. Periodically, she would bang the gavel and demand order in the court, but that would only stimulate a round of laughter from the crowd. Sometimes, members of the crowd would actually raise their voices to directly insult the judge or make jokes at her expense. I was amazed. Back in New York, everyone was terrified of the judges. They would bang the gavel and threaten us with contempt of court charges if they could see us whispering to the person next to us. No one would dare to make an audible sound. But in Raleigh, the courtroom was almost a party.

I hadn't seen any of my codefendants since the day we were arrested, so we took advantage of the situation to get caught up. We made friends and exchanged contacts with the young woman who had joined our group late. I also exchanged contacts with my other codefendants. They all lived in Greensboro, where I would soon be walking, and they were excited to host me on my way through. One of them was very amused to show me his legal paperwork. When he was arrested, the police had found a pack of firecrackers in his pocket, so they had attempted to charge him with "Possession of Pyrotechnics," but the cop who filled out the paperwork had spelled the last word, "pyrochniks." We had a good laugh about that, and I asked them if we could also get in trouble for possessing piroghis.

I was the first one out of our group to get my name called, because my last name starts with a B. Our lawyer stood up from his seat beside us and started walking towards the front of the courtroom. As soon as the prosecutor saw who he was dealing with, his shoulders slumped forward. A look of total defeat washed across his face, and I could swear I saw his lips mouth the words, "Oh shit." Our lawyer glanced back over his shoulder and gave us a mischievous smile. He had seen it too. Apparently, he had owned that courtroom for decades and everyone there knew they couldn't beat him. He told the judge he would like a few minutes to discuss a plea deal with the prosecutor. He then asked the prosecutor if that would work for him. The prosecutor consented, with his eyes still lowered to the ground, and then he and our lawyer made their way to a small conference room off the side of the courtroom that happened to be right next to the bench where we were all sitting.

After about five minutes, the door opened and my lawyer waved for me to come in. They had reached an agreement where I would pay a $500 fine, and do 75 hours of community service. After I completed those two requirements, the charges would be dropped, and expunged from my record. They just needed my consent to make it official. It sounded like a heck of a deal to me, so I agreed.

As soon as that was done, they sent me back out and asked me to send my codefendants in one at a time. They were all offered the same plea deal, and they all gladly accepted it. We had to wait a couple more hours for each of our names to be called, but each time it happened, our lawyer would stand up and tell the judge that they had agreed to a plea bargain and he would make sure she got the paperwork by the end of the day.

I didn't understand why everyone had to be punished for my crime. I thought it was really unfair, and I told them, but all of them just shrugged and smiled and assured me that they were happy with the results. No one wanted to tell me right there in the courtroom that they had all broken various laws that day too, but I found out later. The only one of us who was truly innocent was the hero who had tried to help me escape, but he took it in stride. I suppose he was technically an "accessory" to my attempts to resist arrest.

According to the plea deal, I would get an entire year to complete my community service hours, but for some reason, the court system would not be ready for me to start on those hours until sometime in April. That was frustrating because at that point, I actually had a friend in town who was waiting to go walking with me. I asked my lawyer if I had to do my community service right there in Raleigh, and he said no. He could arrange for me to do it anywhere in the state of North Carolina. I was planning to walk through the city of Asheville, way out in the western part of the state. I figured it would take me more than a month to get there, so I asked the good lawyer if he could arrange for my community service to happen out there. He said he would work on it.

It was always a bit of a trek to get down to Raleigh, so while I was there, I stopped by the police station and found my way to the properties department. I was hoping they would be willing to return my pocket knife to me, but the clerk said he had no record of any such knife. The one thing he did have under my name was a printout of my x-ray from the hospital. That made a good souvenir, so the trip wasn't a total waste of time.

A few days before the court date, someone had given me an even better souvenir. They had gotten ahold of several copies of a Nazi newspaper out of the Midwest somewhere, and there was an article in it about our rally from the Nazi perspective. Their version of the story claimed that I was Jewish, and at one point they referred to me as a "knife-wielding assassin." Watch out!

After the incident, many people advised me to keep my identity secret. They told me not to write about it in my zine, or reveal to anyone that I was the one who initiated the scuffle that day. Their concern was that I had made enemies with a dangerous group of terrorists, so if I reveal my identity, I will make myself a target for revenge.

I understand their point, but I'm really not too frightened. I know it isn't likely that my book will ever get popular enough that any Nazis will even find out about it, but I hope they do, and I hope that they read this someday. On the off chance that actually happens, I'm going to address the following pages directly to the White power movement, and specifically to the mystery man whose throat I chose not to slit.

First of all, I'm not Jewish. My ancestors came from Germany, Scotland, Wales, and a few from Ireland. I am at least as White as you are, if not more. My family came here as impoverished subjects of the British Empire in the early 1700's. That means that at least some of us endured the temporary form of slavery known as indentured servitude. White "servants" were chronically overworked and underfed, and they were housed in filthy, uninsulated shacks. It was not uncommon for them to be whipped just like the African slaves, and any rebellious behavior would be punished by adding years to their sentences. No one knows the actual numbers, but a large percentage of indentured servants died before they could achieve freedom. I am descended from the strong ones who survived.

The story doesn't start there though. Ever since Roman times, my German ancestors were used as serfs. That meant they could not own the homes they lived in, or any land around them, and they had to toil their entire lives making surplus farm products to pay rent to a land baron who essentially owned them.

My ancestors in Scotland, Wales, and Ireland were attacked, captured, and used as slaves by the English for almost a millennium. Many historians have come to see the American Revolution as the ultimate struggle to free the Celts from English domination. One of my ancestors fought bravely in the battle of Trenton- the one where Washington's troops snuck back across the Delaware River at night to surprise the British at daybreak. I hope all Americans appreciate my family's contribution to our shared freedom.

The Englishmen labeled the Celts "Rednecks" to dehumanize us and justify oppressing us. The word Redneck is a racist slur as bad as any other, but I feel comfortable using it in my writing and speech because I am one, so don't fuck with me! It's quite likely that Englishmen forced their way into my family tree without consent. Technically, that would make me part English too, but if there was a way to amputate that part, I would do it.

My ancestors had to be strong to endure so much oppression, but I didn't just inherit their strength. I also inherited a sense of righteous outrage at the injustice they endured. This makes me a natural ally to Black Americans whose ancestors suffered under slavery. When I see a modern Black person being abused by the police, or receiving a ridiculously long sentence for a relatively minor crime, I feel outrage, and I want to help that person. I want to help any person of any race who I see being oppressed. I was born with a sense of righteous indignation towards oppression built into my spirit. I feel like I am always looking for allies to help me gang up on the overseer and defeat him once and for all.

A lot of White Americans are still living under an intense level of economic oppression, and my righteous indignation burns for them too. If you come from a poor White family that's still suffering, then I want to be your ally. I want to help you fight oppression and gain a better future for your family, but I'm not going to help you fight random non-White people. That wouldn't even solve your problems.

Sure. There are definitely some powerful Jewish people, and even a few powerful Black people who are part of the problem. Every race and every nation has its class of oppressive overlords, but here in America, a strong majority of those people are White, just like us.

I don't have any problem with White people in general. Most of the White people I know are awesome. As a race, we have a lot to be proud of, and a lot to be righteously angry about. We are a strong people. Most of us don't deserve to suffer anymore, but you have to understand, history has put us North American White people in a difficult situation.

When the first White people came here as immigrants in the 1600's, there was no policy against immigration. The local people here were very welcoming. In fact, they had to rescue the first several rounds of European immigrants who lacked the skills to survive on this continent.

Those White people, some of whom were our ancestors, thanked the Indians for their hospitality by waging war on them, trying to eliminate them, and stealing their land. Through the combination of this giant land grab, and the enslavement of millions of Africans, many White people were able to amass spectacular fortunes.

Most of our ancestors didn't get rich like that, but they were able to grab small amounts of land. They escaped the worst of Europe's oppression and poverty, and became the largest middle class in history. That's how the USA became the richest and most powerful nation on the planet.

We then went on to conquer half of Mexico, slaughter a million Filipinos, nuke two Japanese cities, and slaughter two million Vietnamese. More recently, we have overthrown democratically-elected governments in almost all of the Latin American countries, as well as various countries in Africa, Southeast Asia, and the Middle East, so we can steal their resources and force their citizens into the closest thing to slavery that we can manage.

In the last several generations, large numbers of non-White people have been allowed into the middle class that buffers the rich from the poor. That's great for us, because it disperses some of the responsibility for the poor people's oppression off of our race. If we treat everyone the way we would want to be treated, and work to end oppression around the world, we can eventually shed the burden of responsibility for the atrocities committed by the White people of the past. But if you join a racist hate group and fight to perpetuate that sick cultural pattern, then you are volunteering to take responsibility for all those past atrocities. In that case, I will not stick up for you, and the whole human race will celebrate when you end up dangling by your neck.

I chose not to stab you that day in Raleigh. I only poked you on the battlefield. I did it to show you I am not afraid, and I did it to warn you that you are making a grave and dangerous mistake.

We cannot make this land into a citadel of Whiteness. Our ancestors came here as immigrants, and they would not have made it without the generous welfare they received from the local people. They conquered the land, and killed off most of the natives, but the spirit of those people didn't go anywhere. It comes from the ground beneath our feet, and the longer we stay on this continent, the more it will work its way into our spirit. We think we own North America, but the longer we stay here, the more it actually owns us.

Europe has a strong spirit too, but thankfully, it's very far away. I am probably the twelfth generation of my family to live in America, and I can't feel the spirit of Europe at all. The Indians warned our ancestors not to kill them off. They warned that their spirits would return in future generations of our own families.

I got to go to Europe when I was younger and it's really not very nice there. I mean, the people were very nice, and the food was much better than ours, but the spirit of the place was super creepy. There was no wild forest left anywhere and that felt really unsafe. We are really lucky to be here, but if you want to be in an all-White paradise, then you should go back to Europe.

If you stay, some future generation of your family is going to come out like me. European culture hit North American culture hard, like the Titanic hit the iceberg. That analogy ends there though, because the people bailing off the titanic European culture aren't going to land in the freezing ocean. We end up here, in the loveliest place on Earth. In North America, we don't have to start conflicts all the time. We don't have to try to establish dominance over each other. We can try to keep that agro, old-world hatred going for a few generations, but the spirit here is more peaceful. A lot of White people have already figured this out. Maybe even most of us, and it's changing our culture.

The change is already underway. Even in the short time our race has lived on this continent, we've already learned to treat women much better. That's because so many White women ran off to join the Indians, and so many more were captured, only to end up thinking of it more like they had been rescued. That's why so many of the eastern tribes look so much like White people. I know our culture still has a lot to work out when it comes to gender relations. There are still a lot of White men and American men of all races who are slow to catch on, but no one can deny that we've come a long way since we met the Indians.

More changes are coming too, but don't be frightened. They are positive changes that will improve life for us and our descendants. Probably the weirdest thing for us to learn will be to love and appreciate nature, and to build mutually beneficial relationships with the wild animals and plants. That's not really a European value, so it may take our race a long time to figure out why it's so important.

There are some values that should make a lot of sense to Europeans though. For example, we need to learn to live as equals and be free from any kind of domination, and we need to raise each child to be excellent. Those are values that White people claim as our own, and North American people would encourage us to live up to them. They would also encourage us to be community-minded instead of selfish, and to define our quality of life by our experiences and accomplishments instead of how much money and things we can horde to ourselves.

I'm sure it's no easy task to overcome racist ideas once they have taken root in our minds. As long as you don't commit any hate crimes or start any race wars, I will give you as much patience as you need.

And to everyone-

Hard-working, trustworthy people come in all colors, and from all corners of the planet. Anyone who writes off an entire race of people as their enemy is going to miss out on a lot of beneficial relationships and opportunities. That puts the racist person at a disadvantage. Villainous scumbags and lazy parasites also come in all colors. A racist person will probably also have the disadvantage of trusting people from their own race who they shouldn't, or feeling responsible to care for the dregs of their race.

I guess I classify people too, and I value different types of people differently. I try to avoid dominant pricks and vampire leeches, and I try to team up with positive, unselfish people who care about the future and work to make things better for everyone. I need all the allies I can get to make a brighter future, so I'm not going to turn down anyone because of what they look like.

45. PHYSICAL THERAPY

Healing a broken bone was an all-new experience for me. For the first two days, the pain was so extreme, I could barely function. Doctors will ask patients to rate their pain on a scale of one to ten, with one being barely noticeable, and ten being the most unbearable. I would say that my pain was somewhere above level eight for two full days. On the beginning of day three, it occurred to me to adjust the straps on my sling. I loosened the strap that supported most of my arm's weight by just a little bit, and instantly felt a wave of relief throughout my entire body. My pain literally dropped down to a five or a six in the exact moment that I adjusted my sling. I then tightened the strap that held my left hand immobile against my right ribs, and dropped down another point on the pain scale.

It was amazing. I had just assumed that the nurse who put the sling on me knew what he was doing and adjusted it to the ideal position for me to heal. In my moment of relief, after I finally thought to adjust the sling, I burst out laughing at the silliness of that assumption. Even if the guy cared about my comfort and well-being, which is not a safe assumption, he still couldn't have known what it felt like to be in my body. He should have at least suggested that I fiddle with the straps until I found the most comfortable position, but I figured it out eventually.

I also assumed that for my bone to heal, that twisted piece in the middle would have to twist back into place. When the doctor declined to do it, I figured that meant that my body would find a way to straighten the broken piece out on its own. I was surprised to discover that's not how a collar bone heals at all.

For the first few weeks, the whole front side of my shoulder filled up with a mass of solid material, so it was impossible to tell what was really going on. Once that started to dissolve away, I was amazed to find that the crooked piece of bone in the middle stayed right where it was while a new segment of bone grew out of nothing to fill the space where a proper collar bone should be. I never knew that's how the body worked, and it felt like magic. The new bone segment grew right around the old crooked one, so the jagged ends of the old one remained, sticking out the top and bottom of my new collar bone. For several years, I had a couple of really gnarly lumps there.

As time wore on, most of the old bone dissolved away, but there are still some noticeable lumps there. Nowadays, they are more like fancy lumps than gnarly lumps.

Less than a week after I adjusted my sling, I was home alone cooking and cleaning. I managed to make a fire in the wood cookstove, breaking up smaller sticks with one hand and stomping the bigger ones with my feet. I am right-handed, so at least my good hand was still functioning. The firebox in a wood cookstove is quite small, so by the time I was done eating, that fire had gone out, and the metal was starting to cool down. I also had a fire going in the heating stove, and ironically, I had the front door of the cabin open so there would be enough light for me to see.

In the process of cooking, I had used up the last of some ingredient that had come home in a large cardboard box, so now I had an empty, dirty box. It was just part of a considerable mess cluttering up the kitchen area, so I took a few minutes to tidy up. When you have no car, and no trash-collection service, anything flammable goes into the woodstove, but this box was too big to fit in the stove. Normally, I would have torn it into smaller pieces and fed them in one at a time, but I couldn't figure out how to tear through cardboard with just one arm. I ended up just stomping the box flat. Then I sort of wadded it up as best as I could, and stuffed the whole thing into the woodstove in one piece.

That was an unwise move. Once the cardboard really got going, a huge tongue of flame reached all the way through the metal stovepipe and up into the chimney. The stove started to roar as it sucked in all the air it would need to feed the giant flame. As soon as I realized what was happening, I closed the vent that lets air into the front of the stove.

Having lived in Maine, I knew about the danger of chimney fires. Creosote from the smoke builds up on the inside of chimney. If no one cleans it out for a long time, the buildup can get thick. Then if a big hot tongue of flame licks up into the chimney, it can catch the creosote on fire. Once that gets burning, it liquifies into a flaming fluid, kind of like napalm. If the air current flowing up the chimney is strong enough, it can splatter this flaming goo out the top where it rains down onto the roof and lights the house on fire. I didn't know what kind of creosote buildup we might have in our chimney, so I closed the flu just to be safe.

Unfortunately, it turned out that we had a huge buildup of creosote inside the chimney, and it had already caught fire by the time I shut off the air. The fire continued to burn with a terrifying roaring sound. For a couple seconds, I was confused. Then I realized it was still drawing air through the cookstove which vented to the same chimney.

Quickly, I closed all the vents that I could close on the cookstove, but they did not close tightly at all. Even in the closed position, they still let in plenty of air to keep the fire going. Worse yet, the entire stove was made out of dozens of individual metal pieces that all fit together quite loosely, so more air was pulling in through large, built-in cracks all over the surface of the deteriorated antique appliance. The loud roar of the chimney fire was accompanied by the whistle and whine from the powerful force of the air sucking in through the cracks of the wood cookstove.

I looked over at the chimney, which appeared to be made entirely of mortar. A big crack ran across the interior face of it, up at about the height of my chest. The crack had been there since before we moved in, but I had never seen it emanating a bright orange glow before. Clearly, air was getting to the fire that way too. This was really bad. I had to do something, but I couldn't figure out what.

I ran out into the yard to get a look at the top of the chimney. It was not a breezy day, and a huge thick cloud of jet-black smoke was billowing over the house. It looked exactly like the cloud of soot you would see in those old films of the original steam locomotives, constantly growing bigger as the fresh smoke shot up into the bottom of it at an alarming speed from the chimney.

I had already closed every valve I could close, and it was still drawing enough air to blast like a jet engine. The roof was made of metal, so it could probably handle a little bit of flaming creosote, but it wouldn't take long for the metal to transfer the heat to the bone-dry timbers underneath. The fire was so intense that I worried it might actually spread to the wood right through the masonry of the chimney, or even cause the chimney to crumble. I knew if I burned down the Kung Fu Redneck's cabin, I would have to get out of the state by nightfall. He had already forgiven me for so many mistakes.

I ran back inside and looked for more vents to close, but I had already closed everything I could. The wood cookstove was just like a giant sieve. It made Swiss cheese look rock solid. Now I was fully panicking. The only thing I could think to do was drag our stuff into the front yard so that something would be left after the house burned down. It felt too risky to go upstairs and get my own stuff though. The wooden staircase was touching the front of the chimney. If I went up to gather my stuff into my pack, I might return to find my way blocked by flames and a crumbling staircase. My one housemate was still living on the couch downstairs, so I ran over and grabbed an armload of his stuff. I used both arms, and with all my adrenaline flowing, I didn't even notice the pain in my left collar bone.

I dropped my friend's things in the front yard, and turned back for another load, but just then I had another idea. A chain ladder led up to the roof, and a heavy, metal wheelbarrow was sitting just a few feet away from it. Maybe I could flop the wheelbarrow over the top of the chimney and suffocate the fire with its own exhaust.

As quickly as I could, I upended the wheelbarrow, dumping several gallons of rainwater onto the ground. Then I hefted the big metal thing up in my right hand. It was heavy, but not quite too heavy to lift with one arm. Then I lifted up my left arm, still strapped into the sling and grabbed the highest rung on the ladder that I could reach. The sling would have allowed me to reach up as high as the top of my head, but the pain made it impossible to reach any higher than my neck. I would just have to take the ladder one step at a time, and stand all the way up before I could reach up and grab the next rung with my left hand. The ladder was made of sturdy aluminum rungs, but they were attached at either end to a pair of chains that dangled loosely from the outer frame of the roof where they were bolted up above. That meant that I swayed and wobbled every which way as I climbed. I would love to see a video of a guy with one arm in a sling, carrying a wheelbarrow up a two-story chain ladder. It must have looked awesome.

I finally got to the top, where I essentially had to swing the wheelbarrow up over my own head onto the roof. My right arm was already tired by then from holding onto the thing all the way up the ladder. I'm pretty sure it only worked because of all the adrenaline. Luckily, the roof was not steeply-pitched, so the wheelbarrow stayed where I put it. Then I had to wriggle my body up over the edge with only one good arm. From there, it was a relatively simple last step to carry the wheelbarrow over to the chimney, and flop it upside-down over the top.

By the time I got there, the smoke had changed to a lighter color, and slowed down a little bit. No globs of flaming creosote had splattered out onto the roof, and it appeared that my efforts were not even necessary. The chimney fire seemed to have run its course without burning the house down. I sat on the roof panting for a few minutes. Then I took the wheelbarrow off the cooling chimney, and dropped it back into the yard as gently as I could. I climbed back down the crazy ladder, gathered my housemate's things up and put them back inside. The house was full of the reeking stench of burning creosote, so I opened the windows upstairs and let it air out.

By the time my friends got home, everything was back to normal. My fire had cleaned all the creosote out of the chimney and thus eliminated the risk of any future chimney fires for a long time. When the guys got home, I let them know the good news.

46. GENUINE JEN

OK. I have to back up now, all the way to the very beginning of *Bug Food*, and fill in an important detail that just didn't fit into the story very well until now. Remember when I had the dream that I had walked to New York City to rescue people from burning buildings, and I woke up and decided to walk across the country? Well, that was a bit oversimplified. Here's how it actually happened.

After the World Trade Center bombing, I quit my job and hid in the woods for a couple weeks. Then I got a job at high-end little grocery store that advertises itself as a co-op. The store has a deli built into one side of it, and after the interview where I got hired, I went to the deli for lunch. I got into a conversation with the girl who fixed my sandwich, and the first moment she looked me in the eyes, I was smitten. It felt like a loud bell went off in my spiritual sixth sense. She did have the most beautiful brown eyes ever, but it was more than that. I could just tell from that first moment that she and I had some kind of spiritual connection, and we would end up being a major part of each other's lives.

Her name was Jen, and I got to know her pretty quickly, since we spent many hours working together. She had her 24th birthday the first week after I met her, so I found out she was born in 1977, same as me. She was a total outdoor adventure girl. She had recently hiked the northern end of the Appalachian Trail, and she told me endless tales about that adventure. She couldn't wait to go on more backpacking trips, and we spent hours talking about all the places we would like to go backpacking.

She was also a rebel activist like me. We found out that in one case, we had been at the same giant protest at the same time. She had an amazing story from another protest where she had made a Philadelphia police officer cry. She started a Recycle-a-Bike program on her college campus, as well as a student club to protest industrial developments and corporate capitalism. She was essentially my dream girl, and it only took a few weeks for her to show up in my actual dreams.

The night of my most fateful dream, I actually dreamed that Jen and I had walked to New York City together, and she stayed with me the whole time, rescuing people from burning skyscrapers and carrying them to safety in the country. When I awoke, I decided to walk across the country, and invite Jen to come with me.

The biggest problem with that plan was that Jen had a boyfriend. She didn't mention him at first, but I met him a few days after I met her when he came into our workplace to give her a nasty attitude about something. As my friendship with Jen grew, we started hanging out outside of work. That pretty much always involved hanging out with her boyfriend too, so I had to pretend to be his friend as well.

It turned out that he always gave her a nasty attitude. That was just his way of interacting with her. I don't ever remember him saying anything nice to her, or even smiling at her, and it was rare for him to go very long without giving her a hard time about something. Not only that, but he also lived off of her like a total leech. Jen had two jobs when I met her, and she picked up a third job after she graduated from college that winter. Her boyfriend didn't have any jobs. Supposedly, he was pulling his weight by selling pot, but he mostly just smoked the pot and then laid around the house doing nothing. It was like watching a patient mother take care of her lazy teen-age son. I decided that a relationship like that couldn't last forever. I would just make good friends with her, and wait patiently for her to ditch the douche bag.

The other big problem with my plan to walk across the country with Jen was that I was pathetically shy around women. Not all women, of course. I had no trouble opening up to women who I felt no romantic attraction to, but Jen was the most attractive woman I had ever met. I could make friendly conversation with her for days on end, but I was a total clam about my deeper emotions. I saw that same twinkle in her eyes every time we looked at each other, so I had myself convinced that she knew, and she had the same feelings for me, but we just had to wait until she could figure out how to get away from Captain Crabby Pants.

It took me until December to tell her about my big idea, and when I finally did, I totally screwed it up. There had been dozens of opportunities to invite her to walk across the country with me while we were at work, but I had chickened out every time. I would literally get short of breath trying to psych myself up, but then I would just fail, and never bring up the subject.

The day I finally found the guts to tell her, we were at the company Christmas party for the store where we worked. We were sitting across from each other at a big long banquet table full of coworkers, and her damn boyfriend was sitting right next to her. I could tell from the look in his eyes that he knew all along how I felt about Jen, and he knew he couldn't trust me around her. We had been exchanging those distrustful glances for two months, but I still went for it right in front of him.

I said, "Guess what Jen! This spring I'm gonna walk across…."

Just then, one of our other coworkers came up and tapped Jen on the shoulder. She turned around to hear what that woman had to say, and her boyfriend just gave me a look that said, "And…."

So, I ended up telling him my plan and not telling her. I didn't tell him I had planned to invite Jen along, but he understood, and he cleverly changed the subject as soon as I was done. By the time Jen turned back around, all my courage to invite her on my big walk had been expended, and we were talking about something else.

It was about five days until the next time I saw her, and when I did, she was very excited. She said, "Guess what Liam! [My boyfriend] invited me to hike the Pacific Crest Trail with him next summer!"

My heart was completely broken, but she didn't notice. She knew I had a bunch of really nice maps of the western states, and she made plans to come over after work that evening to check out the Pacific Crest Trail on my maps.

I ended up deciding that it was a good idea to walk across the country anyway, even if I couldn't share the experience with Jen, and that's how we got the American Odyssey. You could point out that Forrest Gump also took off across the country on foot right after a woman named Jenny broke his heart, but I'd prefer if you didn't.

We remained friends, of course. I saw a lot more of her that winter, and I just kept falling deeper in love. She turned out to be a total do-it-yourself guru. She came from a fairly poor family, but that didn't slow her down at all. She knew how to fix just about everything, and she would make lots of things from scratch.

I had noticed that she had a very interesting sense of fashion. It turned out that she was uncomfortable with the tight fit of most women's clothing, and she needed bigger pockets to carry around all the tools and materials she liked to have on hand, so she just learned to make her own clothing.

She never hesitated to try something new. She had built a huge rack of drying screens above the woodstove in her home. She would gather up all the fruit that was going to get tossed out from our store, and any other free fruits and vegetables she could get her hands on, and dehydrate them so she and her partner could eat them on their big upcoming hike. She also designed and built her own super-light tent.

She had an amazing work ethic and a relentlessly positive attitude. The deli worked her like an ox, but she never seemed to mind. She would take care of all her jobs. Then she would go home to cook for her boyfriend and clean up after him. Then she would dive eagerly into all of her do-it-yourself home projects. She was like a force of nature.

I happened to bump into her by random luck the next summer when I took a couple months off walking, and we ended up hanging out several times. She told me all about her big hike on the PCT. She had lots of beautiful experiences, but her boyfriend had only wanted to fight with her most of the time, and there had been many days when he stomped off ahead of her and left her to walk by herself.

Since her return to Maine, she had squatted an abandoned house on a rural country lane. She had mucked out the old well, and repaired the plumbing leading to and from the kitchen sink. She was in the process of building a garden there, and I spent one whole day that summer helping her till up the hard clay soil with hand tools. She was still unbelievably clever, and motivated, and beautiful, and she was still taking care of her parasitic boyfriend.

She was excited to hear about my walk too, and before I went back on the road, she gave me her email address and asked me to send her updates from the road. She hadn't responded to my emails for months, but then she did. That day I checked my messages in Charlottesville, she had written to say she might be interested in walking with me. Over the winter, there had been several more emails, and then she actually solidified a plan. She would be arriving on the first of March, and we would go walking together at long last!

I was so excited I could barely keep food down. I was always open to hooking up with people like Rooftop Rosie or even Nightmare Jill, but Genuine Jen was the woman I really loved. She was the one I wanted to marry like an old-fashioned Christian and settle down with. Or better yet, we could just go on endless adventures together!

She rode the Amtrak train, and it dropped her off in Durham. She arrived late at night, after the buses had stopped running, so I had to borrow a car to go pick her up. When we got back to the cabin, there was lightning in the western sky, so we climbed up to the rooftop to get a better view. It was the first thunderstorm of the year, and it felt unusual to get a thunderstorm so early in the spring. I took it as a sign that the spirits were rooting for me and Jen to get together, and my heart thundered too. The storm appeared to come towards us for a while, but then it passed by us to the south. We sat on the roof and watched it for about an hour. It was a timeless moment that I felt was very magical and romantic. I should have tried to kiss Jen right there, but I was too shy. We sat very close to each other, but not quite touching.

We had to wait five or six days for my court date before we could actually go hiking, and those days passed without any really memorable events. Jen had plenty of sewing projects to work on, and plenty of books to read, and I remember she came with me on a couple of dumpster-diving missions. It also really stands out in my memory when she told me she was still together with her same boyfriend, but he had become utterly insufferable, and she was finally trying to figure out how to get away from him. That meant that I couldn't kiss her yet, but maybe soon!

We hit the road the morning after my court appearance. I was healed enough by then to ditch the sling and let my left arm dangle. Backpacks are designed so that you carry 90% of the weight on your hips via the hip strap, and just ten percent on the shoulders. I loosened my left shoulder strap and tightened the right one. That way I was carrying almost all of that ten percent on my intact shoulder, and it was comfortable enough. I mean, my healing collarbone was still aching with level three or four pain, but it hurt the same whether I did anything or not.

It was easy enough to walk with the pack on, or to take it off and set it down, but it was very tricky to pick it up and put it on. To do that in a free-standing position would require both of my arms to rotate through their entire range, and that just wasn't going to happen. To put my backpack on with a broken collarbone, I first had to sit it up on something about the height of a table, and then wriggle into it backwards. Luckily, Jen was always willing to lift it up and hold it for me while I fastened the hip strap. She seemed to like helping men who couldn't do things for themselves, so it worked out fine.

We made it into Chapel Hill in time for lunch, and I took Jen to the Cosmic Burrito shop. I was very close to broke at that point, but I was so excited to be walking with her that I felt like indulging. She wouldn't let me pay for her burrito anyway, so I didn't end up spending much money. After that, we got on route 54 west towards Burlington. It was the very beginning of spring time, so none of the leaves had come out yet. All the trees were bursting with buds, and many of them had started to open up, so the trees were covered with little green dots of the most vibrant spring color. It was a most beautiful time of year to be outdoors, and I felt the exquisite romance of it with every step.

That evening, we set up camp at a major crossroads that strangely didn't have any structures near it. All four corners were just thick with young forest, so we walked in just far enough to be out of sight. Jen set up her interesting home-made tent, and I set up mine a modest distance away. We ate some canned supper and chatted until it got dark. Then we went to sleep in our separate tents. It was a very cold night, and I wondered how long it might be before Jen would join me in my tent. My love for her was so pure, it was not even the kind that makes you wish you could have sex. Surely that desire was hiding in my subconscious somewhere, but what I wanted most was just to be beside her all the time.

We awoke to frost, and had a chilly walk for the first few hours of the morning. We walked through a lot of lovely forest and past a lot of small farms and cow pastures. By early afternoon it was comfortably warm. We crossed a large creek, and walked down into the woods a ways to take a break and check it out. After a few minutes, Jen announced she was tired and could use a little nap. I didn't object, so she promptly laid down on her back in last autumn's leaves and closed her eyes.

I needed a break too, but I wasn't sleepy, so I sat down near her where I could watch the beautiful creek flow by. I couldn't help sneaking a lot of peaks at her too. She was a brown-haired White girl of medium height and somewhat skinny build. I found out later that she came from the same German and Celtic stock as me. At that stage in her life, she was trying to work her hair into dreadlocks. It wasn't a very good hairstyle for her, but I didn't care. I had never seen such a beautiful woman before. I wanted to plant a big old smooch on her snoozing cheek, but of course, I was too shy. She awoke after about fifteen minutes, and we continued on.

That evening, we filled up our water bottles from the spigot on the side of a church. Across the road was a broad floodplain leading to a gorgeous mid-sized river called the Haw. The sun was still up, but it was getting late, and we figured we wouldn't find a prettier camping spot than that, so we decided to stop there for the night.

We crossed the highway, climbed over a barbed-wire fence, and scrambled down the steep road embankment covered with thick bushes and small trees. Most of the floodplain had been cleared for a cow pasture, but a good strip of forest remained alongside the river. If you looked back the way we had come, you could see a house and a barn across the pasture, so to remain hidden, we walked along the bottom of the road embankment until the road crossed the river on a bridge. There we intersected with the riparian forest, and we followed it downstream a short ways. Once we had made it a sufficient distance from the noisy road, we set up camp in a comfortable sandy spot, and made supper.

We were in the middle of eating when a heavy old man showed up with his britches held up by suspenders. He hailed us from the edge of the cow pasture up above and asked us what we were doing. He started down over the river bank towards us, and we both stood up and approached him so he wouldn't have to pick his way through al the driftwood and weeds.

He turned out to be the farmer who owned that land. He had spotted us sneaking in, and he felt obligated to check us out. I was not used to being discovered in my secret campsites, and it made me very uncomfortable. I assured him we would be gone in the morning, or we could leave right then if he wanted. It was still a few minutes until sunset. If I had been alone, he probably would have asked me to leave, or something even worse, but Jen was so charming, she just struck up a conversation with him. After a couple minutes, he caved into her charm and said we might as well stay there for the night.

Before leaving, he told us that he kept a bull in that pasture and warned us that we should steer clear of him. After the old farmer left, Jen and I discussed the potential danger of meeting a bull, but we ended up deciding to stay put. The bull wasn't there at the moment to weigh in on the subject, and we were tired. We never did meet the bull, and we left in the morning without incident.

It was a good thing we stopped hiking where we did, because we reached the edge of Burlington early the next morning. Burlington, NC is a small city surrounded by a bunch of large towns. The metro area is home to about 125,000 people. We actually came into a town called Graham first, and then reached Burlington by late morning.

Right downtown, we happened upon a soup kitchen that was serving free lunch, so we got to eat for free. We met a crazy young homeless man there who talked our ears off for almost an hour. I noted with love that Jen had the same affliction as me. It was that concern for all people, combined with that specific type of politeness that had gotten me stuck with that tar pit woman at the Roanoke flea market for so long. Jen had the same problem, so we both made a wacky new friend for longer than we really wanted. When we finally saddled up and started walking again, he came with us, but he gave up after just a few blocks.

Not long after that, we came to a stretch of sidewalk that was just covered with pecans. Someone had recently showed me how to crack a pecan shell open by holding two nuts in the same hand and squeezing them tightly together. I showed Jen the technique and she was delighted. We stopped there and ate pecans until we were stuffed. I felt really cool teaching Jen a new technique for cracking nuts open. That was exactly the kind of thing she was interested in, and I bet she still remembers it to this day. Alas, she was a pure-bred Yankee from the northernmost county in Maine, so I never could teach her how to say the word "pecan" right. Yankees don't realize how ridiculous they sound calling them "pee-cans." The word is actually pronounced "p'kon." Try it. It's derived from a native word that meant "nut" in many different North American languages.

We camped in a small but secretive patch of woods in a town called Elon College, and again I drifted off to sleep dreaming of the day when Jen and I would share the same tent. In the morning she announced that she was leaving that day to get to a women's activist conference in the town of Brevard, up in the North Carolina mountains. Up until that point, she hadn't given me any sense of her itinerary, so I was devastated. I had just planned for us to walk together until she fell in love with me. Then she could call up her old ball-and-chain, dump him over the phone and we would be all set. I hadn't even imagined any other outcome, so I was totally lost.

We got breakfast at a wonderful diner in the little town of Gibsonville, where I managed to hold my emotions together adequately. Even knowing she was about to leave, I still couldn't bring myself to tell her about my feelings for her. Jen gave me a contact number for a friend of hers who I could stay with when I got to Charlotte. After breakfast, we walked about two miles south to a highway junction. Jen gave me a cordial hug, put her thumb up, and in about two minutes, she was gone. I crawled into the bushes where no one could see me and cried and cried. I must have cried for about an hour. Then I got up, crossed the highway, put my thumb up, and hitched back to the ramshackle cabin where I had spent the winter with my friends.

47. TRIANGLE TOUR

When I got back to the cabin, it was mid-afternoon. No one was home, and the squirrels had just committed a major terrorist attack. We had recently gained a bunch of large, sturdy glass containers with screw-on tops. They seemed perfect for storing things like grains and sugar because the squirrels would not be able to bite through them or unscrew the tops. Unfortunately, after filling a bunch of them with foodstuffs, we had then set them on a high shelf in the kitchen. When I got home that day, the squirrels had pushed all of them off the shelf, and most of them had broken when they hit the floor. Broken glass was all over the kitchen, stirred together with rice, flour, cheerios, etcetera.

I had almost finished cleaning up the mess when one of my friends got home. I updated him about the squirrel attack. Then I updated him about what had happened with Jen, and I started crying again. He was very understanding, and he said I was welcome to come back and stay with them for a while longer. He was the storyteller, so he really had a way with words. He told me he knew exactly what I was going through, and then he said, "Sometimes it's hard to get a nice woman to hitch her wagon to your shining star."

He had moved into the master bedroom while I was gone, so I got his old place on the couch downstairs. Looking at a calendar, I can deduce that I must have stayed there for about another week and a half, but I can't recall a single thing that happened during that time, except that I sewed together a new sign for my backpack.

This time, I left all the words out, and just made a bright red flower with a green circle around it on a background of black. I'm going to try to reproduce it on the back of this book.

Back then the American anarchist movement was loosely divided into two main groups. One wing of the movement cared nothing for humanity, and they put all their effort into blocking industrial development and protecting wild ecosystems. Those were the Earth Firsters, and they would rally behind flags of green and black. The other group cared less about nature and devoted their efforts to bringing about equality among humans. Some of them would work with labor unions, while others worked specifically on fighting White supremacists. The human-focused anarchists would identify with a red and black flag.

I had rocked the green and black signs all the way from Maine to Virginia, but now that I had sustained a broken bone fighting the Nazis, I figured I had earned my red stripe. I had never seen any anarchists fly all three colors at the same time, so I flattered myself that I was starting a new trend. It was also a tip of the hat to my favorite hip-hop group, Dead Prez, who were always rapping about tho'in up the red black and green colors of their anti-cop gang.

I contacted my lawyer and had my community service transferred back down to that region of the state. I hope I didn't look like too much of a flake by changing the plan so many times. I still had to wait several weeks to start on my community service, so I came up with a fun idea to pass the time. When I showed up the previous fall, I got picked up in a motor vehicle at the northern edge of Durham. Since then, I had been all over the Triangle cities in buses and cars, but that was not the theme of my adventure. I decided it was high time that I take a walking tour of the cities and finally connect the dots on foot.

I started by walking back through Chapel Hill. It was right nearby, and I had walked and ridden my bike all over town, but I hadn't carried my backpack through it, or flown my fancy new gang colors there. When I finished, I left town on a road headed southeast. In the evening, I crossed a large reservoir called the B. Everett Jordan Lake on a causeway. Just beyond the reservoir, there was a lot of young, piney forest, so I made camp in the soft pine needles.

The next day was the spring equinox. A brief shower had come through during the night and wetted everything, but the sky was clear by sunrise, and the early sun lit up all the little water droplets like magic. A few more leaves had come out in the time since Jen and I went walking, but most of them were still just tiny, or still closed up in their buds. Everything was colored in the glorious green of spring and sparkling wet.

By early afternoon, I made it into a large suburb called Carey where I got lunch and signed up several zine subscribers. There are actually more people living in Carey than in Chapel Hill, but it doesn't make the Triangle into a square because it doesn't have a university. North Carolina State is located in Raleigh. Duke University is in Durham, and the University of North Carolina is in Chapel Hill. So much technological and medical research was happening at those three schools, that corporations started locating their headquarters there. The local governments decided to build upon that economic momentum, and in 1959, they set aside a large piece of land in the space between the three cities to be a tax-free business park. They named it the Research Triangle Park, and ever since then, that urban region has been known as the Research Triangle.

The three cities are not at all similar in size. About three quarters of a million people live in and around Raleigh, but only one quarter of a million live in and around Durham, and only about 80,000 in Chapel Hill. If it weren't for the Research Triangle Park, the region would probably be called "Greater Raleigh," or "the Raleigh Metro Area." Raleigh is also the state capitol.

Chapel Hill didn't even exist in the 1700's, but Orange County, where Chapel Hill now sits, was the epicenter of the rebellious "Regulator" movement. The Regulators were an organization of poor farmers who fought against the British occupation throughout the 1760's. In particular, they opposed what they considered to be an unfair tax on property that served only to enrich the English land barons, without returning any benefits to the people who had to pay the taxes. In some North Carolina counties, the Regulators convinced as many as seven out of every eight farmers to refuse to pay their taxes. On several occasions, they attacked jails and released their comrades who had been taken prisoner.

By 1771, the situation had gotten so out of hand that the British sent in the army and defeated the Regulators in a battle involving thousands of combatants. My New Hampshire friends like to claim that their state started the American Revolution, but it would still be a couple more years before the first edition of the New Hampshire Gazette was published.

North Carolina also played a pivotal role in the Civil Rights Movement of the 1950's and 60's, and I assume it is still a hotbed of cutting-edge rebel activity to this day. In the year 2000, when I first started travelling the country, hopping from protest to protest, every single convergence I want to had a huge squad representing North Kak. That's how I ended up with friends there. For security reasons, I can't tell you much about all the badass warriors I got to hang out with, or all the exciting actions I got to help out with, witness, or hear about, but I can vouch that it's true when they say, "North Kakalakie ain't nothin' to fuck with." Let's just say the winter of 2003/'04 was a really exciting time for a young rebel to visit that state.

***

The End Never Comes

I came into Raleigh on Hillsborough Street. It was the perfect time for supper when I just happened by a really good-looking little country barbecue shack, but I was so broke at that time, I decided I couldn't afford it. I had a bunch of cans of sardines and beans and other cheap stuff in my pack, so I ate that instead. The road was cut into a steep bank on the left side, and all I could see on top were trees, so I scrambled up the bank to sit on top and eat my cold, non-barbecued dinner.

Once I was up there, I realized it would make a perfect camping spot for the night. I was in an undeveloped strip of forest between the road cut on one side, and a railroad cut on the other. It was not a very wide strip of forest, but it was so high above the surrounding terrain that no one could see into it without climbing up the embankment. When trains went by, I couldn't even see the tops of them unless I walked over to the edge of the man-made cliff and looked down. I set up my tent and turned in a little early, but then I discovered a problem with my otherwise perfect campsite. Every so often, I would catch a whiff of the barbecue shack down below, and I kept feeling tempted go back down to it and spend some money.

There was also some kind of large factory across the tracks to the north, and I awoke later that night to the sound of a loud siren going off at the factory. It went off several more times throughout the night, waking me every time, and I realized it must be announcing break times or shift changes for the employees there.

One of the times that the factory woke me, I heard rustling in the leaves nearby, so I poked my head out of the tent to see who it was. There was plenty of ambient light from the city, so it only took a moment for me to spot my visitor. It turned out to be the world's biggest possum. Its body must have been at least as long as my arm, and then it had an equally long tail. I had no idea possums could get that big. I watched in awe as it shuffled by slowly, poking through the downed leaves with its nose, and not appearing to notice me at all. I didn't get much sleep that night, but it was a pleasantly warm spring night, and that queen possum made it all worthwhile.

I found the North Carolina State University early the next morning. I got right into a computer lab, looked up the student activist group, and called them. Someone actually answered the phone, and I had my night's accommodations arranged by eight in the morning. I spent the rest of the day canvassing the campus for zine subscribers, and then checked into a very comfortable activist house that evening.

The house was two stories tall, and a large deck stretched across the entire front of the second story. The expansive deck had two couches, and a number of other chairs, but there was still room for dozens of potted plants, as well as enough bicycles for all the house's residents, and enough bicycle parts to make several more. The railings were all decorated with a combination of beautiful tapestries and old protest signs. Seven or eight students lived there, and most of them were the activist types. I think I spent four nights there in all, and they gave me a couch in the living room downstairs to sleep on. I spent my days wandering the city and selling zines. Then I would spend my nights drinking beer and smoking pot with the kids on their fabulous deck.

One of them got me into a dining hall at NC State for lunch one day. It was a weird experience because it appeared to be an exclusive place, intended only for the richest students and faculty. We rode an elevator to the top floor of a building that was eight or ten stories tall. Only about fifty people were eating there, and we sat at long, fancy wooden tables. We sat down at the table where our placemats were already set with silverware, plates and glasses. Students and faculty sat together at the same table. Then a large staff of all Black people in white uniforms brought food to us from the kitchen.

All the other people who had come there to eat were dressed up like they were going to church, and I felt extremely awkward in my dirty, ripped up shorts, t-shirt and sneakers. I was an official guest of the girl who sat next to me, so no one tried to kick me out, but I obviously didn't fit in there. I failed to make much conversation, so I mostly just ate. The food was exquisite, and the windows gave us a really neat view of the city from up at that height.

The other notable thing that happened while I was in Raleigh was that I got a date. I had gone into a corporate chain organic grocery store to try to sell zines when one of the cashiers took an obvious interest in me. She was extremely skinny, but pretty nonetheless, with straight brown hair and a face full of cute freckles. She had me over to her apartment a couple nights later where she cooked me supper and then kissed me for at least a half an hour. It definitely helped me put my recent failure with Jen out of my mind.

***

There are three large things taking up most of the space in the middle of the triangle created by the three Triangle cities. One is the Research Triangle Park with its miles of glassy office buildings, and another is the Raleigh-Durham airport. The largest of all is a beautiful, undeveloped are of forest called the William B. Umstead State Park. The day I left Raleigh, I camped in the park. It would take about one day to walk from Raleigh to Durham, but if I did that, I would end up in Durham at nightfall with no place to stay. Instead, I left at noon, so I would end up at the Umstead Park when it was time to make camp.

I descended what felt like a very long, steep slope to a beautiful creek at the bottom, and there I made camp. I was so far out in the woods, that I couldn't hear any sounds of the cities around me except for the nearby airport.

I had pocketed maps of all three cities, so I was able to find a nice, quiet backroad leading into Durham the next morning. I passed a sign indicating that I was crossing the line into Durham County around mid-morning. The setting almost looked more rural than suburban, with big manors surrounded by miles of lawn, and even some little patches of forest in between.

I decided I was tired and hungry, and I could use a little break. I should have stopped in one of the little forests, but just as I was considering a rest, I came upon an abandoned-looking garage right out next to the road. The houses were all set back in the distance behind huge expanses of lawn, but the garage was only off the road by about the length of a car, so it felt like kind of a public space to me. I leaned my pack against the front of the small building. Then I sat down and leaned back against it to support my back.

I ate my snack, and then I just sat there for a few minutes enjoying the lovely weather and the spring leaves. Just then, an ancient car came to a stop on the road in front of me, and I saw that it was driven by an ancient White man whose face had turned bright red with fury. His mouth was moving with what appeared to be furious curses, but it took him a moment to lean across the vast interior of the old car and roll down the passenger-side window. Once he got the window down, he yelled some unintelligible, angry nonsense at me, but I understood when he pointed his finger at me like a weapon and yelled, "You! Stay right there! Don't you goddamn move!" Then he pulled into the driveway and raced across the massive lawn to the house behind the garage.

That certainly made me curious, so I stood up and walked to the corner of the garage where I could see around it. I saw the old man get out of his car and hurry to the front door of the house as fast as his legs would carry him. He looked back and saw me, and at that he made another series of aggressive pointing gestures and hollered some more angry words. He was so far away that I could just make out the angry tone of his voice, but not what he was saying.

A moment later, he emerged from the house holding a rifle, and headed back towards the car. At that point, I decided it was time to leave. The trouble was, I was still healing from a broken collarbone. It had gotten considerably better in the time since Jen left. At that point, I could put my pack on by myself, but it was still a pretty slow process. I got it on, and took a few steps down the road, but just then the old psycho came squealing back up the driveway to intercept me. I can't quite say he "jumped" out of the car, because he was too feeble to jump, but he got out as quickly as he could and pointed the gun at me. He shouted, "You just stay put Mister! I called the cops, and they're gonna be here in just a minute!"

I hadn't broken any laws that morning, but I had just recently been busted for Destruction of Property and Resisting Arrest, so I was pretty worried about how a police interaction might go. I told the guy that I hadn't done anything wrong, but he just interrupted me to snarl something nasty.

He told me someone had been vandalizing his garage. He had been trying to catch the culprit for months, and now he finally had me. He was going to make sure they locked me up and threw away the key.

I told him I hadn't done anything to his garage. That was the first time I had ever even been down that road, but he didn't care. He called me a liar, and he said I could explain all that to the police. I sat my pack back on the ground to indicate that I was not going to run. He stopped pointing his rifle right at me after a couple minutes, and we stopped exchanging pointless words, but he remained red-faced and quivering with rage the entire time we waited.

It only took about five minutes for a cop to get there. The old man immediately told him, "I finally caught that weasel who's been messing with my garage!"

I just shook my head "no" in response. The cop checked my ID, and asked if I had any warrants for my arrest. I told him I didn't, but then I went into considerable detail telling him about my recent legal situation. I told him about my next court appearance, which was coming up in the third week of April, and I told him I was very much looking forward to attending it, and getting my name back into good standing with the authorities. The best strategy I could think of was to be as polite and forthcoming with the cop as

I could. He seemed to appreciate my efforts, but as soon as I was done, he opened the back door of his cruiser, and motioned for me to get in.

Here I was going back to jail again, already. Damn! I put my pack in the car, and climbed in beside it, while the cop exchanged a few words with the old man who was just then beginning to calm down. Then the cop got in and we pulled away.

As soon as we got on the road, he turned back to look at me and he said, "Don't worry about that guy. He's insane! He literally calls us about something almost every day."

We pulled around the first corner, just out of sight of the old nut bag's house, and then the cop pulled over. He let me out of the car, and he actually wished me a good day! Luckily, he had taken me towards Durham, so I didn't have to walk back by the same spot.

I made it to downtown Durham in the mid-afternoon where I happened upon a chaotic scene. A large crowd of people had gathered around the railroad tracks, and there were quite a few police cars and an ambulance, all with their lights flashing. The crowd was more-or-less right on the path I was taking, so I stopped and asked someone what had happened. They told me a homeless man had just stepped in front of a passing train and gotten squished. A couple eyewitnesses felt certain that it had been a suicide.

While I was standing there, a younger White guy approached me and asked about my backpack. I told him about my project, and he was fascinated, so we ended up having a lengthy conversation. When I got to the part about how I had to stick around and do community service, he suggested that I could stay there in Durham with him. He and one friend were staying in the abandoned upstairs of a large old commercial building just a few blocks away. They were doing renovation work for the owner who was letting them stay there for free in exchange. He would have to check with the landlord, but he felt fairly certain I would be allowed to stay there too, as long as I did my part to chip in with the work. That sounded awesome to me, so I took down his phone number and thanked him sincerely.

I made it back to Chapel Hill after dark, where a friend let me crash on the couch. I walked back out to the ramshackle cabin the next day, and I stayed there for another two or three days. When I finally got ahold of the young guy in Durham, he told me it was a go, so with that, I moved to Durham.

I would miss my friends, but I had turned out to be such a liability for them that I actually felt good about leaving them behind. I had been a total Yankee to the landlord on numerous occasions. I had turned the squirrels against them, and I had almost burned the entire house down. I had gotten one of their other friends arrested at gun point, and I might have even put them on the radar as enemies of the local KKK. I really needed to get out of there before I completely screwed up their lives.

48. KING BURGERS

There weren't many businesses left open in downtown Durham. All the activity had moved to the strip malls further out. It would be an exaggeration to call it a ghost town, but there were times when I found myself walking down a sidewalk with no other pedestrians in sight. A few cars came by, but I never had to wait for a walk signal to cross Main Street.

One of the last businesses to remain was an old shoe store named Mr. Shoe. The store had been there since the heyday when Downtown Durham was a thriving hub. The business was totally mismatched to the building it occupied. The storefront was at least 25 feet wide, and the space inside was more than four times as deep, but there was almost nothing inside. Several dozen pairs of shoes were on display, each one sitting on its own little shoe-sized shelf along the eastern wall. All the way in the back was a shop space with several workbenches and an array of antiquated equipment for leather-working and shoe repair. A high countertop with a cash register on it mostly separated the busy-looking workshop from the vast, empty retail space. The ceiling was very high, but the space was dimly lit, giving it the feel of a cavern. The store faced south onto Main Street. The entire front was made of huge, glass windows reaching from about knee-height all the way to the distant ceiling, but the sun never shone in because the buildings across the street were too tall.

The proprietor was an extremely popular old Black man who also went by the name of Mr. Shoe. He had no employees, and sometimes whole days would go by without a single customer, but he still kept the store open every weekday, because he loved to entertain visitors. A circle of chairs sat in the middle of the empty retail space, and a steady stream of people would stop by all day, every day, to sit there and converse with Mr. Shoe. He had sold and repaired shoes in that same location since the 1950's.

Back then, Durham was a mecca for successful Black entrepreneurs. It was difficult for Black-owned businesses to get off the ground in those days, but it wasn't impossible. Once a cluster of hard-working pioneers got established there, then Durham got a reputation as a place where Black people could make it. As soon as the word got out, Black people rolled in from all over the state hoping to make a better life for their families. Durham already had a majority Black population before. Once extra Black people started to flood in, the White people who couldn't handle it moved away, and it became an almost entirely Black city. To hear Mr. Shoe tell it, Durham barely participated in the Civil Rights Movement because they didn't need to. The city had become an isolated island of Black prosperity without enough White authority figures around to do them much harm.

Mr. Shoe grew up in nearby Raleigh, but he knew his way around Durham because he had relatives there. He moved to Durham to be part of the scene in his late teens, and he opened the shoe store in his mid-twenties. He was very proud of Durham, and he felt no loyalty for his original hometown. In the four months I had spent in the Triangle cities, I had not previously gotten any sense that there was any sort of rivalry between Raleigh and Durham, but Mr. Shoe and his guests made it sound like a big deal. He was fond of saying, "Raleigh is like talkin' about sex, but Durham is like havin' sex."

Alas, a ring of strip malls popped up around the outskirts of the city in the 1980's, and the younger generations of consumers were not loyal to the businesses that made up the downtown scene. By the end of the 90's, most of the stores downtown were closed and boarded up. The building to the west of Mr. Shoe was torn down, leaving a field of rubble between his building and the next north-south street. Mr. Shoe was able to stand his ground because he had finished paying for the building many years earlier, and he had enough money saved up to keep paying the taxes. His family was doing well enough that they didn't need his help, so he figured he would just stay there until he died.

He acted as a sort of a living history memorial to the glory days of downtown Durham, but he also believed that the city could blossom again someday, and he was a relentless advocate for any scheme that would attract business back into the downtown. He was revered within the region's small business community. About half of his visitors were his old peers who would come to revel in memories of the historical heyday, but the other half were young, aspiring entrepreneurs of all races who came there to soak up his advice and sage wisdom. Mr. Shoe told me the mayor would even stop by to chat with him once in a while.

About a half a year before I showed up, he had teamed up with a pair of White artists in their early thirties who had a plan to make downtown Durham into a hot spot for young artists. Eventually, most of his unused retail space would become an art gallery. There would still be plenty of room for Mr. Shoe to entertain his guests and occasionally fix a pair of shoes, but he would do so surrounded by cutting-edge paintings and sculptures.

A gently-sloping staircase in the northwest corner of the room led up to an equally large second story. That space was being renovated into a series of lofts and studio spaces that he would eventually rent out to young artists. The two younger guys were doing all the renovations, and Mr. Shoe was letting them live in their own construction site for free. One of those guys was the one who had invited me to come live with them, so for the next six weeks or so, I got to be a part of their scene. Mr. Shoe lived elsewhere, so he would lock the front door at five o'clock and go home, but the three of us got our own keys.

The upstairs had an even higher ceiling than the downstairs, and it was as bright as the downstairs was dim. The south face was lined with four very tall windows, and the buildings across the street were not tall enough to shade them. There were also some smaller windows in the western wall, suggesting that the building that had been torn down on that side must have been short enough to see out over. The guys were very good about finishing one project before they started the next, so the chaos of construction was usually limited to just one room, or even one wall at a time. Every surface that wasn't actively being demolished or built was painted or plastered white, so any light coming in the windows would reflect everywhere, making a bright and cheerful atmosphere.

I got a little room on the west side of the building. The day I moved in, one of my new roommates drove me out to his mother's house where we picked up a small, unused mattress that I could sleep on. My room had a window with an awesome view to the west. With nothing but a field of broken bricks in the foreground, I could see significant portions of three different blocks. Straight across from me, the city's main post office was housed in a grand old stone building, complete with Greek-style columns. Diagonally to the north, I was just one block from the city's tallest building, a seventeen-story antique skyscraper from the era when architects designed tall buildings to look attractive, and they weren't all just covered with glass.

I moved in at the beginning of April, and I still had to wait three weeks to start my community service, so I dug right in and helped whenever the guys were working. I had no carpentry skills back then, so I mostly just cleaned up and fetched things, but there are a million and one uses for an unskilled carpenter's helper. The other main thing I did to pay my rent was to go into the dark downstairs and scape black mold off the brick walls with a wire brush. That was very slow going, and it wasn't even halfway finished by the time I moved out. At the time, I had no idea how dangerous black mold can be, so I just wore a little surgical mask to protect myself. I'm lucky I didn't get a toxic mold infection.

When I wasn't working to pay my rent, I was out walking around, scouting the city for sources of free food. There were very few places nearby that served food or sold groceries, so I never found any reliable dumpsters, and I ended up spending more money on food than I was used to. One day I happened by a church picnic and got invited in. A large crew of all Black folks were out in the church yard blasting gospel music and cooking ridiculous amounts of meat on several charcoal grills. Someone noticed me looking at them as I walked by and gestured for me to come in. Next thing I knew I was gobbling up a free plate of barbecue chicken and macaroni salad, and praising Jesus.

I went on two more dates with the skinny girl from Raleigh, but she never kissed me again after that first time. I got the distinct impression she was looking for a guy she could date without having to become a nomad.

One of my new housemates went on a much more exciting date around the same time. Durham had once been the home of a minor league baseball team called the Bulls, and their abandoned stadium still stood, all boarded up, about ten blocks west of our location. My housemate knew how to sneak into the darkened stadium, and he actually convinced his date to check it out with him. Allegedly, they ended up having sex in the middle of center field!

Every Friday and Saturday night, our quiet little block would suddenly come to life with a thick swarm of sharply-dressed people. One of the only other businesses on our block was a night club, just two doors east of Mr. Shoe. If I remember right, the place was called DB's. It was open most nights of the week, but Friday and Saturday were the big party nights. We could hear, and feel the vibrations from the music all the way over in our loft, but it wasn't nearly as loud as the music bumping out of the cars coming and going all night long.

The street out front was a scene of constant activity from about 10pm until the wee hours of the morning. Sometimes I would sit by the front windows and watch in curious fascination. All manner of flashy sports cars and Cadillacs would come and go, all freshly waxed, and many with neon lights along the baseboards or on the hub caps. Many of them would bump the beat so loudly that it was uncomfortable to hear through the closed glass of the window.

The people getting in and out of the cars were dressed up more extravagantly than I could ever describe. Women in tight, bright, sequined dresses of every color, and men in variously colored pinstripe suits. I would need a fashion writer to help me describe all the outfits I saw. Being a nature nerd myself, I can only say that the men reminded me of male birds, growing brightly colored feathers to attract a mate, like peacocks. Almost every rap video depicts a crowd of dancing people who are dressed up like that, but I honestly never knew that real people ever wore clothing like that until I lived next to DB's. All the players came from far and wide.

People would shout across the street to each other all night long too. Usually it was just drunken revelry, but it was not uncommon for hostilities to flare. Sometimes a pair of peacocks would step out front to duke it out, and they would inevitably be followed by a cheering crowd. One night a particularly large fight got so out of hand that the whole street was flooded with shouting people and the cops showed up. Someone actually called Mr. Shoe and woke him up, and then he called us. We assured him that we were all fine and no one had damaged his store front. Mr. Shoe was cordial with the night club owner, but he admitted to me that he didn't like the man, or the atmosphere that his business brought to the neighborhood.

A friend in Chapel Hill heard that I had moved to Durham, and she got in touch to give me a tip on a good place to do my community service. It was called an "industrial reuse center," and it turned out to be just six or seven blocks down the hill to the north of where I was living. The folks there were very accommodating, but I still had to fill out a lot of paperwork to get things set up. I didn't have access to a fax machine, so I actually had to ride the bus down to Raleigh one day to pick up some more paperwork. Finally, my long-awaited court date came, so I could turn my papers in and get started.

There were a lot of manufacturing plants in the Triangle region, and they produced a great deal of waste. Some of that waste came in the form of harmless little pieces of plastic, glass, or metal in interesting colors and shapes. Rather than paying a disposal company to haul that waste away, they would donate it to the industrial reuse center who would sell it at cheap prices. Even if I could remember the details of all the little odds and ends we sold, it would be hard to describe them.

Most of our customers were poor mothers who understood that any bright colored piece of plastic would make a good toy whether it had a brand name on it or not. We also got a lot of artists and crafters looking for cheap raw materials. We did have quite an array of different colored skeins of cloth and balls of yarn that hadn't passed inspection at the local textile mills.

It was a pretty easy job, and I spent a fair amount of time just talking to the employees or the customers. As a convict, I wasn't allowed to work the cash register, so I stocked shelves and cleaned the floors and the bathroom. Sometimes I would sit for hours popping little pieces of plastic out of perforated molds or winding up balls of yarn that had come unraveled.

Before I even started working there, I had noticed that it was only a block away from a notorious hamburger stand called King Burgers. I say notorious because I had heard my North Kakalakie friends talk about it before I ever even came to their state. Apparently, the now defunct Punk mansion known as The Stronghold was close enough that the non-vegan Punks could sometimes get there to eat. King Burgers was widely known to have the best burgers in the state, and possibly the universe.

Though I had noted its location, I had not yet been there to eat, because I was almost out of money. My frugal discipline finally broke down at lunch break on the first day of my community service. I just had to give it a try. It was the kind of food stand with no indoor seating. You just order and receive your food through a window and then eat at a line of picnic tables out on the asphalt. I ordered a bacon cheeseburger, and they only wanted six bucks for it. Not bad. When they called, "Leroy," I went up to the window to receive my burger, pulling cash out of my wallet as I approached. When I got there, the elder woman at the window put up her palm to block my money and said, "No hun. For you it's free." I was confused, but I wasn't about to argue. I went to my picnic table and gobbled it up, and it truly was one of the best burgers I had ever eaten.

Giving out free burgers was a great way to earn my loyalty as a customer. Now that I had gotten a free one, it only made sense to pay for two or three more, so I went back the very next day. The same woman was working the register, and once again she refused to take my money. This time I was really confused, and I gave her a really dumb look. She just smiled and said, "We know who you are hun."

The meaning of this still didn't sink in until I was mostly finished with my second free burger. Slowly, it dawned on me. King Burgers was another Black-owned business, staffed entirely by Black people. I was doing community service as a penalty for physically attacking a Ku Klux Klan rally. I was living in a building owned by a man who talked to everyone in town, and there probably weren't many tall, skinny White boys named Leroy in Durham. It all added up once I got a chance to think about it. Word had gotten around.

After that, I went to King Burgers for lunch every working day, but it only took about a week before I started to feel guilty. I know how hard it is for family-owned businesses to make ends meet, and I couldn't stand the idea that I might be creating an extra burden for one of the world's greatest hamburger stands. One day, probably the seventh or eighth time I ate there, I tried to debate the woman and persuade her to take my money, but she still refused. I stopped going every day after that.

For some reason, the reuse center would only give me six-hour shifts, five days a week, so it took thirteen days, spread over almost three weeks to complete my service hours. I think I ate at King Burgers twice more after my guilt caught up with me. I went one last time on my final day of community service, and I made a big show of thanking everyone at the burger stand, letting them know that I had finished doing my time, and saying goodbye.

All that was left now was to pay my $500 fine, so I organized a fund-raiser concert to raise some money. I actually started setting up the show around the same time I started working off my community service hours. I had made friends with an East Chapel Hill High School kid over the winter, and he was eager to help out. He let me borrow a guitar to practice, and when I was ready, he helped me record a CD. He had a couple really nice microphones and some recording software for his computer, so we put together a decent album. I think I recorded ten original songs and four covers. One of them was a brand-new, super-sad song I had just written to process my recent heartbreak over Jen.

Mr. Shoe and the two young artists had been planning to use the renovated shoe store as a place to hold public events, and my concert ended up being the first one. They brought in a bunch of their friends' paintings and hung them on the walls in time for the show. I had been handing out flyers and inviting people for weeks, and I got almost 40 people to show up. Most of them were friends from Chapel Hill who had driven up or ridden the bus, and there was another large group of high school kids who my young friend had invited.

The highlight of the show for me came when a severely drunk woman stepped out of DB's for some fresh air, noticed our event, and came in to check it out. She interrupted me in the middle of a song to ask some loud, flirtatious question. Almost everyone in my audience was White, and several of them actually gasped at her rude disruption, but I thought it was great. I just gave it back to her and made it part of the show. We went back and forth a few times like a little comic interlude until she was satisfied that she had made enough of a scene. Then I went back to playing music, and she actually stuck around for several songs, cheering louder for me than the rest of the crowd combined.

I sold most of the CDs I had burned and netted a little over $300. It took me several more days to get all the money combined into a single check for my lawyer, and receive a check in the mail from my father. He and I had fought bitterly over our political opinions for years, but when I told him I had gotten busted fighting Nazis, he actually said, "Well at least this time it's for a good cause." I remembered that when I came out almost $200 short of my court fine. I called him the next morning, and he agreed to cover the difference for me. With that all taken care of, my legal status was cleared, and I was finally in good shape to get back on the road.

Benefit Show for:

ECOLOGY

and

EQUALITY

THE BEGINNING IS NEAR
NORTH AMERICAN TOUR

My name is Leroy and I've walked more than 2,000
miles to tell the world that people will prevail over
oppression, and life will prevail over the machines!

49. CIRCLE THAT A

The Research Triangle region had been my home for almost half a year. The day that I was finally ready to go turned out to be my birthday (and Janet's.) I had already walked to Burlington once, and I reasoned that it might be too depressing to retrace those steps, so I dropped twelve dollars on a train ticket as a birthday gift to myself. It wasn't a very good idea. The train didn't leave until 4:30 in the afternoon, and it dropped me off in downtown Burlington around six. Obviously, there wasn't time to get out of the city by nightfall, so I hopped off the train and went directly into the hunt for an urban camping spot.

I ended up in sort of a ditch next to an abandoned auto mechanic shop. The building clung to the top of a very steep hill that dropped off into a deep ravine just behind the shop. I probably could've gotten a more isolated camping spot if I had climbed to the bottom of the ravine, but the hill was dangerously steep, and there really wasn't any need. The ditch where I slept was totally hidden in a thicket of bushes. Of course, I would be screwed if it rained and the ditch filled with water, but I lucked out, and it didn't rain that night.

I hadn't signed up any zine subscribers the first time through Burlington, so I stuck around all morning trying to peddle my wares. I didn't have much success, so I started hiking west right after lunch. I had to walk right back through Gibsonville, the little town where Jen ditched me, and I couldn't help leaking a few more tears. Beyond that, I made it into the little bit of open country that still remained in between Burlington and the eastern suburbs of Greensboro, and a particularly beautiful sunset lifted my spirits.

I found a broad stretch of very flat forest to camp in. A lovely little brook managed to flow through the middle of it without cutting much of a ravine at all, so I hopped across it and camped just beyond it. A thunderstorm blew through just before morning, and I awoke to lightning and heavy rain. I stayed dry inside my tent, and the storm was over by sunrise, but when I got up, my pretty little brook had turned into a raging torrent of murky floodwa-ter. There really wasn't any way to get back to the road other than to wade through it and get my feet wet, but it was fine. By mid-May, it was almost summer in central NC. The weather was warm, verging on hot, and my new sneakers dried out after a couple hours of walking.

The next thunderstorm caught me on the way into Greensboro. I put on my poncho, but it only covered me down to the knees, so my feet got soaked all over again. The storm was brief, and the rainwater was actually warm, so I just kept walking right through it. I made it to the glass skyscrapers of downtown about an hour later, and by that time, the sun was shining again. I had people to stay with in Greensboro, but I couldn't get ahold of them on the phone, and I didn't know exactly where they lived. It was only noon anyway, so I splurged on a deli sandwich for lunch, and then set out to wander around and explore downtown.

Along with its suburbs, Greensboro is home to just under 400,000 people, but it is also part of a larger metropolitan area that has become known as the "Piedmont Triad." The Triad is another triangle of cities, with Greensboro being its northeastern point. The northwestern point is a city called Winston-Salem that is almost exactly the same size as Greensboro. A city called High Point makes the southern point of the Triad, and it is home to about 150,000 people.

Greensboro is also famous for its lunch-counter sit-ins during the Civil Rights Movement. Back then, it was common for restaurants and lunch-counters to refuse to serve Black people, so activists would organize groups of Black college students to go sit in the segregated spaces, and reporters to come document what happened. The restaurant management would behave like barbaric, racist apes, and then the peaceful students would be dragged away violently by police and hauled off to jail. When films of these outrageous scenes hit the news, it made the segregated businesses look really bad, and they were eventually forced to change their policies and serve food to Black people.

In February of 1960, four Black college students sat in an all-White lunch-counter at a Woolworth's department store and refused to leave. They were arrested, but as soon as they got out of jail, they came back to the same Woolworth's with a much larger crowd. It was not the first lunch-counter sit-in of the Civil Rights Movement, but it was the first one to gain national attention, and it is considered to be the catalyst event that inspired dozens of other sit-ins all across the South. Students from that action went on to form the Student Nonviolent Coordinating Committee (SNCC,) which ended up being one of the most influential activist groups of the Civil Rights era. The lawyer who had recently stepped up to defend me in Raleigh actually began his career as a champion for civil rights defending the original Greensboro activists, so I now felt a connection to that history.

There was also an incident in 1979 that came to be known as the "Greensboro Massacre," where a crowd of anti-racist warriors attacked a joint rally of the Nazis and the KKK, just as we had tried to do 25 years later. Back then, the White supremacists were armed and they opened fire, killing five people, and wounding more than a dozen others. The history books claim that the victims of the massacre were communists, but my friends told me that most of them were actually anarchists like us. Interestingly, the courts acquitted all the murderers, claiming they had only acted in self-defense.

Eventually, I got ahold of my hosts, and they were very welcoming. Three of the guys who had come with me to attack the Nazis' cars shared an apartment along with one of their girlfriends. In the safety of their home, they finally felt comfortable telling me what else happened that day. Apparently, after I made my move and stuck the guy's tires, he turned his car directly toward my five allies, and stomped on the gas. They had to jump to either side to get out of the way of his vehicle, but they all had their weapons out, and they managed to thoroughly smash his windshield as he drove past. He sped on to the edge of the parking lot, and made it a little ways out onto the street before his tires deflated enough that he had to stop. They made a brief attempt to pursue him, but they were quickly headed off by several squad cars full of police and arrested.

They had been hoping for a chance to get to know me ever since then, and they lavished me with praise for my courageous behavior that day. They were part of the Anti-Racist Action crew, so I learned a lot about the American anti-racist movement, and the American White supremacist movement during the four days I spent with them. They were pretty serious about researching and tracking their enemies, and they had actually sent away to the FBI for detailed reports on our nation's White power movement. The reports were so extensive that I didn't even have time to read them all, but I read quite a bit, and I found it fascinating.

I was particularly interested to note the geographic locations of the modern racist movement. I lived in New England for most of the last two decades, and it seems like most people there believe that the South is America's hotbed of racist White bigotry. During the Civil War, Union soldiers had to believe that stereotype in order to feel okay about killing Confederate soldiers. 150 years later, an alarming number of Yankees think that modern Southerners are still like that.

Of course, racist hate groups are still active in all the former Confederate states, but their numbers are roughly equivalent to the racist hate groups that are currently active in the Northeast. Neither of these regions come anywhere close to what we see in the Midwest though. In 2004, when I read the FBI report, Illinois was the American White power movement's undisputed capitol. Just by measuring how many people were officially enrolled in racist hate groups, Illinois had the highest per capita rate, and the highest total number, with more than 100,000 people enrolled. Illinois fought on the Union side in the Civil War. It is known as the "Land of Lincoln," because Abraham Lincoln represented that state in Congress before he became president. South Dakota had the second highest percentage of its population enrolled in hate groups, but there aren't enough people in South Dakota for the total number to be very high. Kentucky, another Union state, came in third, and all the other states in the Ohio Valley and the Midwest were above the national average.

So, when Yankees talk about what a bunch of racist bigots the Southerners are, it is not an expression of any genuine concern for non-White people. It is just an expression of ignorant prejudice against Southerners. A huge percentage of modern Southerners are Black. In Alabama, Black people outnumber all the other races of people put together. When Yankees hate on Southerners, who does that hatred actually land on?

The other detail I found in the reports that really amazed me was just how big the federal budget was for anti-racist research and enforcement. There is a whole branch of the FBI that burns through tens of millions of dollars every year keeping track of racist hate groups and busting them as soon as they break any laws. It made me wonder if I was wasting my time chasing the Nazis around when the cops were already working on it with all the authority and resources of the government.

Indeed, the biggest criticism I got from my friends and allies back in the Triangle was that I had gone all out for a cause that, while honorable, was not a very high priority. My friends at the cabin said I had "brought my A game to a B situation." I understood the criticism.

At that time, White power groups posed a potential danger to millions of non-White Americans, but on an average day, they weren't actually causing much harm to anyone. At the same time, US foreign policy was keeping dangerous, White supremacist governments in power across most of Latin America. In those places, the non-White majority had to face potentially deadly levels of oppression every day, and opponents of the government were being imprisoned, tortured, and executed on a regular basis. The FBI budget for fighting American racist groups may have been impressive, but it was nothing compared to the CIA budget for fighting against freedom and democracy in the Third World.

In the years since my attack on the Nazis, it has also occurred to me that White supremacy is a philosophy based on fear. A racist uses their fear to build a psychological barrier around their mind and keep the truth of equality out. Attacking those people is only going to add to their fear and strengthen their mental barriers.

Lately, I have actually been trying to make friends with White racists so I can get inside their heads and try to transform them. In one case, I think I have actually seen some improvement. Nazis are the extreme case, and there may not be anything we can do for someone who is that far gone, but we should definitely be spending time with people who suffer from milder cases of racism. If all of us non-racist people turn our noses up at them, they will have no one to hang out with but other racists. Once they get together without any positive influences, that's when their racist attitudes can snowball into a dangerous situation.

***

On my second night in Greensboro, my hosts took me to see a concert by a band called "Of Montreal." It was a fun show, and it was wonderfully inexpensive. A couple hundred hipsters came out to see the band play in an industrial warehouse that had been converted into a show space. I sold a lot of zines that night. No one gave me very much money, but I still totaled up almost a hundred dollars. It was very encouraging. I was down to the last little bit of the money I had made by selling my car two years earlier. If my project was to continue, I was going to have to find ways to make all the money I needed while on the road. That night at the Of Montreal concert gave me a lot of confidence that I could actually pull it off.

In those days, Greensboro was also the headquarters of the Crimethinc publishing collective. They were operating out of a large residential home, but they couldn't actually put me up for the night because all their couches were already covered with other travelling rebels. They did invite me over to visit though, and we spent the whole day discussing philosophy and our strategies to get important ideas out to the public through radical literature.

I had met some of the Crimethinc writers shortly after I arrived in North Carolina the previous December, and they were big fans of my zine. When I went to visit their headquarters, they asked me to write a column about my walk for one of their quarterly publications. I was honored and thrilled to be working with them, but alas, I dropped the ball. I quit walking less than a month later, and I never submitted a single piece of writing.

Crimethinc used to be the nation's cutting-edge publisher or anarchist philosophy and updates, and I'm guessing they still are. If you enjoy the philosophical discussions in my writing, or if you crave more honesty than you can get from the mainstream political philosophies, I highly recommend you check out the Crimethinc online store at www.crimethinc.org. I consider myself an anarchist, but I can't really speak for other anarchists, because we all speak for ourselves. All I can tell you is what anarchism means to me.

I am here to help you overcome dominant people and oppressive power structures. Anarchists aren't trying to take over the government, and I don't think we really have anything like a blueprint for a perfect economy. We would love to help everyone come up with one, but we can't do it without more universal participation.

The beauty of anarchism is this: You know what's best for you, and I can't tell you you're wrong. The only exception would be if you were oppressing someone else or taking advantage of a situation where someone else is powerless. Then you would be doing wrong, and I would have to try to stop you. The end goal is a culture where I can't dominate you, and you can't dominate me either.

Being really gung-ho as I am, I even want to help you fight off other people or institutions that would dominate you and limit your freedom. If we can actually get free, then we can talk about what to do next, but I'm not the guy to sit around dreaming up theoretical ideas when real things need to get done. Real freedom seems like it's a long way off yet. I don't even expect to live long enough to see it, but I'm still excited to know it's coming.

Back when I went on my odyssey, Republican war-mongers were the most dangerous people, so I wanted to rally around Arabs, Muslims, and the poor

American families whose kids were getting sent to kill and die in the deserts of Asia. Lately, the Democrat fear-mongers have become more dangerous, and I have actually had to make friends with people who think Donald Trump is cool. I assume the political parties will keep going back and forth forever like the Crips and the Bloods as long as we keep eating up the dog-food-grade information they feed us.

I guess I would tell you you're wrong if you squawk at me like a parrot, repeating back ideas that you heard from the liberal or the conservative media. I have to be sassy enough to stand my ground in a world dominated by liars. But I don't judge you if they have fooled you. I was fooled for a long time too. The media is working hard at what they do, and they are good at it. I judge them assholes for trying to fool us.

I will just keep switching to whichever team is the underdog, but I don't have some kind of mental health issue that causes me to need struggle. If humans ever stop oppressing one another; if we release the Third World slaves, and bring production home; I will stop fighting. I will go into party mode, which includes cooking, cleanup, and given enough time, the brewing of fermented beverages.

Anarchists have a proud, centuries-long history of pushing back against oppressive power structures, whether they be monarchal, aristocratic, capitalist, or communist; whether they be governmental, religious, or social. It's our job to stick up for the abused spouses, the oppressed minorities, the poor, and any other underdog that needs our help. We stay on call as much as we can because we enjoy having meaningful lives, but we don't need to be struggling, and we hope to be done someday. We are ready for peace, freedom, and equality as soon as you all are.

That's my take on anarchism, but if you are curious to hear some other people's perspectives on the philosophy behind this righteous tradition, the Crimethinc store is a great place to start. I have not read everything they have published, but I have read most of it, and I thoroughly enjoyed all of that. *Evasion* is another adventure story, much like mine, but with double the smart-assed attitude. *Days of War, Nights of Love* is an appeal for radical lifestyle changes that surprised everyone by selling thousands of copies and providing Crimethinc with the budget to publish several more books. I think you can even see some of the influence of that book on my writing.

The best book they have published so far is a relatively new one called

No Wall They Can Build. As the fanatic fear of immigrants has recently moved from the radical fringe into the mainstream of conservative American thought, this may be the most important book currently available. Neither the conservative, nor liberal media give an adequate or honest picture of what's happening along the Mexican border, or in the countries to the south of it. The author of *No Wall* spent seven years on the border, helping migrants survive their trek across the Sonoran Desert, and they learned volumes of fascinating information from the people they met. They also spent years travelling throughout Mexico, Guatemala, and El Salvador, learning about the situations in those places that motivate people to migrate north. For anyone who is concerned about border and immigration issues, regardless of which side of the debate you support, I highly recommend that you read this book, and arm yourself with some actual information. You will be amazed at how complex the situation really is, and which significant details the liberal and conservative media are covering up.

***

The ARA kids who hosted me in Greensboro were actually pretty weird people. I loved it that they were militant anti-fascists, but they were also militant vegan animal-rights activists, and militantly straight-edge. Their apartment was awkwardly located right next to an apartment full of beer-guzzling, pot-smoking college students. My hosts were constantly criticizing their neighbors for their drug and alcohol habits, but I met the neighbors and found them to be very friendly.

One morning, I encountered a couple of the neighbors out in front of their apartment. They told me they were having a party that night, and they invited me over. Later that evening, my hosts invited me out with them for an evening of fun. Their idea of fun was to walk around looking for drunk college kids and beating them up. I'm not kidding!

I asked them why, and they said it was part of their effort to encourage people to stop doing drugs and alcohol. I had no idea that anyone could be so militantly straight-edge that they would want to force that lifestyle on other people. That's not anarchistic behavior at all. I was baffled, and it took me a while to figure out how to respond.

Finally, I just admitted to them that I would rather get drunk and stoned with the kids next door. Then I asked them if they would beat me up. They looked sad and confused, but they had no inclination to beat me up. They said that my valor at the Nazi rally made me like a brother to them, and they would look for a gentler way to discourage my bad habits. I asked them if they had ever beaten people up for eating meat, and they said no, but one of them had assaulted a man once for abusing a horse.

I did spend the night getting inebriated every which way with the college students next door, and I sold them quite a few zines. Some of them were in a band that performed at the party, and for the finale of the show, they played the song *Baby, I'm an Anarchist*, by Against Me.

50. WALKIN' ANCESTOR

Someone at the Crimethinc house recommended that I hit up the Saturday farmer's market before I left town, and Saturday was only two days out, so I gave it a shot. The market was on the west side of town, so I packed up my backpack and brought it along. I spent the morning selling even more zines at the market, and then I headed out in the afternoon. It was nearing the end of May, and that was the first day I can remember walking through uncomfortable heat. I made it just beyond the airport when I found a perfect camping spot. There were still several hours of daylight left, but I happened by a much larger patch of undeveloped forest than I had expected to find right in between Greensboro and Winston-Salem, so I stopped there. I had just gotten a contact for some people to stay with in Winston-Salem too, so it didn't matter whether I rolled into town early or late.

Winston-Salem is the westernmost city in a solid line that stretches all the way back to Raleigh. The Piedmont Plateau is high and rugged at that point, and the city is draped over a landscape of high ridges and deep valleys. I didn't find any hills there that were too steep for streets to go up and down, but there is no real estate anywhere in that city that isn't on a slope. I kept thinking I must be close enough to see the Appalachian Mountains. I would look for them every time I reached the top of a hill, but if there is someplace in Winston-Salem with a view of the mountains, I never found it.

My hosts there were another large gang of artists who lived in a converted warehouse right near downtown. They weren't like the rebel-squatter artists who I stayed with in Providence. This warehouse had been professionally remodeled, and the artists paid rent and lived there legally. They were exceptionally hospitable, and I felt very comfortable in their home. I stayed there for two nights and signed them all up for zines. Late in the morning of my third day, while I was exploring a neighborhood in a deep valley to the west of downtown, I spontaneously decided I was ready to move on from Winston-Salem. I went back to the warehouse, grabbed my backpack, and bounced.

On my way out of town, I happened through a really neat historic district called Old Salem, where a bunch of structures had been preserved from the original pioneer settlement of the 1700's. I've seen historic buildings preserved like that plenty of times in rural places, but never in the heart of a big city. Just beyond Old Salem, a brief thunderstorm rolled through. I took shelter in a very comfortable coffee shop for about a half hour, and then continued on after the rain.

I aimed myself towards High Point, the last of the Piedmont Triad cities. For reasons I can no longer remember, I went west to Winston-Salem first, so I had to double back towards the southeast to get to High Point, making a big zig on the map. In the evening, the road took me along the top of a high ridge with a long, beautiful view of the rolling hills and valleys to the southwest, all highlighted with the shadows and orange colors of evening sun. Once again, I stumbled upon a much larger patch of forest than I had expected to find in the suburbs, so I settled in for the night. This forest was made of all pine trees, and their needles made a particularly soft bed.

Early the next morning, I passed through a little crossroads called Horneytown. There was a little café there, and I really wanted to stop and eat breakfast, just so I could say I ate breakfast in Horneytown. Alas, it wasn't open yet. The sun comes up really early towards the end of May.

Soon after that, I found myself in High Point, the smaller of the Triad cities. It was a very strange place. For what seemed like miles, the entire Main Street had been cleared of any historic architecture, and replaced by brand-new, box-shaped structures with flat, glassy exteriors. They were shorter than office towers, and they all housed big department stores selling clothing, shoes, and a whole variety of other consumer products. I think it was a long strip of "factory outlet" stores, but I found the whole atmosphere so alienating that I didn't actually investigate what was really going on. It was like a giant outdoor shopping mall, complete with a huge swarm of shoppers. I didn't stop to meet anyone or even attempt to sell any zines. I just put my head down and hiked as fast as I could without tangling up in the thick crowds of pedestrians.

On the south side of town, I came to some residential neighborhoods that felt a bit more comfortable. I stopped in a pleasant park to eat lunch. I sat down at a spot where the mowed grass ended at the top of a steep hill, giving myself a view down into a forested ravine. I whipped up a quick peanut butter and jelly sandwich, and commenced to eat.

Just then, a very haggard-looking White guy climbed up out of the ravine right in front of me. His clothes were filthy, and his hair was stringy and greasy. It looked as if he had been sleeping down in that ravine for days in the same clothes, and without a tent. He had a wild, drug-addled look in his eyes. I'm usually very trusting of even the worst-looking people, but this guy gave me a bad feeling. He was coming right towards me, but I realized quickly that he was walking on a path, and I had sat down right where the path met the mowed grass of the park.

He started talking to me from part way down the hill, and then he sat down with me and continued once he reached the top. He was obviously crazy. I don't remember much of what he actually said, but I do remember him claiming that he had just walked there from Atlanta overnight, and I knew that was not even remotely possible.

After just a minute, he changed gears and tried to sell me some crack. He actually pulled a little piece of plastic out of his coat that had been twisted tightly around a small, white object, and showed it to me. I declined the offer as politely as I could, but that really pissed him off. He cussed me out in an angry tone, stood, and stomped off past the swing-set that was right behind me. He went just a few paces, and then sat down at the nearest picnic table. I turned 90 degrees so I could keep an eye on him. He kept shooting me nasty glances while he fiddled with something on the table top. It looked like he was loading his crack into a pipe in preparation to smoke it himself. I crammed the last several bites of sandwich into my mouth all at once, put on my pack, and hurried away. The man yelled several angry bursts of nonsense at me, but I didn't look back or respond. My mouth was too full anyway.

The guy had really freaked me out, so I hustled away for quite a while. Crack is known to give people short bursts of intense energy, so I kept worrying that I would hear his footsteps come running up behind me. By the time I calmed down enough to notice what was going on, I had walked about a mile in the wrong direction. I had been planning to turn southwest towards Thomasville, but I had gone due south instead. I had a map of the area, so I just picked a new route. I kept going south for a few more miles until I got to a road where I could turn west and get back on track.

I got to Thomasville around suppertime. I'm not sure I would call it a small city, but it was a large town that took me several hours to walk across. The railroad tracks made a straight line right through the middle of town, and a long stripe of green, grassy park had been left on either side of the tracks. It was about the width of a city block, with a railroad track running down the middle, bounded by two streets running parallel to the tracks. It stretched across most of the town, and it led in exactly the right direction, so I followed it all the way. A few of the major cross-streets crossed the park, but most of them stopped at the edge. A small depot building sat right in the middle of town where the passenger train would stop to let people on and off. One big freight train went past, going southwest about three times faster than I was going.

Something spiritual happened to me while I was walking through that park, and it's going to be hard to explain. Remember when I slept in the Devil's Hopyard in Connecticut, I woke up the next morning and I felt like God was looking right at me? It was another very intense spiritual feeling like that. In fact, it was the first time I had a spiritual feeling of that magnitude since that morning almost two years before, but it wasn't exactly the same feeling.

It was more like God was looking at Thomasville through my eyes. I just felt this super-humanly immense love for everything I saw. I loved everyone in town. I loved everyone in *America*. Even the Mass-holes. *Even* the Nazis. I also loved the land, and the trees, and the birds in the sky. I mean, I'm always kind of like that, or I at least try to be as much as possible, but I just carry one little human-sized unit of love. This was like all the love in the universe, flowing through my heart, but without knocking me down, or disabling me like you might imagine.

I don't know what it was, but it felt lovely. I also can't remember anything about where I camped that night. I know I hadn't eaten any ganja food that time, I swear!

The next thing I do remember was walking into Lexington the following morning. You could call Lexington a big town, but I might call it a small city. The chamber of commerce had put up signs claiming that it was the barbecue capitol of the United States. The city was also decorated with pig statues that had all been uniquely decorated by artistic locals. My favorite one was standing up on its hind legs, painted patina-green, and dressed up like the statue of liberty with the torch and the book and the crown.

When I got downtown, it was too early for lunch, so I wandered around for a couple hours. I found a tourist visitor's center that gave me a free map showing all the barbecue places in town. When lunchtime finally came, I got a barbecue pulled-pork sandwich. It was awesome, but I'm not convinced it was any more awesome than barbecue usually is.

That evening, I crossed the next one of the East Coast's mighty rivers.

Coming down from the mountains to the point where I crossed, it's called the Yadkin River, but halfway down to the sea, it changes its name to the Great Pee Dee. Two fairly high bluffs pinched the river from either side, and the bridge crossed right there, high above the water. The river itself had been backed up by a dam into a stagnant reservoir, and I didn't feel much spirit coming from it. When I reached the top of the southern bluff, there was an open stretch of land to my left where most of the forest had just been cut down. There were plenty of places left to hide my tent from the road though, so I camped there on top of the high river bluff. The trees on the steep slope leading down to the water had not been cut, so there really wasn't much view of the artificial lake that was temporarily drowning the great river.

The next small city was Salisbury, and I don't think you could get away with calling it a large town at all. I came in through its little sister, a large town called Spencer, and made it to the middle of Salisbury by mid-morning. I happened by a wonderful looking diner, and decided to treat myself to breakfast. My waitress looked like she spent half of her income at the beauty parlor. She wore huge, fake blonde curls, thick makeup, gaudy jewelry, and giant fake fingernails. And her name was Barbie! She was totally sweet though. She asked me lots of questions about my travels, and she actually signed up to get my zines.

Barbie gave me directions to the public library, and I went there after breakfast to look up the location of an historical site. During the Civil War, when Union soldiers were captured by the Confederate army, they were taken to prison camps, one of which had been located in Salisbury, NC. One of my ancestors, a man named Wilson P. Burnell, fought in the Civil War. He was wounded and captured in the Battle of the Wilderness. He was briefly imprisoned at Salisbury, but he actually escaped, and walked all the way back to Pennsylvania. The military records don't explain how he found his way home, but family legend has it that he found the Blue Ridge, just a few days walk to the northwest of where he was incarcerated, and followed it all the way back to the North.

Now I have to admit, I'm not really proud that one of my ancestors fought in the Civil War. Obviously, it's a wonderful thing that the slaves were freed, but that's not really what the war was about, and it's frustrating that our public schools teach that grossly oversimplified version of the story.

From the way I understand it, the North had been politically and economically dominant over the South ever since independence. Southerners rebelled because they were sick of being pushed around and used as a resource colony. The politicians and plantation owners were certainly keen to preserve slavery, but any slave owners who actually served in the Confederate army got cushy jobs as officers, where they could stand safely behind the men who were actually killing and being killed. None of the men who did the grueling work of soldiering could afford to own slaves, and the practice of slavery meant that there weren't very many paying jobs available to poor White men. Surely, many of them were vicious racists, but it's ludicrous to imagine that most Confederate soldiers cared enough to risk their lives for the institution of slavery.

It's also a fact that most slaves in that era were used on cotton plantations. It's too cold to grow cotton up North, but that's where almost all the textile mills were located that made the cotton into clothing. The South didn't have the capital to build new textile mills very quickly, and they were actually banned from exporting their cotton to other countries by federal law. With the option to seek other customers legally blocked, cotton producers had no choice but to sell their product to the Northern mills. Naturally, the mill owners took full advantage of the situation, and refused to pay anything but the cheapest prices for Southern cotton. Thus, the North was able to point the finger at the South and judge them as backwards racists, while actually soaking up most of the profits produced by the slaves' unpaid work.

Good old "honest" Abe Lincoln didn't give a rat's ass about Black people. For those who may be skeptical, I have looked up some of his own words:

"My paramount object in this struggle is to save the Union, and is not either to save or destroy slavery. If I could save the Union without freeing any slave, I would do it; and if I could save it by freeing all the slaves, I would do it; and if I could do it by freeing some and leaving others alone, I would also do that. What I do about slavery and the colored race, I do because it helps to save this Union."

Lincoln was another two-faced politician in the long American tradition, but he was also very clever. He knew that the South would not be able to continue supplying its army if the slaves stopped working, and he knew that freed slaves could be used as highly-motivated soldiers in the Union army.

I certainly won't complain that slavery was finally abolished, but I wish we could have found a way to free the slaves without sacrificing more than

600,000 lives on the battlefield. It also frustrates me that my fellow Yankees think we occupy some kind of moral high ground over the Southerners to this day. The Civil War was a horrible, bloody mistake that both sides were equally responsible for. There are crucial lessons to be learned from it, and we aren't going to learn anything if we keep perpetuating false histories.

I don't know if Wilson P. Burnell cared about the plight of the slaves either, but I am very proud to be descended from someone who pulled off such a daring escape. That kind of story gives me goosebumps, and I wish I could find out more about it.

What was it like inside the Salisbury prison camp? How did he escape? Did anyone else come with him? It had taken me about a month to walk across Virginia, but I could use roads and trails. Wilson had to stay hidden in the woods. It must have taken him months to hike from North Carolina to Pennsylvania.

How did he eat? Did he find sympathetic civilians to feed him, or did he live off of wild food sources like fish and paw paws? He also would have had to cross the massive James River. Did he know how to swim, or did he wait until the middle of the night and sneak across a bridge somewhere? I wish I could tell you all about my ancestor's heroic and courageous escape, but the details have been lost in the mists of time.

I found the location of the historic prison camp on a computer, and used my modern map to find it on the ground. The library was in the northwest part of the city, but the prison camp was on the southeast side, so I ended up walking all over Salisbury. Eventually, I found a fancy, metal sign that had been erected by the state historical society. It marked the former location of the prison camp, and gave a brief explanation of what had happened there. There was no remnant left of the prison itself. The sign stood between the road and the parking lot of a large, corporate auto-parts store. It was still cool to stand in that spot and think about my ancestor though.

It was late in the afternoon by the time I finally got out of Salisbury. I was walking down the side of route 29, when motion in my peripheral vision directly above me suddenly caused me to look up. I was so startled, I literally jumped. An enormous stealth bomber had snuck up behind me, and it flew over at an alarmingly low altitude. It was one of those planes with no fuselage, just a big pair of broad wings, ending in a jagged series of triangles on the backside, and it was painted pure black. I had seen pictures of them before, but I had no idea they were so large. I am always intimidated by military equipment, but that one scared the bejeezus out of me. I wanted to go hide under the trees, but there was no point. The giant plane was so silent that it got right on top of me before I even noticed it.

A railroad ran along the left side of the highway, and there were some places where the forest had been left to grow up around the tracks. Eventually I crawled into one of those and made camp.

The next day's walk took me through two more small cities called Kannapolis and Concord. On the way into Kannapolis, I passed miles of poor neighborhoods full of small, modest houses. Most of the center of the city was filled with a series of enormous mill buildings that looked fairly new and clean, but there were no cars in their parking lots, and no clouds rising from their smokestacks. I sat down in front of one for a rest, and I was soon joined by a very talkative, middle-aged woman.

I asked about the mills, and she hung her head and let out a big sigh. Kannapolis had been a major center for textile manufacturing, but all the mills had been owned by just one company, and that company had just moved all its production to a sweatshop somewhere in the Third World. It had been less than a year since the mills had closed. Months later, the city was still in shock, and it was really just beginning to collapse. I could swear I remember her telling me that 12,000 people had just been laid off. Roughly 75,000 people lived in and around Kannapolis. For a city that size to lose 12,000 jobs would be absolutely devastating.

The woman didn't want to talk about that though. She wanted to tell me all about Jesus and the Bible. When I put on my pack and started walking again, she followed me, and continued to preach to me for several blocks. She seemed pretty crazy, and I was starting to wonder if this was going to be another tar pit type situation, but then she offered to buy me lunch. She must not have been *too* crazy if she could afford to buy me lunch, so I went for it.

She led me to a nearby restaurant that was modest, and strangely, dimly-lit. Maybe they were trying to save money on electricity. We both ordered sandwiches, and I ate well she got all worked up telling me about the savior. It's funny how some people act like they are the first ones to ever tell you about Jesus. I was too polite to tell her that I had already heard about the guy hundreds of times, and yet I had still chosen not to become a Christian. She was obviously getting a huge kick out of spreading the good word, so I did my best to humor her. When we were finished, I thanked her graciously, and I was relieved when she didn't try to pursue me any further.

Concord looked like a much more prosperous small city than Kannapolis, but I can't report to you about anything interesting that I experienced there. The next city in my path would be Charlotte, the largest city in North Carolina, but first, I would get to visit my cousin again. His place was on the northeastern outskirts of the Charlotte suburbs, right along the route I was walking. It took me until the last light of dusk to reach his apartment, but I made it. His daughter was twice as big as she had been when I saw her at Christmas time, and now she was toddling all over the place and saying all kinds of things that sounded almost like words. I don't remember exactly how many days I stayed there, but I do remember the calendar turning over to June before I left.

51. SOME PIG, HUMBLE, TERRIFYING

I kept calling Jen's friend from my cousin's house, but I just couldn't get ahold of her. (Let's call her Annie, just so she has a name.) After several days, I just gave up and walked into Charlotte. Something always works out when your life is an adventure. At that point, I had seen it happen enough times that I felt confident.

The Charlotte metro area was home to about 1.3 million people back in 2004, when I passed through. I assume it has grown much larger by now. Roughly half of those people live within the city limits, and the other half inhabit a ring of smaller cities and suburbs that surround Charlotte on all sides. It's the biggest city in North Carolina, and if you were to judge by its skyline, you would think it must be one of the biggest cities in the whole country. A large, dense cluster of very tall, glassy skyscrapers looms over the city. Most of them looked like they had just been built in the last few years before I got there, and they had been positioned in a strangely symmetrical pattern, as if the companies that built them were working together to make the city look especially impressive.

I actually found it intimidating. The purpose of skyscrapers is to demonstrate and celebrate hierarchal power, like the Egyptian Pyramids, only much flimsier. Charlotte had recently become the headquarters of several of the world's richest and most powerful banks. Bankers are our modern culture's equivalent of pharaohs, so it makes sense that their home city would be dominated by impressive monuments to their power.

I made it downtown just a little late for lunch and got a bland sandwich at a boring deli. I wandered around all afternoon, calling Annie every so often, and still failing to get her on the phone. Every part of Charlotte I wandered through appeared to have just been built. I'm pretty sure there was a city there before the 1980's, but it looked as if someone had made a conscious effort to eliminate every single historical structure and replace it with something more opulent-looking. All traces of local culture had also been systematically cleaned up in favor of homogeneity.

By that time, I had really come to appreciate how talkative most Southerners are. While some Yankees are friendly enough to handle brief conversations with strangers, a typical Southerner is actually looking for someone to talk to, and they'll keep going for half an hour if you have the time. Not so in Charlotte. The city was teeming with pedestrians, but I couldn't even get anyone into a conversation, let alone sell them any zines. They didn't really seem to interact with each other either. Everyone was just zoned out in their own world, doing their own thing.

As the day grew late, I wandered away from downtown in a vaguely southeasterly direction. The whole city was so new and clean, it seemed like there wasn't a single blade of grass out of place. The prospect of finding a hiding place for the night seemed very daunting. Eventually, right around sunset, I found a public park where a small patch of trees and bushes had been left to grow wild. The little forest was in the middle of the park, surrounded by an ocean of mowed grass where literally hundreds of affluent-looking people were engaged in various sporting activities. It seemed like everyone was kicking soccer balls or throwing frisbees to each other, and they had all dressed in the right spandex or nylon clothing specifically marketed for whatever sport they were playing. If I wanted to take refuge among those trees, I would have to enter them in front of dozens of witnesses.

I wandered back into the city until I found a pay phone. I failed to get ahold of Annie one more time, and then headed back to the park. I could wait until after dark, when all the athletes went home, but then I would have to use my flashlight to set up my tent. That seemed like it might be even more conspicuous, so I just took a deep breath and strolled right into the little patch of woods. The citizens of Charlotte had been pretending not to notice me all day. Hopefully they would stick to that pattern.

I crawled into a thick stand of rhododendron and waited, hoping an errant ball wouldn't come rolling too close to me. I selected a nice flat spot to lay down, but I waited until there was just enough twilight left to set up my tent. By then, most of the athletes had gone home. I was not very well hidden, and I was too nervous to fall asleep for a long time, but I made it through the night without any disruptions. A light rain passed through just before morning, but it was over before it was time to get up.

I spent the early morning wandering around a bunch more sterile, inhospitable neighborhoods. In the late morning, I found a big corporate organic grocery store, and I set up outside the front door to try to sell zines to the customers who were coming and going. I stayed there all through the middle of the day, and I did manage to sign up a handful of subscribers. The nicest people I met were a pair of very fat women and a fat man who told me that they were all in love with each other and living together as a polygamous family. They would have been happy to put me up for the night, but they lived somewhere way out in South Carolina. I kept calling Annie's phone number, but I was starting to lose hope.

I walked around some more in the late afternoon, and I happened across a store that specialized in maps. As I have mentioned, I love maps, so I browsed for a long time. I already had a map of Charlotte, but I picked up maps of the next three cities I would be visiting- Rock Hill, Spartanburg, and Greenville, all in South Carolina. The store was not a corporate chain, so my ethics prevented me from shoplifting there. I think it was the only time I actually paid for maps on my entire journey.

I didn't like the idea of camping in that same park for a second night in a row, so I went south looking for something better. It was after sunset when I finally found something adequate. This time it was a much smaller city park with swing sets and other children's toys. The back of the park bordered on a powerline corridor with lots of bushes for me to hide in. The park itself was completely empty of people, but several dozen houses looked out over it. I didn't like the idea of people looking out their windows to see me messing around in the bushes under the power lines, so I made for a utility shack in the back corner of the park. I figured I would just hide behind it, out of sight until it got dark enough for people to turn the lights on in their houses.

I had just started into the park when I realized that couple of sketchy-looking teen-age boys were walking towards the same shed from a different direction. They both gave me nervous looks, and it was immediately obvious that they were up to something. I gave them my own nervous look and kept walking. We got closer and closer, and we all kept giving each other that same nervous look, like, "You're not going to rat me out, are you?"

At the last moment, I yielded and sat down at a picnic table. I assumed they were just going to make a drug deal and it wouldn't take long. Sure enough, they went out of sight behind the shed, and emerged just a minute later, walking away in the same direction I had just come from. Then it was my turn to hide behind the shed. I waited until almost dark, and then set up camp under the power lines. It was really pathetic as hiding places go, but I got away with it anyway.

As I lay there in my tent, I was finally able to put my finger on what seemed so weird about Charlotte. I had wandered all over the city and I hadn't found a single poor neighborhood. I hadn't even seen very many poor-looking people. How could that be? Upper-class people can't survive on their own. They require a huge serving class of people to cook in restaurants, stock grocery shelves, build and repair things, and clean up the mess. Obviously the serving class was there, working to make the city function, but where did they live? Were they commuting all the way into Charlotte from the smaller satellite cities? It sounds funny, but I felt really uncomfortable in a city without a ghetto. I decided to give up on Charlotte and get the hell out of there.

I tried calling Annie one more time in the morning, and when she didn't answer, I kept walking south. I made it most of the way to the southern edge of the city when I came to another organic grocery/health food store. I always thought of those as good places to sell zines, so I went inside and started canvassing the customers and the staff. Before long, I met the manager, a young Black woman with short dreadlocks. She was wearing a red, black and green wrist-band, so I said, "Hey! I think we're on the same team," and showed her the sign on my backpack.

She took a real interest in my zine and she told me she thought the store owner would support my efforts too. She asked if her store could purchase a whole stack of them and sell them in their magazine section. I was thrilled by that suggestion, so I sold her 50 zines (25 of each episode) for 50 dollars. She wrote me a check, which I had no way of using, but I thanked her and stashed it in my pack, assuming I would eventually figure out a way to convert it to functional cash.

It was not quite noon, and the store had very few customers. The manager was not very busy, and she was very friendly, so we kept up talking for quite a while. Eventually, I told her about how I was supposed to have a contact in Charlotte, but she never answered the phone, so I had given up, and I was in the process of leaving. I can't remember the exact dialogue, but I ended up saying Annie's name. As soon as I said it, the manager asked, "Oh, is it Annie So-and-So," (naming some actual last name.) Jen had never told me Annie's last name, but the store manager had an employee by that name who was off that day, and she thought we should give her a call just in case.

Now I have chosen not to use Annie's real name, but I can assure you, it was not an uncommon name at all. The chances that it would be the same Annie I was looking for, in a city of 1.3 million people, were not very hopeful. Nonetheless, the manager got her employee on the phone, handed the phone to me, and it actually was Jen's friend! I asked her why she hadn't answered her phone any of the last three dozen times I had called, and she said she never answered the phone when she didn't recognize the number. She told me to wait there and she would come pick me up. The deli at the health food store made me a free roast-beef sandwich while I waited. About 45 minutes later, Annie pulled up, chatted with her coworkers for a while, and then drove me back into Charlotte.

Annie lived on the east side of town, on a street that had recently become a dead end. Her street used to intersect with a major boulevard called Independence, but that street had just been converted into a limited access highway. The DOT hadn't made any physical changes to Independence Boulevard yet. They had just set up jersey barricades all along the sides of it, including right across the mouth of the little side street where Annie lived. Her house was the last one before the barricade, so it was like she lived at the end of a dead-end street. She wasn't close enough to Independence to hear all the roaring traffic though. There was a good little stretch of undeveloped forest between her house and the new highway, and there was also a newly-abandoned strip mall that was still dying on the near side of the highway.

The strip mall had been thriving when people could turn into its parking lot from Independence, but ever since the barriers went up, the only way to get there was to snake through Annie's neighborhood, down to the end of her street and in through the back way. Most of the stores were already boarded up, and the last couple were still having their final close-out sales.

The forested area wrapped around behind the backyard of Annie's house, and she told me that it continued quite a ways in towards the center of the city. Normally, it would be awesome to live right next to an island of forest in the city, but this forest was different. Annie explained that eight women had been murdered in the last five years, and all of their bodies had been found in that little patch of woods. Everyone assumed there was a serial killer at work, but the police hadn't caught anyone yet.

Annie had one housemate who she had not met before they moved in together. They both just needed someone to help pay rent, so they had taken a chance with each other, but there couldn't have been any two less similar people in the whole city. Annie was a total Hippy. She smoked tons of pot, couldn't keep track of anything, and didn't seem to have a care in the world.

Her housemate was possibly the most up-tight, stressed-out person I've ever met. She was a student in business school, and she was obsessed with the idea of financial success.

They had a couple of nice couches, but I had to sleep on the floor in Annie's room, because her housemate couldn't stand to have me around. The idea of anyone getting anything for free made her furious. She was so stressed that she would try to blow off steam by running loud machines. I only stayed with them for two days, but in that time, I saw her mow the lawn twice, and she ran the vacuum cleaner so many times that I lost count. She was way off the deep end. Even sober, she would have been pretty scary, but Annie kept smoking me up with some really heavy-duty marijuana. That made her housemate seem utterly terrifying.

Annie was a bit too flakey and airheaded for me to really make friends with, but she made some significant contributions to my story nonetheless. Firstly, she decided that I should have some pot to smoke on the road, so she gave me one nugget of her hyper-potent CIA stash, and I put it in a cannister in my backpack. Secondly, she updated me that Jen had finally managed to break loose from her old ball and chain up in Maine, and was single for the first time since before I met her. That information, combined with that pot were probably the biggest factors that finally ended the era of my walking adventure about two weeks later.

Lastly, Annie let me know that the conscious hip-hop group, Arrested Development had gotten back together after a ten-year hiatus. They were doing a grand reunion tour, and Charlotte was to be the second stop on their tour. The show was happening the very next night, and Annie actually paid something like 30 bucks for me to have a ticket. It was really sweet of her. I loved AD back in the 90's and it was a total surprise to find out they were getting back together.

Unfortunately, she got me stoned again right before we went to the show, and the pot she smoked was way too strong. AD performed for almost three hours and their show was awesome, but I failed to really enjoy it, because I was too stoned to dance, or even feel comfortable in a large group of people.

After the show, Speech (the lead singer) came out to stand behind a table and sign autographs. I had brought copies of my zines in a backpack, so I waited in the line at the autograph table. When I got to the front of the line, I handed the first two episodes of my zine to Speech. I thanked him for the great performance, and I told him, "Your music has inspired some of us to start our own projects."

I'm not sure why I said that. AD is a conscious group that raps about revolution, equality, and Black empowerment, so I think we are probably on the same team. That said, they were not anywhere on the list of things that inspired me to go walking, and I hadn't even thought of them once since I started walking two years prior. Speech just gave me a blank look that suggested he was thinking about something else and hadn't heard what I said, so I left.

Annie had brought two other friends with her, and we all went to a bar after the show. We got uncomfortably high again in the parking lot outside the bar, and once inside, we immediately attracted the attention of the people at the table next to ours. A fairly ordinary-looking woman, dressed mostly in black was sitting with a short-haired man dressed in a brand-new, very clean Grateful Dead T-shirt. Within minutes of our arrival, they both started making pleasantries with us, and it seemed friendly at first. Then the woman got a call on her cell phone and went outside, and the man pulled his chair over to sit right next to me. He continued pretending to be friendly, but he kept asking me where he could get some pot, and it was terribly obvious that he was an undercover cop. Everything from his posture and mannerisms to his vocabulary and tone of voice was screaming, "I'm a cop pretending to be a Deadhead!"

Of course, I didn't know where to get pot in Charlotte. Annie was the one who had the pot, but the cop had latched on to me, and he was ignoring the three women I had come in with. I did my best to keep his attention focused on me, but I didn't return the fake friendly banter. I just kept flatly refusing to hook him up with a pot dealer, and hinting as firmly as I could that he should fuck off and go back to his table. He was a really dumb guy, even by cop standards, but he could tell I was stoned, and he wasn't going to give up. He kept going through the same cycle where he would make about two sentences worth of small talk, and then he would resume interrogating me about where he could get some pot. It got so annoying that I finally said, "Look buddy. I can tell you're a cop. Even if I knew where to get some pot, I wouldn't tell you." He refused to break character. He denied that he was a cop and acted really insulted for a minute. Then he changed the subject.

Eventually, his partner came back inside. She pulled a chair over to our table too and started pretending to make friends with the ladies. Her act was much more convincing, and I realized the she would have totally fooled me if she hadn't brought Bozo along. He just couldn't keep his stupid mouth shut, and it only took a few minutes before he went back to interrogating me. I was having a miserable time, and I eventually lost my temper and snapped at the poor, mentally-challenged cop. I yelled something like, "Look officer, I'm not going to hook you up with any pot! Now would you leave me alone! You fuckin' cop!" He responded by acting offended again, and this time he accused *me* of being a cop.

At that point, Annie and her friends finally noticed how awkward things had gotten and suggested that we relocate to a different bar. I followed them out to the parking lot, and thankfully the cops didn't follow us outside.

I didn't feel like going to any more bars. It was already after midnight, I was tired, and I had big plans for the next day. I had just received an email that afternoon from a friend back in Chapel Hill. It was the guy who had hitch-hiked back from Charlotte with the axe, and he had written to hook me up with some of his rebel friends in the city. I was excited to call them in the morning, so I thanked Annie and hugged her goodnight. She returned the hug and failed to remind me that the door would be locked back at her house.

It took me about 45 minutes to walk back to Annie's house where I discovered that I was locked out. The lights were on inside so I gave the door a polite knock. I waited five minutes, and then gave a slightly louder and more insistent knock. The psycho housemate still didn't answer, so I gave up. I was already standing on a screened-in porch, and it wasn't very cold out, so I just laid down on the hardwood floor of the porch. My hope was that I might be able to catch a few minutes of sleep there until Annie got home and let me in.

After about twenty minutes, a car showed up in the driveway, but it wasn't Annie. Instead, the porch lights flicked on to reveal an aggressive White dude who I hadn't met before. He identified himself as the psycho housemate's boyfriend, and he got right in my face, telling me I had to leave. His hair was trimmed very short, and he was dressed like a total cracker, with some brand-name, collared shirt, tucked into a pair of khaki pants. He was pretty robust, and he struck me as the kind of guy who spends hours working out in a gym, but has no clue how to use a shovel. I tried to stand my ground and explain that I was Annie's guest, but he wasn't having it. He threatened to call the cops.

I didn't like it there at all, so I agreed to leave as soon as he let me in to get my backpack and all my stuff. He refused and repeated his threat to call the cops. He had been doing that bully thing where he stood so close to me that his chest bumped into mine, and I had been slowly backing away, but now I had to stand my ground. I poked him in his fake chest muscles with the tip of my finger and told him he might as well call the cops. If he intended to steal my belongings, then he was the one who was going to get in trouble. It took a couple repetitions for that idea to penetrate his tiny brain, but he eventually figured it out.

He let me in and followed me to Annie's room where he stood in the doorway and continued his intimidating act. It only took me a couple minutes to roll up my sleeping bag, and get my pack all strapped shut. It was obvious that I was packing up quickly and efficiently, but the dog-brained boy couldn't resist barking at me to hurry up a couple of times. After the second prompt, I gave him a steady stream of verbal abuse until I was finished packing, and then I kept it going all the way out the door. I probably failed to inspire him to commit suicide like I was hoping, but at least I got away without having to hear his stupid voice again.

There I was, out on the street with my backpack in America's least hospitable city at 1:30 in the morning. I had a number for some new people to stay with, and they were on the same rebel team as I was. It would be rude to call so late and probably wake them up, but they would understand it was an emergency. They had probably dealt with lots of weirder situations before, but it wasn't just the prospect of a rude introduction that dissuaded me from finding a pay phone and calling them. There was another factor that made it seem like a really bad idea.

Every so often, the national network of anarchist rebels would schedule what they called a "national day of action." Emails would go out to rebel cells in every city requesting that everyone help make some political point by targeting a particular company or government agency with protests, vandalism, or some type of disruptive action.

For weeks leading up to that night, the national network had been calling for a national day of action against the Free Trade Area of the Americas. That was the night that all good anarchists were supposed to be out spray-painting messages on overpasses, or vandalizing the property of a list of companies who had been identified as the puppet-masters behind the FTAA. All the major urban police departments in the country would be on the lookout for suspicious behavior that night, and I would have to walk across the city with a red, black, and green sign stitched onto my backpack at an hour when very few people other than police would be out and about. It was also quite likely that Charlotte would be home to some of the targeted corporations, so my would-be hosts were likely to be busy making mischief at that very moment. It just wasn't a good idea to call them and introduce myself that night.

That meant the murder woods was my last option. Instinctively, I turned left towards the darkness. Normally, a dark patch of forest in a big city would feel like a welcome oasis to me, but not this time. Evil spirits oozed out of the darkness and onto the street like a thick, slow-moving liquid. It could have just been my imagination. I had just learned about the murders, and I was still pretty stoned, so my fear wasn't just coming out of the blue. I shuffled slowly up the dead-end street, feeling nothing but dread at the prospect of entering the forest on my left.

Without really thinking, I walked all the way to the dying strip mall at the corner of Independence. Even at that late hour, there were still some cars racing by on the makeshift highway. I walked right up to the jersey barricade and leaned my belly against it. Looking left, I realized I could see the office towers downtown, glowing against the night sky. They looked ominous, but I just stared at the view for several minutes.

The strip mall was still illuminated by a system of street lights in the parking lot. I felt an idle sense of curiosity about the place and started towards it. I wasn't really that curious, and it wasn't an appropriate time for exploring. I was obviously just stalling the inevitable decision about where I would attempt to rest my head that night.

I had to cut that whimsical little stroll short when I realized there was a security guard standing watch over one of the stores. One of those discount department stores that provides housewares for lower-income people was still trying to sell off all its stock before it vacated the building. A big plastic sign hung from the front of the store declaring, "EVERYTHING MUST GO!" Apparently, cheap bedroom and kitchen sets were enough of a target for looters that it warranted hiring a night guard. The man had spotted me and he was looking at me, but we were too far apart to really shout to one another. Even from that distance he looked nervous, but I suppose working as a security guard would do that to anyone.

I turned and went back in the same direction I had just come from so as to avoid disturbing the guard. Then I walked around behind the strip mall, where the loading docks were also flooded with electric light. I walked about a quarter of the way along the backside of the composite of flimsy buildings, and then I did it. Before my fear could catch up to me, I abruptly turned left and plunged into the murder woods.

I only went in a few paces, just far enough to be hidden in the darkness. Now I was hidden from the security guard and anyone else out in the lights, but anything looking out from the forest would still see a big human silhouette, backlit by the array of lights at the strip mall. As soon as that thought occurred to me, I took off my backpack as quickly as I could, and crawled right into a large bush. Thankfully, it didn't have any thorns. As my eyes adjusted, I figured out the lay of the land. I was on a little strip if level ground that surrounded the parking lot. Just beyond where I had stopped, the ground sloped down into a little ravine, and a much higher hill rose steeply above the far side of the ravine.

Again, it might have just been my imagination, but I felt sure that something malevolent was out there. I felt like I was engulfed in the essence of evil. It knew I was there, and it was checking me out. The fact that I was not female like all the murder victims didn't give me one iota of reassurance. Thinking logically, it didn't make much sense that a misogynistic serial killer would be motivated by some evil, forest-dwelling spirit. That type of behavior seems much more like a predictable byproduct of the sick, patriarchal culture that our ancestors brought to this continent. Still, logical considerations like that provide very little reassurance when you're scared shitless.

As you know, I am pretty open to the idea of spiritual energy. I have travelled all over, and I've experienced all kinds of spirits, but they are almost always neutral or even nice. I can count on my fingers then number of places I have encountered frightening spirits, and the murder woods in Charlotte was one of the absolute worst. There was one place outside the town where I went to college that was even creepier, but I certainly never tried to spend the night out there.

I was too frightened to look around for a comfortable spot, or even unroll my sleeping bag. It was a warm-enough night that I didn't need it anyway. I just laid down right there across the thick stems of my bush and tried to calm down. It was by far the most uncomfortable spot I had ever attempted to sleep. It didn't provide any refuge whatsoever from evil spirits, but it was very unlikely that any humans would ever notice me there. I laid there with my feet pointing out into the darkness, and my head pointing back towards the light of the strip mall. Tingling with fear, and laying on the lumpiest surface ever, I couldn't even come close to sleep.

After a while, I heard something rustling in the leaves up on the hill across the ravine. The sound continued, and after a few minutes, I realized it was moving slowly down the hill. For the next fifteen or twenty minutes, it kept coming down the hill. It was still a ways off, but I couldn't help noticing that it was moving directly towards me.

I have spent many a night in the forest, so I know that it's normal for nocturnal critters to go rustling through the leaves all night long. I also know that everything sounds much larger than it really is in the dark. Mice can sound like cats. Cats sound like bears, and bears sound like dragons. Logic told me that whatever creature was crawling through the leaves had to be pretty small, with very short legs, because it was making such a slow pace. Logic also told me that there was probably a small brook in the bottom of the ravine, and the animal was probably headed there to get a drink of water. Once again, logic had zero effect on the terror that was surging through every cell of my mind and body.

The rustling sound reached the bottom of the ravine and continued. For the next ten minutes or so, I couldn't tell what direction it was moving in, because the nearby lip of the ravine blocked the sound waves from reaching my ears directly, and I could only hear them reflected off the surrounding leaves and tree trunks. Then it emerged onto the nearby lip of the ravine. The sound was much louder and closer now, and it was still making a b-line directly towards me. I had acquired a new pocket knife since I lost the last one to the Raleigh police, so I pulled it out of my pocket, opened the blade, and squeezed the handle tightly in my trembling hand. I sat up and surveyed all the stems around me to make sure I would have a clear swing when I went to stab with my knife.

I had never been so terror-stricken in all my life. It didn't make any sense that some tiny animal would be attracted to me in the night, let alone crawl across a football field's worth of forest to get to me. Something more sinister had to be happening, but I couldn't imagine what. My mind was so flooded with fear, that I couldn't really imagine anything at all. I could stab a physical object with my knife, but I couldn't stab an evil spirit, could I? I had zero experience confronting evil spirits. I had no idea what to expect. I just sat there with my heart thundering, clutching my knife and trembling.

The rustling sound closed the last of the distance between us at the same excruciatingly slow pace. It reached a point that was maybe a leg's length beyond my feet and stopped. Then it made a gentle little cooing sound like a pigeon call. I had forgotten to breathe. The thing cooed like a pigeon several more times. It appeared to be talking to me, and its voice was incredibly reassuring. I was still too frightened to respond, but I realized quickly that it was just a little bird, and it wasn't going to hurt me. It stopped there, and I'm guessing it went to sleep because it didn't make another sound for the rest of the night. I know, because I never did fall asleep until after the dawn finally broke. The place was just too creepy.

The night seemed to last forever, but in reality, it couldn't have been much more than three hours. It was already about 2:00am when I got there, and the nights are very short that close to the summer solstice. As soon as the dawn broke, a nest full of large, black ants awakened to find me lying right in their usual sphere of operations. They had to crawl all over me to figure out what was going on, but I was so incredibly tired that I fell asleep anyway. I slept for several hours with the tickle of ant feet working its way into my dreams. A steady stream of them crawled across my face and hands, but they were not the type of ants that bite very often, and none of them bit me that morning. The daylight washed away enough of my terror that I could finally sleep, and I actually remember feeling thankful for the ants as they were a sign of daylight and safety.

The mysterious pigeon still made no sense. Any biologist who's worth their salt will tell you that no small prey animal would seek out the company of a large predator and sleep next to it. Nor do pigeons use vocal sounds to communicate with humans. At the time, I decided that the forest really was haunted by some spirit that was so evil that it frightened the pigeon too. When the little bird noticed me come into the forest, it decided it would rather take its chances sleeping next to me than be alone in that creepy place. I know the animal scientists are groaning at how hokey that sounds. I can readily admit, I really have no idea why that happened. All I can say for sure is that something beyond the realm of normal scientific understanding took place in the web of Charlotte's murder woods that night.

52. ANARCHIST RAILROAD

I awoke in the late morning and set out in search of a pay phone. I tried to leave all the ants where they belonged, but I kept finding more of them crawling on me for the next hour. When I found a phone, I called my new contact, and they answered. They had been told to expect my call, and they greeted me with great hospitality. I followed their directions, and found their house in less than two hours. It was a modest house in a neighborhood full of other modest houses. I wouldn't call it a ghetto, but I could definitely picture working-class people living there.

I was really impressed with the crew that hosted me on my final days in Charlotte. In those days, almost everyone on the rebel team took great effort to make themselves look counter-cultural. Dreadlocks and other bizarre Punk haircuts were the norm. facial tattoos and big, disgusting piercings were common, and most everyone wore strangely modified clothing that was often covered with patches displaying abrasive messages or images. I loved to see people adorned in those styles, but I never wanted to dress that way myself. Ever since I discovered the thrill and freedom of the rebel lifestyle, I wanted to share it with as many other people as I could. I figured I would get a lot more people to take me seriously if I didn't look like a scary freak. All four of my hosts there in Charlotte had come to the same conclusion. They could blend into almost any crowd of people, and I commended them for their strategic fashion choices.

I would soon find out that was only the beginning. That crew turned out to be like a cabal of elite double agents. With friendly smiles and helpful attitudes, they had infiltrated some of the highest echelons of Charlotte's corporate power structure. They had worked their way into positions where they could literally wreak havoc on corporate America, but they were playing their hands very conservatively. They had inspired a number of very important people to confide in them, and they had gathered a huge collection of fascinating secrets. They believed that if they gathered enough information, they would eventually be able to mastermind some kind of diabolical operation. They didn't even want to destroy the corporations. They were so ambitious, they hoped they might actually be able to bend powerful companies to their own ends, transforming them into agents of egalitarian social change.

My mind was blown. Obviously, I can't tell you any more details, but it was another one of those really inspiring situations like I witnessed in Washington DC. The empire can hire huge numbers of intelligent people to help advance its agenda, but I'm pretty sure that the very brightest people are all working to undermine the empire and liberate humanity.

I stayed with those people for three days, and in that time, I only witnessed one thing that it would be wise to write about. One member of the team had obtained keys to a wealthy person's house, and they happened to know that person was out of town for several days. We piled into a car, drove out to their posh suburban neighborhood, and let ourselves into the house.

We brought our own load of ingredients into the kitchen where we started baking piles of cookies, pizza, and a cake. Before long, car-loads of other anarchists and local poor kids started to show up with beer, hard liquor, chips, and other party favors. The host crew was careful not to let most people into the house so they could avoid making a big mess. Basically, the guests were only allowed inside to use the bathroom or help in the kitchen. No one really minded being denied access to the house though, because the party centered around a giant swimming pool in the backyard. My hosts had brought an extra pair of swim trunks for me so I could go swimming too.

From the backyard, I could see right into the windows of several other neighboring houses, and it made me nervous. We had a raging party of about thirty people who obviously didn't belong there. Surely some neighbor would notice and call the cops. I asked my hosts about it and they said, "Don't worry. We've taken care of everything."

No one ever told me why they were so confident that we wouldn't get in trouble, but they were right. After supper, most of the guests went home. We stayed behind for a couple hours cleaning the kitchen and the back yard until everything looked exactly as it had before. Then we locked up and went home.

The night before I left, my hosts called ahead to another team of rebels in Rock Hill, South Carolina to let them know I was coming. They gave me the number for that house and wished me the best. Rock Hill was a little bit further away than I wanted to walk in one day, but it was definitely less than two full days walk, so I waited until late morning to leave, expecting to camp out for one night in between.

The day started out hot and sunny, but it kept getting windier as the afternoon progressed. By the time I went back past the store where the manager had bought 50 zines, the sky was starting to cloud up. A few miles beyond that store, I turned west on a road towards the South Carolina border. I had been in North Carolina for over half a year at that point, and I was excited to add a new state. My plan was to camp in the first nice place I came to in South Carolina, but it didn't work out that way.

I was still in the suburbs, but they were starting to thin out. The winds from the west reached an ominous level. The sky was threatening something. I was just starting to think about supper when I came to the first big stretch of undeveloped land. Everything up near the road had been clear-cut, but there was a thick, young forest behind it. It wasn't too hard to pick my way across the clear-cut. Most of the slash had been bulldozed up into piles, and the cut was so recent that the new berry canes hadn't grown to full size yet. The forest in back looked like it had grown for about 25 years since the last time it was cut, but the trees weren't so close together that I couldn't move between them. I walked in just a little ways and stopped to eat some supper.

I hadn't even set my pack down before I heard the first roll of thunder from the west. I proceeded to get my food out and eat. That couldn't have taken more than twenty minutes, but in that short time, the thunder got louder and closer at an alarming rate. As I packed up my food stores, I realized I had better set up my tent right away.

The young forest was full of fallen logs and underbrush, so I didn't even waste time looking for a spot in there. I camped right in the middle of an old skidder trail where the ground was clear and grassy. Raindrops had already started falling by the time I finished setting up my tent. I got the poncho all tucked around my backpack and made it into the tent before I got totally soaked.

The wind went absolutely crazy, and thunder cracked all around me from nearby sources. I love thunder, and that was some of the most awesome thunder I've ever experienced. The sound was so loud, I could feel it thumping against my body. I unzipped the door to my tent just enough to peek out and it was thrilling. The wind was whipping in all directions, and the flexible young trees were bending to amazing extremes. A couple of times, I even got to see portions of bright, crooked shafts of lighting between the dancing trees.

I watched for a couple minutes until the rain suddenly increased to a deluge, and I had to zip my little window shut to avoid drowning. For the next ten minutes, the rain came down like a waterfall, while the wind and thunder continued as they had been doing. It was a truly impressive storm. After the crescendo, I got another 30 or 40 minutes of lighter, but steady rain. There was a little less wind, and the sound of thunder retreated steadily to the east.

There were still several hours of daylight left, but I decided I might has well stay there for the night. When the rain was mostly finished, I dug deep into my backpack and pulled out a little wooden pipe. I had bought it way back in New Haven when I was staying with the stoners there, and I had carried it with me ever since. I know that's silly, but the little thing probably didn't even weigh a whole ounce. I got out a little piece of Annie's excessively potent weed and proceeded to get all ashamed about all the things I had recently said and done, and nervous about everything for the next four hours or so.

I had almost made it to South Carolina, and I got there early the next morning. There were still a lot of suburban houses, but the forest around them was thick and shady. I descended into a deep valley to a raging torrent of muddy water. Like most of North Carolina's cities, Charlotte is centered on the top of a hill. Most of the water that runs off the city flows south and accumulates into a large stream called Sugar Creek. Then it flows south into South Carolina. Much of the water from the previous night's storm might have sunk into the thirsty ground, but the rain that fell on the streets, buildings, and parking lots of the city went straight into the creek. When I got to it the next morning, it was a gushing milk-chocolate torrent, complete with lumber scraps and all manner of other trash. It wasn't enough of a flood to endanger the bridge I took to cross it, but it was a thrilling sight.

It was a fairly steep climb up the next ridge, and just before the top, I came to a town right on the slope. The town was called Fort Mill, and it was full of beautiful old houses that had obviously been built before the area was engulfed by Charlotte's suburban ring. The town continued to the top of the hill where there was a little bakery. I stopped in for breakfast, and the girl working the counter made my heart beat a little quicker. She wasn't very busy, and she chatted me up for quite a while. I signed her up for some zines, and she gave me a refrigerator magnet that I still have to this day. It's a red heart shape with the words "I Love Fort Mill, SC" on it. I stayed and flirted with her until a stream of customers started distracting her, and then I rambled on.

The next valley was even deeper with a grand river called the Catawba in the bottom of it. The Catawba flows down from the North Carolina mountains to join two other grand rivers in South Carolina and become the Santee. Where I crossed it, a broad shelf of bedrock made a shallow riverbed with chunks of rock sticking out all over. Some of the rocks were smooth, and others were jagged, but they were all arranged in neat sedimentary layers running perpendicular to the direction of the current. The river braided its way between the rocks in short bursts of whitewater connecting deeper, calmer pools. It was possibly the most beautiful river I had seen on my whole walk, and I lingered on the bridge for a while.

Not long after the river, I found myself on a long, ugly commercial strip leading into Rock Hill. About 150,000 people live in and around Rock Hill, but I would also count those people as part of the Greater Charlotte metro area. When I got to the older part of town, I called my contact, but I got no answer. It was only mid-afternoon, so I wandered around to kill some time. I had only wandered a few blocks when I stumbled upon a good-looking burger place, so I stopped there and sprang for a burger. They didn't mind that I kept hanging out there for a couple hours, and when I called my contact back, he answered the phone.

The next stop on the anarchist railroad was a dorm suite at a place called Winthrop University. My hosts were two enthusiastic young guys who were about halfway through college. They considered themselves anarchists, and they told me there were two more such people on their campus. They were very excited to host me, and they called both of their friends and encouraged them to come meet me. One of them actually made it over, so I got to meet three quarters of the anarchists at Winthrop University. They couldn't wait until night time. They had something they wanted to show me, but they wanted to keep it a secret until I could see for myself. All I knew was that we had to wait for it to get dark.

They actually made me wait until a couple hours after dark, and then we went out walking. Partway across town, we slipped onto a railroad track that quickly exited the glow of the streetlights and into an industrial zone. There was a little bit of moonlight, and our eyes slowly adjusted to make use of it. We made our way along the back side of what looked like a very long warehouse. We had walked past a spectacularly long stretch of the same building, and there was still more ahead of us, when they stopped and turned towards it. All three of my new friends had come along, and one of them said, "Here we are."

Right there, a ladder made of metal railing led to the top of the building, so we climbed up it. Then we walked across the flat top for what felt like a couple minutes. We came to a small rectangle of metal that was raised above the surface a little bit. Just as I realized it was a hatch, one of the guys lifted up on the handle and it swung open. "It's not locked!" He said, mischievously. He climbed down the ladder into the building, and we all followed. Only once we were inside and the hatch was closed did we turn on our lights. They also waited until that moment to tell me what we were actually up to.

We were in an abandoned textile mill, and they just wanted to show me around. Very few things are a fun as exploring an abandoned building. These guys really knew how to entertain a guest!

The building was two stories tall, and it covered several acres of land, so we had to stick together or we literally might not have found each other again. They had already explored every room themselves, so they mostly let me lead the way. The building was laid out in a generally grid-like pattern of hallways connecting dozens of big empty rooms. Many of the rooms had long rows of identical tables, or rows of sturdy metal stands where you could tell machines had been mounted, but the machines themselves were gone, presumably taken to the company's new factories when it relocated overseas. When I pointed that out, my hosts apologized. When they first discovered the abandoned factory, they were also disappointed to find it gutted of all but a few interesting artifacts.

After about an hour of exploring, I found a line of rooms that looked like laboratories. I opened up the cupboards in one of them to discover a whole array of glass containers full of various strangely-colored liquids. I got very excited and called out, "Whoa! Have you guys seen all these chemicals?"

They had. They told me they had found various stashes of chemicals all over the building, and determined that most of them were different colors of dye used for dying fabric. There were a few mysterious chemicals that they couldn't identify, but their best guess was that those were just the ingredients needed to make more dyes. They had already gathered up gallons of dyes and stored them at a friend's house. It seemed like an incredible resource that shouldn't go to waste, so they had been doing research to see if there was some way to use the dyes to stencil messages or images onto clothing. They were also looking for other people who might have a use for clothing dyes so they could distribute the abundant resource. Unfortunately, there wasn't any fabric left lying around, or they could have really gone into business

We explored the building for another hour or so, and then returned to their dorm. When we got back, I took out my address book and gave them contacts for a number of people up and down the East Coast who might be excited to get ahold of some free fabric dye. I only stayed with those guys for one night, but it was a night of unforgettable fun.

53. SPIRIT OF THE SANTEE

In the big picture, I needed to go west, but I had not yet seen downtown Rock Hill, so I started my day by detouring several miles to the southeast. There were no tall buildings in the city, but there was a dense cluster of picturesque old buildings downtown. Some were made of grey stone. Some were made of red brick, and others were a composite of both. The oldest part of the city sat on a level ridgetop between two valleys. The slope dropped off fairly steeply towards the Catawba River on the northeast, while a gentler slope led down into a more shallow valley to the southwest.

Mid-day, and the afternoon were steaming hot, as one might expect June weather to be in South Carolina. I made it to a large town called York in the late afternoon. I stopped for dinner in one of those family-style restaurants where you get an entrée and two sides, but I have to admit the food wasn't very good. Back outside, I got a taste for what kind of town York was when a group of four men rolled down main street on four-wheelers. They stopped at a hardware store where they appeared to be just running a simple errand. York was another hilltop town with spectacular long views to the south and east.

There had been a few last traces of suburban sprawl leading up to the east side of York, but out the west end of town, I made it into real open country. Frequent farms were separated by big swaths of heavily-logged forests. Abundant rainfall and a very long warm season make South Carolina a densely-forested place. Cutting down trees appears to be one of the main jobs available to rural men there, and they keep most of the state pretty closely shaven.

For the second time in three days, I walked across a clear-cut to camp in the forest beyond. This time I walked down a pretty good hill to camp well below the road, and the forest I camped in was much older. I would guess it had been maybe 60 or 70 years since the last time it had been cut over. The soil had recovered to the point that there were no traces of old skidder trails or slash piles. A small brook splashed past my campsite, and its bottom was covered with a bright orange deposit of silt that had just washed down from the new clear-cut up the hill.

The next day was hot and beautiful just like the last. In the morning, I passed through a very attractive small town called Sharon. It was also on a ridgetop, and it seemed to be perfectly self-sufficient, with one small version of each type of store that a town would need. In the early afternoon, I came to another very similar little ridgetop town. This one was called Hickory Grove, and it had a café where I stopped in and got a sandwich.

A very tidy-looking middle-aged White man took the table next to mine, and he struck up a conversation. He was an archetypal Southern gentleman, and he was naturally curious to hear about my walking adventure. After a couple minutes, he asked me what was the significance of the red, black, and green flower sign covering most of the back of my backpack. For some reason, I had never anticipated anyone asking me to explain the sign, and I had no idea what to say. I quickly improvised the line, "It's an anarchist rose."

The man gave me a quizzical look and said, "Hmm." Then he turned away and our conversation was over.

For some reason, out of all the dumb things I've said and done in my life, that remains one of the most embarrassing. For one thing, my flower didn't resemble the shape of a rose at all. If anything, it looked more like a lily. More importantly, I was committed to a strategy of never using the "A" word in front of strangers, because most people had such a negative misunderstanding of what it meant. My goal was to use my lifestyle to demonstrate the appeal of anarchism and avoid repelling people with scary vocabulary. I have said many more dumb things in the eighteen years since then, but for some reason by subconscious won't let that one go. Even now, that memory frequently pops into my head, and my heart floods with intense feelings of embarrassment. Maybe that guy was really important, and if I hadn't made such a dim-witted impression on him, I would have come closer to saving the world.

I walked through blazing heat and beautiful scenery until evening. The road I travelled had very little traffic. At times, I would not see a car go by for half an hour. The Piedmont of up-state South Carolina is an endless series of broad valleys and ridges. The slopes don't usually get very steep, but the difference in elevation between the ridgetops and the valley bottoms is significant. I would spend a half an hour descending into the valley bottoms, cross a creek, and then spend another half hour ascending to the next ridgetop. The views from the ridgetops were long and spectacular in spite of how badly the forests had been devastated by logging.

I didn't detour to make a personal appearance there, but I passed within a few miles of the King's Mountain Battlefield, a much-overlooked battle of the Revolutionary War. The British had already lost a great deal of control over New England and the Mid-Atlantic regions, but a stronghold of loyal Tories in the southernmost colonies of Georgia and South Carolina gave them hope for a rally. They were not aware that a formidable army of Southern Rednecks had amassed in the Appalachians and was making its way down the Piedmont. The Rednecks caught the Brits by surprise and defeated them soundly at King's Mountain, and then again at the nearby Battle of Cowpens. They sent the surviving British soldiers packing back to the coast, and brought America one step closer to freedom. I like to remind Americans that before our politicians trained Northerners and Southerners to hate each other, we all fought together to liberate ourselves from the British Empire.

As the sun sank low in the west, I came to the top of a somewhat steeper hill where I could actually catch a distant view of a great river in the bottom of the next valley. It was the Broad River, the second one of the three great forks that combine to make the Santee. When I reached the bottom of the hill, there was a nice little dirt parking lot on the right, just before the bridge. A strip of beautiful old trees had been left along the riverbank and it looked like a perfect spot to camp, but there was already a guy there fishing. He looked like the friendly type of country boy who wouldn't take any issue with me camping, but it was just my policy to always keep my camping spots a secret from everyone, so I climbed down over the embankment on the left side of the road instead.

I was in the middle of eating supper when I heard the man's truck start up and drive away. The riverbank on my side of the road was too lumpy and choked with brush to make an attractive campsite, so after I finished supper, I crossed over to the little parking lot that had probably been cleared for fishing access. I followed a well-worn fisherman's trail upstream until I was a good distance away from the quiet highway. I found a very comfortable spot to set up my tent on the soft ground just a few paces in from the trail. Once that was done, I sat down to enjoy the view.

The riverbank was an almost vertical cliff made of slippery clay that dropped about the length of my body before it reached the water's surface. I sat with my feet dangling over the edge and smoked some more pot. This time I managed to control my dose enough to avoid freaking out with paranoia. The mighty spirit of the majestic river kept me on a positive track too. The water was turbid and swift. It was probably still charged up from the storms two nights before. There weren't any rapids right there, but the current was so swift that the river's surface churned with ripples and swirling little whirlpools. I am endlessly thrilled by big rivers, but I hadn't actually found a camping spot on the shore of a mighty river since that night in Hartford on the banks of the Connecticut. As I sat there admiring the Broad River, I decided that this was among the loveliest campsites I had found on my entire voyage.

Even after the sun sank behind the ridge on the far side of the river, it was still hot out, and it didn't take me long to decide I could use a swim. There were plenty of sturdy tree roots sticking out of the clay cliff that I could use to climb up and down, so I peeled off my slimy clothes and went for it. The water was too muddy to see through, so I was quite curious how deep it was. I had assumed it would come up to my thighs, or maybe my waist, but as I lowered myself into the current, it pulled my legs downstream before my feet could find the bottom. In the next moment, I found myself in a fully horizontal position, right at the surface of the river, and clinging to the root with both hands to avoid being washed away. The cool water was gloriously refreshing, and it was also really fun to feel the powerful current tugging at my body and swishing me back and forth.

I was still very curious to find out how deep the river was, so I kept thrashing and kicking, trying to orient my body in an upright position so my feet could find the bottom. I literally couldn't do it though. The current was just too strong. I looked behind me and saw that roots were sticking out of the clay bank as far as the eye could see. A bit further downstream, there was a huge, sturdy root that stuck way out over the river, just above the height of the water. I decided to let go of the root I was on, and catch that one as I floated by it.

It was exhilarating to let mighty river current take me. Once my top end was no longer anchored to a fixed point, I was quickly able to orient my body into an upright position. When my feet finally touched the bottom, only my head was sticking out of the water. I was amazed. If the river was that deep right on the very edge, how deep must it be out in the middle? It was mind-boggling to try to imagine just how much water was surging down the Broad River that evening.

It was awesome to feel my feet slide so quickly across the smooth, clay bottom. In a few more seconds, I reached the big root. As soon as I grabbed ahold of it, my legs flipped back up to the river's surface. That root was so close to the water that I could hold onto it with one hand and submerge my head. I gave my hair a thorough washing, and I said many prayers of love and thanks to the river while I was completely inside of it.

Eventually, I climbed back up the slippery cliff on a series of exposed tree roots. My arms and legs got covered with bright orange mud, but at least I had gotten all the old sweat washed off myself. I didn't want to get my sleeping bag all muddy, so I sat there naked until I had dried off enough to scrape most of the mud off. Due to that notorious southern humidity, I had to wait a long time before I was dry enough, but I didn't mind. That was such a beautiful place that it felt like a privilege just to sit there and watch the stars come out. Nothing brings on a peaceful sleep better than a good swim, so I got plenty of restful sleep that night.

It was already hot by the time the sun came up the next morning. By the time I stopped to eat breakfast, it was clear that this was going to be the hottest day yet. I had not figured out a way to filter water out of the Broad River while clinging by tree roots to a slippery cliff, so my water bottle was almost empty. This was a problem I was going to have to solve right away if I intended to survive the sauna-like weather.

Before long, I noticed a guy out in his backyard watering his garden. He already had the hose running, so I yelled hello and waved to him. When he responded with a friendly gesture, I walked around the side of the house to the backyard. He was happy to fill my water bottle, and he picked a fresh cucumber and gave that to me too.

He was a young guy, not much older than me, and he let me know right away that he was a preacher at a small church in the nearby town of Gaffney. We enjoyed a couple minutes of friendly conversation, but things suddenly turned sour when he started preaching at me.

He wanted to make sure I understood that we are all born sinners, but I disagreed. I believe that we are all born with the instincts to live in perfect morality, but our sick culture beats that out of us at a young age and trains us to be sinners. Neither of us would back down, and my temper flared up so suddenly that it surprised both of us. After about three rounds of debate, I was shouting in an angry tone. When he still insisted that we were sinners, I shouted "Fuck you! No we're not!" and I stomped away up the road.

It took a couple minutes for my adrenaline to subside, but once it did, I felt horribly embarrassed for the second day in a row. What kind of asshole flips out and cusses at the preacher man? Clearly he was wrong, but my hysterical behavior had only helped to prove his point. He had filled my water bottle and given me a cucumber. He was a nice guy who was only repeating the dumb things his masters had trained him to say. I was acting like a real Yankee again, and I felt ashamed of myself.

As the day wore on, I kept thinking about it, and I realized what had happened. Back when I was a student at the University of Wyoming, a couple of the local cowboys murdered one of my fellow students for being gay. His name was Matthew Shepherd, and for some reason, his murder became a nation-wide media spectacle.

For some perverse reason, that attracted a swarm of virulent, gay-hating Christians to our town. One church actually rented a billboard along the highway leading into Laramie and painted it to say, "Matthew Shepherd has been in hell for __ days." Every single day, someone would climb up to the sign and add one to the number of days they claimed he had been in hell.

I already had a bunch of gay friends before that, and I made a bunch more through the resulting campaign to pass a hate crimes ordinance in the city council. Many of those people shared heart-wrenching stories with me about growing up in churches that devastated their self-worth and drove them to the verge of suicide. I also heard stories of queer people who did commit suicide after being totally overwhelmed by the judgment of nasty churches. The whole situation left me with a really disgusting impression of Christianity.

That poor guy in his backyard in South Carolina hadn't said anything about gay people, but for whatever reason, his claim that we are all born sinners pressed the button that brought all that righteous anger out of me. It was an awkward mistake. It was another blown opportunity to spread my ideas through friendly conversation, but at least I was able to forgive myself and move on.

In the years since my walk, I figured out why so many Christians are so homophobic. For every man who comes forward to confess that he was abused by the clergy as a child, there must be dozens more who are too frightened to speak up, and there must be even more whose conscious minds won't even let them remember what happened to them. With so many men sharing that terrible experience of male-on-male sex, it's no wonder they think of it as such a scary and dangerous thing.

In reality, that's probably the root cause of most of the really virulent homophobia we see in our culture, church-affiliated or not. I used to get angry whenever I would meet a man who hated gay people so much that he couldn't even shut up about it. Now I remind myself that those guys are crying out for help because something really awful happened to them when they were little, and they still haven't healed from it. That makes it possible for me to forgive them. I'm still going to stick up for queer people, and do what I can to protect them from persecution, but now I can do it with patience and forgiveness.

Really, the last thing I want to do is to pick a fight with Christians. I realize that throughout much of history, the church has been the ultimate advocate for savage patriarchy, and it has been one of the most oppressive institutions of all time. Certainly, I have to take a stance against that church hierarchy and all that it stands for, but the church no longer leads the crusade to justify and validate inequality among humans. That torch has passed to the economists. In these modern times, those economists are my most serious ideological enemies.

The other factor is that I have met so many wonderful people who identify themselves as Christians. Throughout my life, I have been lucky to meet dozens of people whose lifestyle demonstrates that they care more about the good of all humanity than their own personal success or comfort. I would estimate that as much as half of this group are people who call themselves Christians. Many of them are strong, righteous women who probably would have been burned at the stake by the churches of medieval Europe. They are obviously on my team, and I pray that we may never quarrel.

When I observe the behavior and choices of my awesome Christian friends, I can't help but think they must be motivated by the same God that I feel all the time. I have seen Christians do a lot of awesome things. If Jesus was anything like the legends claim, then maybe his spirit really is coming back through those people. I may never understand how the Bible and the patriarchal church get credit for their exemplary behavior, but it doesn't matter if I understand or not. Those people are rock stars, and I support them. I pray that my blunder with the young preacher in South Carolina won't bring about any karma that would screw up my relationships with any other Christians.

The End Never Comes

The morning was so hot and humid that it was almost a struggle to breathe. It was probably around ten in the morning when I first noticed thunder clouds building on the western horizon. The road stuck to the top of a ridge all through the mid-day, but the ridge-crest was not a straight line, and the road had to wind all around to stay on top of it. It was still fairly rare to see a car go by. I trended generally westward, towards the spectacular view of a storm growing more and more giant by the hour. Around mid-afternoon, a shelf of lower, closer clouds blew in and I lost my view of the gorgeous cauliflower tops. It was nice to get out of the searing sun though. The wind picked up right then too. I don't think the air cooled down at all, but it was refreshing to feel it move.

I could still see a gray stripe on the horizon that just kept growing bigger, and darker. I thought it was growing closer too, and I kept my eye out for good places to take shelter. I kept thinking the big storm must be just about to hit, but hour after hour, it just kept getting bigger…… and darker. I started to wonder if it was stuck in one place, and I would only get wet if I walked right under it. I certainly was headed towards it. It took up the entire western half of the sky.

I had looked at a map back in Rock Hill, so I knew I would eventually come to a T intersection where I would need to take a left. It was probably about four or five in the afternoon when I finally got to that left turn. By then the dark gray cloud had moved over top of me. Only about a quarter of the sky was still bright, and the wind was blowing pretty fiercely. I had been hearing the distant growls of thunder for the last hour, but they didn't seem to be drawing closer.

I turned to the south and followed that road along another ridgetop for several miles. I was no longer walking directly into the storm, but now I was finally starting to see clear signs that it was moving towards me. The thunder got louder, frightening shreds of dark, tattered cloud started to swirl past at low altitude, and I started seeing lightning.

Just then I passed a sign that said, "Santee Country." It really caught my attention. The Santee were the biggest tribe of people to inhabit the region now known as South Carolina, but they have no modern reservation. I read a lot about native tribes as a teen-ager, but I had never heard anything about modern Santee people. I had assumed the worst- that they were one of the nations that was completely lost in the genocide. But why would someone put up a sign claiming country for a people who had been gone for hundreds of years?

It made me think that I must have been wrong and there *were* still Santee people. That was a very happy thought. The sign was white lettering on a green background, made out of the same materials as all the other DOT signs. Maybe the Santee had been petitioning the state to recognize them as an official tribe, and that sign was the state's way of recognizing them. That was my best guess.

The storm was even closer now, but it was still moving slowly. I made it several miles south before the first raindrops fell. By then, I had reached the end of the ridge and started descending into the valley of the Pacolet River. The river itself was not that large, but it meandered along a broad, flat flood-plain about a mile wide. The DOT had engineered a huge long bridge, raising the highway up on concrete pillars and spanning the entire floodplain. That was one river-crossing that was impervious to flooding.

Just before I reached the near end of the bridge, a splatter of big, cold raindrops started splashing down, warning me that I might want to take cover under the bridge. Given how slowly the storm had been approaching, I decided I had time to walk to the far end before I got down underneath. I was somewhat right.

The rain kept increasing slowly and steadily most of the way across the bridge. It was so long, it probably took me more than fifteen minutes to get across it, and I was hustling. I was down to the last hundred paces when the rain suddenly increased to a downpour. I broke into a run to the end of the bridge, slid down over the slick embankment, and scurried underneath. I had gotten pretty wet, but I wasn't soaked to the bone, and it was hot out anyway.

The rain came down in a spectacular deluge for more than an hour. Mid-sized hail came down with it for several minutes two different times. The thunder had more bass and less crackle than the last storm I had experienced, and it was less constant. There were even a few breaks between thunders, when all I could hear was rain and wind. Over all though, it was much more impressive than the previous storm just because of its massive scale. It filled the entire sky, and it got amazingly dark underneath it.

Back in Chapel Hill, the guy who got arrested trying to help me escape from the police had told me about storms like this one. He said that when he was growing up, his family called those awe-inspiring storms "turdknockers." I got to ride out a real turnknocker that day.

I ate my dinner while I watched the storm. After watching it approach so slowly all day long, I was surprised by how quickly it finished up and moved along. I didn't have a time piece on me, but I bet it was less than two hours later when the rain finally stopped. It was still daytime, and a few minutes later, the sun actually dipped below the western edge of the cloud, lighting up all the wet trees in dazzling orange and gold.

The floodplain had not flooded, so I put my pack on and set out cautiously to explore it, hoping to get a close look at the river. I walked quite a ways, and found the river meandering much closer to the northern side of the valley. It had risen right to the top of its clay canyon, but it stopped short of flowing out onto the floodplain. It must take a whole series of turdknockers to make a flood that big.

I stayed and admired the flooding, mid-sized river for a while, but then the sun started to set. I took a different path back towards the southern edge of the valley bottom, and I had only closed about a quarter of the distance when I came upon a sandy rise that was several feet higher than the surrounding landscape. Even if the floodwaters did rise higher, that spot would still be safe, and it was covered with soft grass. I pitched my tent on the heavenly softness of the little hill. The floodplain forest had been left to grow for more than a hundred years, and the canopy was so dense that it was already mostly dark underneath. I smoked a big old dose of weed and turned in for the night.

Within minutes, the sound of a hand drum started up. It startled me at first, but I realized quickly that it must be pretty far away. It was a quiet night down in the floodplain. The rainwater still dripping off the leaves was the only other sound. I felt an urge to explore the source of the sound, but I realized quickly that it was coming from somewhere on the far side of the river, and I would not be able to get there.

The mysterious sound of drumming in a place where I thought I was alone could have been unnerving, but I got really excited about it instead. The rhythm was distinctly evocative of a classic American Indian beat. I was really high, so it actually occurred to me that I was hearing the spirit of the Santee. The drumming went on and on while I tripped out, imagining that I was about to make contact with Indian spirits.

After a while, a second hand drum joined in. The two of them carried on together for at least another half hour. Then they were joined by a modern trap set with a snare, cymbals, a high-hat, and a kick-pedal bass. The drums all jammed together for a while, and at that point I started to hear human voices making loud sounds of celebration. The drums jammed their way into more of a modern, rock'n'roll beat, and then an electric guitar came blazing to life. Clearly there was a house on the far side of the river, and they were having a party with a live rock band. I ended up being treated to a couple hours of live, home-made Southern rock. It was awesome.

I also can't say for sure that the musicians weren't at least partly animated by the spirit of the Santee. After all, I never received any data that would disprove that hypothesis.

54. QUITTIN' TIME

I awoke to fog as thick as pea soup, and the air was already hot first thing in the morning. The dense floodplain forest looked positively enchanted, shrouded in the misty fog. Every once in a while, the sense of magic was disrupted by the sound of a vehicle passing by, high up on the flood-proof bridge, but the bridge itself was invisible. I made it back to the roadside and climbed the long, gradual hill up out of the Pacolet River Valley. I was surprised to find that the warm fog was not just limited to the lowlands. It was everywhere.

A gentle rain began falling. The raindrops weren't cold enough to make me uncomfortable, so I didn't even think to put my poncho on until I was already soaking wet. At that point, the poncho would have only made me more uncomfortably hot, so I just left it stowed in my pack.

It took a very long time to reach the ridgetop, and of course, when I got there, I came to a town. This one was called Jonesville. It was a run-down place that looked very dreary in the rain and fog. I was hoping to find a restaurant and get some breakfast, but I had no such luck. I ended up sitting on the porch of an abandoned house where an overhanging roof kept the rain off me, and eating sardines from a can.

I got onto a much busier road headed northwest out of Jonesville, and the fog cleared out shortly after that. The day remained hot and dreary, and the light rain faded in and out all morning. By lunchtime, I arrived in another dumpy little town with no obvious restaurants. This one was called Pacolet. I had eaten right through my food stores, so I had to go into a dumpy little grocery store and replenish before I could eat lunch.

Back on the road, the rain came down a bit heavier for a while, and it was accompanied by a couple of thunderclaps. I was starting to get really tired of walking in wet clothes. They chaffed my skin in ways that dry clothing would not, but there wasn't much I could do about it. The rain stopped falling for a period around mid-afternoon, so I took advantage of the lull to examine my map of Spartanburg. I found that I had just walked into the edge of the piece of land shown on the map, so I could see right where I was, as well as what to expect on the road ahead. I had no contacts in Spartanburg, and I could see that if I kept going, I would end up right in the middle of the city at nightfall. I also saw that I was passing by a large area of undeveloped parkland called Croft State Park, just about a mile away to my left, so I put two and two together and turned left towards the park.

It started raining again before I got there. The near edge of the park was covered with a forest of very young pine trees, most of which were only two or three times taller than I was. I pushed my way in through the dripping wet branches, and it only took a minute before I came to a small, grassy clearing where I could set up my tent. It was fairly unpleasant crawling into a wet tent, but there was a silver lining. I had started keeping all the contents of my backpack inside a big plastic bag, so I had dry clothes to change into, and my sleeping bag was nice and dry.

I had been wearing one of my favorite T-shirts for the last couple of days. It was an off-white shirt made of unbleached cotton with the name of an agricultural fair back in Maine, and a beautiful painting of a chicken on it. When I took it off, I noticed it had grown ugly, dark-grey spots all over it. It took me a while to figure out what they were, but eventually, I realized that mildew had grown all over my shirt *while* I was wearing it. I never had any clue that might be a potential pitfall to avoid. Later on, I tried all sorts of different methods to wash the stains out, but nothing worked. The shirt was ruined.

I had made camp much earlier than usual, so I spent the last quarter of the daylight getting stoned, daydreaming and being bored. The light rain kept coming and going until after dark, but I remained comfortably dry in my tent.

Spartanburg, SC is probably much bigger now, but when I walked through, its metro-area population was just shy of 200,000 people. There was just one lone skyscraper downtown, and it was marked with a big sign up near the top displaying the Denny's Restaurant logo. The day was pleasantly sunny, and considerably less hot than the previous few days had been. I wandered around the city all day, parking in front of different stores and hitting up their customers and staff to buy zines. Most of the city sat up on top of fairly level ridgetops, but it was transected by several deep valleys with medium-sized creeks flowing through them. I did manage to hawk a few zines, including one to a college student who was so excited about it that she actually made me feel awkward. She treated me like I was the second coming of Christ.

Some time in the afternoon, I found one of my favorite targets, a small organic grocer/health-food store. I still can't explain why I thought those were the ultimate places to sell zines. I guess it was just a prejudiced notion that I still hadn't grown out of. I sat my backpack down just inside the front door and strode confidently up to the one person who appeared to be working there. He was a middle-aged White guy, and his behavior suggested that he owned the place.

I launched into a spiel about my voyage and my zine project. The spiel was supposed to end in an appeal for help, whether it be a donation of food, money, or even just letting me sit out front for a while selling zines to customers. I never got to that part though, because the man cut me off.

"I know who you are, and I know what you want," he said, angrily. "People like you come in here every day. I know exactly what you want, and the answer is no! Now get out of my store. Go on! Get!"

I stood there blinking at him for several seconds with my jaw hanging open. He repeated his demand that I leave his store immediately. He made a point of using polite language, but the tone of his voice was still quite angry. His message finally got through on the second try, and I left quickly without another word. My feelings were hurt, and I spent the next hour walking aimlessly, trying to figure out what lesson I should learn from the encounter.

After supper, I made my way to a green patch on the map that was labeled "Milliken Arboretum." When I got there, it was surrounded by a stone wall, but the wall only reached up about as high as my ribs. I looked back at the street, and saw at least two dozen cars whose occupants might notice me climbing over the wall. I stood there for a couple of minutes and then realized that I just didn't even care anymore. I took my backpack off and leaned over the top of the wall to set it down carefully on the other side. Then I hoisted myself up over, and into the park.

The arboretum looked like a neat place to make camp. Various displays of all kinds of different trees and plants were divided by pathways of mowed grass. I climbed to the top of a hill in the middle. The place appeared to be totally empty of people except for one guy far down a slope to the north who was driving laps on a riding lawnmower. Up on the hill where I sat, the grass looked like it had already been cut, so I just waited. Sure enough, the guy finished mowing and left. It was still a few minutes until sunset, but I felt confident, so I set up my tent right then and turned in for the night. I smoked a big crumb of Annie's super weed and had a bit of a reckoning.

The walk just didn't feel right anymore. I had made an ass of myself to a Southern gentleman, flipped out and yelled at a preacher, and been kicked out of an organic grocery store, but those were all just symptoms of a bigger problem. I was convinced that my walk wasn't making a bit of difference. I wasn't making a good impression on anyone except for people who were already on the team. If my walk wasn't going to save the world, then what was the point? I wasn't really a rebel at all. I was just another privileged, middle-class kid dodging responsibility. I was just a slightly less offensive version of Adventure Max paddling along the coast in his kayak. I decided right then and there to quit walking and go back to Maine. It was almost exactly two years to the day since I first started out from Old Town.

I couldn't admit it in my conscious mind at the time, but I think it was also a huge motivation to find out that Jen was single for the first time since before I had met her. She was the muse who had inadvertently set my entire scheme into motion, so she had more power than anything else to end it. If she had come with me, maybe we would have captured the heart of American culture and charmed it into maturity, but she had her own path to walk. Without her help, I just didn't have enough charm to accomplish my lofty goal.

So I failed to save the world back in my twenties, but I gave it a shot. We are gonna make it though, someday. I can't tell if it's coming soon or if we're going to go on suffering like this for another fifty generations. I can just tell that humans keep being born with the instincts for equality. We keep being born with the instincts to cooperate and share, and to treat each other nicely. 6,000 years of oppression hasn't beaten that out of us.

I see neighbors taking care of each other. I see people reaching out to help complete strangers. Someone is always going to keep trying, even in the darkest of times. In every town, there is someone showing us the way back to a safe and social culture. Wherever I end up, I will always keep trying. I have been lucky enough to catch this spirit. I pray that you may be lucky enough to catch it too.

***

So……..like……… I don't have a publishing company to advertise for me, sooooooooo… if you liked my books, please take a minute to recommend them to other people on the social media device of your choice. (/ | \)

55. PUPPY EYES

I had lost all illusions that my walking adventure was making some kind of difference in the world. I understood now that I was the only one benefitting from it, but I wasn't quite ready to go home. My original plan had been to walk all the way to Atlanta, then turn north and spend the hottest months of the summer touring the best swimming holes of the southern Appalachians. When the weather started to cool, I had planned to come down out of the mountains and continue west. None of that ever came to pass, but I decided I still wanted to have one last look at the mountains.

I was already on the north side of Spartanburg, so I headed northwest out of town. It was a beautiful clear day, and I started catching views of the mountains almost immediately. There are some places along the eastern front of the Appalachians where a buffer of foothills divides the Piedmont from the high peaks, but there is no such buffer to the northwest of Spartanburg. The Piedmont Plateau just ends abruptly at the foot of a spectacular range of high peaks. I got to spend the entire day walking towards that view. Each time I got to a hilltop, the glorious mountains would be just a little bit closer.

By evening time, I had crossed the border back into North Carolina. That might make it sound like I was wandering a crooked path, and that is partly true, but the border between the Carolinas is also a fairly crooked line. I had almost reached the front of the mountains when it came time to set up camp. I climbed up a short ridge on the northeast side of the road, and slept on a bed of soft pine needles.

It was cloudy in the morning, but not raining. All I could see from my campsite was the interior of a piney forest, but when I made it back to the road, I was greeted by a spectacular view. A low shelf of clouds was stuck to the mountain front about halfway up, so I could still see mountain tops sticking up above the clouds, and I could see the bottom of the ridge in dark shadows below. I followed route 9 all morning, skirting ever closer to the bottom of the mountains on my left, without actually turning directly towards them. By lunchtime, the clouds had begun to break up, so there were increasing intervals of sunshine.

In the afternoon, the road came alongside a reservoir called Lake Lure. The reservoir was surrounded by miles of sprawling, suburban-style neighborhoods, but without any nearby city to commute to. The housing must just be for retired people, or for people who can afford a house like that without having to work. The road became very twisty to get around all the coves on the shore of the reservoir, so it took me a long time to walk through that area.

I met a very friendly elder woman who had come out to check her mailbox, and we got into a nice long conversation. I had just given up on my mission the night before, so I wasn't trying to sell any zines anymore, but that lady was so friendly that it just came up in the conversation. I let her decide how much she wanted to pay, and she went into her house and brought me back a twenty-dollar bill. She ended up being the final name on my list of zine subscribers.

I was heading for a place called Hickory Nut Gorge. I knew from my obsession with maps and geography that it was one of the scenic wonders of the East. It was a deep, U-shaped valley with a huge granite plume, and a series of high granite cliffs along the southern rim, complete with a great, high waterfall. I had seen all that in photographs.

What I didn't know is that the entire valley bottom is packed with tacky tourist traps. Gift shops, restaurants, art galleries, jewelers, antique stores, hotels, ice-cream stands, and miniature-golf parks- every type of business you can imagine that would cash in on tourism was repeated in dozens of variations. I guess a lot of the people in the suburbs around Lake Lure probably worked right there.

Being such a scenic spectacle, I assumed that the Hickory Nut Gorge would be some kind of park where I could just sneak off the side of the road and camp almost anywhere. That had been my plan, so I was dismayed to arrive there and find that every inch of the valley bottom was covered with tacky development, and it continued right up the hillsides literally until the slopes got too steep to build on.

It turned out that there was some privately-owned version of a park high up the ridge, right around the location of the cliffs and the waterfall, but I found the gate, and discovered I would have to pay some ridiculous fee to go in. As you can imagine, I was deeply offended by the idea of having to pay money to see a wonder of nature, so that wasn't an option.

I decided I was going to have to do some trespassing and find a way to sneak into the woods. I walked slowly back along the impenetrable wall of gimmicky schtick, looking for a crack that I might slip through. There were several side streets that I turned in to explore, but they all ended abruptly in dense housing developments, or clusters of rental cottages. On several occasions, I crossed bridges over the gorgeous little river, splashing crystal-clear over its bed of big rounded stones, and often breaking out into a dead run over stretches of whitewater. It was actually the same Broad River that I had swum in several days earlier, but it was much smaller up there near its source.

After while, I resigned to the idea that I was going to have to pull a fairly brazen move to begin my act of trespassing. I came to the next hive of rental cottages and crossed a flimsy little bridge over the river to get to them. Some people were walking around there, but it wasn't thickly crowded like the sidewalks out on the main drag. No one was giving me any curious looks, so all of a sudden, I turned off the road and hurried across the mowed grass between two of the cottages. The forest started up right behind the cottages, and my plan was to disappear out of sight as quickly as possible.

The trouble was, the slope increased so steeply right behind those cottages, that I couldn't climb it without a bit of a struggle. My shoes tore right through the top layers of soil and old pine needles, leaving muddy stripes on the ground. I had to crawl up the slope on all four limbs, and a muddy wallow hole stayed behind to mark the path I had taken. It was not a quick process, and I was too embarrassed to look back and see if anyone was watching me. No one said anything to get my attention anyways, and I eventually made it up into the cover of the deep, dark Appalachian forest.

The climb got easier up in the forest, because I could grab onto various plant stems and tree trunks with my hands to help pull myself up. There were still quite a few instances though where the surface of the soil gave way, and I fell forwards while sliding backwards, leaving big stripes of opened mud in my wake.

It had not rained at all that day as far as I knew, but everything still seemed to be wet and slippery. I climbed for at least 45 minutes, until I was high above the bizarre little town. I passed several places where the slope leveled out into little shelves of relatively level ground. Finally, I came to one that suited my taste as a particularly good campsite and stopped there. I pitched my tent, ate some supper, and smoked a bit too much pot again. It was hard to control my dose when the tiniest crumb would send my mind right off the charts.

There was still plenty of daylight left, so I left my heavy pack behind, and set out to explore. I thought it would be a real coup to get a close-up view of the Hickory Nut Falls without paying the exorbitant fee to enter the private park. I knew I was right next the creek that went over the falls, because I could hear it cascading down the hill just to the east.

I found my way to the creek quickly, but I couldn't see the waterfall from that particular spot, so I made my way upstream. The going was amazingly slow, because everything was so damp and slippery. The forest thinned out around the creek, making way for a steep field of boulders, every inch of which were covered in thick, emerald mosses. Everywhere my hands and feet touched the moss, it would slough off the rocks, and gravity would deposit me back into the same spot I had just come from. Eventually, I made it up over a little hump, and from there I could see a smaller waterfall, maybe four times the height of my body. That was pretty cool, but I still wanted to look at the actual Hickory Nut Falls, which drops more than 400 feet. If I could get to the top of the little falls right in front of me, then maybe I would be rewarded with a view of the big one.

After several minutes of considerable struggle, I made it fairly close to the bottom of the smaller waterfall. Then I reached a dead end. The slope of the rocks got much steeper there, and I just couldn't find a way up. The rocks were still incredibly slippery even after I had stripped the moss off of them. I fell a couple of times, and while it didn't hurt to land on the thick, soft moss, it was still pretty scary just to fall. I have never felt much of an urge to challenge gravity, so I gave up and turned back.

I was also wreaking havoc on the ecosystem. Moss doesn't grow back over night, and I had stripped a trail of rocks bare along several hundred feet of the remote creek. I was careful to slide my way back down along the same route I had already disturbed.

It was sad not to get a view of the great waterfall, but I figured a nice swim would lift my spirits. It was not nearly so hot up in the mountains, but it certainly wasn't too cold either. The last of the clouds had drifted away hours earlier, and it was still at least an hour until sunset. The arrangement of boulders had backed the creek up into several deeper pools down closer to my camp. When I made it back to that point, I took off my muddy shoes and my reeking clothes, and got right in.

The water was so cold it was almost shocking, but I got used to it after a minute. I sat down in the little pool I had chosen, and only my head and shoulders stuck out of the cold water. I dunked my head in and used my fingertips to scrub at my hair. The spirit of the little creek was so joyful that I started giggling. I made up a spontaneous little song about an Appalachian Mountain bath, and slapped the surface of the water with my hands to make a rhythm while I sang out loud.

My reverie lasted maybe five minutes until I heard the sound of a helicopter approaching. The foreground was totally washed out by the sound of rushing water, so it was impossible to discern where the chopper was or what direction it was going.

I know I've already mentioned that I had developed a touch of post-traumatic stress disorder from all my violent encounters with the police. Well, getting my collarbone broken in Raleigh had made that situation even worse. It didn't even occur to me that the helicopter might not be coming for me. I was trespassing, and I was butt-naked. I could see quite a bit of blue sky right there where the forest had parted to make way for the creek and its surrounding boulder-field. I figured I only had seconds before the chopper would pop into view above the little clearing and catch my naked ass. I jumped up out of the natural bath tub, snatched up my clothing and shoes, and hurried across the slick rocks as quickly as I could in my bare feet.

Back at my tent, I was hidden under a thick forest canopy, but I was still freaking out. The chopper kept circling, and now I heard the sound of sirens down in the valley below. I had left an obvious trail of muddy footprints all the way up the mountainside.

It would take the cops quite a while to climb up to my campsite, and there certainly wasn't anywhere nearby that a helicopter could land. At least I had time to get dressed and pack up my camp.

I was halfway through taking my tent down when I started to think things through. Trespassing was not a very serious crime, and I knew how little motivation most cops had in situations that involved leaving paved surfaces and going into the woods. Would any cops really climb up a steep, slippery slope for 45 minutes just to get to me? Helicopters burn through hundreds of dollars worth of fuel every few minutes. Was that really worth it? The sound of sirens gave me reason to pause. I had already been through several situations where I had heard sirens, but I was with other people who told me they didn't hear any sirens. I stopped packing and listened.

Sirens are only needed to warn people to get out of the way of emergency vehicles. Once those vehicles get to their destinations, they shut the sirens off. The tourist trap down in the valley was an unholy monstrosity, but it was not so large that it would take an emergency vehicle more than a couple minutes to push through it. The sirens I was hearing just kept going and going. The chopper just kept flying back and forth, back and forth, but it never got close enough to me for its volume to get very loud. Maybe my mind was fabricating that sound too.

After waiting for half an hour or so, I finally decided that I was suffering from a paranoid delusion so severe that I was experiencing full-blown auditory hallucinations. My understanding of the situation didn't make the sounds stop.

I set my tent back up, and crawled in for the night. The sirens and the helicopter kept up for at least another hour until it was totally dark out. By then it was obvious that the sounds were only happening inside my head, but they still kept my nerves on edge the entire time. That PTSD is a real bastard.

I slid back down into the tourist trap the next morning, and continued west on route 9. I made it through that strange scene before most of the businesses had opened. Just beyond that, I passed through a little town called Bat Cave. If Forrest Gump had travelled that way, he would surely have encountered Batman, but I was not so lucky.

I saw a sign indicating that I was passing Minnehaha Falls, so I took a detour down the short path to admire the falls. The small, juvenile version of the Broad River made an impressive jump down into a dark rocky gorge. It was not very early in the morning anymore, but the surrounding mountains were so steep and high that the sun still hadn't come up where I stood, looking at the falls from above. The bottom of the gorge was so dark and mysterious, I wondered if the sun ever shone all the way down there.

The road was trending north by northeast all morning and into the afternoon, but then route 9 turned west to go over a pass, and off to the city of Asheville. Right there where the highway turned west, I branched off onto a smaller road that continued in the same direction I had been going. That road took me up over a different pass, and through several miles of terrain that were high, but not quite so steep. There, I was treated to miles of long beautiful views of mountain scenery off to the south and the east.

In the foreground, I passed by several dozen houses whose architectural styles suggested they had been built for rich Hippies. No one in that neighborhood had failed to display their Tibetan prayer flags, and I saw a lot of northern license plates on the cars in the driveways. It appeared to be some sort of Yankee Hippy colony. After that, the road descended a long way down into the next valley.

The day was growing late when a friendly dog came out to the end of its driveway to greet me. It was interesting to note that I hadn't had any trouble with dogs that spring, the whole way across the Carolinas. They had given me so much trouble the previous fall all the way across Virginia. I had just assumed that obnoxious, territorial dogs must be a Southern thing, but I guess it was just a Virginia thing.

This particular dog didn't bark at all. Nor was it territorial. It was so friendly that it wanted to come with me. I have no idea what breed it was, some sort of mid-sized, long-haired mut that didn't quite stand as tall as my knees. I gave it a quick pat on the head to reward its friendliness, and then sent it home. At least, I told it to go home. The poor dumb thing ignored my command and kept following me down the hill. I stopped and yelled at it to go home. I clapped my hands and pointed my finger back towards its house, which I could no longer see. The dog just looked at me like it didn't understand.

It kept following me, literally for miles. I tried all sorts of strategies to convince it to go home, but none of them worked. I don't speak dog telepathy like some people, but when I looked in its eyes, it seemed like it was trying to convince me that we could be a thing. I swear I heard it say, "You're sooooo cool! I could come with you, and snuggle you, and lick you, and love you, and we could be fwends fowever! Don't you wanna be my fwend?"

"No," I said. There was nothing I wanted more than a human companion, but I don't do the dog thing. I just don't have the right hormones for it, or something. Even if I was a dog person, that was not the right time or place to adopt a dog. I was a homeless traveler, without even so much as a car. I didn't even know where I would be sleeping from one night to the next. I tried to explain all that to the poor dumb dog, but it just didn't understand. I wondered what made it want to leave its home and latch onto a someone new so badly that it would settle for me, a guy who doesn't even like dogs. I worried that it must be suffering a terribly abusive home life if it saw me as a good alternative.

After a couple hours, the dog and I came to a town called Old Fort. By then, it had travelled so far from its home that I doubted whether it would even be able to find its way back. I decided I had to draw the line there, before we went into town. The poor thing was so dumb, I was worried it might get run over by a car. I was also fairly certain that it would cause problems with other people, and they would assume it was my dog and blame me. When I came to the first cross street in Old Fort, I stopped. I had tried everything short of physical violence to deter the dog from following me. I had no trouble with the idea of stabbing a vicious attack dog in the throat, but this little guy was such a sweetheart, it felt absolutely awful that I had to give him a whack.

I got a big gulp in my throat. Then I hauled back and gave him a stiff slap across the face. Without waiting to see his reaction, I turned and hurried across the street. When I got to the other side, I glanced back over my shoulder to see if my strategy had worked. It had. The dog was still standing there on the far side of the street where I had left it, but it gave me a look that started me crying. It understood that I had rejected it, and it shared all its devastating heartbreak with me in that final look. It was just awful.

Old Fort looked like an interesting little town with a lot of historic architecture, but I couldn't concentrate on observing very much of it. It took me the whole length of the town to get over the heartbreak of my poor dog friend. At the far end of town, I crossed over the little brook that was actually the very beginning of the mighty Catawba River, and followed its valley downstream for a mile or two. The sun went behind the mountains right about then, but I still had quite a bit of daylight left. I turned left up the valley of a large creek. The road turned to dirt as I entered the Pisgah National Forest. I made it a couple miles without a single car going by. When the daylight finally faded, I picked a spot by the creek and camped out.

56. HIGHEST POINT

The next morning, I went up, up, up the little forestry road, all the way to the top of the Blue Ridge. At that point, I was at least a thousand feet higher than anywhere I had been on the Blue Ridge in Virginia, but I had an even higher goal. Once I got to the top of the ridge, I could see across the next valley to Mount Mitchell. At 6,684 feet, it's not only the highest point in the Appalachian Mountains, it's also the highest point in North America, east of the Great Plains. At the summit of the ridge, I crossed out of the basin of the Catawba/Santee River, which flows east to the Atlantic Ocean, and into the basin of the Tennessee River which flows west to the Ohio/Mississippi River.

I also crossed the Blue Ridge Parkway, and then plunged straight down the west side of the ridge. Thankfully, the bottom of the next valley was not as low as the one I had just come from. At the bottom my little forestry road ended in a T with another forestry road running along the valley. A quick left there, and then it was just a short jaunt to the head of the Mount Mitchell Trail. It was only just lunchtime when I got there, so I fueled up and then started up the trail. It was nice to be walking on something other than a roadway for a change, but the trail was very steep, and I had to take frequent breaks.

By sunset, I had not yet reached the top of the mountain, but I did make it to a beautiful series of meadows, very high up, with a spectacular view to the east. I was at an elevation roughly equivalent to the top of the Blue Ridge, and I could see many miles of it across the valley. To the right it came closer and closer, almost touching the mountain I was on, and to the left it got further away, steadily fading into the hazy distance. It was indeed a blue-colored ridge on that particular evening.

There were no level places to set up my tent at all, and I had to settle for a spot just above a log that had fallen perpendicular to the slope, so the log would prevent me from sliding, or rolling down the mountain.

The next morning, I decided to stay in that spot for a whole day. I had plenty of food and water. Why not? I spent the entire day smoking up the last of the weed that Annie had given me, laying back in the soft grass, and watching a single thunderhead build itself over the Blue Ridge. Something about the air currents kept it stuck in the same place all day long. It had the cauliflower top of a thunderhead, but it never actually got big or strong enough to produce any thunder. It just kept churning and circulating while I watched it in amazement.

By the following morning, I was ready to move along. It only took about another hour to reach the top of the mountain, and when I got there, I was shocked. I knew there was a road leading to the top, but I had no idea there would be such a vast network of parking lots, visitor centers, and other tourist attractions. It was like a miniature Disney World. I guess it wasn't quite as bad as the Hickory Nut Gorge, but they had literally built as many structures and parking lots as would fit on the top of the mountain. That'll teach it to be the tallest mountain!

I realized how lucky I had been to stop and stay right where I did two nights earlier. Obviously, the view from the top was beautiful, but I didn't linger to enjoy it for very long. Summiting Mount Mitchell was the last thing I wanted to do on my journey. With that accomplishment crossed off, I just wanted to get home.

The auto route to the mountaintop was actually just a spur off the Blue Ridge Parkway. A very high ridge connects the mountain to the Blue Ridge itself, and the spur road goes along that ridgetop. I followed it for several miles, and then got on the BRP headed southwest. I knew that road would eventually take me right near the city of Asheville where I could catch a ride home. The BRP and the Mt. Mitchell spur road both had milage signs along them, so I could see that I walked 33 miles that day, plus that last little bit of the trail that I hiked early in the morning. That might have been the longest distance I ever went in a single day, but it wasn't quite enough to reach Asheville.

I walked until it was almost completely dark. Then I just rolled out my sleeping bag a short ways off the side of the road and slept. I felt confident that it wouldn't rain that night, so I didn't even bother to set up my tent.

In the morning, I awoke to discover that I had slept in a huge patch of poison ivy. Luckily, at that young age, I had not yet lost my immunity to it, so I ended up being totally fine. It's actually common for young people to be immune to poison ivy, but if you are one of those lucky ones, you should still learn to identify it and avoid touching it. If you keep touching poison ivy, it will eventually break down your immunity, and you will start to get that fierce, terrible itch. That's what happened to me in the years since then. If I were to lay down in a giant patch of poison ivy now, I would be totally screwed.

Early that morning, I came to the intersection of a different road that took me down off the ridge, and right into the heart of Asheville. Coming in off the ridge like that, I got to skip all the suburbs and start right in the middle of the city.

Asheville, North Carolina is the undisputed Hippy capitol of the southeastern United States. It only took me a couple of hours to find place to stay. The nice young Hippies who took me in actually had a spare bed for me to sleep in. That same day, I also found a guy who was planning to drive right to Chapel Hill in just two days, and he was thrilled at the prospect of someone riding along and keeping him company.

I spent one more day in Asheville, and then I rode with him back to the Triangle. He dropped me off right at the crossroads by my friends' ramshackle cabin. Maine was hosting the Earth First Rendezvous that year, and my friends were about to drive up in their nasty white minivan to attend the party, so I only had to wait a few more days to catch a ride all the way back to Maine.

***

I ended up working on farms for most of the last eighteen years. It's true that farm work doesn't pay very well, but there are a lot of other perks that make it worthwhile to me. I love the feeling of being responsible for everyone's food supply. I get to be outside, soaking up the sun and keeping my body strong, and I always get loads of free, healthy food. It's a healthy lifestyle, and maybe it's just luck, but I haven't had to spend a dime at the doctor's office in all those years. I also discovered that I just love fussing with plants, and I would want to spend much of my time fussing with plants even if I wasn't getting paid at all.

I got to build my own homestead in the forest of Maine, and that ended up being at least as big an adventure as walking across the country. I grew a big garden and tried to catch fish. I learned about a myriad of edible plants, and plants that are useful for all sorts of other purposes as well. I didn't even hook up a single solar panel to my cabin, let alone grid power, but I didn't go cold turkey on technology either. I kept a cell phone charged off the battery in my truck, and I even had a chainsaw. I also still had to buy most of my food from the store. I didn't exactly *have* to spend money so frequently on beer or cheeseburgers, but I did anyway. I don't expect anyone to aim for immediate ecological purity. Just a few steps in the right direction would be nice.

I also think it's important to point out that I paid off eighteen acres of land with money I earned working on farms. Conventional wisdom would say that you can't make enough working on a farm to achieve that kind of independence, but my experience shows that you can. My critics would say that it only worked because of my class privilege, and that may be a factor. It's true that I have not yet had to lift a finger to care for my aging parents, or anyone else in my family. But I spent a total of nine years in relationships with two different single mothers, and I supported their families. I even found money to take the kids on travelling adventures. I just didn't spend a dime on technological gadgets, designer clothing, or any of the other crap that normal low-income people think they need to avoid looking poor. I also figured out how to make almost everything I needed out of materials I could get for free.

The adventures didn't end when I stopped walking. I don't know if I'm actually touched by some spirit that keeps throwing crazy situations at me, or if I'm just blessed to be so easily amused that I find almost every situation interesting. I could write quite a few more books about my adventures, but I'm not going to. The other characters in those stories deserve to keep their privacy, and it's not healthy for me to keep writing about myself. Imagine how weird my social life would be if the people I hang out with all had to worry that they might get written about. If enough people like my writing that I can afford to spend time writing more books, I will take on some other topics. I promise.

I guess that's about it. As Huck Finn would say, "There ain't nothin more to write about, and I am rotten glad of it, because if I'd a knowed what a trouble it is to make a book, I wouldn't a tackled it, and I ain't agoing to no more."

57. BONUS SCENE

I awoke to a pleasant piney smell and the sounds of birds chirping. I poked my face out of my sleeping bag and opened my eyes to see the underside of some very short-needled type of conifer tree. That was weird. I could have sworn it was winter time. How had I come to be sleeping on the ground outside and not freezing? Where the hell was I?

I had worked in the non-profit reform business for three years, and those jobs had me driving, and sometimes even flying all over the country. After I dropped out of that and joined the protest squad, I had been travelling even more frequently. I would usually hitch-hike to nearby destinations, and a hacker friend would hook me up with fake bus passes so I could get to the more distant protests.

Remember at the beginning of *Fight Club* when Tyler Durden is flying around so often that he can't keep track of what city he's in? That's a real thing. Some mornings I would wake up in my tiny rented cabin in the forest of Maine, and that was not disorienting, but it was also common to wake up on couches, in beds, in my tent, or even on hard floors surrounded by squads of other rebels, and have no idea where I was. Sometimes a couple minutes of concentrated thinking would jog my memory. Other times I would literally have to look out the windows or walk around outside looking for clues. There were a handful of times when I just asked other people, but I was usually too embarrassed to go about it that way.

In this particular situation, I had not even set up my tent. I had just rolled out my sleeping bag under some very fragrant evergreens and slept on the ground. Wasn't it the middle of freakin' winter?

I sat up and there it was. The sun had not yet reached the valley bottom where I lay, but the spectacular northeast face of Mount Graham was ablaze with the first rays of daylight.

Oh yeah! A friend and I had ridden the bus all the way to southern Arizona because the Apaches needed our help with something. It was indeed the middle of February. With its summit reaching up 10,720 feet above sea level, Mount Graham was covered with snow, but where I sat, in the valley of the Gila River, it was not too cold to sleep outside. It had gotten chilly overnight, but not enough to frost.

I packed up my sleeping bag and went into the lodge. More than a hundred of us had followed directions to an abandoned resort called Indian Hot Springs. I think we had permission from the building's owner to use the space, but it's also possible that we were breaking and entering. At any rate, the electricity was on, and there was gas running to a pair of large stoves where a small crew was already preparing breakfast. None of my friends were up yet, so I made friends with the breakfast team and joined in to help shred potatoes.

This was the first time I had ever attended an event hosted by the notorious tribe of eco-warriors known as Earth First, and I was totally smitten. These people were so hard core that the politicians of the era labeled them "terrorists." Of course, there has never been a single case of an Earth Firster hurting another human being, or even threatening someone with physical harm. They were only terrifying to that class of people who were trying to get rich quick by ravaging Mother Nature. They were the people who would blockade roads or chain themselves to trees to try to save beautiful wild places from being destroyed by the industrial cancer that was consuming our homeland. Their tactics were usually illegal, so they often had to endure police brutality and jail time, but they weren't afraid. They were the warrior spirits who cared more about the good of all living things than they did about their own personal safety.

I had run with some of these people at the big city protests before, but this was the first time I had ever been called out to the wildlands to help them with one of their own projects. I made a lot of new friends over the next several days drinking, partying, sharing philosophies, and telling stories of all our outlaw adventures. It was there that I met two of my best friends ever, the same two North Carolina boys who I would spend the winter with two years later, toasting bagels on top of the woodstove and telling endless stories.

About half of the crew stayed in the big wooden lodge, and the rest of us camped out front on the desert ground. We could also go swimming in a big concrete pool that was heated by the springs that the vacant resort was named for.

The Arizona team was hosting the event because they needed help to save a tiny area of rare and unique ecosystem at the summit of Mount Graham. In an ecological sense, isolated mountain tops in the desert function much the same way as islands that are isolated out in the ocean. A mountaintop will be considerably cooler, and receive considerably more precipitation than the surrounding desert. If the mountain is tall enough, it can grow a forest, and that forest makes habitat for a whole different roster of animals and plants than you would find living in the desert below. If that forest is far enough away from any other forests, then it's very difficult, or even impossible for some animal species to migrate across the many miles of desert between them. Once the animals become isolated from others of their kind, their gene pool shrinks, and they evolve quickly into unique species. Given how small their habitats are, these species can't grow to very large numbers, so they start off being very rare even before human industry starts destroying their habitat.

Mount Graham is a perfect example of this situation. It's the tallest mountain in southern Arizona, and its upper slopes are crowned by a steep alpine forest that is isolated from any other forest by many miles of bleak desert. That little forest is home to a number of unique species found nowhere else on Earth, including a species of squirrel whose entire world population numbers in the hundreds.

In addition to being a one-of-a-kind ecological gem, Mount Graham is also a sacred site for the local Apache Nation. Being the tallest and most beautiful mountain around, it played a huge role in the Apache spiritual traditions. Notably, whenever an Apache child, male or female, reached the age of puberty and wanted to feel like an adult, they were encouraged to climb to the top of Mount Graham, and sit there until they experienced a vision.

The Apache were not wiped out in the genocide, and many still struggle to maintain their cultural traditions in modern-day Arizona and New Mexico. The trouble is that when modern Apache kids climb up to the summit of Mount Graham, they find themselves in a huge network of parking lots, buildings, and telescopes owned by the University of Arizona. Being far from any sources of city light, and 10,000 feet closer to outer space, the mountain is an ideal place from which to study the heavens. Scientific research is not usually on the list of dangerous industries ruining the planet, but this was a special case. The U of A astronomical research station had already chewed up a huge swath of the tiny and unique ecosystem, and now it was planning to expand even more.

Funding for the proposed new array of telescopes and parking lots was actually coming from an incredibly wealthy church who had openly admitted that they hoped to use the telescopes to make contact with aliens so they could convert them to Christianity. Presumably, the university had worked out a deal where they would get to use the telescopes sometimes for actual scientific purposes. The Earth Firsters didn't think that was a good enough reason to bulldoze any more of the Apache church/incredibly rare squirrel habitat, so they called in the Fraggle Army for help.

After several days of getting to know each other, it was time to make our move. Right at dawn, I piled into a car with too many other people. We had to bring our backpacks too, because we would not be returning to the Indian Hot Springs. It took us almost an hour to drive around the east side of the mighty mountain, and then we got on interstate 10 headed towards Tucson. I'm not sure how long it took us to get there, but it seemed like forever since I was stuck in the back seat with three other people.

We drove straight to the University of Arizona campus where we joined a crowd of other Earth Firsters who were already gathering there. The last couple of vehicles unloaded, and without further adieu, we accelerated into a brisk march across the campus. I would guess there were about 70 of us, and as usual, I was the only one who hadn't dressed up like the cast of a Road Warrior movie. There were definitely some who didn't have dreadlocks or tattoos on their faces, but they were all covered from head to toe with soot and grease from hopping trains. We looked like a more feral version of a biker gang. No one knew what we were up to, but we obviously weren't college students.

I didn't know what we were up to either, but before long, we arrived at the bottom of a ten-story sky-scraper right in the middle of campus. Three very heavy old Apache women were waiting for us there. We had a very brief meeting where I learned that we were about to confront the president of the university in his office. Our scout had reported that the president was in the right place at the right time, so with that, we burst into the building. The three old ladies managed to cram into the elevator all at the same time, while the rest of us poured into a dimly-lit concrete stairwell right beside it. I think the president's office was on the seventh floor, but I don't remember exactly. At any rate, it was a long climb, but we were all in good shape and surging with adrenaline, so we ran the whole way up.

By the time we burst into the lobby, the Apaches already had the president backed up against the wall. Not only did each woman weigh four times as much as him, but two of them also towered over him by almost a foot. Our job was to hold silent and look menacing while they did the talking. We crowded into a tight ring of stinking, savage-looking humanity right behind the Apaches.

We had only been there for about a minute when a campus police officer showed up. He pushed his way through our crowd, which did not yield easily for him, and then stood with his back pressed against the president's right shoulder. He and the president both looked terrified.

The Apache women were calm and collected, and they said nothing in particular to intimidate the sleazy little man who threatened their sacred place. They just explained their grievances to him and demanded that he cancel the plans to build more telescopes. The president agreed to put the project on hold, and then he proposed to schedule some meetings with the tribal leaders.

It seemed like an obvious trick to me. I had no doubt that the university would simply wait for us to leave, lock the doors, and then continue with their sinister plan. I had never come face-to-face with a high-ranking corporate scumbag before, let alone been in a position of power over one. I wanted to pick the weaselly little liar up and throw him out the window.

When the Apaches accepted his offer and scheduled a meeting, I was distraught. Didn't they know that powerful White men always lie? I wanted to warn them, but I managed to keep my mouth shut. Surely they must know. This was their business. They must have anticipated how the president would respond and this was all part of their long-term plan. It would have been a bad idea to throw the president out the window anyway. That would have made Earth First an actual terrorist group, and then the FBI would have hunted us all down and made us disappear.

We were just about to leave when a second campus cop showed up and tried to push his way through the crowd the same way the first one had. A quick scuffle of shoving ensued, and the cop ended up on his butt. He got up wanting to fight, but the other cop grabbed him and calmed him down. The Apaches crammed back into the elevator, and the rest of us shuffled back down the stairs, feeling deflated. I was never very good at following up to see what happened after the protest events that I participated in, so I can't tell you how the situation turned out.

My Mainer friend and I got dropped off at the house where we would be staying that night, and someone fed us lunch. I had never been to Tucson before, so I expressed interest in exploring the city. No one wanted to go with me, but someone offered to lend me a bicycle, so I went pedaling out to explore the less-steep parts of town.

After several hours, I ended up back at the university. I was pedaling past a row of short trees when I noticed that they all had pretty orange balls hanging from them. I thought they were big oranges, but when I picked one, peeled it, and took a bite, it turned out to be a grapefruit.

It wasn't just a grapefruit though. It was the sweetest, tartest, most delicious grapefruit I had ever tasted. I had grown up loving to eat grapefruit that my parents bought from the grocery store, but I had never eaten one fresh off a tree before. It was like watching color-TV for the first time after growing up with black-and-white. I got so excited, I ate two or three right on the spot. I was dumbfounded to think that thousands of students walked by those trees every day without taking any interest the most delectable of treats that they offered.

I had been invited to a Punk show that night, and I really wanted to pick a bunch of grapefruit to hand out at the show. I hadn't brought any kind of container with me, but after a couple minutes, I came up with an ingenious plan. I had worn a pair of long-johns under my jeans, but it wasn't so cold out that I really needed them. I found a hiding spot where a hedge squeezed up close to the side of a building, wriggled out of my extra layer, and then put my jeans back on. Then I tied a knot in the ankle of each pant leg and returned to the grapefruit trees. Once I had filled each leg up to the crotch, I hung the fruit-stuffed pants over my shoulders and cycled back to my host's house in triumph.

(Just this last year, I read Robin Wall Kimmerer's "Braiding Sweetgrass"- another must read- and I laughed out loud with delight when she told the story of her grandfather and great uncle filling their pants with pecans. I know just what that feels like! I plan to send copies of my books to the good professor and pray that she finds time to read them someday.)

Alas, I picked way too many grapefruits, and I was only able to distribute about a quarter of them at the show. The band was amazing though. Their sound was like a perfect mixture of Punk and Country, and I spent hours doing wild and exuberant dances with the feral Earth Firsters. At one point, the band played the "I-Feel-Like-I'm-Fixin'-to-Die Rag" by Country Joe and the Fish, but instead of Vietnam, they sang:

One, two, three, what are we fightin' for?
Who knows I don't give a damn.
Next stop's Afghanistan!

It was awesome.

After the show, I went out walking with four of my new friends. The city was very quiet at that late hour of the night. We were making our way through a trendy neighborhood with lots of little take-out restaurants when one of my companions let out a whoop. He had been rummaging through a trash can and he discovered a tasty snack. He held up the Styrofoam tray, and we all gathered around to share. After that, we all spread out and checked every can along the street. We even found some dumpsters with good stuff in them in the alleys. Every time one of us found something good, we would let out a savage, feral whoop, and the rest of us would come running to share it. It was so fun, we kept laughing, and the whole situation felt like a celebration to me.

By the time I went on my big walk, dumpster-diving and trash-surfing were old hat to me, but that night in Tucson was the first time anyone had ever shown me what an amazing bounty of tasty treats are to be scored for free. The concept totally flipped my lid and put me on a cathartic high for the rest of the night.

The next day, I decided it was time to ditch Earth First and visit some older friends. I had spent a few months in Albuquerque during my brief non-profit career, and I still had a couple really good friends there who I needed to visit. It hadn't quite been two whole years since the last time I saw them, but so much had happened in that time that it felt like half a lifetime.

The bus didn't leave until late in the evening, so I passed a second day in Tucson. I stuffed as many grapefruits into my pack as I could, and walked down to the bus station. First I had to ride to Flagstaff and stay awake through the wee hours of the morning waiting for the bus to take me east along I-40. I arrived in Albuquerque around the time most people would be waking up in the morning, called my friend from a pay phone, and got picked up a few minutes later.

My two best friends in Albuquerque had been my coworkers in the campaign office, but neither of them worked there anymore. One was male and the other was female, and they had gotten together as a couple not long after I left. We had been keeping in touch over email, so I knew they were a thing.

and I was very happy for them. My enthusiasm for their relationship faded within minutes of arriving at the apartment where they were living together.

In the short time since I had last seen them, the woman had completely lost her mind. She was constantly angry at my other friend and she could turn almost any situation into an excuse to yell at him. I can't say she started a lot of fights, because my other friend didn't fight back at all. He would just look sadly at the floor, shrug his shoulders, and try harder to make her happy. It obviously wasn't working. It was obvious to me that he needed to get away from her, but he wasn't ready to even think about that yet. He still really loved her, and I could tell he was clinging to the hope that her mental condition might improve. We had both known her before she went crazy. If she could change so much one time, then I suppose it was reasonable to hope that she could change again.

Like most failing couples, they had just recently gotten a puppy. It was only a couple of months old when I got there. It was some mid-sized, brown and white breed, tough-looking and extremely energetic. Being in the apartment with it was pure hell, because it caused problems at a rate faster than my friends could even keep up with. Between working their jobs and arguing with each other, neither of them had any time or energy to train it. All day long, it would swirl about their apartment destroying things, and my one friend would always get angry at my other friend for everything the puppy did. Ironically, it had been her idea to get a dog.

I had made no specific plans for how long I would visit them, but after two days of that nightmare, I was ready to leave. I would have to wait until 4:00 the next afternoon to catch a bus headed back east, so that meant I would be spending one last night on their couch.

They took me out to eat at their favorite taco place on that last evening, and we actually had kind of a nice time. It was a huge relief to get some time away from the puppy, and the woman calmed down enough that they were actually able to stop making drama for a while and pay some attention to me. We lingered at the taco place for a couple hours and actually had a good time for the first time since I had arrived.

When we got back to the apartment, we discovered that the puppy had torn into my backpack, spread my belongings all over the house, and slobbered on them. For the most part, that wasn't really a big deal, but there was one significant problem. My bus pass had been seriously damaged. I was several thousand miles away from home, and I had about 35 dollars to my name. Normally under those circumstances, you would just go into the bus station, ask the person at the counter to look up your information, and have them print you out a new bus ticket. Obviously, that option was not available to me, because my ticket was fake.

The front side of the bus passes were just a white paper background, printed with black ink words, showing my name, the dates for which the pass was valid, and a variety of other information. It was fairly easy for my hacker friend to forge all that and print it out. The backside of the pass was a different story though. It was printed with dozens of lines of miniscule words, all printed in an odd, light-pink color of ink. I never did endeavor to read what those words said. Clearly, they weren't important. Their only purpose was to make the passes difficult to forge. The hackers could certainly make dozens of lines of tiny words without much difficulty, but no one could get a printer cartridge with that color of pink ink.

To get around this obstacle, we would go into bus stations, dig through the trash, and pull out old tickets that other passengers had thrown away. The hackers would print out the fake fronts, and we would paste those over the front of a real ticket with all the tiny pink words already looking just right on the back. The whole thing was a little bit larger than a dollar bill. A vigilant bus driver might notice that we were handing them two pieces of paper stuck together, so to avoid that possibility, we would get the whole thing laminated to make it much harder to inspect. The bus company didn't sell laminated passes, but they were good for two months to go anywhere in the country, so it wasn't unreasonable to think that customers would get them laminated to keep them from falling apart over that extended period of time.

The puppy had put a couple of tooth holes through my pass, but that wasn't a problem. The real problem arose out of a combination of three things: the puppy from hell, my bus pass, and a pack of condoms. I never did manage to get laid back in those days, but I was always hopeful and polite enough to bring a pack of condoms with me everywhere I went. My backpack just had one small compartment for all the odds and ends ranging from toothbrushes to pens, sewing gear to computer disks, and condoms to fake bus passes. The puppy's teeth had ripped open a condom packet, and that super-slick, chemical lubricant had leaked out, making a big spot on the front of my pass. The grease spot had rendered the paper translucent, so now you could clearly see the words printed on the front of the real ticket underneath showing through the paper of the fake front.

I wasn't sure what to do. I didn't even keep a bank account back then. I had hundreds of dollars cash hidden in a safe place back in Maine, but I had only gone travelling with a tiny bit of money. I decided I would just have to keep using the pass and pray that the bus drivers would be really spaced out. It was a federal crime to use a fake bus pass, and the penalty for getting caught was pretty steep, so it was a dangerous proposition.

I got to the bus station the next day to find it packed with customers waiting to go east. They had all purchased tickets with a specific time and date on them. When it came time to load up, I waited and got in the very last place in the line. That way if the bus was completely filled, I wouldn't cause any paying customers to get bumped off.

Normally, the bus driver would stand next to the front door of the bus, and everyone would show him their tickets just before they climbed aboard. We would hand our passes to the them along with some form of ID, and they would sit them both on top of a clipboard in their hand while scribbling a few notes onto a piece of paper on that same clipboard. This time, for the first time I had ever experienced, something different happened.

When I handed my documents to the driver, he gave me a quirky smile and said, "Okay! Why don't you go take a seat (motioning towards the bus.) I just have to go inside and write this down."

I didn't like that at all. There was always the potential that a bus driver might find our bus passes suspicious, but as long as they were right there in front of us, we could always just snatch our ID and bus pass back off the clipboard, and take off running. I had no backup plan for what to do if the driver took my documents and went into the building without me, but I couldn't very well object to his suggestion. That would only make me look even more suspicious.

Reluctantly, I climbed up onto the bus. There was only one seat left, an aisle seat about halfway back. It was a hot day for February in Albuquerque, and the bus was incredibly stuffy. I sat down and started to sweat. I felt certain that the driver was calling the cops at that very moment, and the bus made me feel trapped. My instincts were screaming at me to get up and flee, but my logical brain reminded me how stupid that would be. The bus driver had my ID card. I wouldn't be able to get very far without it, and the federal marshals would have a handy picture of me to help them with their man hunt. I was just screwed. I was going to prison and there was no way around it. All because of a naughty puppy!

It probably wasn't much more than five minutes, but I sat there sweating for what felt like an eternity. Finally, the driver returned. He stomped slowly up the steps. When he got to the top, he turned to look at us and just stared blankly for a couple seconds. Then, in a stern tone of voice he called out, "Mr. Burnell?"

I raised my hand, and he started walking back the aisle towards me at a casual slow pace. He looked me right in the eyes the whole way back. When he got within arm's reach, he stopped and just looked at me for about one more second. Then he gave me that same quirky smile, handed my documents back to me, and in a friendly tone of voice, he simply said, "Here's your pass." With that, he strolled back to the driver's seat and proceeded to drive us all out of Albuquerque.

I will never know what really happened that afternoon. He must have noticed that my pass was fake and just decided not to turn me in. Maybe the FBI was using our fake bus passes to track our movements and that data was more valuable to them than our asses would have been sitting in prison. I don't know, but I couldn't stop freaking out about it at the time. Paranoia took over my mind, and I became convinced that I was still about to get busted. My mind invented a story that none of the right kind of federal agents had been on duty in Albuquerque that afternoon, but they would be waiting for me at a different station up ahead. I decided to get off at the next stop and make a run for it.

The next stop was called Cline's Corners, and there was literally nothing there but a gas station, some cattle, and an endless panorama of barren desert stretching to the horizon. I could see right away that there were no federal agents, and I couldn't imagine how I would ever get beyond Cline's Corners without just getting on the next bus, so I changed the plan and stayed in my seat. One person actually did get off the bus there, and it took me a few minutes to deduce that there must have been a larger town somewhere nearby.

There were two more stops in eastern New Mexico. They were both small towns where I could conceivably survive, but I decided not to get out there either. It made sense that they would not have their own supply of federal agents, but the towns were so small that I would not be able to blend in with the locals if the marshals did come looking for me. I needed to get to a real city. Amarillo, Texas was the next stop, so I waited to get off there.

The sun was just setting when the bus pulled to a stop in Amarillo. I had already put on my pack and walked to the front so I could burst out the door as soon as it opened. I avoided making eye contact with the driver and hustled out into Amarillo. No cops were waiting outside for me, but I still wasn't taking any chances. Rather than going through the station like a normal passenger, I walked out the road that the bus had come in on and escaped into the city.

In hindsight, it's obvious that no one was trying to catch me. If they were, they would have easily caught me. I just couldn't stop freaking out until I got away from that bus. I was so scared that I hadn't even thought about what to do next.

I found some supper in a trash can and considered my options while I ate. I remembered hearing that truckers were known to sometimes give hitch-hikers very long rides. I had never tried hitching out of a truck stop before, but I figured this was the time to give it a try. After supper, I asked some Amarillo folks how to get to the closest truck stop. They told me it was right beside the interstate about eight miles east of downtown, so I took off walking as the last of the daylight faded behind me.

I had probably made it about half way when a dumpy old car pulled to a stop beside me, and the driver asked if I needed a ride. That sounded great, so I hopped in and told him I was on my way to the truck stop. The man looked to be in his forties with a beer gut and a moustache. His head was bald on top, but where hair remained, he had let it grow down past his shoulders. His name was Kevin and as soon as I got into the car, he started telling me his story.

His mother had died a few years prior and she left her house to him. Kevin had lived there by himself for a while, but he hadn't been able to find steady work, so his finances were scraping bottom. In an attempt to gain a little more income, he had moved into a travel trailer in his aunt's yard and rented the house to a young family. Unfortunately, the tenants had stopped paying rent almost a year ago by the time he met me.

Kevin had tried everything to coax, cajole, or even threaten some money out of them, but all to no avail. He had never been a landlord before, and he hated the idea of evicting anyone. After about half a year, he finally bit the bullet and handed them an eviction notice, but they just ignored it and stayed there. A couple more months went by, and Kevin took someone's advice to try to drive them out by shutting off the water to the house. That involved a process of filing paperwork with the city water department, so it took more than another month before they actually came out and shut off the water. Even without water, the tenants continued to hang out for several more weeks, but eventually, they finally found some other place to go fester, and they moved on.

The place where Kevin was staying was only a few blocks away, so he noticed as soon as they were gone. They had finally left that afternoon while I was riding the bus across eastern New Mexico. Kevin had finally regained access to the house his mother left him to discover that the tenants had utterly trashed the place. He had been cleaning it ever since then, but after about three hours, it occurred to him that he was going to have to take the scummy tenants to court, so he ought to take some pictures to document what had happened. He was on his way to the big box store to pick up a disposable camera when he stopped to pick me up.

With that, he asked if he could hire me to help him clean up the house. I thought for a few seconds and then asked how much he intended to pay me. He took his turn thinking for a few seconds. Then he said he could afford to pay me 70 bucks, and I could quit as soon as I felt like I had done 70 bucks worth of work. Deal! I agreed to help and reached across the cab of the car to shake his hand. I waited in the parking lot while he bought his disposable camera, and then we turned around and headed back towards the city. After a few minutes, we pulled into the driveway of a modest little white-painted house in a modest, working-class neighborhood on the southeast side of Amarillo.

Kevin had told me the place was trashed, but I was still amazed by the scene when he let me in the front door. The whole central room of the house was buried under a pile of garbage and random objects as deep as my thighs. The mess was too huge and complex to really understand simply by looking at it. The house was also full of a thick, unbearable stench, and after just a few seconds, I retreated back to the front yard where I could get some fresh air. Kevin followed me out and explained that the smell was coming from the bathroom. After he shut off the water, the filthy tenants had found somewhere else to go poop, but they had continued pissing in the toilet for weeks

I never knew this before, but the smell of concentrated, stale human piss is one of the most noxious odors on Earth.

Kevin said he would attempt to turn the water back on in the morning, but he wasn't ready to deal with it yet. He proposed that we just tackle the garage that night, and deal with the rest of the house in the daylight tomorrow. That made sense, so we started in on the garage. He had bought a couple big rolls of large plastic garbage bags, so it was mostly just a process of stuffing things into the bags. Once in a while, I would find something that looked like it might be useful and I would hold it up and ask Kevin if he wanted to keep it. We kept a pile of useful things out in the driveway.

As we worked, Kevin told me more about his life. He said he was the last gay man left in Amarillo. All his friends had moved away to Dallas or Austin. He wished he could follow them there, but he could never seem to gather up enough money. It's not easy being a gay Texan. At one point, Kevin pointed to a specific rafter in the unfinished ceiling of the garage and told me that his first lover had committed suicide by hanging himself right there almost twenty years earlier. I could tell he was a very depressed man from the first moment I met him, and the more he told me about his life, the more I understood why.

It was about eleven o'clock when we finished the garage. By some miracle, the nasty tenants had left the master bedroom spotlessly clean, and it even had a bed. The door had been closed, so the smell was much less potent in there too. Kevin had offered it to me as a place to sleep when we first arrived, so I had put my stuff in there and opened the windows to let as much fresh air in as possible. Kevin wished me a good night and headed back to his place, and I went back in to sleep in the master bedroom.

When I got there, the awful smell was almost completely gone, but the room was very chilly. Parts of Texas can be pleasantly warm in February, but Amarillo is all the way at the north end of the state, and it's also pretty high in elevation. It's actually just about half way between Dallas and Denver. I pulled the windows down until they were both only open just a crack. Then I crawled into my sleeping bag and pulled a blanket that had been left there over it. It had been one hell of a day, so I actually slept well despite the strangeness of the situation.

I awoke at the first light of dawn with my stomach grumbling. There wasn't any food left in my pack, so I took a deep breath and went to inspect the kitchen. The fridge was full of disgusting rotten things, and most of the cupboards were empty. I had to take a couple breaths through my mouth, but I eventually found two cans of salmon in a cupboard. I grabbed them and ran back to the bedroom, slamming the door behind me.

Having grown up in the Pacific Northwest, salmon was one of my favorite foods, but I had never tried canned salmon before. I was really surprised to discover how disgusting it was, but I suppose there must be many better ways to prepare it than simply spooning it cold from the can. I was hungry, so I choked down one whole can anyway.

Kevin showed up just after seven, and he had brought me a couple of granola bars as well. He also had a big wrench, which he planned to use to turn the water back on so we could flush the damn toilet. He led me out through the backyard which was surprisingly large given how small the house was. The yard was also cluttered with children's toys and other junk. A wooden fence ran along the back end, and Kevin opened up a gate in the fence. We proceeded into the alley where Kevin squatted down to lift the plastic cover off of a hole in the ground. This revealed a complex network of pipes and valves which Kevin started tinkering with, trying to turn the water back on to his house. It probably wasn't legal for him to mess with the water lines, but it ended up being irrelevant. After ten or fifteen minutes, he still couldn't figure out how to do it. I had no experience with such systems, so I was of no help either, and we just ended up giving up on that plan.

We grabbed a couple buckets out of the garage, hopped in Kevin's car and drove about four blocks over to his aunt's house. When I saw where he lived, I felt even sorrier for him. It was one of those little campers that fits on the back of a pickup truck, but there wasn't even a truck underneath it. Kevin filled up the buckets from the spigot on the side of his aunt's house, and I carried them to the trunk of his car.

Back at the house, I went around and opened all the windows while Kevin bucket-flushed the stale old piss down the commode. There was a decent breeze that morning, so the stench reduced to a tolerable level fairly quickly.

The heaviest of the mess was located in the big living room/dining room that took up the whole center of the house, so we started there. It took us about four hours to dig through all of it, and I developed a real distaste for Kevin's ex-tenants through the process. We came up with a much smaller pile of useful things than we had in the garage the night before, and we found some disgusting things too. Items of rotting food were scattered throughout the pile, and we found three dirty diapers. I found the first one, and I was lucky enough to notice what it was before I touched it. I was able to improvise a tool to pick it up with and put it in the bag without contaminating my hands. (We hadn't thought to bring gloves.)

Kevin found the second diaper, and he lucked out the same as I had, noticing what it was before he touched it. A half an hour later, the poor guy stuck his hand right into the third and final diaper of the day. We each had our own bottle of drinking water, but we didn't have any to spare for hand-washing. Kevin had flushed the toilet twice for good measure, so all that water had been used up. Luckily, we had found a good roll of paper towels and put it the keep pile, so he was able to clean up pretty well and get back to work.

We filled bag after bag and set them in the front yard. Kevin said he would drive them all to the dump after I left, two at-a-time in his little old car. I couldn't help notice how much Jesus paraphernalia had been left behind. Beautifully-scripted prints of prayers still hung in glass frames on the walls, and about a quarter of all the clutter on the floor was made of kitschy little crafts and sculptures depicting Christian Bible themes. Apparently, collecting that stuff had been a higher financial priority than paying rent. I tried to joke with Kevin about it. I said, "Hey, do you think these people thought if they prayed hard enough that God would clean up after them?" Kevin was too depressed to think anything was funny.

He brought a little radio with him, and we spent the whole day listening to an awesome local Blues station. I had never been much of a Blues fan. I lived right near Rockland Maine for years, and that town hosts a giant Blues festival every summer. I went to it a couple times. I even got a job at the festival one year, but all the acts that came to Rockland were just terrible. Based on those experiences, I had come to believe that good Blues music was a historical phenomenon that had come to an end sometime in the past, so that Amarillo station really gave me a pleasant surprise. I must have heart 50 to 75 really good contemporary Blues songs that day, all by different contemporary artists. I don't remember the radio playing a single song I didn't like all day long.

I wish I could tell you what station it was, or who some of the bands were. I actually wrote a diary entry about my whole Amarillo experience, but I can't find it now to quote from it. My life has been too much of an adventure to keep track of things like that. I just remember being excited to learn that the Blues are alive and well in Texas. If I ever want to hear some really good Blues, that's where I'll go.

After we finished the living room, we braked for lunch. Kevin drove back to his aunt's house to wash his hands, and I gulped down my second can of cold, nasty salmon. Luckily, I had saved my second granola bar for dessert.

We went for the kitchen next. It was a smaller space, with less total volume of mess, but it had a lot more decaying organics. We also had to deal with the fridge, which meant releasing a powerful eruption of odors. We got everything from the fridge into a bag as quickly as possible, dragged the bag out front, and then took a long break in the front yard until we stopped feeling nauseous.

Kevin had brought more buckets of water back at lunch time, so after we got all the solid pieces of trash out of the kitchen, we were able to wash the sticky surfaces. The tenants had been level ten slobs, but it was at least nice to see that they hadn't vandalized anything on purpose, so there wasn't really any damage to the structure of the house.

It took us a couple more hours to finish the kitchen. After that, Kevin declared that I had done my share. He said if I did any more work, he would feel guilty for taking advantage of me, and he couldn't spare any more money to pay me. I told him I didn't mind. I felt bad for him, and I wanted to keep helping until the whole job was done. There were still two smaller bedrooms where God knows how many children had lived, the bathroom, and the backyard left to clean. After a couple minutes of negotiations, we decided to clean the back yard together and then call it a day. That didn't even take a whole hour, and there was nothing gross there at all. It was just a lot of children's toys, and stuff that I would classify as "construction and demolition debris."

When that was done, we were getting on towards late afternoon. Kevin handed me three twenties and a ten, just as promised, and then he declared that he wanted to take me out for supper. I had done a good job, and he wanted to do something to show his appreciation. I thought that was a great idea, so we hopped in the car and drove to a strip mall. He treated me to supper at one of those corporate chain restaurants where you sit down and a waitress serves you. The food was good enough, and I ate heartily. I don't remember what I said to cause it, but at one point during the meal, Kevin actually smiled. The worst of his ordeal was over, and he didn't have a job, so he would have plenty of time to clean up the rest of the mess on his own.

After dinner, he dropped me off at the bus station as I had requested. I had about a hundred dollars, so I walked up to the ticket counter and asked the woman how far east I could get for that amount of money. I was dismayed to learn that was only enough to get to Tulsa Oklahoma, but what else could I do? I bought a ticket to Tulsa, and I didn't even have to wait two whole hours before the bus showed up.

I got to Tulsa right around midnight where I learned that I could catch the next easterly bus at 4:30am. I knew I would not be able to sleep under fluorescent lights on the cold tile floor of the bus station, so I set off on foot to explore the city, backpack and all. The night was frigid. It was probably right around freezing temperature, with a stout wind that cut right through my winter coat. I had never been to Tulsa before, and I found it interesting, even in the dark. I wandered northwest through miles of ghetto where the streets were completely deserted due to the cold weather.

After a couple hours, I came to an odd place where the ghetto ended abruptly at a large street running north-to-south. Across the street, there were no human structures at all, just alternating patches of prairie and forest. I had only ever seen ghetto neighborhoods in the middle of cities before. I didn't know you could have one right on the edge of town.

I walked along that road that made the boundary between ghetto and wilderness for quite a while. I was still on it when the first pickup truck ever made pulled to a stop beside me. An elderly Black man rolled down the window and said something I couldn't understand. After several repetitions, I realized it was the a basically a variation of the same thing elderly Black folks always said when they found me walking around the ghettos. I was not safe there, and he wanted me to get in the truck so he could take me some place where I would be safer. It seemed like it was way too cold for ghetto thugs to be out prowling, but I was also very cold, so I climbed into the ancient truck and didn't argue.

First, the man took me to a Church's Fried Chicken with an all-night drive-thru, and bought me an order of chicken with mashed potatoes and gravy. The food was absolutely disgusting, but it was hot and I was hungry, so I thanked him as much as I could. We kept trying to make friendly conversation, but I was surprised to find myself struggling with a real language barrier. I was all smug a couple of years later when Nightmare Jill couldn't understand Black people, but in truth, my linguistic skills were pretty limited to the East Coast Ebonic dialects. Oklahoma really has its own thing goin on, and I hope I get to spend enough time there someday that I can learn t communicate effectively with Black Okies too.

He dropped me back off at the bus station a couple of hours earlier than had wanted, but I managed not to die of boredom. By then my paranoia ha worn off enough that I was ready to take another chance with my half-ruine bus pass. I noticed that the grease spot was not so obvious in the dim, artif cial lights of the parking lot. The bus driver scribbled my info into his ledge and returned my pass to me without any sign of suspicion.

After that, I decided I would just wait out the daylight in all the other citie where I would have to transfer, and only use my pass in the dark of nigh I ended up having to transfer four more times, in Saint Louis, Columbu Pittsburgh, and New York. As I recall, the Pittsburgh and New York transfer happened at night anyway, so I didn't even have to wait any longer in thos cities than usual. I ran into another whole episode of hijinks in Columbu but you must be tired of reading about this stuff by now, so I'm just goin to skip that part.

I made it safely back to Maine where it would be less than four month before I set off on the big walking adventure that has come to be known a the American Odyssey.

Interestingly, I slept in a different place almost every night on my walk, bu I never once woke up feeling confused about where I was. Based on that dat I would hypothesize that the Tyler Durden effect is only caused by travellin long distances at high speeds in cars, trains, or airplanes. Walking won't mak you lose your mind like that.

Well, I guess that's about it. Now don't go stickin' this book in a pile in th attic. Pass it around!

ABOUT THE AUTHOR'S SISTER

Did you know that my sister writes books too? She has actually been doing this a lot longer than I have, and she has already published thirteen books. They are all fabulous fantasies full of epic characters and amazing systems of magical physics. My personal favorites are the entire *Foreign Sorcerer* series, and *Into the Darkbower*, but really, they are all excellent. Her name is M.C. Burnell. Check her out at meaghandreams.com

A NOTE FROM THE AUTHOR

Thanks so much for reading my book! Please take a minute to share your thoughts in a review on Goodreads or your favorite online book vendor, it helps indie authors like me enormously.

Made in the USA
Middletown, DE
15 March 2022